CONFESSIONS

CONFESSIONS

SAINT AUGUSTINE

TRANSLATED BY
ANTHONY ESOLEN

TAN Books
Gastonia, North Carolina

Cover design by David Ferris—www.davidferrisdesign.com

ISBN: 978-1-5051-2686-0
Kindle ISBN: 978-1-5051-2687-7
ePUB ISBN: 978-1-5051-2688-4

Published in the United States by
TAN Books
PO Box 269
Gastonia, NC 28053
www.TANBooks.com

Printed in India

CONTENTS

TRANSLATOR'S NOTE

It is a daunting thing indeed, to translate the first and, for all I can tell, the greatest autobiography ever written, the *Confessions* of Saint Augustine, especially when the acts of speaking and writing, of prayer and praise, are central to the work itself. For Augustine was trained up in the art of rhetoric, and he taught young men how best to choose their words, arrange their material, and craft their sentences so as to be most persuasive in courts of law, and though he looks upon his former line of work with disgust, knowing the immoral uses to which the art would often be put, he was still the rhetor, and he aimed to persuade.

Yet there is a difference between that old pagan rhetoric and the rhetoric of Augustine the Christian, and it means all the world. We hear the clear ring of the difference from the first sentences of the *Confessions:*

You are great, O Lord, and to be praised indeed: great is your power, and your wisdom is beyond reckoning. And man, a mere part of your creation, desires to praise you, man, who bears his mortality about with him, and the testimony of his sin, and testimony that you resist the proud; and still this man, this part of your creation, desires to praise you. You rouse him up to take delight in praising you, for you have made us for yourself, and our heart is restless until it rests in you.

That is not mere stylishness. The pilgrim Dante would later say, when he stood in the presence of God, that whatever he could say of what he saw would be no more than what a baby could say, "who wets his tongue still at his mama's breast"[1] What can the finite creature say of the infinite God? That is the paradox of praise. We are a part, a tiny part, of creation, but we are made in the image and likeness of God, made to praise God, and to revel in his love. What can we say? But what can we not say? What Sidney's Astrophil says of his beloved Stella, Sidney the poet, thinking of Augustine, intends that his readers should apply to God:

> Not thou by praise, but praise in thee is raised:
> It is a praise to praise, when thou art praised.[2]

The wisest of pagans could but stand upon the shores of this mystery, because even if they—I am thinking here of the Neoplatonic philosophers[3] whom Augustine himself read before his conversion and to whom he gives generous credit for seeing what they did see, though there was much they did not see—knew somehow that the divine must

---

[1] *Paradiso* 33.108.

[2] *Astrophil and Stella,* 35.13–14.

[3] Plato (428?–348?), the first and perhaps greatest titan of ancient philosophy, taught that there was a realm of changeless and non-material "Forms" or ideas, things to gaze upon with wonder, whereof the objects in the material world were but shadows. Objects, as he taught, possess different levels of existence, depending upon how closely they approach to the changeless and therefore eternal. Man is meant to hunger for what is true and beautiful, and thus was Plato the father of what we might call a philosophy of attraction and love. The highest and most beautiful object of man's contemplation is the form of the Good. The Neoplatonist philosophers whom Augustine read—Iamblichus (c.242–325), Porphyry (c. 234–305), and their leading light, Plotinus (204–270)—were less interested in Plato as a political philosopher than as a mystic and a contemplative, someone searching, with all the energy of love, after the changeless source of existence itself, which Plotinus called "the One." It was not difficult for Christians to see in the Neoplatonists, who themselves used the term "Logos," "Word," to identify the mediating principle between the One and the soul, a kind of natural insight into the existence of God, especially as Saint John had used the word "Logos" to refer to Christ himself: "In the beginning was the Word" (Jn 1:1). We must keep in mind, though, that for the Neoplatonists, the Logos was not a personal being, nor indeed was the One, which overflowed, by its own nature and not by any free decision, into the lower levels of existence, as the water of a fountain flows from the highest basin to the lower basins. It is also quite likely that the Neoplatonists were influenced, if grudgingly, by Christianity and by the more mystical strains of Jewish thought and worship. Porphyry, for one, wrote a fifteen volume work, *Against the Christians.*

be the object of their love, they did not see that they had first been the object of God's love. "God is love," says Saint John, filled with joyous contemplation of Father and Son and the Spirit of love they mutually enjoy.[4] The One, the distant and divine Alone to whose contemplation the pure Plotinus aspired with all his heart, spilled forth a measure of his being to all subordinate beings, automatically, impersonally, inevitably, as a fountain spills its water. There can be no story in that, no story whereof the divine is the author, because story implies decision, not necessity, and personhood, not impersonality. Only the God who creates can, if I may be permitted the metaphor, write a story: and then God is not simply an agent in the story of the universe he has made, but is the author and comprehender of all, the originating spring and the final end of all.

If we are going to speak about God the Creator, God who spoke that we may speak, God in whose eternal Word all things were made, we require a style that is not shy of paradox, because whatever we predicate of God may be true and not true at the same time, depending on how we mean it. And the paradox is not just an obstacle to our thought, but an invitation to penetrate more and more deeply into the divine, into God's self-revelation, and into his very life of love. It would be absurd to say that Augustine merely employed the artifices of rhetorical paradox, such as he had learned in the pagan schools, and turned them to Christian use. Scripture itself is full of paradox. God has a name that may not be uttered, the name that is beyond all naming, as it is an expression of his pure being, not to be qualified, not to be penned in—a name utterly unlike Zeus or Osiris or Baal. God is love, and he is a consuming fire. His glory is set above the heavens, and yet he visits the son of man and cares for him. He made the stars as it were in an afterthought, but he cares for the young of the ostrich though she does not care for them herself, and not a sparrow falls to the ground without his will. The very person of Christ is a scandal, a paradox, for, as Saint

---

[4] 1 Jn 4:8.

Paul says, the Greeks seek wisdom and the Jews demand a sign, but we preach Christ crucified. For the foolishness of God is wiser than men.

Then it is not artfulness but joy, the rush of intellectual seeking and finding and seeking all the more, that we find in these fine early expressions of wonder, in paradoxes that both express a truth and open our minds to the mystery of it:

You love, but you do not burn with passion; you are jealous for what is yours, though you are secure in your possession; you regret, though you do not grieve; you grow angry, though you are at peace; you alter your works but not your counsel; you take up what you find though you have never lost it; you are never needy, but you are glad in your winnings; you are never covetous, but you exact interest. Men pay and overpay you, that you may be in their debt, and yet what does anyone have that is not already yours? You pay debts though you are in debt to no one; you forgive debts, and you lose nothing.

The art of such sentences, then, is not decoration, not "style" in an ornamental and arbitrary sense, but a formal embodiment of the truths Augustine is attempting to name, and in naming to describe, and in describing to praise and to give thanks. The style is indivisible from the matter, just as, let us say, the form of Michelangelo's *David* is indivisible from the monumental stone.

What, then, shall the faithful translator do? I have long believed that when it comes to works of literary art, and the *Confessions* is one of the most stupendous ever wrought, the best translations are those that retain and reveal the figurative *by hewing as closely as possible to the literal*, both in the significance of individual words and in the manner of the author's expression. And that is what I have tried to do here, though I have avoided English archaisms and I have attempted to render the sentences with some speed, occasionally dividing one long sentence into two or three, when the division did no harm to the meaning or the emphasis. I have paid close attention to the literal meanings of words we may be tempted to consider merely abstract, so that we may hear what Augustine assumed his careful readers would hear. "The comforts of your mercy took me up," he says of his infancy, and the verb there, *susceperant*, might easily be rendered as *sustained*, without any apparent injury to the meaning. But Augustine really does think of the action of God as bearing him up from below, and as the life of sinful and redeemed man is one of fall and rise, of loss and restoration and elevation infinitely beyond the initial loss, it behooves the translator to keep that literal-figurative in mind, and to suggest it to the mind of the reader. Unless the attempt would result in something ridiculous or glaringly conspicuous, I have attempted always to do so.

And then there is the matter of prayer. We, in our strangely inartistic time, find it hard to imagine that common people, often enough illiterate people, *prayed in artistic form*, in immemorial songs and poetry. The great prayer book of the Jews was a book of poems, the psalms, and many of the Lord's own sayings, including the beloved prayer he taught to his disciples, are Semitic poems too. Saint Paul urges the Ephesians to encourage one another in "psalms, hymns, and spiritual songs,"[5] and Saint Ambrose, the man whose careful and learned and poetically sensitive readings and expositions of Scripture first taught Augustine how to read those writings at once humble and highly exalted, was himself a composer of hymns, which Augustine must have heard and sung, and which moved his heart so powerfully, he wonders sometimes whether the joy of it were not beyond what is permitted in due measure.

Prayers, then, must not be translated as office memoranda, or as mere colloquial requests, as if you might ask a waiter for a hamburger and a bottle of beer. The *Confessions* is one continued and coherent prayer, a profound profession of faith, and a plea for more, ever more wisdom, ever more love. It is artistic in its whole conception, in its parts and their arrangement down to the merest sentence. It is closer to the Gothic cathedrals that would grace Europe eight hundred years later than to anything that you or I might write about ourselves and our lives. Then the translator must not be embarrassed by prayerful

---

[5] Eph 5:19.

expression, by the heightened word, the unusual phrasing, the order of petitions, and the music of contemplative thought.

This too have I attempted to render into English, again with expressions I hope will speed the reader along:

Then tell me, O God to whom I bend the knee, have pity on your pitiable servant and tell me, did my infancy follow upon some other age of mine that had died?

If I were writing in the mode of a memorandum, I might simply say, "Then I beg you, God, to have mercy on your miserable servant, and tell me whether," and so forth. The reader would understand the request, but he would not hear the prayer in it. The words would be objects to process, containers to open and then to toss aside once you had gotten the meaning out of them. But that, I believe, does injustice to the form and matter of the work, to what Augustine intends by the work to move in the soul of those who hear it.

One final point: Before his baptism, Augustine and his friends would sometimes call on the bishop Ambrose, and they often found him reading silently, perhaps to save his voice, which was prone to going hoarse, or perhaps to grasp more fully with the mind the import of what he was reading. At such times, they would not disturb him. But Augustine remarks on it as unusual, even unexampled, and that leads me to consider that he assumed that his own readers would *hear* his work, and thus did he write not simply to be read but to be *heard.* And that returns us to the matter of song. When God made the world, the sons of morning sang for joy,[6] and indeed J. R. R. Tolkien, thinking of that verse from Job, and thinking as any medieval artist would have thought, presents in his *Silmarillion* the creation of all things as having come about not by declaring merely, but by singing. The proper song has a beginning, a middle, and an end, not randomly or arbitrarily set in this or that way. For the end of the greatest songs is present from the beginning, and all times are present, in the song, in any single note, just

---

6 Job 38:7.

as the infinite God is present in his totality and eternity in each least particle of matter and each fleetest moment of time. Then the story of Augustine is but the whole story of salvation made manifest in this matter, in this time, and so also the stories of salvation that Augustine hears about or reads, those of Victorinus, of Anthony, and of the imperial guardsmen, for the stories are incorporated into the stories, as human artists can with all their intelligence but flail about and attempt in a small way to do, but as God has done and always does, in his creation and his providence. Then the *Confessions* is a vast human song in praise of the song of God, timeless not because it is great literature, though it is, but because its root is in the Word through whom all things were made, and its crown reaches toward him who sits upon the throne, and says, "Behold, I make all things new."

—Anthony Esolen

BOOK ONE

1

You are great, O Lord, and to be praised indeed:[7] great is your power, and your wisdom is beyond reckoning. And man, a mere part of your creation, desires to praise you, man, who bears his mortality about with him, and the testimony of his sin, and testimony that you resist the proud;[8] and still this man, this part of your creation, desires to praise you. You rouse him up to take delight in praising you,[9] for you have made us for yourself, and our heart is restless until it rests in you.

Lord, give me to know and to understand which comes first, to call upon you or to praise you, to know you or to call upon you? But who could call upon you without knowing you? For without knowing it, he might call upon another instead of you. Or rather must you be called upon, to be known? But how can they call upon him in whom they have not believed? And how can they come to believe, without a preacher?[10] And more: They shall praise the Lord who seek him, for

---

[7] Ps 144:1.

[8] Jas 4:6; cf. Job 22:29, Mt 23:12, 1 Pt 5:6.

[9] Cf. Ps 122:1. Praise is the gift whereby we who receive the gift of grace participate in the being and the goodness of God, the giver.

[10] Rom 10:14. Notice that reason alone, without the revelation of Christ, cannot attain to faith.

they who seek him shall find him,[11] and they who find shall praise him. I shall seek after you, O Lord, as I call upon you, and I shall call upon you, believing in you; for you have been preached to us. My faith calls upon you, Lord, the faith you have given to me and breathed in me by the humanity of your Son, through the ministry of your preacher.

2

And how shall I call upon my God, my Lord and God, seeing as when I invoke him, I seem to invoke him into myself? For what place is there in me, where my God might enter?[12] What place for God to enter, God who made heaven and earth? My Lord God, is it so? Is there anything in me that can contain you? Why, even the heavens and the earth you have made, wherein you have made me—can even they contain you? Or is it this way: because without you nothing that is could ever have come to be, it follows that whatever does exist must contain you? I too exist, and so what do I beg for when I ask you to enter me, when I would not exist in the first place unless you were in me already? For I am not in the nether world, and yet you are there too. And "even if I should descend to the world below, you would be present there."[13]

So, my God, I could not be, I could not be in the slightest, unless you were in me. Or is it rather that I would not be, unless I were in you, from whom and through whom and in whom all things are? This too, this too, O Lord. But if I am in you, why do I call upon you? From what place can you enter into me? Where can I go beyond heaven and earth, so that my God can enter into me from there, my God, who has said, "I fill heaven and earth"?[14]

---

[11] Cf. Jer 29:13, Mt 7:7–8. Augustine will end his work with the same echo of Scripture.

[12] Augustine had been a materialist, so that his emphasis here on place is quite significant. What, in fact, does it mean that God is "in" us if we conceive of things only as bodies taking up space?

[13] Ps 138:8.

[14] Jer 23:24.

3

Do heaven and earth then contain you, because you fill them? Or, after you have filled them, does some part of you remain that they cannot grasp hold of? When you have filled heaven and earth, where do you pour out that part of you that is left over? No, you have no need of that, no need for a place to contain you, because all that you fill, you fill by containing it. Those vessels that are filled with you do not provide for you a settled place of rest, because if they were shattered, you would not be spilled. And when you shed yourself upon us, you do not fall, but you raise us up; you do not trickle away, but you gather us together.

You fill all things, and it is with all of yourself that you fill them. Or, because all things cannot contain the whole of you, do they hold only a part of you, and do they all hold the same part? Or do various things contain various parts, the greater containing the greater, and the lesser the lesser? Or are you everywhere in your totality, even though no one thing can contain you wholly?

4

What then is my God? What, I ask, but the Lord God? "For who is Lord, but the Lord? And who is God, but our God?"[15]

Supreme, best, most mighty, most omnipotent, most merciful and most just, most hidden and most immediately present, loveliest, strongest, steadfast and impossible to grasp, unchanging and yet changing all things, never new, never old, making all things new; driving the proud to the decay of old age though they know it not; ever in act, ever at rest, gathering up and never in need, bearing and filling and sheltering, creating and nourishing, bringing to perfection, seeking, though of nothing are you in want.[16]

---

[15] Ps 18:31.

[16] Augustine's emphasis here is on the personhood of God and his free and providential action as the Creator and the fulfillment of all things.

You love, but you do not burn with passion; you are jealous for what is yours, though you are secure in your possession; you regret, though you do not grieve; you grow angry, though you are at peace; you alter your works but not your counsel; you take up what you find though you have never lost it; you are never needy, but you are glad in your winnings; you are never covetous, but you exact interest. Men pay and overpay you, that you may be in their debt, and yet what does anyone have that is not already yours? You pay debts though you are in debt to no one; you forgive debts, and you lose nothing. Then what shall we say, my God, my life, my sacred sweetness, or what does anyone say, when he speaks of you? But woe to them who keep silent about you, when those who chatter most are like the dumb.

5

Who shall give me the gift, to take my rest in you? Who shall give me the gift, that you may enter my heart and so fill it with drink,[17] that I may forget all my ills and embrace you, my only good? What are you to me? Have pity on me, that I may speak. What can I possibly be to you, that you command me to love you, and if I do not do so, you grow angry and threaten me with mighty sorrows? Is it then by itself only a little sorrow, if I should not love you? Ah me, tell me, my Lord God, in your mercy tell me what you are to me. Say to my soul: "I am your salvation."[18] Say it aloud, so that I may hear. Behold, O Lord, the ears of my heart are before you; open them, and say to my soul, "I am your salvation." I shall run after that voice, I shall take hold of you. Hide not your face from me![19] Let me die to see it, lest I die.[20]

---

[17] Cf. Ps 23:5, 42:1. We thirst for the living God, while the drink of this world can provide a brief satisfaction at best.

[18] Ps 35:3. The Latin means also, "I am your health."

[19] Ps 27:9. Isaiah cried out that he was a dead man because he had seen the face of God, 6:5, but now the Son has come into the world, and we can seek the face of God with confidence.

[20] Death is the lot of all men, but God gives us the grace of dying with Christ, that we may live; cf. Rom 6:8.

The house of my soul is too cramped for you to enter: make it more spacious. It is falling to ruin; repair it. Much inside it offends your sight; I know it and I confess it. But who shall cleanse it? To whom else but you shall I cry: "Cleanse me, O Lord, from my hidden sins, and from the sins of others deliver your servant"?[21] I believe, and that is why I speak. You know this, O Lord. Have I not given witness before you against my own crimes, my God, and have you not forgiven the impiety of my heart? I shall not contend in judgment with you,[22] who are Truth yourself; and I do not want to deceive myself, lest my iniquity bear false witness in its own behalf. So I shall not contend in judgment with you, for "if you, O Lord, should mark iniquities, who shall stand?"[23]

6

Nevertheless, permit me to plead before your mercy, though I am but earth and ashes.[24] Permit me to plead, for it is to your mercy that I speak, and not to some man who smiles at me in scorn. And maybe you smile at me also, but when you turn you will have pity on me. What do I want to say, O Lord, except that I do not know from what place I came into—what shall I call it—a dying life, or a living death? I do not know. And the comforts of your mercy took me up, as I have heard from the parents of my flesh, from whom and in whom you formed me in the course of time; I myself have no memory of it. And so the comfort of human milk came to me, though neither my mother nor my nurses filled their breasts. It was you who by their means gave me the nourishment my infancy required, according to the natural law you have established, and the riches you have shed even upon the least of your creatures.[25] And you gave me the desire to want no more

---

[21] Ps 19:13.
[22] Cf. Job 9:32.
[23] Ps 130:3.
[24] Cf. Job 42:6.
[25] We should try to enter into the wonder that Augustine here expresses at the beauty and the mystery of creation and the natural laws that govern it, whereby God provides for all

than what you gave, and to those who nourished me, the desire to give me what you gave to them; for they were willing to give to me by well-ordered affection what they had from you in abundance. For it was good for them that my good should come from them, though really it was only by their means, as indeed all good things come from you, O God, and from you comes all my health. It was only later in life I took note of this, as you were calling me by those faculties you had endowed me with, both within and without. For then I knew how to suck at the breast, and to rest content with what pleased me, and to cry whenever something hurt my flesh. That was all I knew.

Then I began to laugh, first while I was sleeping, and then when I was awake. At least, so was I told about myself, and I believed it, because we see other babies doing the same; but of what I myself did, I remember nothing. And sure enough, little by little I began to be aware of where I was, and I had a will to express my desires to those who would fulfill them, but I could not do so, because the desires were within me while the people were without, nor could they by any power of their senses enter my soul. So I thrashed about and I spluttered, and made signs that somehow were like what I wanted, only a few, and only such as I could make. And when the people did not obey me, either because they could not understand me, or what I wanted would hurt me, I would grow indignant with my elders, because they were not my underlings, and with free-born children, because they were not my slaves,[26] and I avenged myself against them by wailing. And this is the way all speechless babies are, as I have since learned by observation, and they have shown me, without their knowing it, that I was just the same—shown me it better than did my nurses who knew.

And see, my infancy of long ago is dead, and I am still alive. But you, Lord, live forever and nothing in you dies, for you are God and Lord of

living things; cf. Job 39.

[26] The words for "slave" and "servant" are the same in Latin, as in Hebrew and Greek. Notice that man's fallen nature expresses itself, from our earliest years, in the desire to dominate others, to be first rather than last.

all the things you have created, before the beginning of the ages, before anything that can be said to come before.[27] In your presence stand the causes of all things that do not stand still; in your presence abide the changeless founts of all things that suffer change; in your presence live the eternal reasons[28] of all things temporal and unreasoning. Then tell me, O God to whom I bend the knee, have pity on your pitiable servant and tell me, did my infancy follow upon some other age of mine that had died? Was it the time I spent in my mother's womb? For I have been told a little about that too, and I myself have seen women with child. And before that age, was there another, my God, my sweet delight? Was I somewhere? Was I anyone at all? I have no one to tell me about it, neither my father nor my mother, nor anyone else by experience, nor my own memory. Do you laugh at me for wondering about these things, you who command me to praise you and to confess to you for what I know?

I confess to you, Lord of heaven and earth, and praise you for the first stirrings of my infancy, which I do not remember; and you have made men to guess from other people at many things about themselves, and to believe many such things upon the credit of weak little women. For I existed then, even then was I alive, and as my infancy drew to its end, I sought out the signs to make my meanings known to other people. Whence could such a living soul come, O Lord, but from you? Can any man be his own craftsman, to shape himself? Whence could any stream of being and life flow into us apart from you who made us, Lord, you for whom to be and to live are not separate things, for the summit of being and the summit of life are one and the same?

---

[27] God does not dwell in time as created beings do; he is the creator of time. Augustine will address the question of what God did before He created the world, affirming that the question has no meaning, since "before" and "after" come into existence only with time, which God has created.

[28] We may think here of the immaterial laws which govern the created world. When the modern physicist says that the "nothing" that existed before the physical universe burst into being was not "nothing" but rather full, we may say, of potentiality and the laws that would govern the matter about to exist, they are not doing philosophy very well, and they have, besides, unwittingly said nothing that Augustine has not said here more precisely.

For you are the highest, and you do not change. Nor is this present day past in you, and yet in you it does pass, for in you are all such things, and they would never have their ways to come and pass except that you hold them in your grasp. And because your years never fail, your years are this present day, and no matter how many are our days and the days of our fathers, through this present day they all pass, and thence do they receive their manner of being, and that they have being at all; and then other days come and likewise pass away. But you, Lord, are the selfsame, and all the tomorrows and beyond, and all the yesterdays and before, you are creating today, you have created today.[29]

What is it to me, if someone should not understand this? Let him be glad anyway, and say, "What is this?"[30] Let him be glad, and let him love to find you in not finding it, rather than in finding it to fail to find you.

7

Give ear to me, O God! Woe to the sins of men![31] But it is a man who says this, and you have mercy upon him, because you made him, but the sin within him you did not make.[32] Who shall recall to my mind the sins of my infancy? For no man is clean of sin in your sight, not even the infant whose life is but one day upon the earth. Who shall recall it to my mind? Why not any little child at all, in whom I now see what I cannot remember about myself?

---

[29] Again, Augustine insists that God does not suffer time, as the false gods of the pagans do, because they are conceived as existing on the same plane with everything else. If we ask when God created the world, we must be careful lest we identify a specific time after which God, like any lesser craftsman, might cease to work. The creation was at the beginning, and it is now, and it shall be till the world comes to its consummation.

[30] Ex 16:15. The Israelites found flakes like hoarfrost on the ground, and they said, "What is this?" – in Hebrew, mah na, "manna." Even if we do not understand these tremendous mysteries about God's being and his creation, we should be glad, and partake of the bread of heaven.

[31] Mt 18:17.

[32] Cf. Ws 11:25. God loves all the things he has made, but he hates sin; he is its punisher, not its author. Augustine will return to the question of what evil can even be, seeing that it is not something God made, who made all things.

How did I sin then? That I wailed open-mouthed for the breast? For if I wailed like that now, not for mother's milk, but for some food fit for my years, I would be laughed at, even reprehended, and rightly too. So I did reprehensible things, but since I could not understand anyone who might blame me, neither custom nor reason permitted me to be blamed. For as we grow, we root out such things and throw them away, nor have I ever seen anyone who knew what he was doing clean out the bad and throw away the good. Or are we to think that for the time being it was good to cry for something that would hurt me if it was given, to be bitterly angry with freemen and elders and even those who gave me birth if they did not truckle to me, to lash out as much as I could and try to hurt those who were wiser than I, for not obeying the nod of my godlike will, because they did not heed my commands, which would have done me harm had they heeded them? Then it is not the will of the infant that is harmless, but the weakness of his little limbs. I myself have seen and observed a little baby rife with jealousy. He could not yet speak, but he went pale and cast a bitter glare at the child nursing at the breast beside him.[33]

Who is unaware of this? Mothers and nurses say they have some remedies or other to allay such things. But is it really innocence, to be full fed from a fountain flowing and dripping with milk, and not to suffer a poor fellow nursling to share in the one nourishment he needs to stay alive? We bear with these things, we smile, not because they are nothing, or little and insignificant, but because they are going to pass away as the child grows older. To prove it, one can consider that the same things, if an older person should do them, would be condemned and not to be borne with a patient mind.

You, O Lord, who have given life to the speechless baby, and a body, as we have seen, furnished with senses, fitted with members, and shaped in beauty, and for his integrity and safety have instilled in him

---

[33] For Augustine, man's fallen nature is evident from his earliest days on earth. He is not saying that such a child is evil, but that our inclinations have been distorted by the effects of the sin of Adam.

all the powers of a living being, you command me to praise you for them, and to sing psalms to your name, O Most High. For you are a God almighty and good, even if you had made these things and no more, which none other than you could have made, you single and one, from whom comes all measure, you most beautiful, who lend form to all things and set them in order by your law.[34] So then, O Lord, I consider this age of my life which I cannot recall, which I have learned of by crediting the accounts of others, and guess at by observing other infants, and indeed the guesses are much to be trusted, and only grudgingly do I count it a part of the life that I live in this time now. In the darkness of my forgetting, it is like the age I passed in my mother's womb. Now if I have been conceived in iniquity, and if in sin my mother fed me in her womb, then where, I beg you, my God, where and when, O Lord, was I your servant ever innocent? But now, see, I shall let that time pass. What does it matter to me now, when I cannot recall a trace of it?

8

What happened then? From infancy did I pass into boyhood? Or did that come to me, following upon my infancy? Nor did my infancy depart—for where would it have gone? And yet it no longer was. For I was no longer an infant that could not speak, but a gabbling little boy indeed. I do remember this, but it was only later that I became aware of how I learned to talk. For the grownups did not teach me how to talk by giving me words in a certain plan of instruction, as they did when they taught me my letters a little later on, but I myself, with the mind you gave me, my God, by moaning and making various sounds and moving my limbs, tried to bring forth the senses of my heart, so that my will would be obeyed, though I could not express everything I wanted to, no matter for all the signs I made. Then I remembered the word they used when they called something by a name and moved their

---

[34] Cf. Ws 8:1.

bodies toward it, and I saw it and I grasped that the thing was called by the sounds they made when they wanted to show it to me. That they wanted to do this was clear to me by the movement of the body—by natural words, so to speak, common to all peoples, made by the face or a wink of the eye or the motion of other members or the sound of the voice, to show the affections of the soul, to ask for things, or grab hold of them, or shove them aside, or flee them. So, little by little, by words set in their right places in various sentences and heard time and again, I gathered what they were the signs of, and my mouth was tamed to these signs, and through them I expressed my will.[35]

So did I learn to exchange, with the people among whom I lived, the words people use to tell what they want. And I set forth more deeply into the whelming ocean of human society, dependent upon the authority of my parents, and at the beck and call of those who were greater than I.

9

O God, my God, what miseries and mockeries did I suffer in that age! For then it was put to me, when I was just a boy, that to live a good life meant to obey those who urged me to flourish in this world, and to excel in the arts of the tongue, arts that go slaving after false riches and honor among men. And so I was sent to school to learn my letters, and, poor lad that I was, I did not know what use there was to it. Yet if I was sluggish in learning, I got beaten. The adults praised this form of discipline, and so did many people who led this life before us, and it was they who paved the way for these troublesome roads we had to travel, multiplying labor and sorrow for the sons of Adam.

---

[35] Augustine will devote much of his treatise *On Christian Doctrine* to the nature of signs, their fitness to the things they signify, and the degree to which they participate in those things, rather than being merely arbitrary. Language, after all, must be near to the heart of a Christian who meditates on what it means for God to speak, whether in words to the prophets or in signs and wonders.

Yet, Lord, we observed people calling upon you in prayer, and from them we learned to think of you, so far as we were able, as someone great, who even though you did not appear to our senses could hear our cry and come to our aid. For while I was but a boy I began to call to you, my help and my refuge, and in prayer to you I loosened the knots of my tongue, and small though I was I begged you, with no small feeling, that I would not be beaten in school. And when you did not hear me out, and it was by no means foolishness in me, my elders took these plagues of mine in sport, even my own parents, who never wished me any harm. But for me then it was a great and burdensome evil.

Is there any man, O Lord, so great of soul, cleaving to you with so strong a love, is there, I ask, anyone—though sheer dullness can sometimes make a man so—is there, then, anyone who by piously cleaving to you is so profoundly moved that he can reckon as trifles the racking-horse, the hooks, and other tortures of that kind, which make people all over the world beg you with great fear to help them to escape, going so far as to make fun of people he loves who are terrified of them, as our parents laughed at the torments which we boys suffered from our masters? For we were no less afraid of them, and no less did we pray to you to escape them. And still we sinned by not writing or reading or pondering our lessons as much as we were told to.

It was not, Lord, that we were lacking in memory or in native intelligence. You had willed to bestow on us as much as we needed for our age. But we loved to play games, and people who did the very same thing took it out on us. For the frivolities of grown men are called business, yet they punish children for the like, and no one has pity on the children or on them or on both. But maybe some good judge of things would say I was rightly beaten, because I was a schoolboy playing ball, and so it took me more time to learn the lessons I needed for more disgraceful foolery once I was grown up. Or did my master who beat me do anything other than what I did?[36] If some other schoolmaster

---

[36] Augustine has said that if a grown man should wail like a baby because he was hungry,

defeated him in some petty question, he was racked worse with gall and envy than I was when I lost a game of ball to my playfellow.

10

Despite it all I did sin, O Lord my God, ruler and creator of all natural things, but of sin the ruler only; O Lord my God, I did sin by acting against the commands of my parents and those masters. For I could have gone on to put those lessons to good use, no matter what my people had in mind. I did not heed them, not because I had better things to choose, but because I loved to play, relishing in my sports the pride of victory, and loving to have my ears scratched with stories full of lies, which inflamed them to itch all the more.[37] And then the same sort of curiosity flashed from my eyes, to gape at the spectacles and the plays my elders put on. And the producers of these plays rise to such honors that almost everyone would wish the honors for their own children, whom they are glad to see bruised if the plays keep them from their studies. And why do the parents want them to study, but to grow up and put on the very same? Look upon these things with pity, O Lord, and deliver us who call upon you now, and deliver also those who do not yet call upon you, that they may call upon you to deliver them.

11

When I was still only a boy I had heard of the life eternal you promise to us, by the humility of our Lord God who descended to our pride, and I was signed with the sign of his cross, and was seasoned with his salt as soon as I came forth from the womb of my mother, whose hope in you was great. You saw, Lord, how when I was yet a boy I was seized one day by a sudden fever and cramps in the stomach, and was close

---

he would be laughed at and reproved. Now, though, he suggests that in fact grown men and women do often behave as children—as spoiled, irresponsible, and willful children.

[37] As we will see, worldly desires are like itches: they grow worse when we try to allay them by scratching.

to dying—you saw, my God, for you were my keeper then, with what passion and faith I begged, of the piety of my mother and your Church that is the mother of us all, for the baptism of your Christ, my Lord God. Then the mother of my flesh, deeply troubled, for with a chaste heart that trusted in you she was most dearly in the throes of labor for my everlasting salvation, now took all care and haste to see that I might be initiated and washed clean by the health-giving sacraments, after I had confessed to you for the remission of my sins; but all of a sudden I recovered. So then my cleansing was put off, as if I must needs get even filthier in sin by living longer, for obviously it would be a more serious and dangerous thing to be fouled with sins after the bathing than before.[38]

So I was a believer at that time, as were my mother and the whole household except for my father, though he did not overrule in me the law of my mother's devotion, to hinder my belief in Christ, just as he himself did not yet believe. For she did all that she could so that you, my God, would be my Father, rather than he. And you came to her assistance, so that she overcame her man whom she served, though she was the better of the two, for in serving him also she was serving you, who had commanded her to serve.[39]

I beg of you, my God, for I wish to know, if it should please you to tell me, to what end was I then put off, so that I was not baptized? Was it for my good that the reins of sin were then relaxed? Should they have been relaxed at all? Why then are our ears abuzz even now from this person and that person all around us, who say, "Leave him alone, let him do what he wants, he hasn't been baptized yet!" But when it comes to the health of the body, we do not say, "Let his wounds grow worse awhile, because he hasn't yet been healed!" How much better it would

---

[38] It was not the custom in North Africa to baptize infants and small children. Augustine sees in the delay an attempt to play God, as if we could arrange our times and seasons by our own efforts, and as if God must submit to the arrangement, or must be deceived by a sort of temporal trick.

[39] Saint Monica's submission to her husband, Patricius, may scandalize some of us now, but she did exactly what Peter recommends for wives of unbelievers; cf. 1 Pt 3:1.

have been for me to have been healed right away! And then, for my own diligence and that of my family to have made sure that my soul's health, which you had bestowed upon it, would remain safe under your guardianship! Surely that would have been better. But how many and how violent were the waves of temptation that were going to loom above me when my boyhood should pass! Of these my mother was well aware. So she would sooner expose to them the earth from which I was formed, than the image and likeness that had been created first.

12

Still, in that boyhood of mine, wherein there was less to fear for my sake than in my adolescence, I did not love my lessons, and I hated to be forced to do them. But they forced me anyway, and it did me good, though I did nothing good myself, for I never would have learned a thing if I had not been compelled. No man does good if he does it against his will, even if the thing itself is good. And those who compelled me did not do well either, but what was good for me came from you, my God. For they who made me learn could not see what I would do with my learning, unless it was to sate the insatiable lusts of a plentiful neediness and an ignominious glory.[40] But you, to whom every one of our hairs is numbered, made use, for my benefit, of the error of all those who insisted that I should learn, while you made my own error, since I did not want to learn, into the whip I deserved for my punishment, such a little boy as I was, and so great a sinner. So you did well for me from those who did not do well, and you paid me most justly what I as a sinner deserved. For you have commanded it and so it is, that every man's disordered soul shall be his own punishment.[41]

---

[40] As always, Augustine stresses the paradox of sin, that it should be and not be; it is a contradiction in being. Its glory has no glory, and its fulfillment empties the soul.
[41] That evil is its own punishment was taught also by the Greek philosophers. It gives the lie to those whose idea of God is of an arbitrary and cruel avenger. Sin is a self-inflicted wound, a self-infecting disease.

13

But why I hated Greek, which I was steeped in when I was little, I still have not quite puzzled out. For I fell in love with Latin—not with the rudiments, but with what those who are called men of letters teach. As for those rudiments, to read, to write, and to do numbers—they were no less a burden and a punishment for me than was everything Greek. Since I was but flesh, and a breath that passes and does not return,[42] where could this come from, if not from sin and the vanity of this life? For those rudiments were better, as they were more certain. From them was first wrought in me what I still possess, the skill to read what I find written, and to write what I want to. Better, than those later lessons whereby I had to commit to memory the wanderings of some Aeneas or other, while I forgot my own, and to weep for the death of Dido, who slew herself for love, when at the same time I, most pitiable, bore with dry eyes my own dying to you, O God, my life.[43]

---

[42] Ps 78:39.

[43] With remarkable insouciance, Augustine has reduced the legendary founder of Rome, Aeneas, to "some Aeneas or other." The story of Aeneas is told by Virgil, in his epic *Aeneid*, the basic text for schoolboys in the Latin-speaking world for centuries. Aeneas, it was said, was a prince of Troy, and on the night when the city was being destroyed, he and other refugees fled the land, guided by a prophecy that he would settle the people in a new land, Italy, and there be the progenitors of a great nation and empire. Aeneas thus wandered about the seas, like Odysseus before him, but unlike Odysseus, who was notable for his cunning and trickery, Aeneas was notable for piety, which the poet Virgil wished to identify as the most Roman of all virtues, combining duty to one's family, to the household gods, to the fatherland, and to the great gods. Amid his journey, Aeneas and his ships were blown by storm to the shores of a newly founded city in North Africa, Carthage. There, the queen Dido, herself a refugee and a victim of evil and cunning, welcomed Aeneas and the Trojans, and, by the machinations of the goddess Juno, who wanted to keep the Trojans from reaching Italy, and the goddess Venus, Aeneas's mother, at enmity with Juno, she falls madly in love with Aeneas, going so far as to offer to make the Trojans equal to her own people. But when Aeneas, warned by the gods, must abandon Carthage after all, Dido erupts into fury, and curses Aeneas and his descendants, as she dies by her own hand. The wandering of Aeneas, whom the learned of Augustine's time knew was but a fictional character, proceeds from Troy to Carthage to Italy, and thus to the Rome that is to be. Augustine's history would bring him also to Carthage and then to Rome—but his will be the history of a true pilgrimage. Since the *Aeneid* was for the Romans a sacred text, Augustine's dismissal of it was a direct challenge to the heart of imperial paganism and the myths upon which it attempted to found itself.

For what can be more pathetic than this? That a pitiable fellow should have no pity on himself, but should shed tears for Dido who died from loving Aeneas, but shed no tears for his own death, which comes from not loving you, God, the light of my heart and the bread for the mouth of my soul within, the virtue that weds my mind and the bosom of my thought? I did not love you, and I fornicated against you, and from everywhere came cheers for the fornicator, "Well done, well done!" For to be friendly with this world is to fornicate against you, and so often do we hear, "Well done," that we are abashed not to be so. But I did not weep for that. I wept for *Dido who came to death by the sword, seeking after the last things,*[44] all the while I sought the lowest of your creatures, abandoning you; I, mere earth, sinking to earth. But had I been forbidden to read these things, how sad I would have been—sad, not to read what made me sad! Such mindless stuff was thought to be more profitable and commendable than those lessons by which I learned how to read and write.

But let my God now cry out in my soul, and let your truth speak to me, "It is not so, it is not so; that first learning was far better." For look now, I am far readier to forget the wanderings of Aeneas and everything else like that, than to forget how to write and read. Sure, they hang curtains to veil the entry to the grammar schools—not as a cloth of honor for some mystery, but as a cover for error. Let those buyers and sellers of literature not cry out against me, my God, for I do not fear them anymore, as I confess to you what my soul desires, and I take my rest in reprehending my evil ways, so that I may love your ways that are good, let them not cry out, if I should put them to the test and ask, "Is it true that Aeneas once came to Carthage, as the poet says?" The less learned among them will say they do not know. The more learned will say it never happened. But if I ask them with what letters "Aeneas" is written, everyone who has gotten so far in learning will reply with the

---

[44] *Aeneid*, 6.457. The words are spoken by Aeneas in the underworld, when he sees the shade of Dido, and he appeals to her to speak to him, since he did not leave Carthage willingly. Dido will turn away without a word.

truth, according to the rule that men established among themselves to govern these signs. And if I should go on to ask which would make for more difficulty in this life, to forget how to read and write, or to forget these figments of poetry, who would not see right away how to respond, unless he had forgotten himself completely? And so I sinned, still but a boy, when I gave more love to those empty things than to these that were better for me—rather, I hated these outright, but I loved those. To tell the truth, "one and one are two, two and two are four," was for me a detestable jingle, but what a sweet spectacle of emptiness it was, the wooden horse full of men at arms, the burning of Troy, and *even the shade of Creusa*.[45]

14

But why then did I hate Greek literature, that sings of such things? For Homer was skillful at weaving tales, and is a most delightful liar,[46] and still he was a bitter pill for me when I was a boy. I suppose Virgil is the same for Greek boys when they are forced to study him, as I was forced to study Homer. The difficulty, the sheer difficulty of learning a language from a far-off land, sprinkled with gall all the Greek delicacies of those fabulous stories. I understood not a word of it, and yet was I threatened with savage terrors and punishments to make me understand.

Now, when I was a baby, I did not understand a word of Latin, but by observation I learned it without any fear or torture, just by the sweet baby-talk of my nurses, and the jests of those who laughed

---

[45] *Aeneid*, 2.773. Creusa was Aeneas's wife. She was to follow him as they made their way through the burning city of Troy, but she lost the path, and when Aeneas tried to retrace his steps, crying out for her, her shade appeared to him and told him to leave Troy, to be at peace, and to care for their child, the boy Ascanius.

[46] Plato had accused Homer of weaving lovely falsehoods about the gods, and that is why, in the *Republic*, his Socrates banishes the poet from the ideal city he is imagining. Thus was pagan instruction based upon what the most learned men acknowledged were fictions, but perhaps useful fictions for governing the people.

with me, and the happy chatter of my playmates. So I learned to talk without any grievous pain to goad me on, as my own heart led me to make its conceptions clear, and it never would have been so, unless I had learned words not from teachers but from people who talked to me, into whose ears in turn I brought forth whatever I was thinking. Hence it is clear that for a child learning a language, free curiosity has more power than does enforcement, bristling with threats. But by your laws that enforcement restrains the wild tossing of liberty, your laws, O God, from the birch rod of the master to the trials of the martyrs, your potent laws that mingle the wholesome and the bitter, to call us back to you from the plague-ridden pleasure whereby we had first wandered away from you.

15

O Lord, hear my prayer, and let not my soul faint under your discipline, let me not grow faint in confessing to you your mercies, by whose means you pulled me up from all my worst ways.[47] Hear me, that you may be sweeter to me than all the enticements I always followed, and that I may love you with all my strength, and lay hold upon your hand with all my heart, and that you may draw me away from every temptation, unto the end.

For behold, O Lord, my king and my God, let whatever useful things I learned when I was a boy serve you, let whatever I speak and write and read and reckon serve you, for you gave me discipline while I was studying those empty lies, and you forgave the sins I committed in taking delight in them. In those studies, I learned many useful words, though I could have learned them from things that were not mere vanity. And that is the truly safe path for children to walk.

---

[47] Cf. Ps 6:1–2. Discipline is literally a means of instruction. The worldly teachers applied the rod to beat falsehood and false ambitions into their young charges. God's discipline is at once gentler and sharper, to bring the soul to humility and the truth.

16

But woe to you, river of human custom! Who can stand against you? How long must it be before you run dry? How long shall you keep on tossing the sons of Eve into that great and terrible ocean, which they who have set sail by the mast-tree hardly manage to cross? Was it not in you that I read of Jove thundering and committing adultery?[48] In truth he could not do these two things at once. It was all put-on, that someone might have the authority to imitate adultery in fact, with the false thunder playing the part of a pander. But which of our long-robed teachers can with a staid ear hear a man of their own field crying out and saying, "Homer made these things up, and gave human features to the gods—I'd rather he had given divine features to us!"[49] But it is closer to the truth to say that Homer made these things up indeed, attributing godlike features to wicked men, so that crimes would not be reckoned as crimes, and anyone who committed them would seem to be imitating not lost men but the gods in heaven above.

Nonetheless, O floodwater from hell, the sons of men are cast upon you, and they even pay money to learn these things. And a great production is made of it, when they stage the fables in public, in the marketplace, and the teachers by law are granted a salary over and above the tuition the students pay. And you crash against your rocks and roar, "Here, here are words to learn, here you gain skill in speaking, the skill you need above all to persuade when you need to persuade, and to make your thinking plain!" Else we would never have understood these terms, the Shower of Gold, the Lap, the Makeup Trick, the Temples of Heaven, and all the other words written in that place, where Terence

---

[48] Augustine is perhaps thinking of the myth of Danae, whom Zeus (Jove) impregnated by means of a shower of gold. In general, the adulteries of the chief of the gods were frequent and utterly untrammeled from considerations of good and evil.

[49] Cicero, *Tusculan Disputations*, I.26.65. Cicero (106–43 BC) is discussing the nature of the gods and of the human soul, in part to console himself after the loss of his beloved daughter, Tullia. What divine features? "To live, to know, to find things out, to remember." Augustine will return, in the final books of the *Confessions*, to those divine features of the soul.

leads on stage a lewd young man who wants to use Jove as a model for his own corruption. For he gazes at a painting on a wall, portraying the tale in which Jove pours a golden shower into Danae's lap, a makeup trick to fool the girl. And look how he rouses himself to lust, as if by some teaching from heaven:

> *What god do I follow, but him who shakes the heavens with thunder?*
> *Shall I, but a man, not do the same? I have, and I love it!*[50]

There is no way, none, that these words are more easily learned by this filthy stuff. Rather, by these words is the filthy deed perpetrated with the firmer confidence. I do not accuse the words, which are like choice and precious vessels, but the wine of error in them which our drunkard teachers gave us to drink, and unless we drank, they beat us, and we had no sober judge to appeal to. And even so, my God, in whose sight my memory can rest secure, I learned these things with a will, I took delight in them, poor fellow, and was accounted a lad with good prospects.

17

Allow me, my God, to say a little about my inborn talents, your gift to me, and upon what raving nonsense I wasted it. I had a task to do, full of trouble to my soul, with praise for a reward if I did well, and shame and the dread of beatings if I did not. I was to speak the words of Juno in her wrath and sorrow, because she could not *turn away from Italy the king of the Trojans.*[51] I had heard that Juno never uttered those words,

---

[50] Cf. Terence, *The Eunuch*, 585. Terence (d. 159 BC) was, with Plautus, one of the two great comic playwrights of ancient Rome. The play hinges on a trick played by a young man who uses Jove as an excuse for his wickedness. Since he does not have a beard, the boy passes himself off for a eunuch and slave, and once he is admitted into the household, he rapes the girl he is in love with.

[51] *Aeneid*, 1.38. Rage and inordinate desire are, in Virgil's poem, the two most destructive forces in human life. Augustine has criticized the adulterous lust of Jove; now he strikes at

but we were compelled to wander off and follow in the footsteps of these poetical fictions, and to speak in free prose what the poets had spoken in metered verse. And the boy won the most praise if, in accord with the dignity of the personage he was shadowing forth, he gave the most lifelike semblance of wrath and sorrow, dressed up in words most fit for the meaning.

But what was that to me, O my true life, my God? What was it to me, that for my recitation I got more acclaim than did so many of my fellow readers, my own age? Was that not all just smoke and wind? Was there nothing else for me to exercise my talents and my tongue on? Your praises, O Lord, your praises, through your Scriptures, might have propped up the young vine of my heart, and it would not have been ravaged by empty frivolities, a prey to winged spirits of filth. For there is more than one way to offer sacrifice to the transgressing angels.

18

What wonder was it that I was carried along into vanities, and that I left you and your house, my God? For I was encouraged to imitate men who, if they recounted things they had done that were not evil, and they slipped into some bad style or bad grammar and were criticized for it, would be covered with confusion; but if they told of their lusts in a polished style, rich in words well-chosen and properly placed, they would glory in the praise they got. You see these things, O Lord, and you keep silence, for you are long-suffering, but shall you keep silence forever? Even now you will draw up out of this most horrible pit the soul that seeks you and thirsts for your delights, whose heart says to you, "I have sought your face, your face, O Lord, will I seek."[52] For I had wandered far from your countenance, in the dark fog of my desires. For we do not depart from you or return to you on foot, by

---

the fury of Juno, Jove's much sinned-against wife.
[52] Ps 27:8.

22

change of place. Truly, that younger son of yours[53] did not look for horses or wagons or ships, nor did he fly away on a wing that could be seen, or move his legs to go on that road where he might live in a far country and spill away what you had given him, you the sweet and gentle Father, for you gave him his portion when he set out, and you were sweeter still to him when he returned destitute. No, he left you by the lust of his desire. That was the darkness, that was to be far away from your face.

See it, O Lord my God, and see it with patience, as you ever do; see how careful the sons of men are to observe the rules of letters and syllables they have received from speakers before their time, and how careless they are with the rules of everlasting salvation they have received from you. Suppose someone holds to and teaches the old rules of pronunciation, and suppose, contrary to good grammar, he fails to aspirate the first syllable and says *'uman* instead of *human*. He will make men more disgruntled than if he should hate a human being, though he himself is one. It is as if he thought that some enemy of his could be more pernicious to him than his own hatred that goads him on against the man; or that he could work more destruction on the man he persecutes, than on his own heart by his enmity. Surely the knowledge of letters is not more interior than is this law written in the conscience, that we are doing something to another person what we ourselves would not endure.[54]

How secret you are, dwelling in silence in the heavenly heights, O God who alone are great! By a tireless law you cast blindness as a penalty for unlawful desires. When a man seeking fame for his eloquence stands before a human judge, surrounded by crowds of men, assailing his enemy with the most savage hatred, he is on the strictest watch lest by a slip of the tongue he say *among 'uman beings*. But he has no

---

[53] The prodigal son: cf. Lk 15:11–31.

[54] Cf. Mt 7:12, Lk 6:31. The sin, again, is a self-contradiction, setting man not only against his fellow man but against himself.

fear lest by the fury of his mind he take from *among human beings* the human being he hates.

19

So there I was, a wretched boy, lazing about at the threshold of these customs. And that was the arena where I was more wary of committing a grammatical blunder, than I was of glaring with envy, supposing I did commit one, at those who committed none. I say these things and confess them to you, my God. For such was I praised, and to please the sorts of men who praised me seemed a life well lived. I did not see the whirlpool of filth into which I had been cast from your eyes. What in your sight was fouler than I was? For I displeased even such people, and told any number of lies to deceive my tutor, my masters, and my parents, all for the love of play, and for my restless passion to gape at spectacles that meant nothing, and to imitate what I saw on stage.

I even stole from my parents' pantry and table, either because my gullet commanded me, or because I needed something to give to the boys to play games with me, because they sold their play, though they enjoyed it as much as I did. And in these games, overthrown by an empty desire to be regarded as excellent, I would often cheat to win. So what I would never put up with, but would most bitterly protest if I caught someone else at it, I would do to others. But if I were caught, I would protest, and would rather rage than give in.

Is that childlike innocence? It is not, O Lord, it is not. I beseech you, my God; for these are the same things, the very same, as we go from tutors and teachers, from nuts and sparrows and balls, to governors and kings, gold, booty, property for sale, just as we grow older, as the birch rod gives way to greater punishments. It was therefore, O King, the stature of the child you approved as a sign of humility, when you said, "Of such is the kingdom of heaven."[55]

---

[55] Mt 19:14.

20

Nevertheless to you, our Lord and God, I owe thanks, to you, most excellent creator and ruler of the universe, even if you had willed that I should be no more than a boy. For I existed, I was alive, I could perceive things; I took care for my well-being, and that was a trace of the most secret unity whence I had my being; by an inner sense I brought my outward senses into one fold, and in these little things and in my thoughts about them I delighted in the truth. I did not want to make mistakes; I had a vigorous memory; I was well taught in speaking; I was soothed by friendship; I fled from pain and sorrow and ignorance. What in such a living soul was not marvelous and worthy of praise?

But these were all gifts my God gave me; I did not give them to myself. And they were good, and all together they made up myself. Good, therefore, is he who made me, and he himself is my good, and I rejoice before him for all those good things that made my being when I was a boy. But this was my sin: I sought delights, and lofty places, and truths, not in him, but in his creatures, in myself and in others. And so I rushed headlong into sorrows, defeats, and errors. Thanks be to you, my sweetness and my honor and my trust, my God, thanks be to you for your gifts! But preserve them for me, and so shall you preserve me too, and what you have given me will grow and be brought to perfection, and I shall be with you, for my very being is your gift.

BOOK TWO

1

I wish to call to mind the ways I was befouled, and the fleshly corruptions of my soul, not because I love them, but so that I may love you, my God. I am doing this for the love of your love, retracing my wicked paths in the bitterness of my remembrance, so that you may become sweet to me, you, the sweetness that does not beguile, sweetness that is happy and free from care. So may you gather me up from the shattered fragments into which I was strewn, when I turned aside from you who are whole and one, and I wasted myself upon the many.

For I burned in my youth to get my fill of hell, and I made bold to go wild in the dark woods of various loves, and my beauty faded away, and I stank in your sight, while I pleased myself and longed to please the eyes of men.[56]

---

[56] Augustine here touches upon another of the transcendentals: oneness. When we sin, we lose our integrity, our being properly ordered, with all our faculties in harmony with one another. We fall, so to speak, from oneness into duplicity, divided against ourselves. God, however, does not possess faculties in the partial and fragmentary way we possess them; he is his own power, his own goodness, his own truth.

2

And what was it that delighted me, but to love and to be loved? But I did not hold to the due measure, the bright boundary-path of true friendship, that binds one soul to another. Mists came breathing up from the muddy cravings of the flesh and the springs of puberty, and they overcast and darkened my heart, so that I could not tell the difference between the clear skies of genuine love and the fog of lust. Both love and lust roiled in confusion, and they swept my weakling youth over the falls of desire and plunged me into a gulping whirlpool of crimes. Your anger against me rose in strength, but I was not aware of it. I had been drummed deaf by the clashing chains of my mortality, the penalty for my soul and its pride. I went far away from you, and you let me go, and I was tossed here and there, spilled out, overflowing, frothing over in my fornications, and still you kept silent. O my joy, so late in coming! You kept silent then, and as for me, I took my way farther and farther from you, into more and more fields where no seed can grow but sorrow, proud in my downheartedness, restless in my languor.

If only someone had been there to ease my trouble, to turn to good use the fleeting beauty of those new things I loved! Someone might have set an aim to their sweet delights, so that my youth's tides, if I could get no rest from them, would break at last upon the shores of marriage, and would be content to have children, as your law, O Lord, prescribes. For it is you who fashion the new scions of our mortality, laying a gentle hand upon us, to blunt the thorns that you once shut out from your paradise.[57] For your omnipotence is not far from us, even when we are far from you. Surely I might have kept a better watch, and heard your thunder, when you said, "Those who marry shall have trials in the flesh, but I wish to spare you," and, "It is good for a man not to touch a woman," and, "He who has no wife spends his time thinking

---

[57] Cf. Gn 3:18. Augustine reads the verse both literally and allegorically: the thorns that spring from man's own earth after the fall are the pricks and stings of concupiscence, of disordered desire.

of the things of God, but the married man must think of the things of the world, to please his wife."[58] I should have been awake, I should have listened to these words, and made myself a eunuch for the kingdom of heaven, to be the gladder as I waited for your embraces.[59]

But I was all in a fever, poor fellow that I was, following along my headstrong course. I had left you behind, and I overtopped the lawful bounds you had set, but I did not escape the whip. What mortal man can do that? For you were at my side always, mercifully severe, seasoning all my illicit merriments with most bitter disappointment, so that I might seek delight that does not disappoint. And if I found it, what could it be but you, O Lord? Only you, who have decked the moral law with sorrow, you who smite us that you may heal us, who slay us that we may not die apart from you. Where was I, and how far had I banished myself from the delights of your house, in the sixteenth of my years in the flesh, when the delirium of licentious craving had gotten the scepter over me, and I gave myself up to it utterly? For men it is but a blot, a fault, but by your laws quite forbidden. My elders did not trouble to snatch me from ruin by getting me married. But they took great care that I should learn how to work up a mighty speech and persuade people by my words.

3

That was the year my studies were interrupted, because when I returned home from Madaura, the nearby city where I first learned to roam the fields of literature and oratory, my father was gathering up the expenses for a journey to Carthage farther away, more by his spirited determination than by his wealth, since he was just a rather poor freedman from Thagaste.[60] To whom am I telling this? Not to you, my God, but

---

[58] 1 Cor 7:28, 1, 32.

[59] Cf. Mt 19:12. Those who make themselves eunuchs for heaven's sake, Augustine suggests, do so from an ardent desire for the embraces of Christ. Thus do they want more love, not less.

[60] Patricius, Augustine's father, is notably generous and self-sacrificing, even, we might say,

in your presence I tell it to those of my kind, my fellow human beings, whatever little part of them may happen upon these writings of mine. And why? Why else, but that I and whoever reads them may consider the depths from which we must cry unto you. And what is nearer to your ears than a confessing heart and a life lived by faith? For who was there who did not praise that man, my father, to the skies, because, going beyond the means of his household, he furnished his son with everything necessary for me to go so far away to study? Many far richer citizens undertook no such business for their sons. Meanwhile that same father did not bustle about to see how I was growing toward you, or how clean my life was, so long as I became a man of culture, or rather uncultivated, a desert not tilled by you, you the good and one true landlord of my heart.

But while in my sixteenth year, furloughed from school because we did not have the money, I lived idly at home with my parents, and the thorn-bushes of lust grew rank over my head, and there was no hand to root them out. Rather, my father saw me one day at the baths and noticed how I was coming of age, endowed with the restless stirrings of first manhood, and he told my mother about it with joy, as if grandchildren were already on the way. He rejoiced like a drunken man, drunk with the wine the world drinks when it forgets you, its Creator, and loves the creature in your place—that invisible wine of its own crook-backed will, bent toward the lowest of things. But you had begun to raise up your temple in my mother's heart, to lay the foundations of your holy dwelling. For my father had only recently become a catechumen. But she was startled with a pious fear and trembling, and though I was not yet one of the faithful, she was still afraid of those crooked ways that people walk in, when they turn to you the back and not the face.

Woe to me! And dare I say that you kept silent, my God, when I wandered ever farther from you? Did you really then keep silent from

---

providential in his care for his son's career in the world; it is just that he has neglected the greater care for his son's soul.

me? Whose words were they but yours, that my mother, your faithful one, was always singing in my ears? But nothing of them descended into my heart to move me to action. I well remember that she took me aside and urged me, warning me with great care, not to commit fornication, and especially not to defile any man's wife. These seemed to me just what women worry about, what I would blush to pay any heed to. But they were your warnings, and I did not know it, and I thought that you were silent and that it was she who spoke, through whom you were not silent to me. And I held you in contempt when I held her so, I, her son, the son of your handmaid, your servant.

But I was ignorant, and I ran headlong on a course so blind, I was ashamed among the boys my age to be any less shameful than they were. For I heard them brag about their wicked deeds, taking more glory in them the fouler they were, and I took pleasure in doing them not only for the pleasure but for the praise.[61] What is more worthy of blame than vice? Yet what did I do? I steeped myself more deeply in vice, so that they would not blame me. And when I had nothing to put me on a level with the lost, I made things up, and said I had done what I had not, lest I look the more contemptible as I was the more innocent, or held to be a coward, because I was more chaste.

See with what a gang I haunted the squares of Babylon, and I wallowed in its slops as if they were cinnamon and precious oils. And to make me cleave fast to the navel of sin, my invisible enemy trod me down and seduced me, because I was easy to seduce. For even the mother of my flesh, who had already fled from the center of Babylon,[62] was still lingering awhile in its neighborhood. She had admonished me to keep myself chaste, and now she gave ear to what her husband said, and she thought it was best to trammel up within the bounds of con-

---

[61] Augustine is careful to distinguish motives. We want more than bodily pleasures. We want friendship, and we want the praise that true friends give us for what we have done well. The desire for praise is, in itself, natural and good: recall the praise that the master gives to the faithful servants (Mt 25:21).

[62] Cf. Jer 51:6.

jugal love what she knew was an infection now and a dangerous threat to come, supposing that it could not be cut back to the quick. But she did not take enough care for this, because they were afraid that a wife would be a ball and chain to my prospects. I do not mean the hope my mother had in you for the world to come, but the hope in learning, which both of my parents wanted very much that I should attain, he, because he hardly ever thought about you, and about me thought only empty things, and she, because she reckoned that the usual subjects of study would not only be no hindrance to me, but would help me on toward reaching you.[63] That is my best guess, as I recall, as to my parents' motives. And so I was given free rein to sport myself, quite beyond the rule of severity, and I poured myself out into dissoluteness, and suffered all kinds of afflictions because of it. And in all these things, a fog shut out from me the peaceful skies of your truth, and my iniquity came forth from me, as from a greasy fatness.[64]

4

Your law, O Lord, surely forbids stealing, as does the law written upon the human heart, which wickedness itself cannot expunge. For what thief will calmly put up with another thief, even if he is rich and the man who robs him is driven by poverty? I too wanted to steal, and so I did, not compelled by need, unless it was a poverty of justice, or boredom with doing the right thing, or being fatted up with iniquity. For I stole what I had plenty of, and much better besides, nor did I want to relish the thing itself, but rather the theft, the very theft and the sin.[65]

---

[63] Saint Monica was not a learned woman. We have no evidence that she could read. But her attitude toward the learning Augustine was acquiring was wiser than her husband's, and in fact Augustine did eventually read works that brought him closer to the faith. He did not read himself into the faith, for that would make of faith an intellectual conviction that we persuade ourselves of, rather than a free gift from God.

[64] Cf. Ps 73:7. The echo of the psalm is ironic, since Augustine and his family were not rich; the fatness he refers to is that of sin, that shuts up the eyes of the soul.

[65] Plato had said that men do evil because of ignorance, and thus we can make men good by teaching them what the good is. And in fact, as Augustine will show, we do evil under

There was a pear tree near our vineyard, laden with fruit, not appealing either to the eye or the taste. But a group of us wicked young lads went in the middle of the night to shake that tree down and spirit away the fruit, for in our pestilent way we had kept on playing till that hour in the public squares. And we carried off a great load of pears, not to feast on, even if we did eat a little of it, but to throw to the pigs. We loved it, because we had no leave to do it.

Behold my heart, O God, behold my heart, which you pitied in the bottom of the abyss. And now behold, let my heart tell you what it was seeking, that I should be so free with my evil, that there should be no cause of my malice but the malice itself. It was foul, and I loved it; I loved to go down to the lost, I loved my failing, not the thing for which I was at fault, but the failing itself. My soul was vile, shrinking back from you, my mainstay, and holding fast to destruction, seeking nothing in shame but the very shame.

5

There is a splendor in beautiful bodies, as in gold and silver and the like; and in the flesh's touch we prize what we find agreeable, and likewise there is some proper form of body most accommodating for each of our senses. Temporal honor also has its grace, in commanding and overcoming by its own power, and even the eagerness to avenge a wrong springs from that source. And yet, in seeking these things, we must not depart from you, Lord, or stray from your law. And this life we live has its allurement, in its own measure and grace, and in its harmony with all those lower things of beauty. Friendship among men, too, is sweet, because of the dear bond that binds many hearts in one. On account of all these good things and

---

the impetus of seeking something good. But Augustine also suggests that Plato underestimated the depravity of the human heart. For Augustine, the theft of the pears was terrible not because of the value of the things stolen, because they were only pears, and they were not very good at that, but because he sought the evil for its own sake, or, more precisely, for the power the evil deed seemed to have to unite him with his fellows in theft. It is a terrible parody of the body of Christ.

others like them we sin when we lean toward them beyond fit measure, for they are but lower goods, and we desert the best and highest—you, O Lord, and your truth and your law. For even these lower goods have their delights, but not like my God, who made them all. In him does the just man delight, and he is the joy of the upright of heart.[66]

So when we ask about some wicked deed and why it was done, the usual reply is that it came from a hunger for one or another of these good but lower things, if we think we can get it, or from a fear of losing it. For they are beautiful, and they have their fit place, though if we compare them with goods that are higher and that bring more blessings, they are but mean and poor. Someone has murdered a man. Why did he do it? He was in love with the man's wife. He coveted the man's estate. He wanted to rob him to get something to live on. He was afraid the man would take the same from him. The man hurt him, and he was on fire to avenge it. Would anyone murder a man without cause, but just from the pleasure of murder? Who would believe it? It has been said of a certain savagely cruel and senseless man, that he was evil and cruel just for the sake of it. But he had already given the cause. It was, he said, "to keep my hand or my heart from growing sluggish, from doing nothing."[67] And what about that in turn? Why? So that after he had assaulted the city with wickedness and taken it captive, he could hunt down honors and power and wealth for himself, with no fear of the laws, and not cowed by any difficulty that might arise from want of means or a guilty conscience. So even Catiline did not love his villainy, but something else for which he played the villain.

---

[66] Cf. Ps 97:11.

[67] Sallust, *The Conspiracy of Catiline*, ch. 16. Lucius Sergius Catilina (c. 108–62 BC) has gone down in history as a man of immense ambition, extraordinary cruelty, and shameless treason, as he sought control of the Roman state. Cicero delivered his four famous orations against Catiline, quashing Catiline's candidacy for the consulship. Catiline attempted to lead an armed insurrection against the senatorial armies, but he was defeated and slain in battle in 62 BC, and his army was obliterated. Cicero went on to write a poem, in the epic style, about his own consulship and his having saved Rome. But Julius Caesar, who favored Catiline, was waiting in the wings.

6

You thievery of mine, you deed of night in my sixteenth year, what did I love in you, wretch that I was? You were not beautiful, for thievery cannot be so. Are you anything at all, that I may have it out with you? Those pears we stole were beautiful, because they were your creations, O most lovely Creator of all things, God of goodness, God the supreme good and my true good. The pears were beautiful, but they were not what my miserable soul was craving. For I had plenty of pears that were better. I plucked those pears just so I might steal. No sooner had I plucked them than I threw them away, and I feasted only on the sin, the fruit that made me glad. If any bit of the pears did enter my mouth, wickedness was its spice.

And now, O Lord my God, I ask what it was in the theft that delighted me. Nothing lovely to behold; and I am not talking about the loveliness we see in plain dealing and prudence, or in the mind of man, or his senses, or his flourishing life in the flesh; nor the splendor of the stars set each in its proper place, or in the earth and the sea filled with the fry of the generations, those that are born succeeding upon those that pass away. I am not even talking about that sort of shadowy and faulty loveliness we find in vices that deceive.

For haughtiness mimics the height of majesty, while you, O God most high, are alone above all. And what does ambition seek but honors and glory, while you alone are to be honored before all, and are glorious forever? Men of might are fierce so that they may be feared; but who is to be feared if not God alone? What can be wrested from his power, or what can be taken away, and when, or where, or how, or by whom? The sweet nothings of the wanton long to be loved; but nothing is more soothing than your charity, nor can anything be loved more wholesomely than your truth, most handsome and filled with light. Idle curiosity pretends to pursue knowledge; while you, Most High, know all things. Even ignorance and dullness go draped in the garb of simplicity and innocence, but nothing is more essentially simple than

35

you are. And what is more innocent than you, when it is their own deeds that are enemies to the wicked? Sloth itself hankers after a sort of rest; but what sure rest is there, apart from the Lord? Luxury likes to be called bounty and having one's fill; but you are the fullness and the never-failing bounty of incorruptible sweetness. Squandering pretends to spill itself freely abroad; but you are the most flowing bestower of all things good. Avarice seeks to possess many things; but you possess all. Envy wrangles over excellence; what is more excellent than you? Anger seeks to be avenged; but whose vengeance is more just than yours? Fearfulness shies away from sudden and unusual things that threaten what it loves, ever on the alert for its security. But what can strike you as unusual? What to you is sudden? Or who can sunder from you what you love? Where but in you is security steadfast? Sadness pines away for what it has lost, which it once loved to enjoy. It wishes it could never lose a thing, just as nothing can be taken away from you.[68]

So the soul goes whoring when it turns away from you and seeks outside of you what it can never find pure and clear unless it returns to you. All men imitate you in a twisted way when they set themselves far from you and lift themselves in glory against you. But even in so mimicking you they show that you are the creator of the whole natural world, and that there is no place where they can hide away from you.

What then did I enjoy in my thieving? How did I, in a crooked and vice-riddled way, imitate my Lord? Was it just this, that I took delight in a false show of overruling the law, since I could not do so by sheer might? Was it that I, a captive, should mimic a crippled liberty, doing something unlawful and not being punished for it—a gloomy likeness of omnipotence? Look here, a slave, fleeing his lord and gaining a shadow! What stink of rot, what monstrosity of life, how deep a pit of death! Can it be that a lawless deed could give delight, and for no other reason than that it was not lawful?

---

[68] All sin thus seeks God in objects that are not God; and ultimately, this means that man is seeking his good by his own devices and not by the gift of God. "Ye shall be as gods," said the serpent (Gn 3:4).

7

What thanks shall I render to the Lord, who gathers up these memories of mine, so that my soul does not shudder at them? I shall love you, Lord, and give you thanks, and confess your name, because you have forgiven me so many evil and unspeakable deeds. I account it to your grace and merciful heart, that you have melted my sins away like ice.[69] To your grace also do I give credit for whatever evil things I did not do. For what was I not capable of doing, when I loved the crime as a kind of grace? And I confess that all these things have been forgiven me, both the evil I did by my own will, and the evil I did not do, because you were my guide.

What man is there who can consider his frailty and yet dare to attribute his chastity or his innocence to his own powers, so that he might love you the less, as if he were less in need of the mercy you give to sinners who turn to you? Whoever may read what I remember and confess, if he has been called by you, and has followed your voice, and has shunned the sins I record, let him not laugh at me, for I was sick and was made whole by the same Doctor who prescribed for him what kept him from falling ill, or rather what made his illness milder. Then let him love you so much the more indeed, seeing me delivered by you from the maladies of my great sins, and seeing himself protected by you from falling into their tangles to begin with.

8

What fruit did I, a miserable fellow, enjoy, from the deeds I now blush to recall? Especially from that thievery, when I loved the thieving itself, nothing else, though itself was *a nothing* and I was the more miserable for it. Yet had I been alone, I would not have done it—or so I remember what my mind was then; alone, there is no way I would have done it. Then it was the company I loved, the gang I did it with. So it was not

---

[69] Cf. Sir 3:15.

that I loved nothing besides the theft. Or rather it was *another nothing*, since it too was a kind of nothing.[70]

But what was it, really? Who else can teach me, but he who sheds light upon my heart and reveals its shadows? What is it that comes to my mind, to inquire into, to discuss, and to ponder? For had I loved those pears I stole, had I craved to enjoy them, I might have done the evil deed on my own, supposing I could get my pleasure by that way. I would not have needed the friction of guilty minds to inflame my desire and its itch. But there was no pleasure for me in the pears. It lay in the crime itself, committed by a company of sinners together.

9

What was then the state of my soul? All too base, and woe to me who kept it. Still, what was it? Who can understand his crimes? Our hearts were tickled and we laughed, because we had tricked those who did not know what we were up to and would have most heartily disapproved. Yet why did I delight in the fact that I did not do it alone? Is it that laughter is not easy to come by, when a man is alone? True, it is not easy. Still, once in a while laughter will overcome a man even when no one else is around, if something really ridiculous strikes his mind or his senses. Yet I, alone, would not have done the deed; I would never have done it alone.

Behold, my God, I lay before you the living remembrance of my soul. Alone, I would not have done the stealing, when what delighted me was not what I stole, but that I stole. I would have gotten no pleasure from doing it alone, and so I would not have done it. O friendship, all too unfriendly! Seducer of the mind, leaving no clue! Eager craving to hurt someone else, making a game of it, a joke! Thirst, not for my gain but for someone else's loss, and not from a lust for vengeance, but only because we said, "Come on, let's do it," and we were ashamed not to be shameless.

---

[70] Augustine will learn what he did not know when he was a youth, that evil has no existence of itself. What we call evil is a turn toward non-existence, toward emptiness.

10

Who will pick apart these most crooked and tangled knots?[71] It is foul, and I wish not to think about it, or look at it. It is you I long for, O justice and innocence, lovely and graceful to the light of honest eyes; you I crave, with a fullness that can never be filled. With you there is true rest, and life that can never be troubled. He who enters into you, enters into the joy of his Lord,[72] and he shall not fear, and he shall possess himself best with him who is the best. But I, I slipped away in the days of my youth, and wandered from you, my God, far afield from your steadfastness. And I made of my own self a kingdom of want.

---

[71] Cf. Dn 5:12.
[72] Cf. Mt 25:23.

BOOK THREE

1

To Carthage I came, and a fryingpan of disgraceful loves sizzled roundabout me. I was not yet in love, yet I loved to be in love, and from a neediness more deeply hidden within me, I hated myself for being less in need. I sought for something to love, loving to be in love, and I hated security and a path without snares, because the famine was within me, a starving of that interior food, of yourself, my God. Yet that famine did not make me hungry, for I had no desire for incorruptible nourishments, not because I was filled with them; the emptier I was, the more they nauseated me. And so my soul was not hale and strong, but it broke out into open sores, miserably longing to scratch itself against things of the senses, things which, if they were not alive, would never be loved at all. Still I found it sweet to love and to be loved, especially when I could enjoy the body of the one I loved.

And so I polluted the springs of friendship with the filthy things I craved, I clouded its bright gleam with a hell of lust, and I was foul and base, but in my overflowing emptiness I passed myself about as quite the sophisticated and elegant fellow. I hurled myself into love, longing to be taken captive. Merciful God, my God, how good were you to sprinkle so much gall on that sweetness of mine! For I was loved in return, and I pressed on to the bonds of enjoyment, glad to be tied up in wearisome tangles, to be whipped by the iron lashes of jealousy and suspicion and fear and anger and wrangling.

2

Stage-shows swept me away, filled as they were with images of my miseries and fuel for my fire. Why is it that a man in the theater is willing to be saddened by tragic and tearful things, which in his own person he would never want to suffer? And still he likes to suffer sorrow from them as he looks on, and the very sorrow is his delight. What a pathetic madness this is! For the more such things move you, the feebler you are, and the more prone to suffer. Now, when a man suffers in his own person, we call it misery, and when he shares in another man's suffering, we call it kindheartedness. But what kindheartedness can you give to things pretended on a stage? You hear them, and you are not stirred to help anyone; you are invited to feel sorry, and that is all, and the sorrier you feel, the more you cheer the author of the images. And if the calamities that befall the persons on stage, whether they are made up or come from olden times, are portrayed so that the spectator feels no sorrow, he walks out on the show, bored and grumbling, but if he does feel sorrow, he stays in his seat, riveted, and enjoying himself mightily.

And so tears and sorrows are loved. No doubt, every man likes to enjoy himself. Is it then that although no man finds it pleasant to be miserable, he does find it pleasant to be merciful, and since you cannot be merciful without sorrow, that is the one reason why sorrows are loved? This too has friendship as its spring.

But where does the stream go? Which way is it flowing? Why does it empty into a torrent of boiling tar, those vast heaves of nasty lust, wherein it is changed utterly, and at its own nod it wrests itself away from the clarity of the skies above, and makes itself warped and base? Shall we then repudiate a merciful heart? Not at all. Therefore let sorrow sometimes be loved. But beware, my soul, of uncleanness! Under the watchful eye of my God, the God of our fathers, worthy of praise and exalted forever—beware of uncleanness![73]

I still do feel compassion, but in those days I rejoiced with the lovers on stage, when by disgraceful means they got to enjoy one another, although the wicked deeds were but pretended images to delight the theatrical eye; and when they lost one another, I was saddened with them, as if I were full of mercy. Either way, I was pleased. But now, in truth, I pity far more the man who takes joy in his wickedness, than the man who can hardly bear it when some pernicious pleasure is scraped away, and he loses a felicity that is miserable. This really is a more genuine mercy, but sorrow takes no delight in it. Granted, a man who feels sorry for the miserable is to be commended. He has done an office of charity. But if he really has the heart of a merciful brother, he would rather there were no cause for him to feel sorry. Supposing the impossible, that a good will can wish for evil, then he who truly and sincerely shows mercy might desire that there be poor wretches for him to be merciful to. Some sorrow, then, is to be commended, but none is to be loved. For you, Lord God, love our souls far better and far more purely than we do, and you are more incorruptibly merciful, as you are not wounded with sorrow. What man can be that way?

But, poor fellow, I loved in those days to be moved with sorrow, and I went seeking what would make me feel sorry, when in those troubles of mere pretenders leaping about on stage, the actor pleased me more and led me along with all the more powerful lure, who wrung the most tears out of my eyes. And no wonder, that I, a luckless sheep, straggling away from your flock, unwilling to put up with your protection, should be fouled with the mange. That was where my love of sorrows came from. Not that they penetrated to my inmost heart—for

---

[73] Cf. Jgs 13:4. Augustine was perhaps too powerfully attracted to the stage, especially tragedies, to agree with Aristotle that the experience of watching a good but imperfect man go from happiness to misery is meant to be cleansing for us, as we experience a kind of fear and pity. Augustine would ask, "Exactly what good do these feelings do, since the object of them is merely fictitious?"

I did not love to suffer what I did love to look upon. These fictions I listened to scratched me lightly on the hide, and then, as after fingernails that tug and dig, came the angry boil and the liquefaction and the disgusting pus. Such was my life then, my God—but was it a life?

3

Still did your mercy, ever faithful, hover above me from afar. In how many iniquities did I waste myself away,[74] and what an unholy curiosity did I pursue, so that, once I had deserted you, it might drag me down to the bottom of infidelity, to the service of demons with all their sleight of hand! To them, I burnt my sacrifice, my evil deeds—and in all these things, you laid on me with your flail. For I made bold one day, within the walls of your church, during the celebration of your solemn rites, to desire and to accomplish a business to procure the fruit of death.[75] So you scourged me with heavy punishments, but they were nothing compared with what my guilt merited, O my God, my tremendous mercy, my refuge against those terrible harms into which I had wandered, cocksure, stiff-necked, falling farther from you, loving my ways and not yours, loving the freedom of a man in flight.

And those studies of mine too, which were called honorable, led but to the law courts and their quarrels, and I was supposed to excel in them—the bigger the fraud, the louder the praise. Men are so blind, they will glory in their blindness. And I was a top student in the school of rhetoric, and I was glad and proud and blown up with arrogance. Yet I was a good deal more reserved, Lord, as you know, than the Subverters, and I kept clear of their works of subversion—for this savage and devilish name was a banner to show off how sophisticated they were. I lived among them, shamelessly abashed because I was not like them. Still I kept

---

[74] Cf. Ps 31:10.

[75] We do not know what the deed was, but Augustine's reticence suggests it was something shockingly wicked, which the young man felt to be of little consequence. His sin is exacerbated by the setting. A miracle of grace was occurring within his field of vision, but he was blind to it.

company with them and sometimes liked their friendship well enough, though I always shrank back in horror from what they did, that is, from the wreckage, the subversion. For they would assail the shyness of the new students, giving them no end of trouble, for no reason at all, making fun of them and feeding their own malevolent fun. Nothing could be more like the actions of demons. What better name for them could there be, than Subverters? For they were subverted and perverted beforehand, by spirits who jeered at them behind their backs and seduced them and deceived them, in the same way as they loved to jeer at and deceive others.

4

Among such companions of my weakling youth, I studied books on eloquence, wherein I longed to stand tall, for a damnable end, full of wind, to gain the joys of human vanity. Then by the usual course of study I came upon a book by a certain Cicero, whose tongue almost everyone admires, but his heart, not so. This book urges the reader to pursue philosophy, and it is called the *Hortensius*.[76] It changed my affection. It turned my prayers toward you, Lord, and it gave me other aims and other desires. Suddenly every vain hope seemed petty to me, and I hungered with an incredible fervor for wisdom that cannot die, and I began to arise, that I might return to you. I bought that book, I think, with the allowance my mother gave me when I was nineteen, as my father had died two years before. I did not use it to file my tongue, no, not to file my tongue, for it persuaded me not by its manner of speaking, but by what it said.

---

[76] Cicero's dialogue, actually a conversation among four men, is named for his friend and rival orator, Quintus Hortensius Hortalus. He wrote it in 45 BC, in part to console himself after the death of his beloved daughter, Tullia. The work is now lost, though we have fragments of it quoted by various authors, and though it was quite well known. The conversation is on how one should best use his leisure time; more specifically, on what one should read. Cicero himself stands up for philosophy. This now is the first work that will move Augustine, in the providence of God, toward his conversion, and he has set it against the epic poetry of Virgil and the works of the dramatists.

How did I burn, my God, how did I burn to fly from earthly things toward you, though I did not know what you were doing within me! For wisdom is with you. But in Greek they call the love of wisdom "philosophy," and that was what the book kindled in me. There are some who use philosophy to seduce, and by that great and comely and honorable name they color their errors and trick them up with rouge. Almost all such, from those times and from times before, are noted in that book and are shown up for what they are. There too he makes clear that wholesome warning your Spirit has given us by your good and dutiful servant: "Watch, lest anyone deceive you by philosophy and vain seduction, following the tradition of men and the principles of this world, and not following Christ. For in him dwells in bodily form all the fullness of divinity."[77]

And at that time, as you know, you the Light of my heart, I was not yet familiar with your apostle's words. But I was delighted by the exhortation anyway, just because it did not urge upon me this or that sect, but rather wisdom itself, whatever it might be, that I should thirst for it and seek it and follow it and hold fast to it, or rather be caught in its embrace. So was I roused up by its teaching, and it lighted a fire in me, and I burned, and yet one thing damped the heat of that fire: the name of Christ was not in that book. For by your mercy, Lord, this name of Christ my savior and your Son had my tender heart drunk devoutly even with my mother's milk, and it still held that name deep down inside. Whatever was missing this name, no matter how learned and polished, no matter how well it spoke the truth, could not utterly sweep me away.

5

So then I set my mind to look into your holy Scriptures, to see what they were like. And what do I see, but what is not found out by the proud,[78] or stripped bare for mere children, but humble at the entry

---

[77] Col 2:8. What passes for philosophy can also be an empty thing, full of misdirections and lies.
[78] Cf. 1 Tm 6:4. There are people who love not wisdom but disputation, especially if it is tricked out in fancy dress.

and lofty beyond, and veiled in mysteries. And I was no such person as could enter them or bend my neck to get inside the door. The way I speak about the Scriptures now is not what I felt then, for they seemed unworthy to be compared with that high Ciceronian dignity. My swollen pride shunned their plain style,[79] and my sharp wit could not penetrate their depths within. For they really were fashioned to grow up along with your little ones. But I disdained to be a child, and, engorged with arrogance, I thought of myself as quite a big man.

6

And so I fell in with men who raved in their pride, all too fleshly and full of words, upon whose lips lay the fowling-snare of the devil, and a bird-lime[80] with ingredients cooked up from the syllables of your name, and that of the Lord Jesus Christ, and that of the Holy Spirit, the Paraclete, our Comforter. These names were constantly in their mouths, as far as

---

[79] Augustine will later see that the plain style of Scripture is a mark of its greatness, not like the adornments of rhetoric that he himself was being prepared to teach to young men, to make them persuasive speakers in courts of law and government. Cicero was considered the master of Latin style, and yet we see in him more than occasional flashes of self-conscious pride.

[80] Cf. Ps 91:3. Birdlime is a sticky substance that fowlers use for catching birds, whose feathers get tangled up in it. The men whom Augustine is referring to are the Manicheans, followers of Mani (216–274), a Persian heretic and mystagogue. Mani claimed, among other things, to be the Holy Spirit foretold by Christ. He preached a form of dualism that had long been a feature of the ancient Persian teachings of Zoroaster, who lived, at the latest, in the sixth century BC. There are, in this dualism, two principles of the universe, the good and the evil; the good is associated with spirit, the evil with matter and with bodies. Manicheans believed that Mani himself was born without any act of human intercourse and even without parturition, as those would have defiled him, being bound up with fleshly reality. For the Manicheans, it was not only fornication that was wicked, but all forms of sexual intercourse, so that the "perfect" among them must abstain from sex and marriage, and eat no meat, drink no wine, till no fields, and own no goods. The "imperfect" among them would be reincarnated again and again until their final purification. Of course, the Manicheans could not acknowledge God to be the Creator of the physical world, since matter was the realm and the tool of the evil principle. In a strange way, we can see how a mistaken reading of the New Testament—or of Plato, for that matter—could cause you to draw the wrong conclusion, since we are warned about "the world" and "the flesh"; but then we would have to ignore the central mystery of the salvation of man, that "the Word was made flesh, and dwelt among us" (Jn 1:14).

the sounds and the clacking of the tongue go, but aside from that, their hearts were empty of the truth. And they used to say, "Truth, Truth,"[81] and were always saying that word to me, but the Truth was never in them. They uttered falsehoods not only about you, who are Truth indeed, but even about these elements of the world, your creation. There are philosophers who do tell the truth about these matters, and yet I should have passed them by also, preferring the love of you, my good and supreme Father, beauty of all that is beautiful. O Truth, Truth! How did the marrow of my soul, even at that time, pant after you, all while those men were sounding your name to me, so often and in so many ways, with the voice alone, and in a load of heavy books! And on these platters, when I was starving for you, they served up for me the sun and moon, beautiful works of yours, but still only your works and not you, nor even the prime of your works. For your spiritual works come before these bodily works, no matter how heavenly they are, and full of light.

But I was starving and thirsting not for these first things of creation, but for you, the Truth, in whom there is no change, and upon whom no shadow of influence falls. And they put before me dishes full of glittering fantasies, and it would have been better for me to fall in love with the sun, which at least is true to our eyesight, rather than with those false dreams, fooling my soul by means of the eyes. Nevertheless, because I thought it was you, I took to the meal, but I did not eat heartily, because you did not savor in my mouth as you really are—for those inane fictions are not you; and they did not nourish me, but they drained me instead. Food in our dreams looks just like food when we are awake, but the sleepers are not fed—they are asleep. But those dreams were nothing like you, as you have since told me. They were fleshly fantasies, false bodies.[82] Far more trustworthy

---

[81] Mt 7:21: Not all who cry, "Lord, Lord," shall enter the kingdom of heaven. When Augustine uses the word "Truth" here, he is clearly thinking of it as a name for Christ himself, the Way, the Truth, and the Life (Jn 14:6).
[82] The irony is that the Manicheans, who despise the flesh, are themselves the most "fleshly" of all, as Saints John and Paul use the word.

are these genuine bodies we see with our fleshly sight, whether in the heavens or on the earth. The birds and the beasts can see them as well as we can, and they are more certain than any images we can form of them. And so on too, we are on more sure footing when we form those images, than when we use them to guess at things greater than they are, infinite—fictional things that do not exist at all. On such empty husks did I feed, and I was not fed.[83]

But you, my love, whom I faint for that I may be strong, you are neither those bodies we see, not even those we see in the heavens, nor those things there that we cannot see, for you established them all, nor do you hold them as the highest of your creations. So then, how far you were from those phantasms of mine, phantasms of bodies that do not even exist! More certain than these were the images of bodies that do exist, and more certain than the images were the bodies themselves—yet you are none of these. Nor are you the soul, which is the life of bodies—though the life of bodies is a better thing and more certain than the bodies themselves. But you are the life of souls, the life of living things that live by you alone, nor are you changed, you the life of my soul.

Where then were you for me, and how far away? For I had wandered far afield from you, forbidden even to feed on the husks I was to feed the swine. How much better were even those fables of the schoolteachers and the poets, than were those booby traps! For their verses and their songs and Medea flying through the air were surely of more use than the Five Elements, dolled up in various ways for the Five Dens of Darkness, which do not exist but can kill the believer anyway.[84] For

---

[83] Cf. Lk 15:16. The prodigal son in Jesus's parable was more fortunate than Augustine. He did not get to eat the husks that the swine ate; Augustine did.

[84] Medea, in Greek mythology, was a sorceress from Colchis, on the Black Sea. She used her powers, against her father and her brother, to help the hero Jason, whom she loved, to gain the Golden Fleece and to sail back home to Corinth with it. Jason took Medea for his wife and she bore him two sons, but then he abandoned her for a princess named Glauce. Enraged, Medea gave to Glauce a poisoned robe and coronet, and then, after her rival died an excruciating death, she slew the children and flew off to Athens in her dragon-led chariot.

I can turn a verse and a song into good pottage. Even when I sang about Medea on the wing, I did not assert that it was so, and when I heard someone else sing it, I did not lend it credence; but these things I did credit. Woe, woe! By what steps was I led down to the pit of hell, laboring and sweltering from a poverty of truth! My God—I confess it to you, who had mercy upon me even when I did not yet confess—I sought you then not by the understanding of the mind, wherein you willed that I should be more excellent than the beasts, but by the sensations of the flesh. But you were more intimate to me than my most inward being, and loftier than my loftiest height.[85]

So I stumbled upon that brazen woman, prudence-poor, Solomon's riddle, sitting on a stool at her door and saying, "Come, eat with relish the secret loaves, and drink the sweet and stolen water."[86] She seduced me, because she found me lingering outdoors in the eye of my flesh, chewing the cud, gnawing the same food it had given me to gnash down before.

7

For I was ignorant of that other wisdom, which truly is, and I was tickled by subtleties. So I lent my approval to those deceitful blockheads,

---

See Euripides's play *Medea*. Augustine has gone out of his way to compare the Manichean myths—for that is what they are, outrageous and fantastical stories—with one of the most bizarre tales from pagan mythology, whose heroine is singularly vindictive, impassioned, and savage. The Five Dens of Darkness were, in Manichean myth, the forces of the Father of Evil, who envied the Father of Good and desired to devour as much of his light as he could, and to defeat the Good's Original Man, who ends up trapped in darkness, till the Father of Good goes on the counteroffensive. We see here a melange of Scripture, worked upon by a febrile imagination, and animated, as Augustine perceives, by pride—because the Manichean myths are esoteric and clotted with symbols that only those most in the know could really understand. They are thus opposed both to the precision and rationality of philosophy, and to the humility, the ease of initial access, and the profound mysteries of Scripture.

[85] Cf. Ps 139:2.

[86] Prv 9:17. Folly is a prostitute, calling out to passersby to come inside her house. Augustine will come to see that grave sin is an act of fornication against God.

50

when they asked me, "Where does evil come from? And how should God be bound up in a bodily shape, and have hair and fingernails? And how can we reckon men as just, when they had many wives at once, and slew other men, and engaged in animal sacrifices?"[87] Know-nothing that I was, these things disturbed me, and I thought I was making my way to the truth all while I was slipping farther away. For I did not know that evil was nothing else but a privation of good, even to the point of nonexistence.[88] How was I to see this, when I could see only bodily things with my eyes, and only phantasms with my mind? I did not know that my God is a spirit,[89] who does not possess members with length or breadth or any material bulk. For what has mass is less in a part than in the whole, and if it is infinite, it is less in a part that occupies a certain finite space than in its infinite extent, and is not whole and entire everywhere, as a spirit is, as God is. And as for what it was within us that causes us to be, and how we are in Scripture said to be made in the image of God, I was altogether ignorant.

And I knew nothing of that true inward justice that judges not by common habit, but by that most straight law of the all-powerful God, which gives form to the customs of various places and times as best fits the places and times, itself remaining always and everywhere the same, not one thing here and another thing there, or one thing now and another thing then. According to this law, Abraham and Isaac and Jacob and Moses and David were all just men, and they were all praised

---

[87] The heretic Marcion (c.85–c.160) taught that the Creator in the Old Testament was wicked, limited in knowledge, and not at all the Father whom Jesus came to preach of. Like the Manicheans to come, Marcion seemed to suggest that physical nature itself was bad, so he denied that Jesus's body was truly material. Augustine's fleshly imagination is likewise turned against the fleshliness of Christ, and the specific and fleshly commands and permissions we find in the old Law.

[88] Evil does not have any independent existence. What we call "evil" is a distortion, corruption, or privation of some real and specific good. A bad man is not bad because he possesses an existent thing, "badness," but because he has corrupted, or deprived himself of, a genuine good: he uses his mind, perhaps, not to discover the truth but to fix himself and others in falsehood, and soon he ends up with reason enfeebled and crippled.

[89] Cf. Jn 4:24.

by the mouth of God. But unskillful men, judging by the human day that passes, and measuring the moral customs of all mankind by their one portion of it, judged them as wicked. It was as if someone knowing nothing about armor and what piece is fit for what member should try to stick a greave on his head or a helmet on his heels, and grumble when they don't fit; or as if in one same day, when public business is forbidden in the afternoon, someone should bellyache, because he wasn't given leave to sell his goods as he had done in the morning; or if, in one same house, he should see that some servant might handle stuff that would not be permitted to the butler serving drinks; or if you could do something behind the woodshed which you mustn't do at the table; or he should take it ill that for one family in one dwelling, the same things are not granted equally to each person and in each place.

Just like that are people who take it ill when they hear that in ages past something was permitted to righteous men which is not permitted to righteous men in this age; and that God has commanded one thing for those times and another for these, for reasons having to do with the times, while both commands served the same justice. But they may see that in one same man and one same day and one same house, different things are fit for different members, and what is lawful at one time is not lawful at another; and what is permitted, even commanded to be done in that corner there is not permitted right in the open, but it is punished. Then is justice at variance and changeable? Not at all. But the times that it governs are not the same, for they are only times. But men, whose life on earth is brief, cannot connect in their minds the reasons of other ages and other peoples they have no experience of with the reasons of their own. They can readily see what is fitting in one body or one day or one house for this member or these times or these rooms. But they submit to these, and they are offended by those.[90]

---

[90] This is not moral relativism. God commands nothing that is in itself evil, but he may command, forbid, or permit something in one age, for one people, which he does not command, forbid, or permit at another time for other people, and he does so precisely in accord with the unchanging justice that the differing commands, prohibitions, and permissions serve.

I did not know these things then, and did not bother to notice them, though they struck my sight from all sides, and I did not see. I even used to compose songs, and I was not permitted to place any poetic foot wherever I pleased, but for this meter it had to go here, and for that meter it had to go there, and even in one verse alone the same foot could not go anywhere.[91] Yet one and the same art that governed my poetry did not vary in its rules, but it kept all of them at once. Still, I did not perceive that justice, which good and holy men observe, possesses all at once in a far more sublime and excellent way all that it commands, not varying in any part, though not granting and commanding everything at once to different times, but rather what is fit for each. And I, a blind man, blamed those holy fathers, not only because they made use of present things as God had commanded or inspired them to do, but even because they were the heralds of things to come, as God had revealed.

8

Can it be unjust anytime or anywhere to love God with all your heart and soul and mind, and to love your neighbor as yourself? So it is that crimes against nature, such as the men of Sodom committed, are everywhere and always to be detested and punished. Even if all peoples should practice them, divine law must hold them alike guilty of the crime, for it did not fashion men that they should use themselves in this way. Indeed that friendship that should bind us with God is violated when nature, whose author he is, is befouled by a perversion of lust. But crimes against the customs of men are to be shunned, according to the differences among those customs; so that what citizens or nations have settled and confirmed among themselves by law or tradition should not

---

[91] Unlike English poetry, classical Latin and Greek poetry was *quantitative:* each syllable counted as long or short (a long syllable had a long vowel, or a short vowel followed by two consonants) and the meter determined where those syllables must go. Each meter prescribed a different pattern.

be violated at the pleasure of anyone, whether a citizen or a traveler. Vile is the part that does not accord with the whole.

But when God commands something contrary to the customs or the constitutions of any nation, it must be done, even if it has never been done before. If it has been neglected, it must be reestablished. If it has not been set in law before, it must be set in law now. For if it is lawful for a king to command something in the city he governs, which neither he nor any of the kings before him have commanded before, and if it is not against the common life of the city to obey him— rather, it would be so if he were not obeyed, for by the general consent of human societies, people should obey their kings—how much more then is it lawful to obey God, the ruler over the whole created universe, in all that he commands, and without any wavering! For as in human society the greater power is set over the lesser, which must obey, so too God, over all.

The same thing applies to heinous crimes, done from a lust to do harm, either by slander or by violence. Sometimes it is for revenge, as of enemy against enemy, or to get something belonging to someone else, as of the bandit against the traveler, or to avert an evil, as of someone afraid of another; or out of envy, as of the wretched fellow who hates the man who is happier than he is, or the prosperous man who fears that someone may grow to be his equal, or who grieves when the other is so; or for the sheer delight to see someone suffer, as with spectators at the gladiatorial games, or mockers and tricksters generally.

These are the wellheads of iniquity, bubbling up with the love of playing the prince, of seeing things, and of feeling things, whether one alone or two together or all of them at once. So do we live badly, set against the three and seven, your psaltery of ten strings, your ten commandments, O God most sublime and sweet.[92] But what crimes can

---

[92] Augustine compares the stringed psaltery, of the Old Testament, with the Decalogue— that is, the Ten Commandments. These are "three and seven" because the first three deal with our duties to God, while the last seven deal with our relations with other human beings.

be committed against you, who cannot suffer corruption? What evil deeds can touch you, who cannot be harmed? But you avenge the evil that men perpetrate against themselves, for when they sin against you, they commit impiety against their own souls, and iniquity tells lies to itself.[93] For men corrupt or pervert the nature which you created and ordained for them; or they make use of permissible things, but out of all good measure; or they burn in lust for things that are not permitted, things against nature; or they are held to blame, raving against you in mind and speech, kicking against the pricks;[94] or they are glad to break the bonds of human society, and they come together in gangs or sects, according as something pleases or offends them.

And that is what men do when they forsake you, O Fountain of life, who are the one and true creator and ruler of the universe, and in their selfish pride they love a mere part, which they mistake for a whole unity. The way to return to you is by a humble piety, and then you burn out of us our evil habits, and you look with favor on those who confess their sins, and you hearken to the groans of those who are bound hand and foot, and you loose us from the chains we ourselves have forged. You will do so, if we do not raise up against you the horns of a false liberty,[95] by an eagerness to have more even at the risk of losing all, loving our own private good more than we love you, the Good of all.

9

But along with these vices and crimes are the mistakes of those who are on their way to learn. Good judges, hewing to the rule of perfection, will reprove the sins but praise the sinners in the hope of fruit to come, as the green stalk comes before the corn. Then there are things that look like vice and crime but are not sins at all, because they offend neither you, our Lord God, nor social fellowship; for instance, as when

---

[93] Ps 26:12.
[94] Cf. Acts 26:14.
[95] Cf. Ps 75:5–6.

people gather up things fit for the occasion and for ordinary use, and we cannot tell if their motive is a desire to have and hoard; or when a proper authority punishes deeds to correct them, and we cannot tell if the motive is a desire to hurt.

Many deeds, then, seem fit to be disapproved by men, but you have testified that you approve them, and many are praised by men that you testify against and condemn. That is because the look of an action is one thing, but the mind of the doer and the need of the time are another. But when you suddenly command something unusual and unforeseen, even what you had once forbidden, and even though for the time being you might conceal the reason for your command, and the thing runs counter to the compact of some human society, who shall doubt that it must be done? For no human society is just unless it obeys you. But blessed are they who know it was you who gave the command. For they who serve you do all they do, either to show what is needful for the present, or to foretell what will be needful in the times to come.

10

But I knew none of these things, and so I laughed at those holy servants and prophets of yours. And what did I accomplish when I laughed at them, but to be mocked by you? For little by little and step by step I was led along to such nonsense as to believe that a fig weeps when it is plucked, and its mother tree sheds milky tears. But if some saint of a Manichee ate that same fig, plucked of course by the sacrilegious deed of another man and not his own, he would mix it up in his innards, and from it he would breathe forth angels, genuine particles of God, sighing in his prayer, or belching. And those particles of the true and most high God would have been all bound up in that fruit, if the elite saint had not set them free with his teeth and his belly. Pathetic, I was, and I believed that more mercy should be shown to the fruits of the earth than to the men for whom they were born. Why, if a starving man who was not a Manichee should beg for that little bit, it would be like condemning it to capital punishment to give it to him.

11

And you stretched forth your hand from on high, and you snatched my soul from that smoking pit,[96] when my mother, your faithful servant, wept for me more than mothers will weep over their children's dead bodies. For by the faith and the spirit she had from you, she saw my death, and you, Lord, heard her plea. You heard her plea and you did not despise her tears, when they poured from her eyes and watered the earth beneath, wherever she prayed; you heard her plea. Hence came that dream you gave her to console her, that she might consent to live with me and share the same table in one house—as she had begun to refuse, loathing and detesting the blasphemies of my errant way. She saw herself standing on a kind of wooden rule, and a splendid young man came toward her, of good cheer, smiling, while she was grieving and broken with sorrow. When he asked her why she was sad and why she wept every day—asking, as ever, not to learn, but to teach—and she answered that she was wailing on account of my utter loss, he told her to rest secure, and said that she should take a good look and see that where she was, I was also. And when she looked, she saw me standing beside her upon the same rule. How could this be, unless your ears were turned toward her heart, O almighty Good, who care for each one of us as if you cared for him alone, and for all of us together, as for each single person?

And this too, that when she told me what she had seen, and I tried to twist it round, saying that she should instead not despair, because someday *she* would be where I was, she said most firmly and without any hesitation, "No, he did not say to me, you will be where he is, but where you are, he will be." I confess to you, Lord, that as far as I can recollect, nor have I kept silent about it, I was even at that time more

---

[96] Cf. Ps 30:3.

deeply moved by the response you gave through my mother than I was by the dream itself. For the obvious falsehood of my interpretation did not disturb her, and she saw straight off what there was to be seen, which I certainly did not see before she spoke. And in that dream, to console the pious woman in her present care, you foretold so long beforehand the joy that would be hers. For it was a full nine years that I wallowed in the mud of that pit and in that darkness of falsehood, and every time I struggled to rise, I was flung down with all the heavier weight. Yet all this while that chaste and reverent and sober widow, such a woman as you love, now livelier in hope but no slower to sigh and weep, never let up in all her hours of prayer to cry out to you for my sake. And her prayers entered into your sight, but still you let me stagger and stumble in that fog.

12

Meanwhile, you gave her another response, as I now recall. Yet I pass over many things, so I can hasten toward what is urging me on to confess to you, and there is much beside that I do not remember.

So then, that other response you gave her came from your priest, a certain bishop raised up in the church, and well trained in your books. When that woman begged him to be so good as to speak with me, to give the lie to my errors, to un-teach the evil and to teach me the good (for he did that whenever he found those who were ready for it), he declined, and wisely too, as I later understood. He replied that I was still unteachable, and that I was all puffed up with that newfangled heresy, and that I had already pestered unlearned people with a lot of niggling questions, as she had told him. "But let him alone," he said. "Keep praying to the Lord for him. By his own reading he will find out what is wrong about what he believes, and how great its impiety is."

Then he told her about how when he was a little boy his mother, who had been seduced by them, gave him over to the Manichees, and how he not only read almost all their books, but even copied them out again and again. But at last, without anyone around to dispute them or to win him over, it became clear to him how much one ought to fly from that sect—and fly he did. So he said, and when she still would not let the matter rest, but kept insisting all the more, weeping freely and begging him to see me and talk to me, he said, fed up with it, "Go away, and as sure as you live, know that it is impossible that the son of these tears should perish." And as she often said to me when she recalled it in our conversations, she took that answer as if it had sounded from heaven.

BOOK FOUR

1

For nine years, from my nineteenth to my twenty-eighth year, we were seduced and we seduced others, deceiving and deceived in a variety of lusts. In the open we did it by teachings that are called liberal; in private[97] we did it under the false name of religion; here proud, there superstitious, everywhere vain. Here we sought the hollow sound of popular acclaim, going so far as to mount the stage for applause, contending with one another in song, striving for crowns of grass,[98] putting forth nothings for people to gaze upon, and indulging our unbridled desires. There, meanwhile, we longed to purge from ourselves these smutty things, so we brought food to those who were called saintly and elect, so that they would hammer out gods and angels for us from their smithies in the paunch, and those would set us free.[99] Those were my pursuits; I did these things, I and my friends, who were deceived by me, and along with me.

---

[97] It would have to be in private, because Manicheanism had been condemned by the Church, and it was against the imperial law to preach it.

[98] Grass is weak and fleeting; cf. Is 40:6: "All flesh is grass." A crown of grass—think of the laurels to honor a poet—is not the crown of precious stones that the Lord set upon David's head (Ps 21:4).

[99] Think of the "spirit" or wind liberated from the material food when it is digested in the belly of a supposed saint.

Let arrogant men laugh at me, whom you, my God, have not yet dashed to the earth to heal them, but let me still confess to you my shame, in praise of you. I beseech you, let me go roundabout in my memory to recall the past circuits of my wandering ways, that I may offer to you a sacrifice of jubilation. Without you, what am I to myself but a guide to my own downfall? And what am I, when all is well with me, but a child nursing at your milk,[100] and feeding upon you, the incorruptible food? And what kind of man is anyone, seeing that he is only a man?[101] But let the big and strong laugh at us, and let us, the weak and needy, confess you.

2

Those were the years when I taught the art of rhetoric. Vanquished by a desire for gain, I put up for sale the art of gabbling for victory in the courts. Still, as you know, Lord, I preferred to have good students, such as are called good, and without guile I taught them guile, not that they might seek the heads of innocent people, but that sometimes they might save the head of a man who had done harm. And from afar you saw me, God, stumbling along that slippery way,[102] and you saw a glint of my good faith in all that smoke, as in that school of mine I became a comrade to those who were in love with vanity, and who sought a lie.[103]

In those years I kept a woman,[104] not one I knew in what is called a lawful bond of marriage, but one I had scared up in my wandering lust, as I had no prudence at all. Still, she was the only one, and I kept faithful to our bed. Here I might well learn by my own example how far

---

[100] Cf. Is 66:11.

[101] Cf. Ps 9:20. The princes of this earth are but men; what then of teachers of rhetoric?

[102] Cf. Ps 73:18.

[103] Ps 4:2.

[104] We do not know the name of Augustine's mistress. She gave birth to his son, Adeodatus, whose name means "Given by God," a euphemistic name for a child born out of wedlock. Some critics have interpreted Augustine's failure to name her as motivated by misogyny, but that does not follow.

the moderation of conjugal pleasure, mutually agreed upon for the sake of children, is from the bargain of lust, where a child is born against our wish, but once he is born he compels us to love him.

I recall once, when I decided to enter a theatrical competition, that some reader of animal innards sent to me to ask what I would pay him to win the prize. But I loathed and detested such filthy rituals, and I replied that even if the crown were of deathless gold, I would not permit a fly to be slain for my victory. For he was going to slay living creatures in those sacrifices of his, to honor the demons so they would favor me. But, God of my heart, it was not chaste love for you that made me repudiate so wicked a thing. For I did not know how to love you, not when I could think of you only as certain flashings of physical light. Swooning over such fictions, does not the soul fornicate against you, and pledge its faith in false things, and feed the winds? Sure, I did not want him to sacrifice to demons for my sake, but to those demons by my superstition I sacrificed myself. For what else is it when we feed the winds, but to feed the demons, when we go wayward, much to their delight and their laughter?

3

So those traveling cheats, whom people call mathematicians, I never ceased to consult, because they hardly ever engaged in sacrifices, and they never aimed their prayers at any spirit to help them divine the future.[105] Nevertheless, with good reason does true and Christian piety reject and condemn them. For it is good to confess to you, Lord, and say, "Have mercy upon me, and heal my soul, because I have sinned against you,"[106] and not to abuse your indulgence so that we might have

---

[105] Astrologers. The Roman pagans practiced divination, often by slaying an animal and examining its entrails; the job was performed by someone specifically designated as an *haruspex*, literally one who looks at guts. The astrologers did not do that, nor did they call upon any evil spirits to assist them. The Old Testament warns against divination (Dt 18:10–14), including the star-gazing that was central to Babylonian religious practices.
[106] Ps 41:4.

the license to sin, but to keep in mind the Lord's words, "Behold, you are made whole; now sin no more, lest something worse come upon you."[107] They seek to put that good health to death, when they say, "The cause of your sin comes from the skies, and is inevitable," and "Venus did this," or Saturn, or Mars, so that the sinner, flesh and blood and towering stench that he is, might not bear the blame, but rather the creator and ruler of heaven and the stars above. And who is that but our God, the sweetness and wellspring of justice, you who render to each according to his works,[108] and who do not spurn the humble and contrite heart?[109]

There was at that time a wise man, most skilled and renowned in the art of medicine, who had, as a proconsul and not as a physician, set upon my unsound brows that crown of victory in the poetry contest. Of this disease you are the healer, you who resist the proud but give grace to the humble.[110] But did you fail me even by that old man, or did you cease to tend to my soul? I grew familiar with him, and I visited him all the time, and I clung to his conversation, which was both cheerful and serious, and that came from the liveliness of his opinions, which he did not dress up in fancy words. When he had found out in our talk that I had given myself up to the books of the birthday-astrologers, in a most kindly and fatherly way he admonished me to throw them all away, and never to waste on that vain stuff any care or labor I should spend on things of use. He said he had once studied them too, and in his youth he wanted to make it his profession and get his living by it, saying that if he could understand Hippocrates, he could understand those teachings too. But for all that, he gave them up and pursued medicine, and the only reason was that he had found them to be utterly false, and as a good sober man he did not want to put food on his table by deceiving people. "But as for you," he said, "you have rhetoric to sustain you,

---

[107] Jn 5:14; Jesus's words to the man born blind.
[108] Rom 2:6.
[109] Ps 51:19.
[110] Cf. Jas 4:6.

and here you go after this trumpery by your own free will, and not for anything you need at home. So you ought to credit my advice about it all the more, because I worked hard to learn it to perfection, thinking to live on it alone."

When I went on to ask him why so many things they foretold happened to come true, he responded, as well as he could, that it was the force of chance that made it so, diffused as it was throughout the nature of things. Suppose a man consults by chance the pages of some poet or other, who sang and intended things far from the matter at hand. Quite often a verse will show up that is marvelously in tune with his business. So it is no wonder, he said, if from the human mind, by some higher instinct, ignorant of what is going on within itself, something should ring out that jives with what the interrogator is thinking or is busy with, and not by art but by chance.

And so, from him or by means of him you took care for me, and you traced out in my mind the outlines of what I would afterwards find out on my own. Still, neither he nor my dear friend Nebridius, quite a good and chaste young man, who laughed at that whole business of divination, could persuade me to reject it, since the authority of those writers swayed me more than they did. I had not yet happened on the proof I was searching for, that would show me without any ambiguity that the true things these counselors said were spoken by good luck or chance, and not by the art of men who peered into the stars.

4

In those years, when I first began to teach in the town where I was born, I had made a very dear friend who shared the same studies with me, a lad of my age and blooming with me in the flower of youth. He had grown up with me when we were boys, and we attended the same school, and we used to play together. But back then he was not yet the friend he would later be, and later too we were not truly friends, for no friendship is genuine unless you have been the glue, bonding together those who cleave to one another, by that charity that you pour forth into our hearts by the Holy Spirit, who is given to us.[111] But it was sweet to us, forged in the warmth of the studies we shared. For I had bent his mind away from the true faith, as he was a young fellow and he had never held the faith deep down and with full conviction. I led him along into those superstitious and noxious fables, the same that made my mother weep for me, and now that man went along with me wandering in his mind, and my soul could not be without him. Yet there you were, right at the back of your runaways, God of vengeance and wellspring of mercy at once, you who in wondrous ways turn us back to you;[112] there you were, and you bore that person out of this life, after he had hardly filled up a year in my friendship, sweeter to me than all the sweet things in that life of mine.

What one man can number all your praises that he has come to know in himself alone? What did you then do, my God, and how unsearchable is the abyss of your judgments?[113] For when he lay laboring in fever, lying a long while insensible in the sweat of death, and there was no hope, he was baptized without knowing it. I was nonchalant about it. I presumed that his soul would retain what he had gotten from me, and not what had happened to his body when he was unconscious. But it turned out far otherwise. For when he had recovered and was safe again, as soon as I could talk with him—and that was as soon as he could talk, because I never left his side and we depended on each other so much—I tried to get him to join me in laughing at a baptism he had gotten when his mind and his senses were far away. By then, though, he had learned about the baptism. Yet he looked on me with horror, as if I were an enemy, and with a sudden and admirable liberty he warned me that if I wanted to be his friend, I must stop saying such things to him. I was stunned, I was, and troubled, but I kept my feelings to myself. Let him get well, let him be fit again in the power of health, and then I

---

[111] Cf. Rom 5:5.
[112] Cf. Ps 85:4.
[113] Cf. Rom 11:33.

could do with him whatever I wanted. But he was snatched away from my madness, that with you he might be saved for my consolation. A few days later, when I was not there, the fever returned and he died.[114]

My heart was made dark with grief, and whatever I looked upon was death. My homeland was to me a prison, my father's house a place of unhappiness to stun the heart, and whatever I used to share with him, without him became a cruel torment. My eyes sought him everywhere, and he was not to be found. And I hated all things because he was not there, and they could not say to me, "Look, here he comes," as when he was alive and had been away for a time. I became a great question to myself, and I would ask my soul why it was downcast and why it troubled me so sorely,[115] and it could give me nothing in reply. And if I said, "Hope in God," it did not heed me, and rightly so, because that most dear person I had lost was truer and better than the phantasm I commanded my soul to hope in. Weeping was the only thing I found sweet, and it took the place of my friend in my soul's delights.

5

And now, Lord, these things are long gone, and time has soothed my wound. Can I hear from you, for you are Truth, can I set the ear of my heart near your mouth, that you may tell me why weeping is sweet to those in misery? Have you, though you are everywhere, cast our misery far away from you? And you abide in yourself, while we are tossed about in our trials; and yet unless we turn our weeping to your ears, no trace of our hope should remain. How does it come about, then, that

---

[114] Augustine lays stress here on the miraculous effects of God's grace, which transcend human wisdom and calculation. The sacrament was not a mere human action, to be counteracted by human strategy, for it had changed his friend's heart and taken root in his inmost being. But Augustine, having no faith in the sacrament, behaves here like all those who believe they are the ruling providence of their own lives, and can thus plot and plan, even to outwitting or anticipating and preventing God himself. Compare his attitude here with that of the Christians he has described, who delay baptism so that they can enjoy a youth full of sin while they can.

[115] Cf. Ps 42:11.

this fruit we pluck from the bitterness of life is sweet to us, to groan and weep and sigh and wail? Is it sweet because we hope you will hearken to us? That can be said rightly of our prayers, because they desire to come into your presence. But what about the woe and the mourning that then overwhelmed me for what I had lost? I had no hope he would come to life again, nor did I seek such a thing by my tears, and still I mourned and wept. I was wretched, and I had lost all my joy. Or is weeping a bitter thing, but when we are sick of things we used to enjoy and we shrink from them, it somehow pleases us?

6

Why do I speak of these things? This is no time to ask questions, but to confess to you. I was miserable, and miserable is every soul caught in the bonds of friendship with things that die, because it is torn apart when it loses them, and then it feels how miserable it was even before it had lost them. Such was I at that time, and I wept most bitterly and found some rest in bitterness. I was so miserable, that my miserable life was dearer to me than my friend was. For however much I wanted to change it, I was less willing to lose it than I was to lose him. I do not know if I would have done for him what we are told about Orestes and Pylades, supposing that the story was not just made up, that each one at the same time would have died in place of the other, because for them it was worse than death if they could not live together.[116] But in

---

[116] Orestes and Pylades, in Greek mythology, were the classic emblems of unshakeable friendship. In *Orestes,* by the Greek playwright Euripides (484–406 BC), the two friends are caught in the land of Tauris, where strangers are to be sacrificed to the goddess Artemis. The priestess, Iphigenia, is Orestes's long lost sister, though neither one recognizes the other. She takes pity on the two young men, and says that only one of them need be sacrificed, at which point each of them insists that he should be slain in order to save the other. Cicero recounts, in his treatise *On Friendship,* what happened at a performance of a play by Pacuvius on the two friends; the king of Tauris agrees to have Orestes slain and to let Pylades go free, but he does not know which is which. Then each of the young men insists that he is Orestes. When the audience heard it, they gave the actors a standing ovation (7.24). It is notable here that Augustine does *not* say that he would have given his own life to save the

me arose a strange sort of feeling quite contrary to theirs. A tedium of living weighed heavy upon me, and yet I was afraid to die. I believe that the more I loved him, the more did I hate and fear death, as my most savage enemy. For death had taken him from me, and I imagined death might all at once devour all men, because it could do so with him. Such were all my feelings, as I remember.

Behold my heart, my God, and search it through! See it, for I remember it so, you my hope, who cleanse me from the uncleanness of such affections, turning my eyes straight to you, and plucking my feet from the snare.[117] For I marveled that other mortal beings should live, since he, whom I delighted in as if he would never die, was now dead; and I marveled more that I should still live when he was dead, as I was his second self. Well did someone once say of his friend that he was half of his soul.[118] For I had felt that my soul and his were really one soul in two bodies, and life was a horror to me, because I did not want to live as a mere half. So maybe I was afraid to die, lest he whom I had loved so much should die utterly.

7

O madness, not knowing how to love human beings in a human way! O foolish man, unable to suffer with moderation the trials of human life! And such was I. So I stormed, and sighed, and wept, and tossed about in confusion, and there was no rest, no counsel. For I carried about my crushed and bleeding soul, which could not bear that I should carry it; and I found no place where I could lay it down. Not in pleasant groves, not in games and songs, not in sweet smelling gardens, not in fancy banquets, not in the pleasures of the bedroom and the bed, not even in books and poetry—nowhere could it rest content.[119] All things

---

life of his friend.

[117] Cf. Ps 25:15.

[118] Horace, *Odes*, I.3.8. The poet Horace prays to the gods to rule over the winds and bring back to Italy, unharmed, his friend the poet Virgil, "half of my soul."

[119] Cf. Rom 13:13, the verse that Augustine will read at the crucial moment of his conversion.

were a horror. The very light, and whatever was not what he was, was worthless and wearisome to me, all except moaning and tears. In those alone did I find a little peace. But as soon as I left off my weeping, a great burden of misery weighed me down. Only you could lift it from me and cure my sorrow. I knew it, but I did not will it, nor was I able to will it, because whenever I thought about you, you were not, for me, something whole and firm. For not you, but my own error, an empty phantasm, was my god. If I tried to let my burden rest there, it fell through the emptiness and collapsed again upon me; and I remained an unhappy place where I could not settle, nor could I get away. For where could my heart go to flee my heart? Where could I go to flee myself? Where would I not come after myself in pursuit? Still, I did flee from my homeland. For my eyes would not seek him so much, where they were not used to seeing him. So from the small town of Thagaste I came to Carthage.[120]

8

The times never take their rest, nor do they roll idly through our senses; they work remarkable effects in the mind. See, the times came and passed from one day to the next, and they sowed in me other hopes and other memories, and little by little they patched me up with my old pastimes, and my sorrow gave way to them. Other sorrows did not follow upon them, but the causes of other sorrows did. How, after all, could that sorrow have penetrated so easily and so deeply within me?

---

[120] Carthage, literally, in Punic, "New City," near to the site of modern Tunis, in North Africa, had been Rome's inveterate enemy in the three Punic Wars. When, at the end of the third war (146 BC), Scipio Aemilianus besieged the city and crushed its defenses, the Romans slew the entire population or sold them into slavery, and sowed the lands with salt. A hundred years later, Carthage was refounded as a Roman city. Carthage was, as I have noted, the city where the legendary ancestor of the Roman race, Aeneas, seemed content to settle down in, as Virgil tells the story in his *Aeneid*. But the gods would not permit it, and Aeneas had to abandon the queen, Dido, who had fallen into a madness of love for him. Her curses as she died by her own hand foretell the three Punic wars, though, ironically, they would prove to be the destruction of Carthage herself.

Unless it was that I had spilled my soul onto the sand, loving someone who must die as if he would never die.

No doubt, the solace of other friends did much to restore me and refresh me, among whom I loved what I would go on to love again. And that was a great fable and a long stretch of a lie, itching in the ears and corrupting our minds with the pettings of a whore.[121] But that fable did not die in me, even if one of my friends did. There were other things that occupied my mind when I was with my friends—to talk together and laugh, and happily do good turns for one another; to read eloquent books together, sometimes to joke around, sometimes to be in earnest; now and then to disagree without any hate, as if somebody might do with himself; and to enjoy that quite rare dissension as the spice to our more frequent agreement; now to teach the others and now to learn from them; to miss those who were away, and to greet them with gladness when they came back. These signs and others like them, coming from the hearts of those who love and who return the love of their friends, signs from the countenance, the tongue, the eyes, and a thousand free and easy gestures, were the tinder to set our minds afire, and to forge, from the many, but one.

9

This is what we love in our friends, and we love it in this way, that a man's conscience will blame him if he does not love someone who returns his love, or if he does not return the love of someone who loves him, demanding nothing from his body other than the tokens of good will. Hence the mourning when a friend dies, hence the dark clouds of sorrow, and the heart moist with tears, as sweetness is turned into bitterness, and the dying of those who live, caused by the lost life of the dying.

Blessed is he who loves you, who loves his friend in loving you, and who loves his enemy because of you. For he alone loses no one dear,

---

[121] Cf. 2 Tm 4:3. Augustine is referring to the fables of the Manicheans.

who loves all men in the dear One who never can be lost. And who is that but our God, who made heaven and earth, and who filled them, because it was by filling them that he made them? No one loses you unless he sends you away, and if he does send you away, where can he go and where can he flee but from you well pleased unto you in wrath? For where will he not find your law in the punishment he suffers? Your law also is truth, and truth is what you are.[122]

10

O God of hosts, turn us to you and show us your face, and we shall be saved.[123] For whatever way the soul of man may turn, unless he turns to you, he nails himself to sorrows, regardless of whether the things he clings to outside of you and outside of himself are beautiful. There would be no such things at all, unless they came from you. They rise and they set, and in their rising they begin to be, and they grow, and they come to their perfection, and once they have done so they grow old, and they pass away, and even if they do not all grow old, pass away shall they all. So when they rise and they strive to be, the faster they grow, the faster comes the time when they will be no more. That is the rule of their being. You have given them this measure, because they are parts of things that do not all exist at the same time, but by their going and coming they all make up the whole universe whereof they are parts. Why, so too our speech is made up of signs that make sound. No sentence could be complete unless one word gave way when it has sounded through all its parts, for another word to follow it.

By these things let my soul praise you, O God, creator of all things, but let it never be stuck to them by the glue of love that comes through the bodily senses. For they go where they were going, that they may no longer be; and they tear the soul by sickly desires, for the soul wills to exist and it loves to rest in what it loves. But such things have no place

---

[122] Cf. Ps 119:142.
[123] Ps 80:19.

of rest, for they do not stand still. They fly away, and who can follow them by the sense of the flesh? Who can even grab hold of them, when they are standing right there?

The sense of the flesh is sluggish, for it too is flesh; that is its way. It suffices for what it was made to do, but it does not suffice to seize things that race from their due beginning to their due end. For in your word, by which they were created, they hear, "Thus far and no farther."[124]

11

Do not be a fool, my soul, do not go deaf in the heart[125] from all the riots of your folly. You too must give ear—the Word himself calls to you to return. With him is the place of quiet that cannot be disturbed, where your love is never forsaken, unless you forsake love. Behold, these things pass away, that others may succeed them, so that this lowest universe may stand stable in all its parts. "But do I depart to some place?" says the Word of God. Set there the foundation of your house. Entrust to it, my soul, weary with disappointments, whatever you have from there. Entrust to Truth whatever you have of truth, and you shall lose nothing; what in you has begun to rot will flower again; what in you has languished will be made whole; what in you has trickled away will be given form again, will be made new, and will be bound again to you. They shall not pull you down to where they are falling, but they shall stand with you and they shall abide forever before the ever-standing and ever-abiding God.

Why then, my wayward soul, should you follow your flesh? Turn round, and let it follow you. Whatever you understand by its means exists only in part, and you do not know the whole whereof they are but parts, and still they delight you. For even if your fleshly sense were fit to comprehend the whole, rather than, for your punishment, being confined to only a part of the universe, still you would wish that things

---

[124] Job 38:11.
[125] Cf. Zec 7:11.

present should pass on, so that all things together might please you the better. For by that same fleshly sense you hear what we are saying, and you do not want the syllables to stand stock still, but to fly away so that others may come and you may hear the whole. That is the way with all things that are made up of parts that do not exist all at once. And all things in their entirety delight us more than do their single parts, if the things can be sensed all together. But far better than these is he who made all things, and he is our God, and he does not depart, for nothing can come to take his place.

12

If bodies please you, praise God for them, and turn your love to their artisan, lest in the things that please you, you should displease him. If souls please you, let them be loved in God. For they too are changeable, and they stand firm only in him; else they would pass on and perish. Then love them in him, and carry away to him all the souls you can, and say to them, "Let us love him; for he made these things, and he is not far. For he did not make them and then go away, but from him and in him, they are. Behold, wherever he is, the savor of truth is there. He is most inward to the heart, but the heart has gone wandering from him. Turn back to the heart, all you double-dealers, and cleave unto him who made you. Stand with him and you shall stand indeed. Rest in him and you shall find rest. Where are you going, along these rocky ways? Where are you going? From him comes the good you love; insofar as it is turned toward him, it is good and sweet. But if not, it shall go bitter, and justly so, for it is unjust to love what comes from him while you forsake him. What good is it for you, to keep straggling farther and farther along these hard and toilsome roads? There is no rest where you are seeking it. Seek what you do seek, but it is not where you are searching. You seek a blessed life in the lands of death. It is not there. How can a blessed life be where there is no life at all?

"And our Life came down to us and bore our death, and slew it from the abundance of his life, and he thundered and cried to us to return to him, to enter that secret place whence he came forth to us, that first virginal womb, where the human creature, mortal flesh, was wedded to him, so that it might not be mortal forever. And thence like a bridegroom coming forth from the marriage bed, he rejoiced as a giant to run his course.[126] For he did not tarry, but he raced, and he called out in words, in deeds, in his death, his life, his descent, his ascension, ever crying out that we should return to him. And he withdrew from our eyes, that we might return to the heart and find him there. He went away, and behold, he is here. He did not wish to stay long with us, and he did not leave us behind. He has returned to the place he never left, for the world was made through him, and he was in this world,[127] and he came into this world to make sinners whole. To him does my soul confess, and he heals it, because it has sinned against him. Sons of men, how long must you be sluggish of heart? Even after life has descended to you, will you not arise and live? But where shall you rise, when you already perch up high and lift your faces to the heavens? Come down then, that you may rise and ascend to God. For you have fallen by rising up against God."

Say these things to those you love, that they may weep in this vale of tears,[128] and so you may carry them captive with you to God, for it is by his Spirit that you say it, if you say it as you burn with the fire of charity.

13

At that time I did not know all this, and I loved beautiful things of a lower order, and I sank deeper into the pit. I said to my friends, "Do we love anything unless it is beautiful? What is it to be beautiful? What is

---

[126] Cf. Ps 19:5.
[127] Cf. Jn 1:10.
[128] Cf. Ps 84:6.

beauty? What is it that entices us, and binds us to the things we love? Unless there were something graceful in them, something pleasing to behold, they could never move us."

And I bent my mind to it, and I saw that in these bodily objects it was one thing to be whole, and to be beautiful in wholeness, and another thing to be comely as being suited for something else, just as a part of the body is suited for the whole, or a shoe is fit for the foot, and suchlike. And this consideration welled up in my mind from the deepest recesses of my heart, and I wrote *The Beautiful and the Fitting*, two or three books, I think. You, O God, know what it was, as it has escaped me. For we do not have them anymore, and I do not know how we lost them.[129]

14

What was it that moved me, O Lord my God, to dedicate those books to Hierus, an orator in Rome? I did not know him by face, but I loved that man by his reputation for learning, which was eminent, and I had heard some sayings of his that I liked. But he pleased me all the more because he pleased other people, who were wonder-struck in their praise—that a man born in Syria should first learn eloquence in Greek, and then become so marvelous a master of the Latin tongue, and be most knowledgeable in all things pertaining to the pursuit of wisdom. So is a man praised and loved, even when he is not present. Does this love pass from the lips of him who praises to the heart of him who hears? Not at all. Rather does one lover enkindle another. That is how someone who is praised comes to be loved, when we believe he has been set forth by someone with an unfeigned heart, that is, when the praise comes from someone who loves.

---

[129] We see that Augustine's mind was turned toward considerations that might lead him to God, but that he was burdened with a merely fleshly way of seeing things. Just as his conception of God was as an entity occupying space and time, and thus divisible into portions, so he could conceive of beauty only in terms of an arrangement of parts.

So did I then love men by the judgment of men, and not by your judgment, my God, wherein no man is deceived. Still, why did I not also love some well-known charioteer, or some fighter of wild beasts in the arena whom all the people raved about? My love was far different and more serious, and I would have liked to be praised in the same way Hierus was. For I would never want to be praised and loved as the stage-players were, even though I myself praised and loved them—no indeed, I would rather go into hiding than to have their notoriety, and I would rather be hated than be loved as they were loved.[130] How are all these weights of love, so various, scattered every which way, distributed within one single soul? What could it be that I love in another man, but also hate in myself, because unless I hated it I would not detest it and reject it, seeing as the two of us are human beings? And it is not the same as a man who loves a good horse but would not want to be a horse, if he could; for the actor is a fellow to our human nature. So then, do I love in a man what I would hate to be, precisely as a man? A great deep is man, whose very hairs you have numbered, Lord, nor do they dwindle in you.[131] But it is easier to number the hairs of his head than the affections and the movements of his heart.

But that orator was of the sort that I loved so much that I wanted to be like him too. And I went wandering in arrogance, helter-skelter in every wind that blew, and yet in a most secret way you were my helmsman. And how do I know, and how am I sure as I confess to you, that I loved him more for the love of those who praised him than because of what they praised him for? For had the same people not praised him but reviled him, and had they told me the same things about him in their reviling and despising, I would not have been kindled and roused up to love him. Yet neither the person nor the facts would have been different; only the feelings of the people recounting them.

---

[130] Romans loved the stage, but it was considered to be beneath the dignity of a well-born man to take up acting as a profession.
[131] Cf. Lk 12:7.

See then where the weakling soul lies, when it does not cling to the good solid truth! As by the winds from flapping tongues when people must belt out their opinions, so is the soul whisked along and whirled about, tossing and turning, and its light is overcast with clouds, and it does not discern the truth. But look, it is right in front of us! And it was a big thing for me if I could get my style and my studies noticed by that man. If he approved of them, my love for him would blaze up all the more, but if he disapproved, my vain heart, empty of all your solid truth, would have been deeply wounded. Yet it was with a free and contemplating mind that I had considered that subject of *The Beautiful and the Fitting*, which I wrote about and dedicated to him, and I admired what I had done, even with no one beside me to praise it.

15

But I could not yet see that the hinge of this matter lay in your craftsmanship, you the Almighty, for you alone are he who works wonders,[132] and my mind went along the track of bodily forms. I defined the beautiful as what was so in itself, and the fitting, as what was gracefully accommodated to something else, and I propped up my argument with examples I took from bodies. Then I turned to the nature of the mind, but my false supposition about spiritual things kept me from discerning the truth. The power of that truth kept beating at my eyes, but I turned my dazzled mind away from the incorporeal, toward shapes and colors and swelling magnitudes, and since I could not see them in the mind, I reckoned that I could not see my own mind, either. And because in virtue I loved peace, and in vice I hated discord, I noticed that there was a sort of unity in the one, and division in the other. So I thought that in that same unity lay the rational mind and the nature of truth and the highest good. But in that division of a life contrary to reason, pitiful fool that I was, I really thought there was some sort of substance, the very nature of the greatest evil, and this would be not

---

[132] Cf. Ps 77:14.

only an existing thing, but life in fact. Yet it would not have come from you, my God, from whom all things come. And I called that first thing a *monad*, as if it were a sexless mind. The second I called a *dyad*, such as anger in cruel crimes, and lust in deeds of shame. But I did not know what I was talking about. For I did not know and I had never learned that evil is not a substantial thing, and that our own mind is not the highest and unalterable good.

For crimes are committed when the motive force of a soul is riddled with vice, and it flings itself into insolent and tempestuous action, and deeds of lust are done when that affection of the soul by which we drink carnal delight is given free rein. Just so, errors and false opinions defile a man's life, if the rational mind itself has gone vicious. So was mine then. I did not know that the mind must be enlightened by another light in order to participate in the truth, because by itself it is not the very being of truth. For you shall light my lamp, O Lord, my God; you shall bring light to my darkness, and of your fullness we have all received.[133] You are the true light, which enlightens every man who comes into this world, for in you there is no change, or the least shadow of falling away.[134]

But I struggled toward you, and you thrust me away, so that I might get the taste of death, for you resist the proud. And what could be more high-and-mighty than this, that with a remarkable madness I should declare that I was by nature what you are? I was changeable, and that was quite clear to me, because I wanted to be wise, and so to proceed from the worse to the better, and still I preferred to think of you as changeable, rather than admit that I was not what you are. So I was thrust away, and you resisted my stiff-necked frivolity. I imagined forms that were bodies, and, being flesh, I blamed the flesh. Being a spirit, I did not turn back to you, but I took my ambling way, stumbling along into things that do not exist, neither in you nor in me nor in any bodily object. They were not created for me in your truth, but

---

[133] Cf. Ps 18:28, Jn 1:16.
[134] Cf. Jn 1:9, Jas 1:17.

in my folly they were fancied out of a body. I said to your little faithful ones,[135] to my fellow citizens from whom I had exiled myself without knowing it—I would say, inept and ever chattering, "Why does the soul that God made wander into error?" But I did not want anyone to say to me, "How, then, can God err?" I would rather fight to hold that your unchangeable being might be compelled to err, than confess that my changeable being might go astray of its own will, and that to err was my punishment.

And I was about twenty-six or twenty-seven years old when I wrote those books, turning these corporeal fictions round and round that clashed and clanged in the ears of my heart, even as I was straining to turn my ears, O sweet truth, to your inward melody. I thought all the time about the beautiful and the fitting, desiring to stand still and to hear you and to rejoice at the sound of the bridegroom's voice,[136] and I could not do it, because I was hustled out of the house by the call of my error, and from the sheer weight of my overweening pride I sank into the depths. For you did not give joy and gladness to my hearing, nor did my bones rejoice, for they had not yet been humbled.[137]

16

And what did it profit me that when I was hardly twenty years old, I got hold of some books by Aristotle, which they call the *Ten Categories?*[138]

---

[135] Cf. Mt 18:6. Augustine sees that he had played the part of an underminer of the faith of God's servants; better, says Jesus, that such a person should have a millstone hung round his neck and be thrown into the sea.

[136] Cf. Jn 3:29.

[137] Cf. Ps 50:10.

[138] Aristotle (384–322 BC) wrote that everything could be identified according to ten different modes of predication: substance (that a thing is *this particular thing*), quantity (measuring the space or time it takes up, and also whether or not these are continuous, and whether its parts are in relation to one another), quality (such as color, weight, shape, taste, temperature, and so forth), relation (whether, for example, it is twice something else, or subordinate to something else, or the result or cause of something else), place (e.g., in New York), time (e.g., today), relative position (as the result of an action, so that you may be lying down, standing, walking, etc.), condition (whether you are clothed, for example),

That was the name my master of rhetoric in Carthage knew it by, he and the others who were taken for learned men, their cheeks fairly bursting with pride, while I gaped upon it in suspense, as if it were something great and godlike. What did it profit me that I read them and understood them by myself? But when I conferred with those who said they could hardly understand them at all, and then only when they had things explained by the most learned teachers, and not just by words but by a lot of tracing figures in the dust, I saw they had no more to teach me about them than I could get by reading them on my own. And it was all plain to me, when the books spoke about substantial beings, such as a man, and about what chance features there might be in a man, such as his shape, what it was like; his stature, how many feet tall; his kindred, whose brother he was; or where he was placed, or when he was born, or whether he was standing or sitting, whether he was wearing shoes or armor, whether he was doing something or something was being done to him, and the countless other things that can be classed under those nine categories, of which I have given some examples, or in that same category of substantial being.

What good did it do me, when it even got in my way? That is because, reckoning that anything that exists must be included under those ten predications, I strove to understand you, my God, who are wondrously simple and immutable, as if you yourself were the subject of your predicated greatness or your predicated beauty, as if they existed in you as they would in a subject, as in a body; when instead you simply *are* your greatness and your beauty.[139] But a body is not great or beautiful insofar as it is a body, because even if it were smaller or less beautiful, it would be a body all the same. It was falsehood whenever I thought and thought about you, not the truth. It was a figment of my misery,

---

action (what you are doing to something else), and affection or passion (what you are suffering to be done to you by something else). The *Categories* became the most influential part of Aristotle's work on logic and dialectic, through the Middle Ages and beyond.

[139] We do not say that "God is good" in the same way as when we say that "John is good" or "bread is good." That is because God does not possess his goodness as a characteristic separable from his essence. He is his own goodness; goodness is what he is, not what he has.

not the firmament of your blessedness. For you commanded it, and so it was in me, that the earth should bring me forth thorns and thistles, and with toil I must earn my bread.[140]

And what did it profit me, that I, a most idle slave to my evil desires, should read and understand on my own whatever books I could find of those arts that are called liberal? And I was right glad to read them, though I did not know the source of whatever in them was true and sure. I had my back to the light and my face toward what the light shone on. So that face of mine by which I discerned things in the light was itself not in the light. Whatever I understood of the art of speaking and reasoning, whatever I understood of the dimensions of geometrical figures, of music, and of number, without any difficulty and with no one handing it on to me, you know, O Lord my God, because a quick understanding and sharp vision are your gifts. Yet I made sacrifice of none of it to you. So they were of no use to me, but rather they were a powerful force for my ruin. For I did all I could to keep that good portion of my substance in my own power. I did not keep myself strong to move toward you, but I set forth from you into a far country, to spill it away in whorish desires.[141] For what did the good thing profit me when I did not use it well? I was not aware that even the studious and the naturally talented found those arts quite hard to understand, until I tried to explain them and found out that anyone who could follow me without slogging along was held to be most excellent at these things.

But what did it profit me,[142] as I was all the while thinking that you, Lord God and Truth, were some measureless gleaming body, and I a fragment of it? What perversity! Yet such was I. But I do not blush now to confess to you the mercies you showered upon me, and to call upon you, as I did not blush to profess my blasphemies before men, and to keep yapping against you. What good then was my inborn talent to me, nimble at learning those things, what good were all those knotty

---

[140] Cf. Gn 3:17–19.
[141] Cf. Lk 15:13.
[142] Cf. Mk 8:36.

books I unraveled without any help from human teaching, when in the study of piety I went far afield, misshapen, disgraceful, profaning sacred things? Did a far slower wit get in the way of your little ones? They did not fall far away from you, but they dwelt safe in the nest of your Church, and got themselves feathers, and they fed the wings of charity on the food of wholesome faith.

O Lord our God, under the shadow of your wings let us hope.[143] Protect us and carry us onward. You shall carry us, you shall, from when we are little children till when we are old and gray. For our firm assurance is firm indeed when it is you; but when it is ours, it is but infirmity. Our good ever lives with you, and because we have turned away from it, we are quite turned out of the road. Let us now turn back, Lord, that we may not be overturned, because our good dwells with you, dwells without any falling or failing, for you yourself are that good. And we shall not fear that there will be nowhere to return to, though from thence we fell headlong. For though we were gone away, our house has not fallen to ruin—our house, which is your eternity.[144]

---

[143] Cf. Ps 17:8.
[144] Cf. Lk 6:49.

BOOK FIVE

1

Accept the sacrifice of my confessions from the hand of my tongue, which you formed and have stirred that it might confess to your name, and make all my bones sound, that they may say, "Who is like you, O Lord?"[145] For he who confesses to you does not teach you what is working within him; the shut heart cannot shut out your eye, nor can men's hardness keep back your hand. But you melt it when you will, either to have mercy or to avenge, and from your heat no man can hide away. But let my soul praise you, that it may love you, and let it confess to you your mercies, that it may praise you. The whole creation never ceases and never falls silent in your praise, nor does the spirit of man, by the mouth that is turned toward you; nor do the animals or other bodily creatures, by the mouths of those who consider them well; so that our soul from its lassitude may rise up to you, leaning upon the things you have made, and passing on to you who so wonderfully made them.[146] For there we find refreshment and true strength.

---

[145] Ex 15:11.
[146] Cf. Ps 139:14.

2

Let restless sinners go and flee from you.[147] Still do you see them, and you can tell one shadowy thing from another, and behold, the universe all these things make up is beautiful, while the sinners in their midst are ugly. And what harm could they do you? How could they disfigure your rulership, which is just and whole from the heavens down to the lowest things of all? Where did they fly to, when they fled from your face? Where shall you not find them? No, they have fled so that they would not have to see you seeing them, and they plucked out their eyes that they might stumble against you—for you do not abandon anything you have made[148]—that they, the unjust, might stumble against you, and be justly vexed by it, withdrawing from your gentleness, stumbling against your justice, and falling into your severity. See, they do not know that you are everywhere, whom no place can encompass, and that you alone are present even to those who have fled far from you. Then let them turn round and seek you, for you are not like them; they have forsaken their Creator, but you have not forsaken your creature. Let them turn round, and behold, you are there in their hearts, in the hearts of those who confess to you, who cast themselves upon you, and shed tears upon your breast after all the hard roads they have traveled. And you, most kindly, wipe away their tears, and then they weep and they rejoice all the more in their weeping, because you, Lord, and not some fellow man, not flesh and blood, but you, Lord, who made them, make them over again and bring them comfort. And I, where was I when I went seeking you? But you were right before me, and I had even departed from myself and I could not find myself—much less could I find you.

3

I shall declare in the sight of God the twenty-ninth year of my age. At that time, a certain bishop of the Manicheans, one Faustus by name,

---

[147] Cf. Is 57:20.
[148] Cf. Ps 138:8.

had come to Carthage.[149] He was one of the devil's great snares, and many were the fowl that got themselves caught by the lure of his smooth tongue.[150] I too praised his eloquence, yet I drew a distinction between it and the truth of things I was eager to learn about, and I kept an eye out not for the platter and its style, but for the meal of knowledge that their much-named Faustus would set before me. For his fame had preceded him, and I heard he was quite an expert in all kinds of honest study, and most polished in the liberal arts.

And because I had read many books of the philosophers and kept fresh in mind what they said, I compared some of it with what I found in the far-gone fables of the Manicheans. And what they said seemed more probable to me, because they had the intellectual strength to reckon up this passing world, though its Lord they could not find in the least. For you are great, Lord, and you look kindly upon the humble, but the high and mighty you acknowledge only from afar.[151] To the contrite of heart alone do you draw near, nor shall you be found by the proud, even if by their curious skill they should number the stars and the grains of sand on the shore, and measure off the constellations, and track the paths of the planets.

By the minds and the inborn power you gave to them they searched out these things, and they made many findings. They foretold many years ahead of time the eclipses of those luminaries the sun and moon,[152]

---

[149] Faustus was a Manichean bishop, reputed as the most learned of all the teachers of that religion. He had come from a humble background, and, as we learn from Augustine, he was not particularly well-read. He had died before 400, when Augustine wrote his treatise *Against Faustus,* wherein he refutes the shockingly arrogant teachings of a man who treated the Old Testament with contempt, who denied that Christ was born of Mary, and who asserted that much of the New Testament had been falsified by imperfectly formed Christians too firmly bound to the Jewish religion. These attitudes are not unknown in our own time.
[150] Cf. Ps 91:3. Faustus is an eloquent speaker, and that is just what Augustine prided himself for, and what he was hired to teach young men to be. Eloquence, however, is not the same as truth.
[151] Cf. Ps 137:6.
[152] Cf. Gn 1:14. The astronomers can discover the numbers, so to speak, that govern the paths of the sun and moon, but they do not discover the Creator. The ancients knew that the moon shone by the reflected light of the sun, and that eclipses occurred when the moon

what day, what hour, and how far the light would fail, and their numbers did not deceive them. Things happened as they foretold, and they wrote down the rules they discovered, and their books are read to this day. From those rules one can foretell in what year, what month of the year, what day of the month, what hour of the day, and what portion of the light of the sun or moon is going to fail; and it will happen just as foretold.

Men who do not know these things are stunned with wonder at it all, and those who do know them glory in it and are praised to the heavens, all the while they are falling away by their ungodly pride and going into eclipse from your light. They see the future eclipse of the sun so far before it happens, but do not see their own eclipse here and now. That is because they do not seek out with a religious devotion where they have gotten their inborn intelligence from, by which they do their seeking. And even if they do find out that you made them, they do not give themselves over to you that you may preserve what you have made. They do not slay to you what they have made themselves to be. They do not slaughter their lofty fancies that are like birds of the air; or their troublesome probing that is like the fish of the sea, as they roam the secret byways of the abyss; or their fat lusts that are like beasts of the field,[153] so that you, God, a consuming fire,[154] should swallow up their dead cares and recreate them for immortal life.

But they did not know the Way, your Word, by which you made the things they number, and those who do the numbering, and the senses whereby they see what they are numbering, and the mind they use for numbering; and of your wisdom there is no number.[155] But that same Only-Begotten Word has been made Wisdom for us, and Justice, and Sanctification, and he was numbered among us, and he

---

blocked the sun's light from the earth, or the earth blocked the sun's light from the moon. Of course, they also knew that the earth, like the sun and the moon, was a sphere.

[153] Cf. Ps 8:8–9. Augustine here condemns pride, vain curiosity, and the lusts of the flesh.

[154] Cf. Dt 4:24, Heb 12:29.

[155] Cf. Ps 146:5, Jn 1:3.

paid the tribute to Caesar.[156] They did not know this Way, whereon they might descend from themselves to him, and through him to rise again to him. They did not know this Way, and they counted themselves as lofty and splendid among the stars, and behold, they plunged to the earth in ruin, and their foolish hearts were darkened.[157] And about the created world they say many true things, but they do not seek Truth, the architect of creation, with a pious heart. So they fail to find him, or if they do find him and know that he is God, they do not honor him as God or give him thanks, but they dwindle away in their imaginations, and they profess themselves to be wise, paying as tribute to themselves what belongs to you. And they go on from there, with a most perverse blindness, to find ways to tax you with the evils that are their own. They put their lies upon you who are Truth, changing the glory of the incorruptible God into the image and likeness of a corruptible man, or of birds and four-footed beasts and things that crawl, converting your truth into a lie, and adoring and serving the creature rather than the Creator.

Nevertheless, I had kept in my mind many of the true things these people said about the created world, and I was struck by their rational order, based on numerical calculation, the succession of seasons, and the visible witness of the stars, and I compared them with what the Manicheans said. For they in their raving had written plenty about it, and I found in them no such order, no way to explain the solstices, the equinoxes, the eclipses, or anything else I had learned from the books of natural philosophy. But I was commanded to trust their works, even though they did not concur with the rational order proved by numerical calculations and what I saw with my own eyes. No, it was far otherwise.

---

[156] Cf. 1 Cor 1:30, Rom 4:25, Mt 17:27.

[157] Cf. Rom 1:18–32. Augustine applies the famous passage from Saint Paul to the intellectual life of those who do not seek the Creator when they investigate the creature. The result is a virulent form of pride, whereby man attributes to God his own wickedness or incapacity.

4

O Lord God of truth, tell me, if a man knows these things, does he please you? Unhappy is the man who knows them all, if he does not know you; but blessed is he who knows you, even if he does not know them. And whoever indeed knows you and those other things besides is not more blessed for all that, but only because of you is he blessed, so long as in coming to know you he gives you glory as you are, and gives you thanks, and does not grow vain in his imaginations.

For a man is better off if he knows he possesses a tree and he gives you thanks for the fruit, even if he does not know how many cubits tall it is or how wide its branches spread out, better off than is the man who has measured the tree and numbered its branches but does not own it and does not know and love its Creator. It is that way with the man of faith. His are all the riches of the world, and as if he owned nothing at all he possesses all things[158] by cleaving unto you whom all things serve, even if he does not even know the rounds of the Big Dipper.[159] How stupid it would be to doubt that he is better off than some measurer of the heavens and reckoner of the stars and weigher of the elements who is negligent of you, who have disposed all things in measure, number, and weight![160]

5

But who asked some Mani or other to write about such things? One can learn piety without having any skill in them. You have said to man:

---

[158] Cf. 2 Cor 6:10.

[159] The constellation known in Roman times as Ursa Major, the Great Bear; it is, for people in the northern hemisphere, the easiest constellation to recognize, and one that is always visible in a clear night sky, as being near to the pole star, Polaris, which does not appear to move at all from one hour to the next.

[160] Cf. Ws 11:20. It is one of Augustine's most beloved verses in Scripture, and it provided a ruling principle for the artists, musical composers, and poets of the Middle Ages and the Renaissance.

behold, piety is what wisdom is.[161] He could have been ignorant of piety and still have known those other things to perfection. But because, when he did not know those at all, in his great impudence he still dared to teach them, he could never come to know piety. It is a vanity for someone to profess these worldly matters even when he does know them; it is piety to confess to you. So Mani had gone out of the right way, and talked a lot about them, and to what end? He was convicted by people who had learned the truth, and anyone might manifestly see how much good sense he might have in other matters that were more difficult to find out. He did not want to be reckoned as some little fellow, no indeed. He tried to persuade everyone that the Holy Spirit, the Comforter, the giver of riches to your faithful ones, dwelt with full authority within his person. So when he was caught saying false things about the heavens and the stars and the motions of the sun and moon, though they have nothing to do with religious doctrine, it was plain to see how brazen he was in his sacrilege. For he went around talking not only about things he knew nothing of, but about things he had falsified, and he did it with such a stark raving vanity and pride, that he tried to give himself tribute for them as if he were some divine being.

So whenever I hear this or that brother Christian who is ignorant of these matters and mistakes one thing for another, I can regard him with patience as he gives his opinion. As long as he does not believe things unworthy of you, Lord and Creator of all things, I cannot see how it gets in his way if he happens not to know the position or the regular action of a bodily creature. But it will get in his way if he decides that it strikes to the very essence of pious doctrine, and he dares to be stiff-necked about it, affirming what he knows nothing about. Yet our mother Charity can bear even this frailty in the cradle-time of faith, while the newborn is still growing up toward the perfect man, and he is not carried roundabout by every wind of doctrine.[162]

---

[161] Cf. Job 28:28.
[162] Cf. Eph 4:13–15.

But what of him, the teacher, the authority, the leader and chief of all those who fell to his sweet-talking, as he dared to make them believe they were following no mere man but your Holy Spirit? Who would not judge such madness as something to detest and cast aside, especially when the man had already been shown up as a liar? But it was not yet perfectly clear to me whether the lengthening and short-ening of days and nights by turns, the alternation of day and night themselves, the waning of light in an eclipse, and everything else of that sort that I read in other books, could still be explained in accord with his words. If so, I would not be sure whether the matter was this way or that, but I would put my trust in his authority, on account of the holiness I believed was his.

6

And so for those nearly nine years, when my wayward mind gave ear to the Manicheans, I waited, with desire stretched to the snapping point, for the coming of this Faustus. Others of the sect whom I happened to meet, unable to answer the objections I put forth about such things, promised me that when Faustus came and spoke with me he would easily unravel all the knots, and even solve whatever greater questions I might propose.

When he came, then, I found him to be an agreeable fellow and a delightful talker, much more pleasant in his chatter than the rest of them when they talked about their usual teachings. A most decorous butler, with costly cups in hand—but what was all that, to my thirst? For my ears were long surfeited with such stuff, and they did not seem to me any better because they were better said, or true because they were elegant; nor was his soul wise because he looked the part and he had fit words for it too. For those who had promised me so much from him were not good judges. He seemed prudent and wise to them because he delighted them when he spoke.

I have met another sort of person who would hold truth itself in suspicion and would be unwilling to acquiesce, if it were put forth in rich and well-adorned language. But as for me, you had already taught me in wonderful and hidden ways, my God, and therefore do I believe what you have taught me, for it is the truth, nor is there any teacher of the truth besides you, no matter when or where his fame may shine. For I had already learned from you that nothing should seem true to us for its eloquence, or false to us for its harsh sound on the lips; and the converse, too, that rough speech does not make a thing true, nor does brilliant elocution make a thing false. Rather, wisdom and folly are like foods that are wholesome or worthless, and either one can be served up in words that are polished or unpolished, as food can be served in fancy or homely platters.

Therefore the eagerness with which I had waited so long for that man was delighted by his bearing and his sensitiveness in conversation, and the apt words he readily found to robe his thoughts. I was delighted, and along with many others, and even more so than many of them, I praised him and bore him aloft; but it vexed me that with all the press of people listening to him I could never go up to him and share with him the questions that troubled me—to discuss them in a familiar way, in the give and take of conversation. When at last I got to do it, I began along with some friends of mine to lay siege to his ears, at a time not inopportune for discussion. I put to him the questions that moved me, and I discovered right away that the man was not skilled in liberal learning, except for grammar, and that only in the usual way. He had read a few of Cicero's orations, and a very few books by Seneca,[163]

---

[163] Lucius Annaeus Seneca (4 BC–AD 65) was a Stoic philosopher and one of the great essayists of the ancient world. He had been a teacher to the young Nero, but the emperor in his vanity and suspicions commanded the old man to take his own life, in the year 65. Saint Paul met Seneca's brother Gallio (Acts 18:12–17), who dismissed charges that the Jews had made against him. Since Paul was in Rome at the same time as Seneca's break with Nero was complete, and since both men died by Nero's command, some early Christians believed that Paul and Seneca must have known one another, and that supposition prompted an unknown Christian of the fourth century to write several spurious letters between Paul and

and some of the poets, and whatever books of his own sect that had been written fairly well in Latin, and he had daily practice in public speaking. That was how he got up his eloquence, which was made more seductive, easier to receive, by the modest government of his native talent and a kind of natural grace. Is it not as I recall it, O Lord my God, judge of my conscience? My heart, my memory stand before you; for you were working then in the hidden secret of your providence, turning my shameful errors round to stand before my face, that I might see them and hate them.

7

Now, once it was clear to me that he was not skilled in those arts I had thought he excelled in, I began to lose all hope that he could make plain and unravel the difficulties that troubled me. Still, though he was ignorant, he might have gotten hold of the truth of piety, if only he were not a Manichean. For their books are full of far-fetched fables about heaven and the stars and sun and moon, and when I compared their accounts with the calculations I had read elsewhere, I could no longer judge him able to do what I so much desired, that is, to untangle the matter and to show me that things were as the Manichean books say, or that some certain or at least equally strong explanation might be gotten from them. Still, when I brought these things up to consider and discuss, he was quite modest about it, and not so bold as to shoulder that burden. For he knew that he did not know, nor was he ashamed to admit it. He was not like those many prattlers I had put up with, who tried hard to teach me and had nothing really to say. This man did have a heart which, though it was not right with you, was still not too careless with himself. He was not wholly ignorant of his ignorance, nor was he so bold as to get himself cornered in a dispute without any easy way to get out or to back off. And I liked him all the better for that, because the temperance

---

Seneca, letters that became well known and that were taken as genuine, until methods of textual analysis developed by Renaissance scholars showed otherwise.

of his confessing mind was lovelier to me than the very things I wanted to know about. And I found him to be the same way with all the subtler and more difficult questions I had.

So it was that the study I aimed at Mani's books was blunted. All the less did I put hope in any of their other teachers, since in the many things that disturbed me this much talked-of Faustus appeared unable to help. But we were together quite a lot, as he was all on fire to take up the literature I was then teaching as a master of rhetoric to the young men at Carthage, and I read with him whatever he had heard of and wanted to read, or what I reckoned was best suited to his talents.

Meanwhile, all my effort to advance in that sect fell away, once I had gotten to know that man. I did not break with them altogether, but as I had not found anything better than what I had somehow or other stumbled upon, I made up my mind to stay content where I was, until something preferable should come to light. Thus did that Faustus, a deadly snare for so many, begin to undo the bonds I had been caught in, neither willing it nor knowing it. For your hand, my God, in the recesses of your providence, did not abandon my soul, and a sacrifice for my sake was offered up to you day and night, a sacrifice of the blood of my mother's heart, sent up by her tears; and you wrought with me in mysterious ways.[164] It was your working, my God. For by the Lord shall a man direct his steps, and he shall like his way.[165] How can we obtain the gift of health, but by your hand that shall make anew what you have made?

8

You were working, then, within me, so that I was persuaded to go to Rome and teach there rather than at Carthage. How I was persuaded, I will not pass by in my confession to you, since in these matters too we find the deepest recesses of your work, and your mercy most near at

---

[164] Cf. Job 11:7, Hb 1:5.
[165] Cf. Prv 16:9.

hand, to meditate upon and to proclaim. I did not want to go to Rome for the better pay and the more prestigious position that my friends held out for me when they urged me to do so, though these things did then draw my mind on. No, the prime reason, almost the only reason, was that I heard that the young men there were quieter in their study and were kept under the rein of a more orderly discipline. They did not barge in upon a teacher's class where they were not enrolled, impudently and whenever they pleased, nor were they even allowed through the door unless the teacher permitted it.

By contrast, at Carthage the students are allowed an unseemly and unruly license. They are not ashamed to break into a class and, looking like madmen, to disrupt the order that a teacher has established for the good of his students. They do all kinds of harmful things, remarkable for their stupidity and warranting punishment by law, except that custom is their patroness. That shows they are the more miserable, because custom lends a color of lawfulness to what they do, when by your eternal law it shall never be so, and they suppose they have acted with impunity, when they are punished by the very blindness of their deeds, and what they suffer is incomparably worse than what they inflict. When I was myself a student, I did not want to take up such ways, and now that I was a teacher, I was forced to put up with them from others. Hence, I wanted to go where everyone in the know said that such things were not done. But the truth was this: you, my hope and my portion in the land of the living,[166] spurred me on for the health of my soul to change the land where I lived, to get myself out of Carthage, and you set the snare to allure me to Rome, by means of men who loved this dead life, working madness here, promising vanity there; and to direct my steps aright you secretly made use of their perversity and my own. For those who disturbed my peace were blind in their foul frenzy, and those who were inviting me to something else savored merely of

---

[166] Cf. Ps 142:5.

earth. But I, who detested the genuine misery here, had an appetite for a false happiness there.

But why I went from here to there, you knew, O God, nor did you show it to me or my mother, who cruelly wailed over my leaving, and followed me to the seaside. But I deceived her even as she hung on to me by main force, begging me to go back with her or to let her come along with me. I pretended that I had a friend I did not want to leave before the wind rose for him to set sail. So did I lie to my mother—to such a mother as mine!—and I got away. Even this have you forgiven me, mercifully saving me, full of the squalid and execrable, from the waters of the sea to bring me into the water of your grace, so that once I had been washed clean in it, the streams flowing from my mother's eyes would be dried, with which she had for my sake daily watered the ground she looked upon.

And still she refused to leave without me, and I hardly managed to persuade her to stay the night in a place near to our ship, an oratory dedicated to the memory of blessed Cyprian.[167] But that very night I sneaked off and got aboard, leaving her behind to pray and weep. And what did she beseech you for, my God, with all those tears, but that you would not allow me to sail away? But deep was your counsel, and you heeded the turning point of her desire, caring not for what she sought at that time, so that you might do for me what she had sought at all times. The wind blew and filled our sails, and the shore faded from our sight, where she on that morning raved in her sorrow and filled your ears with sighing and complaining. And you disregarded them, as you swept me up in my desires to put an end to those desires, and in justice you plied the rod of sorrow to her desire that was merely

---

[167] Saint Cyprian of Carthage (d. 268), bishop, confessor, and martyr, beheaded in Carthage during the persecutions enacted by the emperor Decius. Augustine does not draw out the dramatic irony, but any of his readers who knew about his life and the life of Cyprian would have appreciated it. Cyprian too had been a pagan, and an orator and a teacher of oratory. After he converted to the Christian faith, he was notable for his learning and his powerful defense of orthodoxy in the many and various theological and ecclesiological controversies of his time.

of the flesh. For she loved to have me with her, as mothers do, but far more than most; and she did not know what joy you were going to make for her out of my absence. She did not know it, and so she wept and she wailed, and by those punishments she proved what in her remained of Eve, groaning in sorrow for what she had brought forth in groans.[168] But after she had accused me of falsehood and cruelty, she turned again to praying to you for my sake. She left and went home, and I went to Rome.

9

And lo and behold, there was I greeted with the lash of bodily illness, and I was going down to the netherworld, carrying with me all the evil deeds I had committed against you and myself and other men, so many, so heavy, over and above the fetters of that original sin whereby we all die in Adam.[169] For you had not yet forgiven me any of them in Christ, nor had he dissolved upon the cross the enmities I had contracted against you by my sins. For how could he dissolve them upon the cross of a phantasm, as I had believed him to be?[170] As false and unreal as the death of his flesh seemed to me, so real and true was the death of my soul, and as true as was the death of his flesh, so false was the life of my soul that did not believe in it.

And as my fever grew worse, I was on my way, I was perishing. And where would I have gone if I had gone then and there, but into fire and the fit torments for my deeds, in the truth of your dispensation? My mother knew nothing of this, but still she prayed for me in her absence. But you, who are present everywhere, hearkened to her where she was,

---

[168] Cf. Gn 3:16. Again, Augustine allows the dramatic irony to remain implicit. When Aeneas abandoned Dido at Carthage to sail to Italy, the queen raved in her wrath and despair, cursed him and his people, and committed suicide. Saint Monica weeps indeed, but she does not cease in her love for her son and in her prayers to God on his behalf.

[169] Cf. 1 Cor 15:22.

[170] The Manicheans were Docetists, from Greek *dokesis, semblance*. They believed that Christ had no genuine fleshly body, but only the semblance of one.

and you had mercy on me where I was, that I might recover the health of the body, while I was still raving in the sickness of my ungodly heart. In such peril as I was, I still did not desire your baptism. I was better when I was just a boy and I begged for it from my mother's piety, as I have recalled and confessed. But I had grown up in my shame, and now quite out of my mind I scoffed at the medicine you prescribed, while you did not permit me to die two deaths at once.[171] If such a wound had struck my mother's heart, it would never have been healed. For I cannot say enough of how much she kept me in her mind, and how much more labor she suffered in giving birth to me in the spirit than she had when she bore me in the flesh. Then I cannot see how she could have been healed, if my death in such a state had pierced right through the inward parts of her love. And where would all those many prayers have gone, so frequent, never letting up? Nowhere, except to you. Would you, God of mercy, really have spurned the humble and contrite heart[172] of that chaste and sober widow, so constant a giver of alms, who obeyed and served your holy ones, who never let a day go by without making an offering at your altar, who went to your church twice a day, morning and evening, without cease, and not to hear empty fables and old wives' tales,[173] but so that she might hear you speaking to her in your lessons, and that you might hear her in her prayers? Would you have scorned her tears, a gift you bestowed upon her, and repelled them from your assistance, when she sought from you not gold or silver or any shifting and fleeting good, but the health of her son's soul? Never, O Lord. For you were there, and you heard her plea, and you wrought all things in the order you had foreordained for them to be done. Never let it be thought that you would deceive her with those visions and those replies she received from you, both those I have recalled here and those I have not, which she held fast in her faithful heart, and ever in her prayers she would bring them before you as if they were written by

---

[171] Cf. Rv 21:8.
[172] Cf. Ps 51:17.
[173] Cf. 1 Tm 4:7.

your own hand. Because your mercy is everlasting,[174] you have deigned, for those whose debts you have forgiven, to become a debtor yourself by your promises.

10

So then, you recovered me from that illness, and for the time being you made the son of your handmaid whole in the body, that he might still live and receive the better and more certain health you were to give him. And even then at Rome I joined up with those false saints, full of deceit, and not just with people who listened to them, such as the man in whose house I fell ill and then got back my strength again, but even with those they call the "chosen."[175] For it still seemed to me that it is not we who sin, but some alien nature within us, and it tickled my pride to think that I was beyond fault, and whenever I did something evil, not to have to confess that I had done it, so that you might heal my soul because it had sinned against you. No, I loved to excuse myself, and to accuse that something or other instead, something that was with me, though it was not myself. But the truth was otherwise. It was all me, though my impiety had divided me against myself, and my sin was all the more incurable because I reckoned myself to be no sinner at all. It was an accursed iniquity, God Almighty, for me to prefer that you, even you within me could be overcome to my deadly harm, than that I should be overcome by you to my salvation.

Therefore you had not yet set a watch before my mouth,[176] or the door of continence round my lips, to keep my heart from stooping to evil speeches, excusing excuses for sins among men who worked iniquity, and that was why I still kept company with their chosen ones.

---

[174] Cf. Ps 100:5.
[175] The Manicheans were divided into two groups: the "chosen" and everyone else. These "chosen" lived lives of strict and somewhat absurd asceticism, spurning marriage, the eating of meat, and other ordinary goods in this world, not for the sake of prayer but out of a vain desire for preeminence.
[176] Cf. Ps 141:3.

Nevertheless, I had no hope that I could get on in that false teaching, and though I decided I would rest content with it if I could find nothing better, I was now a little looser and more careless in holding it.

And a notion rose up in me that maybe those philosophers they call the Academics[177] were wiser than the rest, because they judged that everything should be held in doubt, and declared that man was incapable of grasping any of the truth. That at least was what they clearly seemed to me to believe, as common wisdom would have it, though I did not yet understand what they meant. And I made no pretense, but I tried to tamp down the too much trust I saw my host placing in all that fabulous stuff the Manichean books are full of. Still, I made more familiar use of my friendship with them than with other people who did not share their heresy. But I was not as spirited in defending them as I used to be. And yet our familiarity—for Rome harbored a lot of them in those days—made me more sluggish in looking for something else, especially as I had no hope to find the truth in your church, O Lord of heaven and earth, Creator of all things visible and invisible,[178] for they had turned me away from there. For it seemed downright gross to believe that you had the shape of human flesh, and that you could be enclosed within the lineaments of our bodily members. Whenever I wanted to think about that god of mine, though, I could conceive of nothing but a mass of corporeal stuff—for I could not imagine that anything could exist otherwise—and that was the greatest and nearly the sole cause of my inevitable error.

---

[177] The Academics (whose founder was Carneades, 213–128 BC) were a branch of the philosophical descendants of Plato and Socrates. They took as their lead not Plato's dogged search for truth, nor his insistence that truth can be found, but Socrates's habit of playing one side against another, and his claiming that he was wiser than other men only in that they believed that they had knowledge, while he believed he had none. The philosopher Arcesilas, as Cicero reports in *On the Academics* (I.12.45), went so far as to deny that you could even know that you knew nothing. It is not clear that Augustine's tentative movement away from the Manicheans toward the Academics is a good thing, but we may consider it, at least, as his first effort to clear out the falsehoods from his mind. Augustine would go on to write a treatise *Against the Academics*.
[178] Cf. Col 1:16.

As a result, I believed that evil had such a substance too, and its own mass, ugly and shapeless and gross, which the Manicheans called earth; or slender and subtle, like the body of the air, which they imagined as a malignant intelligence creeping through the earth. And because a kind of piety compelled me to believe that a good God never created any evil nature, I posited two great bulks, each averse to the other, each of them infinite, but the evil narrower, the good broader, and from this plague-ridden beginning other blasphemies pursued me. So whenever my soul tried to return to the Catholic faith, it was rebuffed, because the Catholic faith was not what I thought it was. And I thought it was more pious, O my God to whom I confess your mercies upon me, if I believed that although you were infinite on all other sides you were bounded on the one side where the evil mass was set against you, than if I believed that on all sides you were bounded by the form of a human body. And it seemed better to believe that you did not create anything evil—for to my nothing-knowing self, evil seemed to be some sort of substantial and even corporeal thing, because I could not think even of the mind except as some subtle body poured out to fill up a certain space—than to believe that from you could come what I imagined the nature of evil to be. Why, our Savior himself, your Only-begotten Son, I thought of as something protruded, for the sake of our salvation, out of the mass of your light-filled substance, since I was unable to believe anything about him besides what I could imagine in my vanity. And so I judged that such a nature could never have been born of the Virgin Mary, unless it had been all commingled with flesh. But, as I imagined things, I could not see how it could be so commingled without being defiled. So I dreaded to believe that he was made flesh,[179] lest I be compelled to believe that he was defiled by the flesh. Your spiritual sons now may well laugh at me, in a kindly and loving way. But such was I at that time.

---

[179] Cf. Jn 1:14.

11

Besides, I thought there was no way to defend the things in your Scriptures which those men condemned. But now and then, I really did wish I could bring up these various things with someone fully versed in those books, to find out what he thought. For even at Carthage, the statements of a man named Elpidius had begun to stir me, when he spoke and disputed with the Manicheans face to face, bringing up things from the Scriptures that could not easily be refuted. And their response seemed feeble to me—not one that they would offer out in the open, but rather in secret, when we spoke apart. They said that the writings of the New Testament had been falsified by some unknown persons who wanted to smuggle the Jewish law into the Christian faith. But they themselves could not provide any uncorrupted copies.

So did these massive imaginary things press me down, holding me somehow captive and fairly choking me, as my thoughts were fixed upon bodies, and I gasped for the air of your clear and simple truth, and I could not breathe.

12

I began to work with a will, doing what I had come to Rome for, teaching the art of rhetoric. Soon there were students gathering at my house, among whom and by means of whom I began to be well known. But straightaway I saw that they did things in Rome that would never be tolerated in Africa. True, I did not find here those "subversions" that I had gotten from young men on their way to perdition. But, people said, the young men would get together secretly and all at once transfer themselves to another teacher, in order to defraud the first teacher of his pay. They would forsake their good faith, and hold justice in contempt, all for their precious love of money.

My heart hated these people, but not with a perfect hate. Perhaps I hated more what I was going to suffer from them, than that they did such lawless things with anybody at all. Such people are surely vile, and they commit fornication against you,[180] loving the fleeting trifles of the times, and filthy lucre[181] which befouls the hand that grabs it, and hugging to themselves the passing world, while they spurn you who abide, who call them back, who pardon the harlot, the human soul that turns back to you. And now I hate such warped and crooked persons, though I love them as men to be made straight again, so that they might love their learning more than they love money, and still more, that they might love you, God, who are Truth, and the wellspring of sure good, and the most chaste peace. But in those days I was more unwilling to put up with them for my sake than I was willing that they should become good, for yours.

13

That was why, when a message came from Milan to the city prefect in Rome, requesting a teacher of rhetoric, his travel to be at the public expense, I put myself in the running for it, with the help of those same people drunken with the Manichean frivolities. I went there to get free of them, though neither I nor they knew it. Symmachus,[182] who was prefect then, proposed that I give a speech to prove myself, and after I had done so, he sent me there. So I went to Milan, to the bishop Ambrose,[183] well praised all the world over, a devoted tiller of

---

[180] If we are to love the Lord our God with all our heart, when we sin we wrench ourselves away from him and turn in love, in fornication, toward a mere created thing.

[181] Ti 1:11.

[182] For many years, Rome had ceased to be the real center of political activity in the empire. Constantine had moved his court to the ancient city of Byzantium, on the critical waterways linking the Mediterranean and the Black Seas, but even before that, the emperors had had to station themselves nearer to the frontiers of the empire to repulse invasions from Germanic and other tribes, and to keep peace in the outlands. Milan was therefore the real seat of power in the west. Quintus Aurelius Symmachus (345–402) was a Roman politician and a man of letters. He was not a Christian, and when he appealed to the young emperor Valentinian II to restore in Rome the altar to the goddess Victory, Saint Ambrose wrote in opposition, begging the emperor to utter the name of Christ alone (Letter 18.10).

[183] Saint Ambrose (c.340–397), bishop of Milan and traditionally praised as one of the

your fields, whose cheerful eloquence in those days ministered to your people the fatness of your wheat, the gladness of your oil, and the sober inebriation of your wine.[184] To him did you lead me, unknowing, that by him I might be led knowingly to you.

That man of God welcomed me like a father, and was delighted at my coming, as was most seemly for a bishop. And I began to love him, not at first as a teacher of the truth, which I quite despaired of finding in your church, but as a man kindly disposed toward me. I took great care to hear him in public disputation, not with the intention that I should have had, but to gauge his ability as a speaker, whether it was up to his reputation, or whether it flowed with more or less force than what people said about it. And I hung intent upon his words. But as for *what* he was saying, I did not trouble myself over it, and I stood at a distance, in scorn. But I delighted in the sweetness of his speech, for he was more learned than Faustus was, though not so cheery or amusing. That is as regards the manner. As for all the rest, there was no comparison. For Faustus rambled here and there, plying his Manichean devices, while Ambrose most wholesomely taught salvation. But salvation is far from sinners,[185] such as I was then. And yet, little by little, I drew nearer, though I did not know it.

---

four great doctors of the ancient western Church. To him are attributed several of the most powerful of all Christian hymns, such as the *Aeterne rerum Conditor,* which seems to have made a deep impression upon Augustine. Ambrose's writings are far too extensive for comment here. Though he was personally gentle, Ambrose was a steadfast opponent of the Arian heresy, which had been favored for a time by the most powerful forces in Rome and Milan. Yet when the orthodox emperor Theodosius I engaged in a slaughter of Arians at Thessalonika in 390, Ambrose wrote to him, as a kindly and stern father writing to a son, telling him that he must do penance for his sin before he could receive the Eucharist again. Such was the man's authority. We should keep in mind that by this time, the old senatorial families in Rome had abandoned their traditional civic duties, largely on account of the stagnant or shrinking economy of the fourth century, and it was the Christian bishops who took them on instead, making sure, for example, that the poor were fed, the aqueducts and streets repaired, and so forth. Ambrose was likely the busiest man in northern Italy.

[184] Cf. Ps 81:16, Ps 45:7, Ps 23:5.
[185] Cf. Ps 119:155.

14

For though I did not work very hard to learn the things he said, but only to hear the way he said them—for that frivolous care remained in me, though I had no hope to find any clear way for a man to come to you—still some things I paid no attention to entered my mind along with the words I delighted in. For I could not keep the two separate. And while I opened my heart to how finely he spoke, at the same time, step by step, there came to me how truly he spoke. For the first time I began to see that those things could be defended, and that the Catholic faith, on whose behalf I had thought nothing could be said against the attacks of the Manicheans, could be asserted without embarrassment. That was especially when I heard Ambrose speak about one or two points from the Old Testament, mostly by way of untangling the threads of an allegory, whereas when I had read the words in their literal sense alone, I was slain. Hence, when so many of the passages in those books were explained in a spiritual sense, I reprehended my despair, my thinking that the law and the prophets could never stand up against those who hated them and scoffed at them.[186]

Still, I did not yet think that I must hold to the Catholic way, just because it had preachers and defenders learned enough to refute, with plenty of sound arguments, the objections made against it; nor that what I had always held should be condemned. For the defenses seemed equal on either side. I did not think the Catholic faith had been defeated, but it was not clear to me that she was the victor. Then did I ply my mind more determinedly, to see if by certain other proofs I could convict the Manicheans of falsehood. Had I only been able to

---

[186] Cf. 2 Cor 3:6: "For the letter kills, but the spirit gives life." Augustine had been unaware of the great and intelligent tradition of reading the prescriptions, the rituals, and the laws of the Old Testament allegorically, as God-ordained signs pointing toward their fulfillment in Christ. Nor were Christians the originators of this way of reading; the Jews themselves, for example, had long interpreted the Song of Songs allegorically, as expressing the mutual love of God and his chosen people. The most notable proponent of such methods of reading was the titanic Christian scholar Origen (c.185–c.253).

conceive of a spiritual substance, all their subtle artifices would have melted to nothing, and I would have cast them out of my mind. But I could not do so.

Nevertheless, when it came to the body of this world, and the whole of nature that the fleshly senses can touch upon, considering them more and more closely and comparing them, I thought that the philosophers understood more things and that their conclusions were far more likely. So, after the manner of the Academics, as they are commonly supposed to be, doubting all things and wavering among them all, I determined that I must leave the Manicheans behind. For I judged it wrong, in that time of my vacillation, to remain in that sect, when I thought that many of the philosophers were to be preferred. Even so, I declined to commit to those philosophers for good and all the healing of my sickly soul, because they were without the healing name of Christ. Therefore, I decided to be a catechumen in the Catholic Church my parents had commended to me, until something more certain should come to light to steer my course.

BOOK SIX

1

O my hope, even from my youth,[187] where were you then for me, where had you gone? Had you not made me, and set me apart from the four-footed beasts, and made me wiser than the birds of the air?[188] And I kept walking in the darkness, over the slippery ground,[189] and I sought you outside of myself, and I did not find the God of my heart; and I went down to the depths of the sea[190] and I had no confidence, no hope of finding the truth.

By now my mother, brave in her piety, had come following me over land and sea, sure of your help in all perils. For when the voyage was at a critical point, she comforted the sailors themselves, who usually are the ones to comfort fearful passengers inexperienced with the deep. She promised them that they would arrive safely where they were going, because that is what you had promised her in a vision. And she found me in dire straits, in despair of finding the path of truth. Still, when I admitted to her that I was no longer a Manichean, while not yet a Catholic Christian, she did not leap for joy, as someone might do

---

[187] Cf. Ps 71:5.
[188] Cf. Ps 8:8–9.
[189] Cf. Ps 73:18.
[190] Cf. Ps 107:26.

when he hears good news he never expected. For she had already been sure concerning that part of my misery, which had made her shed tears before you as if I were dead and you must revive me again; and in her thoughts she laid me upon the bier and carried me to you, that you might say to the widow's son, "Young man, I say to you, arise," and he would come to life once more and begin to speak, and you would give him to his mother.[191] So her heart did not flutter in a frenzy of joy, when she heard that a good part of what she had been begging of you, with tears, had been accomplished already, that I had been rescued from falsehood, though I had not yet attained to the truth. In fact, she was quite certain that you who had promised the whole would give the rest. Calm, and with a heart full of confidence, she replied to me that she trusted in Christ, who had assured her that before she was to pass from this life, she would see me a faithful Catholic. That was what she said to me. But to you, the fount of mercy, she sent up more frequent prayers, she shed more tears, that you might come to my assistance more quickly, and enlighten my darkness.[192] And she was all the more zealous to run to church and hang upon the lips of Ambrose, to the fountain of water that springs up unto life everlasting.[193] For she loved that man as if he were an angel of God, because she saw it was he who had led me in the meantime to the fluctuating state I found myself in. She was sure that I must pass through this state from sickness to health by the narrows of some fresh and more dangerous peril, which physicians call the crisis.

2

One time, as she used to do in Africa, she brought some meal-mush and bread and wine to the tombs of the saints, but the doorkeeper

---

[191] Lk 7:12–15.
[192] Cf. Ps 18:28.
[193] Cf Jn. 4:14.

would not let her in.[194] As soon as she understood that the bishop had forbidden it, she so piously and obediently took the command to her heart, that I myself was amazed, that she so easily condemned her old custom rather than presuming to judge the prohibition. No weakness for drinking assailed her spirit, nor did love of wine goad her to hate the truth, as it does to many people, both male and female, who get sick to the stomach at a song of sobriety, as drunks at a drink of plain water. But when she used to bring her basket with the festival treats, which she tasted a little of and then bestowed at large, she would not set aside for herself more than a little cup of wine well watered-down for her sober palate, which she would drink from for courtesy. And if there were many such tombs of the departed to be honored in this way, she would go around everywhere with the same little cup, not only watered-down but, by this time, quite lukewarm, and this she would share with her companions in tiny sips. For she went there for piety, not for pleasure.

But when she found that so brilliant a preacher and so pious a bishop had given word that this must not be done, not even by those who were sober about it, lest drunkards be given occasion to guzzle, and because these ancestral devotions were too much like the superstitions of the Gentiles, she gave them up most willingly. And instead of her basket full of fruits of the earth, she learned to bring to the memorials of the martyrs a heart full of petitions more cleanly purged. So did she give what she could to the needy, and she celebrated the communion of the Lord's body in that place, where, in imitation of his passion, the martyrs had been immolated and crowned.

And yet it seems to me, O Lord my God, and as I think of it my heart stands in your sight, that my mother might not so readily have forgone this old custom had someone else forbidden it, someone whom she did not love as she loved Ambrose. For she loved him dearly for the sake of my salvation, and he loved her indeed for her deeply religious

---

[194] Saint Monica obeys the direction of the doorkeeper or porter, who had taken minor orders to be so. The custom probably was a survival of a pagan rite for honoring the dead, and thus did Ambrose forbid it.

ways, for she went to the church again and again, so fervent in the spirit and full of good works. Often when he saw me, he would break out in praise, congratulating me for having a mother like her, though he did not know what kind of son she had in me, who doubted and dallied in all these things, and who hardly believed that the way to life could be found.

3

I did not then do much sighing in my prayers that you would help me, but my soul was restless, intent upon learning and discussion. I considered Ambrose a man most fortunate as the world goes, honored by so many persons of authority. His celibacy was the only thing that seemed toilsome to me. What hope he bore, how he might have wrestled against the temptations that his eminence exposed him to, what solace he felt in adversities, and what savory joys he tasted in the secret mouth of his heart, ruminating upon your bread, I could not guess, and I had not experienced. He for his part did not know about my waves of doubt, or the pit that imperiled me. Nor was I able to ask him what I wanted to, in the way I wanted. For crowds of people were always coming to him with their business, and he was a slave to their infirmities, and they shut me out from his hearing and his speaking. And in those brief moments when he was not with them, he would refresh his body with a little sustenance, or his mind by reading.

But when he read, his eyes went through the pages, while his heart spied into the sense, and his voice and his tongue were still. Often, when we were there—for no one was kept from entering his house, nor was it his custom to have visitors announced—we would see him reading in this way, silently, and never otherwise.[195] We might then sit

---

[195] It is clear that Augustine and his friends had never seen anyone reading silently. We should keep in mind that a Latin text would be written in all capital letters and without spaces between the words, so that the voice was of great assistance in reading, as one could hardly just glance at a text and discern a phrase.

in daylong silence—for who would dare be a burden to someone so intent?—and finally take our leave. We guessed he did not want to be summoned to some other matter, when for that little while he had a furlough from the noise of other people's troubles and could repair his mind. And maybe he was wary, we thought, if perchance the author he read should put forth some murky point, and someone listening might catch it and fix upon it, and then he would have to explain it, or get involved in discussing some rather difficult questions, and with all the time he would spend at this work, he would not be able to go through as many volumes as he wished. Or maybe this was the real reason he read quietly, that he wanted to save his voice, which easily went hoarse. But whatever was his reason for doing so, no doubt that man did well.

But I never had time for the inquiries I desired to make of that most holy oracle of yours, his heart, except when the matter could be heard briefly. I had to find him quite at leisure, if I was going to pour out to him those sweltering troubles of mine; but I never could. Yet on every day of the Lord, I went to hear him before the people, rightly handling the word of truth,[196] and more and more was it confirmed for me that all the shifty knots of calumny which our deceivers had knit up against the divine books could be solved. To tell the truth, I found out that your spiritual sons, whom you have by grace caused to be born again by our Catholic mother, did not understand your having made man after your image as if they believed or supposed that you were hemmed in by the shape of a human body; and even though I still had not the slenderest or vaguest inkling of what or how a spiritual substance might be,[197] I rejoiced, and I blushed, because I had spent all those years snarling and snapping not at the Catholic faith, but at the figments of a carnal imagination. In so doing I was reckless and ungodly, because what I

---

[196] Cf. 2 Tm 2:15.
[197] Augustine's trouble is with us again, as many people assume that only matter and material things exist, even while, with staggering inconsistency, they invoke the notion of a physical *law* to rule out the miraculous, a law that itself is not material and not subject to change.

should have asked about and learned, I talked about and accused. But you, O Most High and most near, most secret and most present,[198] who do not possess members, some bigger and some smaller, but who are everywhere in your wholeness, and never confined to location, you are not at all this corporeal form, and yet you made man in your image, and behold, from head to foot he is contained in place.

4

Since I was ignorant of how your image could subsist in us, I should have knocked and asked how it was to be believed,[199] rather than gloating in opposition against something as if it actually were believed. I was eaten up inside with anxiety over what I should hold for certain, and it was all the bitterer to me as I was now ashamed of myself. I had been deluded for so long, taken in by the promise of certainties, and I had blathered, with all of a boy's enthusiasm for his errors, about one unsure thing after another, as if they were sure. And those things were in fact false, as was clear to me afterward. But I was certain of this already, that at the least they were uncertain, though I had all this time held them as sure, whenever I would attack your Catholic Church with all my blind belligerence. I had not yet come to see that she taught the truth, but I did see that she did not teach the things that weighed the most when I accused her. So I was whirled in confusion, and then turned rightly about, and I rejoiced, my God, that your one and only Church, the body of your Only-Begotten, wherein when I was a speechless baby the name of Christ was laid upon me, had no relish for babyish frivolities. She never held in her wholesome teaching that you, the creator of all things, should be crammed up in the shape of human limbs, occupying a certain bounded space, no matter how great or vast.

I rejoiced too, that the ancient writings of the law and the prophets were set before me now to read, but not with the same eye as before,

---

[198] Cf. Ps 91:1, Col 1:26.
[199] Cf. Mt 7:7.

when they seemed absurd to me and I took to arguing against your holy ones as if they thought what they did not think at all. And I went again and again to hear Ambrose giving sermons to the people, and I was glad to hear him most diligently commend this verse as a rule to guide one's reading: "The letter slays, but the Spirit gives life."[200] For what seemed to teach perverse doctrines when read literally, said nothing that offended me when he opened them up by the spirit, lifting the mystical veil. But I still did not know whether what he said was true. I held my heart back from any assent, as I was afraid to pitch myself into something too rashly; and that very hanging in suspense was the more deadly to me. For I wanted to be as sure of the things I could not see as I was that seven and three make ten. I was not so mad as to think that not even *that* could be grasped as true, but I wanted everything else to be that way, both bodily things that were not present to my senses, and spiritual things, which I could not conceive except as bodies.

I could have been made sane and whole by believing, so that my mind's eye would have been cleansed and directed somehow into your truth, which abides forever[201] and in no part fails. But, as it often happens that a man who has suffered under a bad doctor is afraid to commit himself even to a good one, so it was with the well-being of my soul. Only by believing could it be made whole, but lest it believe what was false, it refused to be cured. It held aloof from your hands, you who have compounded the medicines of faith and spread them on the diseases of all the world, endowing them with so great a power.

5

Nevertheless, from then on I began to prefer the Catholic teaching. I thought it was far more modest and not at all shifty when it commanded men to believe what was not proved—whether it was proved, but not perhaps to this or that person, or whether it was not capable of

---

[200] 2 Cor 3:6.
[201] Cf. 2 Jn 2.

proof—than was the ridiculous credulity of the Manicheans, with their brazen huckstering of knowledge. For they would then demand that you believe a lot of fabulous and absurd stuff precisely *because* it could not be proved.

Then, little by little, Lord, with a most gentle and merciful hand, you treated my heart and made it calm.[202] I considered how innumerable were the things I believed, though I had not seen them, nor was I present when they happened; so many things in the history of nations, so many things about places and cities I had never seen, so many things about my friends, about physicians, about countless other people; things which, if we did not believe, we could get nothing done in this life at all. Then I thought about what I held with an unshakable faith, that I was born of such parents, which I could not know but had to take on faith from what I heard. You persuaded me that blame was to be laid not on those who put their trust in your books, which you have poured out abroad with such authority among almost all nations, but rather on those who did not put their trust in them. They should not be given a hearing, if perchance they say to me, "How do you know that those books have been imparted to mankind by the spirit of the one true and trustworthy God?" That above all was to be believed. No wrangling and slanderous questions, no matter how many I had read in philosophers conflicting with one another, could twist my mind so badly that I should not believe that you are whatever you are, though I did not know then what that was, or that the government of human affairs did not belong to you.

Sometimes I was sturdy in my belief, and sometimes a weakling, but I always believed that you exist and that you care for us, even though I did not know what I should believe about your essence, or what way leads—or leads back—to you. And so, because we were too frail to find the truth by pure reason alone, we needed the authority of the sacred Scriptures. I began thus to believe that you would never

---

[202] Cf. Ps 18:35.

have granted to those Scriptures so lofty an authority all over the world, unless you wanted them to be the means by which we believe in you and seek after you. Any absurdity which used to trip me up when I read those writings, once I had heard many things in them explained most plausibly, I attributed instead to the depth of the sacred mysteries. To me, their authority appeared the more venerable and worthy of sacrosanct trust, in that they were ready at hand for all to read, while they guarded the dignity of their hidden truth under a deeper meaning; they offered themselves to everyone in plain words and a lowly style, while they exercised the attention of those who are not slight in mental power.[203] In this way, they receive everyone into their common bosom, while they send the rarer souls on to you by narrow passageways. Still, these few are many more than they would have been, had the Scripture not stood forth on so high a summit of authority, or had it not drawn the crowds into its bosom of holy humility.

I thought about these things, and you were with me. I sighed, and you heard me. I tossed about on the waves, and you were at the helm. I went down the broad highway of the world, and you did not forsake me.[204]

6

I panted for honors, wealth, marriage, and you laughed at me. In these desires I suffered the most bitter difficulties, and you looked kindlier upon me, the less you allowed anything that was not yourself to grow sweet to me.

---

[203] Unlike the works of the philosophers, the Scriptures, whose author is God himself, are written in such a way as to invite the simplest of people, even children, while possessing and presenting mysteries that exercise the most penetrating of minds, and some of these mysteries shall remain beyond the human grasp until God reveals them in glory. Nothing in the ancient world was comparable. Nothing in our own time is comparable.

[204] Cf. Jas 1:6, Mt 7:13.

Behold my heart, O Lord, you who have willed that I should recall this and confess it to you! Let my soul cleave to you,[205] now that you have drawn it out of the most tenacious glue of death. How wretched it was! And you pierced my wound in its tenderest spot, that it might abandon all other things and turn round to you, who are above all things and without whom all things would fall to nothing—that it might be converted and healed. How wretched, then, was I—and how did you work that I might feel my wretchedness!

It happened on the very day when I was getting ready to recite a speech in praise of the emperor,[206] wherein I would tell many a lie, and yet I would gain the approval of people who knew I was lying. My heart was pounding with these cares, seething in a fever of thoughts that wasted me away. So then, I was walking down one of the streets of Milan, and I noticed a poor beggar, soused, I think, and glad and full of jests. And I heaved a sigh, and I spoke to my friends who were with me about the many woes that followed upon our mad way of life. For with all our great struggles—which at that time I labored under, stung by the lash of desire, dragging along with me the burden of my unhappiness, which grew greater and heavier by the dragging—we really wanted nothing else but to come at last to a gladness safe and sure. But this beggar had gotten there long ahead of us, and we might never get there at all. For what he had got hold of by a couple of little coins he begged for, I was seeking round and round by my ambition, back and forth with all kinds of trouble, namely, the gladness of a good fortune that could not last.

Not that the beggar's joy was a true joy, but I with all my helter-skelter ambition sought a joy that was falser still. And that man certainly was cheerful, while I was gripped with cares; he was carefree, and I was full of fear. Now, if anyone would put the question to me whether I would rather be merry or fearful, I would reply that I would rather be merry. But if he should ask whether I would rather be as the beggar was,

---

[205] Cf. Dt 13:4.
[206] Valentinian II (372–392), who was just a boy at this time.

or as I then was, I would choose myself, though all compounded with cares and fears. I would choose so out of sheer stubbornness. For how could it be true? I had no cause to prefer myself over him just because I was more learned, since I got no joy from that, but I sought instead to use it to please men, not to teach them, but only to please. For this reason too you cracked my bones with the rod of your discipline.[207]

Begone from my soul, then, those who say to it, "It all depends on what you take joy in. That beggar took joy in being drunk, but you, in glory." What glory, O Lord? As his was no true joy, so mine was no true glory. No, it turned my mind to consider things more closely. That night, he would digest his drunkenness, but I had fallen asleep with mine and had risen in the morning with it, as I was going to do again—and look how many days! Indeed, it does matter what you take joy in, I know it well, and the joy of a faith-filled hope is incomparably beyond such vanity. But even in that regard he was farther along than I. For he was happier than I was, not only because he was drenched in good cheer while my insides were torn up with cares, but more truly because he got his wine by wishing somebody good luck, while I sought after a windy pride by telling lies.

I said much along these lines to my dear friends, and I often pointed out to them how things were with me, and I found they were ill indeed; and I was sad to see it, and that made things twice as bad. And if any fair hope smiled upon me, I was leery to take hold of it, because as soon as I had got it, it would fly away.

7

We friends who lived together bemoaned these things together, and most of all I would talk them over with Alypius and Nebridius.[208] Of

---

[207] Cf. Prv 22:15. The irony is rich. Augustine was prepared to give a flattering speech before the boy-emperor, while he himself was spiritually but a schoolboy, in need of the rod of correction to spur him on to the truth.

[208] Augustine's younger friend Alypius, recognized as a saint by Gregory XIII (1584), eventually became the bishop of Thagaste, their hometown in North Africa, following in the

the two, Alypius was born in the same town I came from. His parents were among the prime citizens there, and he was younger than I was. He had also studied under me when I first began to teach in town, and later at Carthage too. And he loved me dearly, because I seemed to be a learned man and to be kindly disposed toward him, and I loved him in return for his great natural inclination to virtue, outstanding for one of so tender years. And yet, for all that, the undertow of Carthaginian ways, which were all in a froth for idle shows, sucked him down into the madness of the circus.[209] But while that was tossing him round so miserably, and I was setting up in public as a teacher of rhetoric, he did not then come to hear me lecture, on account of a grudge that had arisen between his father and me. And I found out he had fallen into a lethal love of the circus, and it wrung my heart, because I thought he was going to squander his great prospects, or that he had squandered them already. But I had no means to warn him or to compel him to turn back, neither as a friend who wished him well, nor as a teacher laying down the law. For I thought he felt the same about me as his father did, but it was not so. Laying aside his father's disposition in the matter, he began to say hello to me and sometimes to come to my school room, to listen to me for a while and then go away.

In the meantime it had slipped my mind to deal with him, so that he would not ruin such fine talents by a blind, headstrong concentration upon frivolous pastimes. But you, O Lord, who sit at the helm of all things you have created, had not forgotten him, who would one day be among your sons a chief priest of your sacred mysteries. You worked in such a way as to make it clear that he owed his correction to you, bringing it about through me, though I did not know it.[210] One day I was sit-

---

footsteps of Augustine, who was bishop of the nearby Hippo Regius, west of Thagaste, now the site of Annaba, in Algeria. Nebridius too became a Catholic Christian, a wise and holy man, though he did not live long after their conversion to the faith.

[209] The circus was the oval track for horse races, and then as now, the track was the site of gambling.

[210] As so often, Augustine marvels at the providence of God, who brings about his ends despite what we have planned, or despite our not having planned anything at all.

ting in my usual place with my students, and he came by, greeted me, sat down, and set his mind to what we were doing. By chance I had in hand a reading I wanted to explain, and I thought it fit to use a comparison taken from the games, to make what I was suggesting wittier and clearer, and to aim a biting jest at people whom that madness had enthralled. You know, our God, that just then I was not thinking about healing Alypius of that disease. But he took it to heart, believing that I had aimed it straight at him. And what someone else would have taken as cause to be angry with me, that honest lad took as cause to be angry with himself, and to love me the more warmly. For you had said it long ago and set it in your Scriptures: "Rebuke a wise man, and he will love you."[211]

But I had not rebuked him, not I. It was you who make use of all men, those that know and those that do not know, by the order you know, and that order is just. Out of my heart and my tongue you wrought burning coals to scorch the open sore of so promising a mind, and to heal it. Let the man be silent in your praise if he will not consider your mercies, which I am confessing to you from the marrow of my bones.[212] After those words, he dragged himself out of that deep pit into which he had plunged himself with a will, where he had been dazzled by bizarre delight. He shook his mind with a strong self-control, and all the filth of the circuses slipped away, and he never went back there again.

So he won over his reluctant father to let me be his teacher, and his father gave in and permitted it. And when he began to hear my lectures again, he got tangled up with me in that superstition, because he loved that show of continence the Manicheans made, taking it as true and genuine. But it was senseless, a seductive lie, taking captive souls of great price that still did not know how to touch the height of virtue, souls easy to fool by a fair surface, a bit of play-acting, a shadow of virtue.

---

[211] Prv 9:8.
[212] Cf. Prv 3:8.

8

He had not left behind the worldly way his parents had persuaded him to pursue, as if they had laid a spell on him, and he came to Rome before I did, to study law. And there, with a gasping passion not to be believed, he was swept away by the gladiatorial combats.[213] How it happened too is incredible. At first, he was averse to such things and he detested them, but some friends and fellow students of his, meeting him on the street while they were coming back from dinner, led him along with a friendly kind of violence, he refusing most strenuously and resisting them, into the amphitheater when those cruel and deadly games were going on. "Even if you drag my body there," he kept saying, "can you fix my mind and my eyes on those shows? I will be there, but I will be absent, and so I will overcome both them and you."

Hearing that, his friends were none the slower to bring him along, perhaps wanting to try him out, to see whether he could do what he said. When they had gotten there and found what seats they could, the whole place was seething with the most savage pleasures. Alypius shut the doors of his eyes and forbade his soul to go out into such evils. If only he had stopped up his ears too! For when one man fell in the fight, and a mighty roar from all the people pounded against him, Alypius was overcome with curiosity. He thought he was well-armed to see whatever it was and to condemn it and enjoy the victory, so he opened his eyes. And he was struck with a more grievous wound in the soul than the man he wanted to look at was in the body, and he fell more miserably than did the man at whose fall the shout went up. That cry got into his ears and shot the bolt of his eyes, so that his mind was struck and thrown to

---

[213] Gladiatorial combats were on the decline in Augustine's time, partly because of the economic shrinkage of the third and fourth centuries, and partly because of Christian opposition, which, however, was often inconsistent. Honorius would ban the games in 399, but they seem to have continued anyway, as he banned them again in 404. Augustine's account of the fascination that the games could have for an unguarded soul might well have been penned in our time, with pornography rather than cruelty as the driver of the evil addiction.

the ground, not yet as strong as it was rash, and all the weaker, because he had presumed to rely on himself, rather than relying on you.

As soon as he saw the blood, he drank savagery in with it, and he did not turn away, but fixed his gaze on it, and poured the furies down his throat unawares, and delighted in the wickedness of the contest, and got drunk with bloodthirsty lust. He was not the same man who had come there. He was one of the crowd he had joined, a thorough comrade of those who had brought him. What more can I say? He looked, he cried out, he took fire, and he carried the madness away with him, which goaded him on to go again, and not only in the company of those who had first dragged him to it. He would get there before they did and drag others along too. And still with a most mighty and merciful hand you set him free of this, and you taught him to put his trust not in himself but in you. But that came much later.

9

There was something else too that was laid up in his memory, as a medicine for times to come. It happened when he was still attending my lectures in Carthage. It was in the middle of the day, and he was walking along in the marketplace, going over in his mind the recitation he had to give, as a typical exercise for students. You permitted the officers to apprehend him as a thief, and for no other reason did you permit it, as far as I can judge, than that he, who was going to become an important man, would begin to learn that people should not be condemned too easily—we should not be too rash to believe we know the facts of a case.

He was walking by himself past the courthouse, with his notebook and his pen, when look, a certain one of the young students who was the real thief, smuggling a hatchet under his cloak, got up to the leaden grill work that overhangs the street of the silversmiths, and started to hack away at the lead. Alypius never noticed him. But the silversmiths from below heard the noise of the hatchet, and they whispered together, and sent some of them up to catch whomever they might find. The thief heard their voices, though, and got scared, running off and leaving the tool behind. Now Alypius, who had not seen him going in, heard him leaving and saw him running, so he went into the place to find out why. He found the hatchet, and he stood there, wondering about it, when all at once the men sent there discovered him alone, with the iron tool whose noise had roused them. They seized him and dragged him away, with all their fellow tenants of the marketplace flocking round, and, boasting as if they had caught a thief red-handed, they led him to the judge.

But he was to be instructed no farther. For you were right there, O Lord, to stand for his innocence, whereof you were the sole witness. While he was being led to prison or to punishment, a certain architect, the man in charge of the public buildings, met them on the way. They were glad to meet him of all people, because he had long suspected them of taking things from the marketplace that were missing, and now, they thought, he would know who was responsible. But that man had often seen Alypius in the home of a senator he used to call upon, and straightaway he took him by the hand and led him apart from the crowd, asking what had brought about so bad a business. When he heard what had happened, he commanded all the rabble, seething and full of threats, to come along with him.

Then they went to the house of the young man who had done the deed. Now at the door there was a boy, so little that it would be easy to get him to tell everything, without his being afraid he would do his master any harm, because he had tagged along after him in the market-place. At that, Alypius recalled the fellow, and mentioned him to the architect, who showed the little boy the hatchet and asked him whose it was. "It's ours," he said right away, and they plied him with questions, and he revealed all the rest. So the blame was laid on that house instead, and the crowd, that had begun to crow in triumph over Alypius, was put to shame. And Alypius, who was to become a dispenser of your word, and an examiner of many cases in your church, went away a better taught and more experienced man.

10

So then, I found Alypius at Rome, and he stuck by me with a bond most strong, and he came with me to Milan, because he did not want to leave me, and he thought he could do something there with his study of the law, more to fulfill his parents' wishes than his own. Three times had he already sat as a judge, with an impartiality that others marveled at, while he marveled rather at those who would prefer gold before innocence. His character had been tested not only by the bait of covetousness, but by the sting of fear. At Rome he had been an assessor for the Count of the Italian treasury.[214] There was at that time a very powerful senator, whose good favor had bound many people under obligation, while others were subdued by terror. This man then wanted, by his usual show of force, to get something permitted which was forbidden by law. Alypius stood against him. The man offered a bribe. Alypius scoffed at it. He tried threats. Alypius trampled them underfoot. Everyone was amazed at such a rare spirit, that would neither choose such a man for a friend, nor fear him as an enemy, a man notorious for his countless ways to help a man or to hurt him. The judge himself whom Alypius served as counsel did not want to do it, but still he did not refuse it openly. He threw the whole responsibility upon Alypius, asserting that Alypius would not let him do it, when, to tell the truth, if he had done it, Alypius would have resigned.

The one bait that nearly caught Alypius came from his love of literature—to set about getting books copied for him at a discount, as the praetors did. But, consulting the justice of it, he turned his purpose to a better course, judging equity, which would forbid it, to be of more profit than power, which would allow it. A little thing, this; but he who is faithful in a little thing will be faithful in a great thing too. Nor

---

[214] Subordinate to the imperial treasury were the various provincial treasuries, such as this one, the Italian. As Alypius was learned in the law, he was assigned to the Count as an advisor. We see that Alypius used his knowledge of law for the sake of justice, and not to find ways to circumvent the law, to win the favor or to avert the hatred of rich and powerful persons.

can anything be null which has proceeded from the lips of your Truth: "If you have not been faithful in the mammon of unrighteousness, who will trust you with true riches? And if you have not been faithful in what belongs to another man, who will give you what belongs to you?"[215] That was the man who then clung to me, and who wavered along with me, as to what course of life we should take up.

Nebridius was with us too. He had left his home village near Carthage, and Carthage itself where he often stayed, leaving behind his father's rich farmlands, leaving his house, leaving a mother who did not want to follow him, all to come to Milan and to live with me in a most ardent study of truth and wisdom. With me he sighed, with me he was tossed on the waves, an ardent man on the quest for the blessed life, and a keen examiner of the most difficult questions. So there we were, three beggars with empty mouths, each one gasping to the others in his poverty, all of us looking to you, that you might give us our food in due season.[216] And in all the bitterness that by your mercy followed upon our worldly pursuits, we tried to find the end, the reason why we suffered. But darkness fell upon us, and we turned away mourning, and saying, "How long must it be?"[217] We said it all the time, and even as we said it we did not forsake the things we did. For nothing certain came to light that we might take hold of, once we had forsaken them.

11

And I was astonished at myself, recalling again and again how long a time had passed since my nineteenth year, when I began to grow warm with the desire for wisdom, determining, once I had found it, to put away all the idle hopes I had set on vain desires and their lying fits of madness. And here I was, nearly thirty, stuck in the same mud, still

---

[215] Lk 16:11–12.
[216] Cf. Ps 145:15, Mt 24:45.
[217] Cf. Ps 13:1–2.

hankering after present pleasures, fleeting as they were, and spilling my substance away, while I said:

"Tomorrow I shall find it. It shall be plain and clear, and I will grab hold of it. Look, Faustus is coming, and he will explain everything. You great men, you Academics! Is there nothing certain, nothing sure to grasp, for how we are to live? Well then, let us search more diligently and not give up hope. See, the things that seemed absurd in the Church's books are not absurd, for they can be understood in another and a more reasonable way. I shall set my feet on that step where my parents set me when I was a boy, till I can see the truth right through. But where shall I seek it, and when? Ambrose has no leisure for it. We have no leisure for reading. And where shall we look for the books to read? Where and when can we get them? Or from whom can we borrow them? Let's set aside certain times and devote certain hours for the health of our souls. A great hope has dawned: the Catholic faith does not teach what we once supposed, and what we in our vanity had accused her of. Her learned men hold it as an unspeakable blasphemy to believe that God is bounded by the form of a human body. And do we still hesitate to knock, that all the rest might also be opened unto us? Our students take up all our morning hours, but what about the rest of the day? Why are we not doing this? But when shall we call upon our influential friends, whose favors we need? When are we going to prepare works for the scholars to buy? When will we refresh ourselves, relaxing the mind from its cares?

"Let it all go to perdition, let's put away all these empty and pointless matters! Let's put our heads together and seek only the truth. Life is miserable, death is uncertain. If it snatches us up, in what state shall we be when we leave this world? Or where must we learn what we neglected to learn here? Shall we not rather pay the penalty for our negligence? What if death itself should cut short and put an end to all our troubles, along with sensation? We should look into that too. But let it not be so! It is no vain trifle that the lofty and eminent authority of the Christian faith should be spread abroad through all the world.

Never would God have done so many and so great things for us, if at the death of the body the life of the soul were consumed as well. Why do we dawdle then? Why shouldn't we give up hope in the world, and devote ourselves to seeking God and the blessed life?

"But watch out—worldly things are pleasant too, with no little sweetness of their own. It is not easy to cut our ties to them, and it would be a foul shame to go back to them again. And we have done so much already to gain a position of honor. What is more to be desired? We have plenty of powerful friends, and so long as we don't rush after too much, we might even get a governor's place. Then I could get a wife, too, with some money, so our expenses will not weigh too much. That would be the scope of my desires. Many great men most worthy of imitation have given themselves to the study of wisdom, though they were married."

And while I kept saying these things, and the winds shifted hither and yon and tossed my heart about, the time passed, and I was slow to convert to the Lord, and I put off from one day to the next to live in you. But I did not put off my daily dying inside. I loved the blessed life, and I was afraid to find it in its proper place, and so I fled from it even while I sought it. I thought I would be the most miserable of men if I were deprived of a woman's arms. About the medicine of your mercy, for healing that disease, I never gave a thought, because I had no experience of it. I thought that continence lay within our natural powers, and I was conscious of no such power in me. I was a fool not to know, as it is written, that no one can be continent unless you grant it to him.[218] And you would have given it to me, if with inward groaning I had knocked at your ears, and with a solid faith cast my care upon you.

12

It was really Alypius who kept me from taking a wife, always sounding the same tune, saying that if I did that, there would be no way we could live together, free of care, in the love of wisdom, as we had for

---

[218] Cf. Ws 8:21.

so long wanted to do. In that regard, he was himself so very chaste, it was a wonder to behold. For at the very beginning of his adolescence he had tried sharing a woman's bed, but he did not stick to it, but was sorry about it instead and held it in scorn, and ever afterward he was most continent in his way of life. But I opposed him with examples of married men who did cultivate wisdom, and who deserved well of God, who had kept faithful to their friends and who loved them too. As for me, I was far from their greatness of soul. I dragged my chain along, fettered by a disease of the flesh, deadly sweet. I was afraid to have the chain undone, and I repelled his good and persuasive words, as if they were the hand knocking off the chain and chafing my wound to do it.

Worse still, the serpent spoke through me to Alypius himself, contriving sweet snares and using my tongue to lay them in his path, to catch and tangle his honest and unbound feet.[219] For he was amazed that I, whom he regarded so highly, should be stuck so fast in the trap of that pleasure as to affirm, whenever we talked about it, that I could never live a celibate life. But when I saw him wondering, I defended myself, saying there was a big difference between what he had tried in haste and stealth, something he could hardly remember and what he could despise without any regret, and the delights I was accustomed to. And if you added to those the honest name of matrimony, he need not wonder why I could not reject that life. Then he too began to want to be married, not at all overcome by lust for such pleasure, but out of curiosity. He said he wanted to know what it could possibly be without which my life, which pleased him so much, would seem to me no life but a punishment. Free from those fetters, his mind was amazed at my servitude, and from amazement it went on to desire the experience, and had he gotten the experience he might well have fallen into the same servitude that now amazed him. For he wanted nuptials with death, and he who loves peril shall fall into it.[220] Neither of us was more than slightly attracted by

219 Cf. Rom 14:13. Augustine was playing the part of a tempter, laying a snare before his friend's feet.
220 Cf. Sir 3:26. Augustine is the stubborn man in love with peril, tempting his friend to

129

whatever is comely in marriage, whether the good order of a married life or the raising of children. For the most part, I was seized and tormented by my habit of trying to satisfy an insatiable desire, while he was to be caught by his wonder at me. That was our state, until you, Most High, who did not abandon our poor clay,[221] having pity on the pitiable, came to our help in mysterious and wonderful ways.

13

And I was pressed, with no letup, to get a wife. Soon I asked for a girl's hand in marriage, and we were betrothed, with my mother doing most of the arranging. Uppermost in her mind was this. She thought that once I had gotten married, I would be washed in the health-giving waters of baptism, which she rejoiced to see me preparing for, day by day, as her prayers and your promises were being fulfilled in my faith. And at my urging and at her own desire she besought you, every day, with a mighty outcry of her heart, to show her in a vision something about my future matrimony, but you never willed it. She did see some insubstantial and fanciful things, driven by the force of the human spirit when it is preoccupied with something like this, and she recounted them to me, but not with the same confidence as when you showed something to her. Rather she made light of them. For she said there was a kind of savor, which she could not explain in words, that let her distinguish between when you were revealing something to her, and when her soul was merely dreaming. Still, she kept up the pressure, and she got a promise for a girl who was still about two years shy of the marrying age.[222] But I liked the girl, so I decided to wait.

14

And all of us many friends set our minds to it, and we talked together about how we detested all the troublesome upheavals of human life,

---

join him in it.
[221] Cf. Is 64:8; Ps 103:14.
[222] She was then a small girl. The age of consent for girls was ten.

and we were on the verge of resolving to live at ease, far away from the crowds. We would provide for that leisure by pooling together what each one had, and so from everyone we would forge one common household. In the sincerity of friendship, nothing would belong to this one or that one, but what had been made up from all of us into one would belong to every single person, and all things would belong to all. We thought there would be ten or so persons in our society, and some of them were quite wealthy, especially our countryman Romanianus, a close friend of mine from childhood, whom weighty affairs of business had brought to court.[223] He was quite forward in this matter, and his authority was powerful and persuasive, because he was much wealthier than the rest of us. And we thought it would be good to have two men act as magistrates every year, to take care of everything we needed, while everyone else could live quietly. But then we began to wonder whether our wives would put up with it, because some of us were already married and I wanted to be married, and the whole pleasant design we had drawn up so well dwindled away in our hands, fallen to pieces and cast aside. Then we went back to sighing and groaning and following the broad and well-beaten ways of the world.[224] For many were the thoughts in our heart, but your counsel abides forever.[225] By that counsel you laughed at ours, and prepared for us your own, for you would give us food in due season, and you would open your hand and fill our souls with blessing.[226]

15

Meanwhile my sins were multiplied,[227] and the woman with whom I shared my bed was torn from my side as an obstacle to my marriage. My heart, which cleaved to her, was crushed and wounded, and it bled.

---

[223] Rominianus, also from Thagaste, was a rich and generous man, and he had financed Augustine's move to Carthage and then to Italy.
[224] Cf. Mt 7:13.
[225] Cf. Prv 19:21.
[226] Cf. Ps 145:15–16.
[227] Cf. Sir 47:24.

And she went back to Africa, vowing to you that she would never know another man, and leaving with me our natural son.[228] Unhappy man that I was, unable to imitate a woman, too impatient to wait, since it would be two years before I could take the girl promised to me, and since I was no lover of marriage but rather a slave to lust, I procured myself another woman, but not, of course, as a wife. By her means, my soul's sickness would be sustained and led right into the kingdom of marriage, either whole and entire or more powerful than before, under the convoy of inveterate habit. Nor did it heal the wound made when my former mistress was cut off, but after the first fever and the bitterest pangs were over, the wound began to fester, and though the pain was cooler, so to speak, it was more desperate.

16

Praise be to you, glory to you, O fountain of mercies! I grew the more miserable, and you drew nearer to me. Your right hand was ready to catch me up from the mire and wash me clean, but I did not know it. The only thing that called me back out of a still deeper gulf of carnal pleasures was fear of death and of your judgment to come, which through all my changing opinions never did leave my breast.

And I discussed with my friends Alypius and Nebridius the final ends of the good and the evil, and to my mind Epicurus would have won the palm of victory, save that I believed that after death something of life remained for the soul, a drawing-out of our merits, which Epicurus refused to believe.[229] And I put this question. Suppose we never had to

---

[228] We do not know the name of Augustine's long-time mistress. No doubt Augustine did not want to cast aspersions on her name, and that explains his tact here. The woman, too, promises to God that she will not repeat the sin, nor even take a man in marriage. She leaves behind their natural son, the boy Adeodatus.

[229] Epicurus (341–270 BC) taught that the chief aim in human life was to avoid pain and trouble, and to pursue pleasure, mainly the pleasure of friendship and the exercise of the mind; he believed that to indulge the sexual passion, especially in its form as ardent love, was to invite unhappiness and disappointment. He was a strict materialist, teaching that the whole world was made up only of atoms—literally, particles that cannot be split into

die, and we could live in perpetual pleasures of the body without any dread of losing them. Why should we not then be considered happy? What more could we ask for? I said so, not knowing that that itself was a part of my great misery, that I was so blind, I was sunk so deep, that I could not conceive of the light of a virtue and a beauty to be embraced for its own sake. The eye of the flesh does not see it; it is seen from the inmost soul. I did not even consider, poor fellow that I was, the stream that fed me my highest pleasure. For the things I said, though they were filthy enough, were sweet to talk about with my friends, nor could I really be happy without friends, even according to the opinion I held at the time, regardless of my flood of fleshly delights. In fact, I loved those friends with a free heart, and I felt that they loved me freely in turn.

What winding roads! Woe to my brazen soul, hoping that if it retreated from you, it would find something better! It tossed and turned on its back, on its sides, on its belly, and every place was hard, and you alone were its peace and quiet. And behold, you are near, and you deliver us from our wretched wandering, and you set us firmly in your way, and you console us, saying, "Run, and I shall carry you, I shall bring you to the end, and I shall carry you there."[230]

---

parts—and empty space. That included the mind and the soul, which he said were also material, composed of the most subtle of atoms, whose coherence and organization were easily dissolved with the death of the body. Thus did the gods neither reward virtue nor punish vice. Epicurus's teachings were spread most effectively among Latin speakers by the poet Lucretius (c.99—c.55 BC), in his didactic philosophical epic *On the Nature of Things*.
[230] Is 46:4.

1

By now, my wicked and unspeakable adolescence was dead, and I went on into young manhood, older in years, grosser in vanity, unable to conceive of any substance unless I could see it with my own eyes. But I did not conceive of you, O God, in the form of a human body. From when I first began to hear something of wisdom, I always shunned that thought, and I was glad that I found agreement in the faith of our spiritual mother, your Catholic Church. But what else I was supposed to think of you never occurred to me. I strove hard to think about you, though I was only a man, and such a man, too! I tried to conceive of you, the highest and only and true God, and I believed to the marrow of my bones that you were incorruptible and inviolable and immutable, for I saw quite clearly, though I did not know how I saw it or where it came from, that what could be corrupted was a lesser thing than what could not be corrupted, and what could never be violated I did not hesitate to prefer to what could be violated, and what does not suffer change was better than what can be changed.

With violence did my heart cry out against all those phantasms of mine, and with one blow I tried to drive out of my mental sight the whole fluttering troop of unclean things. But at a stroke, in the blink of an eye, they would be there again in a mass, and they would take my vision by storm, and cloud it over. So although I did not conceive of you in the form of a human body, I was compelled to think of you as some other corporeal thing spread out through all space, a thing infused all through the world, or even diffused beyond the world in endless space, but incorruptible for all that, and inviolable and immutable, which I set above the corruptible and violable and mutable. For anything that I deprived of such location seemed to me to be nothing, nothing at all, not even empty space. I thought that if one takes some bodily thing away from a location, the location would be what it was, empty of everything bodily, whether of earth or water or air or the fire of heaven, but still an empty location, a kind of nothing taking up space.[231]

That is how thick-hearted I was, unable to peer into my own self. I reckoned that whatever was not stretched over some spatial extent, whether poured out or clumped together or bulging up, whatever could not assume such a form or be assumed into it, was downright nothing. Just as my eyes were used to go on from shape to shape, so my heart went on from image to image. I did not see that the very intention of mind whereby I gave a shape to these images was itself no such thing. But were it not a great and real thing, it could never have formed them to begin with.[232]

And so I thought of you, life of my life, as something vast in endless space, penetrating the whole mass of the world, extending beyond it on all sides in space without measure, without limit. So, then, the earth would possess you, and the heavens above, and all things besides, and they would have their limits in you, but you would have no limit

---

[231] That is the spatial equivalent of the mistake often made with God and time. Just as there is no space before God created it, and therefore space—as modern physicists have come round to saying—is a feature of this universe and not an independently existing thing, so also there is no time before God created it.

[232] The mind is not a material thing, though its substrate in man is the brain; for the thought whereby I conceive of a thing, or a truth, or a law, is irreducible to the physical inducements that lead me to think of it, and is more and greater than the object of my thought. One human thought is greater in being than the entire solar system, because it can conceive of that system, which cannot conceive of itself or of the least thing in existence.

anywhere. I thought of the sunlight, and how the body of air that lies above this earth does not obstruct it, but the light passes right through, and it penetrates the air not by breaking it or cutting into it, but by filling it all. Just so, I reckoned that all bodies, not only of the heavens and the air and the sea, but even of the earth, give you free passage, penetrable in all their parts from the greatest to the least. They take your presence within them, while from within and without, by your secret inbreathing, you govern all things you have created. That was my guess, because I could not conceive of anything else; but it was false. For, by this reasoning, a bigger portion of earth would possess a bigger portion of you, and a smaller, likewise. All things would be filled with you in such a way that the body of an elephant would get more of you than the body of a sparrow would, just insofar as it is bigger and takes up a bigger place. So too you would make your own parts present in them bit by bit, big parts for big things and little parts for little things. It is not so. But you had not yet illumined my darkness.[233]

2

For me, O Lord, it was a decisive answer against those self-deceived deceivers, who chattered and were dumb at once, because your word never sounded from their lips—answer enough, what Nebridius used to say at Carthage long ago, and it staggered us who heard it. "What," he asked, "would that who-knows-what 'nation of darkness' the Manicheans set against God have done to him, if he declined to fight it?" If they replied that it would hurt you, then you could suffer violence, and you would be corruptible. But if they said that it could *not* hurt you, then there would be no point in fighting it, especially since, in the fight, some portion of you or some member or some offshoot of your substance would get mixed up with enemy powers and with natures you had not created, and they would so far corrupt it and change it for the worse. It would be turned from beatitude to misery,

---

[233] Cf. Ps 18:28.

and it would need help to get out of there and be purged of the evil. This offshoot they would identify as the soul, which your Word came to aid, the free to aid the slave, the pure to the befouled, the whole to the broken. But then the Word too would be corruptible, as it came from the same substance. Now if they say that whatever you are, the substance whereby you exist is *incorruptible*, then they must hold that all these other opinions are false and execrable. But if they say you are *corruptible*, that right there would be false and abominable as soon as it is said. It was a sufficient answer, against those whom in every way I should have puked up from a swollen gut. They had no other way out, unless they committed some horrible sacrilege of the heart or the tongue, believing and saying such things of you as they did.

3

Up till then I did most firmly believe and say that you, our Lord, the true God, who made not only our souls but our bodies too, and not only our souls and bodies but all things, cannot suffer contamination or conversion into something else or change in any way. But for all that, I could not grasp the cause of evil, I could not untangle the matter. Whatever the cause might be, I thought it must be what would not force me to believe that it could change the unchangeable God, or else I would end up being the very evil I sought to explain. So I felt safe in my search, certain that what the Manicheans said, whom I fled with all my heart, was not true. For I saw that their search for the cause of evil had filled them with malice, as they would rather believe that your substance could suffer evil, than that they themselves had committed it.

And I bent my mind to understand what I often heard, that the will's free judgment was the cause of the evil we committed, and that your righteous judgment was the cause of the evil we suffered. But I was not strong enough to see it clearly. Every time I struggled to raise my mind's eye out of the deep, I was plunged back under, and as often as I struggled, so often did I plunge, again and again. But this did raise me up toward your light: I knew I had a will as surely as I knew I was alive. For whenever I willed a thing or declined to will it, I was as sure as sure can be that it was I and no other that willed or declined to will.[234] And that was the cause of my sin, as I was on the point of perceiving. But what I did against my will, it seemed I suffered it rather than did it, and that, I judged, was not my fault but my punishment. And because I thought of you as being just, I said straightaway that it was just for you to upbraid me.

But then I turned round and said, "Who made me? Was it not my God, who is not only good, but the very good itself? Then how does it come about that I should will the bad and decline the good? Is it so that I might justly undergo punishment? Who was it that set and engrafted in me this sprig of bitterness, seeing that the whole of me was made by my God most sweet? If the devil was the author of it, where did that devil come from? If by his perverse will he went from being a good angel to a devil, how did that evil will get into him, seeing as he had been made all angel by the best Creator?" By these thoughts I was thrown down again, and I gasped for breath, but I was not dragged all the way down into that hell of error where no one confesses to you, while they think that you suffer evil rather than that man commits it.

4

So I fought on, trying to find out the rest, now that I had found that it was better to be incorruptible than to be corruptible, and as a result I declared that whatever you are, you must be incorruptible. No soul

---

[234] The freedom of the will is a fundamental datum of human thought and experience, and it is, as Augustine suggests here, bound up with the knowledge that we are ourselves and no other. I may be prompted to do one thing or another, but my experience of choosing is far different from my experience of being compelled by force from without. But this freedom cannot be reducible to matter. The Epicureans themselves were aware of the problem, and that is why, long before any theories regarding the quantum fluctuation of subatomic particles, they posited a random "swerve" in the downward and everlasting and otherwise wholly deterministic rain of atoms in empty space. That element of uncertainty, they thought, would suffice to save the experience of freedom, which otherwise they would be compelled to deny, in the teeth of universal human judgment.

was ever able, and none ever will be able, to conceive of anything better than you, who are the best and highest Good.[235] For just as it is most true and certain that the incorruptible is to be preferred to the corruptible, and that is what I now did prefer, I could then attain by thought to what would be better than my God, supposing you were *not* incorruptible. I should have sought after you just at that point where I saw that the incorruptible was to be preferred before the corruptible. From there I could have turned my attention to where evil comes from, that is, whence comes the corruption that can in no way violate your substance, your essential being. For corruption cannot infect our God at all, not by any will, any necessity, any unforeseen chance. He is God, and what he wills for himself is good, and He himself is that same good. But to be corrupted is not good. Nor are you ever compelled to act against your will, because your will is not greater than your power. It could only be greater, if you could be greater than yourself: for the will and the power of God are God himself. What can strike you as unforeseen, you who know all things? For no nature exists, unless you have known it. And why should we ask all the time, "Why should the being of God not be corruptible?" If it were, He would not be God.

5

And I sought an answer to where evil comes from, but I sought it in an evil way, and I failed to see the evil in my own inquiry. And I set before my spirit's view the whole created universe, all that we can discern in it, such as the earth and sea, the air and the stars, the trees and all living things that die, and all that we cannot see, such as the

---

[235] This affirmation would be crucial for Saint Anselm (1033–1109), in his demonstration of the necessary existence of God, "that than which nothing greater can be conceived" (*Proslogion,* ch. 2). We must be precise here. Augustine is not merely saying that God is the greatest of all existing beings. That would still set God on the same plane of existence with other beings; it would be a version of the error he struggled so long to abandon. For what is infinite in space is still bound to space, and what is everlasting in time is still bound to time. God is not simply the greatest of existing beings, but the greatest conceivable being.

firmament of the heaven above, and all the angels and the spiritual beings that dwell there, even these, as I imagined them, possessing bodies and arranged in these places or those. And I made of it one vast mass, distinguished by a variety of bodies, your creation, whether they were bodies indeed, or whether I fancied them as such instead of spirits. I made it vast, not as big as it really was, which I did not know, but as big as seemed proper, and yet bounded in all directions. Meanwhile, Lord, I imagined you as ambient on all sides and penetrating it, while you yourself were boundless everywhere. It was as if there were a sea, a single sea, extending everywhere through immeasurable and infinite space, and there were inside this sea a sponge, huge indeed but still finite. And that sponge would be filled in every part by the boundless sea.[236]

That is how I thought your finite creation could be filled with you, the infinite, and I would say, "Behold, here is God! Behold what God has created! And God is good, far and away more outstanding than any of these things. Nevertheless, the good God created good things, and see how he surrounds them and fills them. Where then does evil come from? Where and how does it creep in? What is its root? What is its seed? Does it even exist at all? Why then do we fear and beware what does not exist? If our fear is in vain, then the fear itself is an evil, stinging and tormenting our hearts for no reason, and so much the more ponderous evil, because what we fear does not exist, and yet we fear it anyway. Therefore, either an evil does exist, which we fear, or our fear itself is an evil. Well then, where does it come from, since the good God made all things good? The greater and indeed the highest good has made lesser things that are good, but even so, both he who creates and all things he has created are good. Where does evil come from? Maybe there was some evil matter[237]

---

[236] Cf. Plotinus, *Enneads,* IV.3.9. Plotinus says that the cosmos is permeated by the "soul," which is the second level of emanation from the One; this soul is infinite in extent, while the cosmos is like a net in the sea, encompassing all material things, but itself not in act.

[237] Again we find a trace of the supposition that matter is the wellspring of evil, common

that he made things from, and he gave it shape and order, but he left something in it that he did not turn to good? But why would he do that? Was he not strong enough to change and convert the whole thing so that none of the evil would remain, he who is all-powerful? Besides, why would he make anything of it at all? Why not instead, in his omnipotence, reduce it to nonexistence? Really, could it have existed against his will? If this evil material had always been, why did he suffer it to exist for all that endless stretch of backward time, and then, after so long, why did it please him to fashion something out of it? Or if he suddenly willed to do something, why would he, the all-powerful, not rather cause the thing not to exist, so that he would abide alone, the whole true and highest and infinite good? But supposing it were not good, that he who is good should refrain from framing and fashioning something else that is good, why not then take away that evil material and reduce it to nothing, and then replace it with good material, to make all things from? For he would not be omnipotent, if he were incapable of creating some good thing without the help of some material he did not create."[238]

Such things did I turn round and round in my miserable heart, laden with sharp biting cares from the fear of death, and from truth not found. But the faith of your Christ, our Lord and Savior, to be found in the Catholic Church, was fixed fast in my heart, though I was still unformed and I wavered in many ways from the straight rule of doctrine. Still, my mind did not forsake it, but drank in more and more of it every day.

---

enough in the mysticism of pagans all the world over, and only with difficulty ruled out by the Neoplatonists and their system that assigns to matter the lowest level of existence, farthest from the One.

[238] In his dialogue *Timaeus,* even Plato seems to have supposed that there was some primal or chaotic matter, pre-existent, which a divine but not all-powerful Demiurge converted into the cosmos. The notion of pure creation, rather than of rearrangement of pre-existing matter, was foreign to the ancients, though Plotinus and his followers, perhaps influenced by Judaism and Christianity, come close to suggesting it.

6

By now I had rejected the astrologers and their deceitful divinations and the impious ravings. For this too, my God, let your own mercies confess to you from the most inward reaches of my soul! It was you, all your doing—for who else calls us back from our dead waywardness, but Life that knows no death, and Wisdom that enlightens minds in want, itself in want of no light, Wisdom by whom the world is governed, even to the leaves that rustle on the trees? It was you who took care for my being so stiff-necked, when I wrestled with Vindicianus,[239] that sharp-witted old man, and with the lad Nebridius and his marvelous mind. The former was vehement, and the latter just a bit hesitant, but both said over and over that there was no art for foreseeing the future, and that when men guess at things they are often corroborated by chance. Men say many things, so it happens that many a thing they say will come to pass, regardless of what they know or do not know. They stumble upon it just by not keeping their mouths shut.

Therefore you got for me a friend, a man not slow to consult the astrologers, nor all that skillful himself in their writings, but, as I said, a curious consulter. Still, he knew something that he said he had heard from his father, but he did not know how far it would go to overturn my opinion of that art. This man, Firminus by name, liberally educated and well taught in public speaking, consulted me as a most dear friend about various of his affairs, as his hopes were on the rise. He asked how it looked to me according to his constellations, as they call them. Although in this matter I had begun to lean toward Nebridius's thinking, still I did not refuse to make a conjecture, or to tell him what occurred to me, doubtful as I was. But I did add that I was nearly persuaded that these things were ridiculous and silly.

---

[239] Vindicianus, a Christian, was the prefect in Africa who awarded the young Augustine with the crown of victory in a contest of rhetoric (376; see book 4, ch. 3), and he was the personal physician for the boy-emperor Valentinian II.

Then he told me the story of how his father used to pore over such books all the time, and that he had a friend who was as devoted a follower as he. These two were so hot to study and discuss these frivolous things, fanning the fire in their hearts, that they even observed the precise moments when the dumb animals they had in the household were born, and they made note of the position of the heavens, to rack up some proofs of the art, so to speak. Well, he heard his father say that when his wife was pregnant with him, Firminus, some female slave of his friend was big with child at the same time. She could hardly hide it from her master, who went so far as to examine most diligently when his dogs littered. And it so happened that, while with the most painstaking calculation they were figuring out the days and hours and the least little particles of the hours, he for his wife and his friend for his servant, the two women bore children at precisely the same time. That meant they were forced to draw up the same horoscopes for each child, down to the minute, one for his son, the other for his little slave boy. For when the women went into labor, each man gave notice to the other as to what was going on at home, and they got messengers ready to send instant news as soon as a child was born. It was easy for them to give immediate notice, as each was like a king in his own domain. And Firminus said that the messengers ran into each other exactly halfway between the houses, so that neither of them could note down any other position of the stars or any other small moment of time than the other had done. But despite it all, Firminus was born to an ample position in his family home, and he ran his course along the fair white ways of the world, increasing in wealth, and rising high in honors, while the other was but a slave, and his yoke was never made easier, and he served his masters still. It was Firminus who told me, and he knew the man.

When I heard these things I believed them, because the teller was a trustworthy man, and all my reluctance melted and fell away. The first thing I did was to try to call Firminus himself back from that study. I said that if I were going to look into his constellations and utter true predictions, I would already have had to see parents prime among their fellow citizens, a noble family in their city, gentle birth, an honorable education, studies fit for a free citizen; but if that slave born under the same constellations, for they were his too, had consulted me, and if I had to tell true things about him, I would have had to go back and see an utterly downtrodden family, the condition of a slave, and other things far different and far distant from the first. Inspecting the same patterns, I would have to come up with different things to say if I was going to speak the truth, but if I said the same things, I would be speaking falsely. Thence did I gather, with full certainty, that whenever people read the constellations and say things that turn out to be true, they say them not by art but by luck, and whenever they say things that turn out to be false, it is not that they are clumsy in the art, but that chance has tricked them.

Taking this approach to the business, I ruminated within myself about such things. What if one of those dolts who read stars for a living—whom I now wanted to attack right away and refute, and make a laughingstock of them—should confront me and say that what Firminus told me or what his father told him was false? So I turned my attention to people who are born twins. Most of them slip out of the womb so closely one upon the other, that human observation is incapable of determining that small interval of time, no matter how much force they contend it has in the nature of things, nor can it be signified in the tables that the astrologer looks into so that he can foretell the truth. And it will not be true. For if he had inspected the same tables for Esau and Jacob, he would have had to say the same things about them, but the same things did not happen to them at all. He would have had to say what was false, or, if did say what was true, he would have had to say different things of each child, even though he would have been inspecting the same tables.[240] Therefore when they do speak truly, it is not art but luck.

---

[240] Esau and Jacob, of course, were twins (Gn 25:21–33), and when they were in the womb, the Lord said to their mother, Rebecca, that two nations were struggling in her womb, and that the younger would be stronger than the elder. The point is that Esau and Jacob were

For you, O Lord, most just governor of the universe, work by so secret an indwelling, though both those who consult and those they consult know nothing about it, that when a man does consult an astrologer, he may hear what he deserves to hear, according to the hidden merits of men's souls, out of the abyss of your righteous judgment. Let no man say to you, "What is this? What is it for?" Let him not say it, let him not say it—for he is but a man.[241]

7

By this time, my Helper, you had slipped me from those chains, and I still asked, "Where does evil come from?", and there was no way out. But you did not allow those waves of thinking to carry me away from the faith I had, that you exist, that your substance is unalterable, and that you care for men, and you judge them; and that in Christ, your Son, our Lord, and the holy Scriptures which the authority of your Catholic Church commends, you have laid down the way of man's salvation, on to the life after death, that is to be.

These things were safe and settled in my soul, strong and unshakeable, and I kept asking, in my sweltering mind, "Where does evil come from?" My God, what groans, what torment of my heart, laboring in the pangs of birth![242] But your ears were open, though I did not know it. And when in silence I sought more boldly for the answer, the speechless contrition of my soul was a mighty cry for your mercy. You knew what I suffered, you and no man. How much of it did my tongue direct to the ears of my closest friends? Did the tumult of my soul, when neither time nor my tongue could suffice to tell of it, ever ring in their ears? Nevertheless, the whole of it went forth into your hearing, what

---

very different in personality and in their ways of life, and that though Esau was the mightier warrior, the greater nation would spring from Jacob. Yet their horoscopes were exactly the same, as Jacob followed upon Esau immediately, gripping his brother's heel as they came from the womb.

[241] Cf. Ps 9:20.
[242] Cf. Mi 4:10.

I roared out of the groaning of my heart,[243] and my desire was before you, when the very light of my eyes was with me no more. For that was a deeply inward thing, but I was outside, and it was not in any place. But I focused my mind on things that are contained in places, and there I found no place to rest, nor did those things welcome me in, so I might say, "This is all I need, this is well." Nor did they let me go back along the way to where it might really be well with me. For I was superior to those things, though inferior to you, and you are my true joy, as I am subject to you; and all the things you created inferior to me you subjected to me.

This was the right and well-tempered order, this was the center of my well-being, to abide in your image, and in serving you, to be the lord over my body. But when I rose in proud revolt against you, and I sallied forth against the Lord with the thick neck of my buckler,[244] even the meanest of things lorded it over me and put me down, and they never eased up or let me breathe. They rushed against me in heaps and troops as I looked upon them, and if I gave them a thought and I tried to retreat, those same images of bodily things blocked my way, as if they said, "Where are you going, you worthless and grubby thing?" And they had grown fat upon my wound, for you have humbled the proud man as if he were wounded, and in my swelling infection I set myself far from you, and the overblown fat of my face shut up my eyes.[245]

8

Truly, O Lord, you abide for everlasting, nor are you angry with us forever, for you have mercy upon dust and ashes, and it was pleasing in your sight to reform my deformities.[246] And you roused me up by stings within me, that I would grow restless and not suffer delay, till

---

[243] Cf. Ps 38:8.
[244] Cf. Job 15:26.
[245] Cf. Ps 17:10, Is 6:10.
[246] Cf. Ps 103:9, 14.

you should appear as certain to my inward sight. And my swollen sore began to subside under the hidden hand of your medicine, and then the baffled and darkened sight of my mind, day by day, by the pungent eye-salve of healing sorrows, began to clear.[247]

9

And first of all, you wanted to show me how you resist the proud, and give grace to the humble, and how great a mercy it is that you show men the way of humility, in that the Word was made flesh, and dwelt among men.[248] You provided for me, by means of a certain man puffed up with a perfectly monstrous arrogance, certain books of the Platonists, translated from Greek into Latin.[249] And there I read, not indeed in these words, but the very same thing, set forth persuasively with many reasons of various kinds, that "in the beginning was the Word, and the Word was with God, and the Word was God: He was in the beginning with God; all things were made through Him, and without Him nothing was made, that was made; in Him is life, and the life was the light of men, and the light shines in the darkness, and the darkness has not comprehended it."[250] And that the soul of man, though it gives testimony to the light, is not itself the light. And that

---

[247] Cf. Rv 3:18.

[248] Cf. Prv 3:34, Jn 1:14.

[249] This chapter is one of the most significant and influential pieces of writing in the history of the Christian West. In it, Augustine shows that certain truths of the Christian faith, among them the very doctrine of the only-begotten Son of God, the second Person of the Trinity, were discoverable by reason or by intuitive insight apart from the Scriptures. He gives to the Neoplatonists as much breadth of interpretation as possible, and indeed he suggests to us that God used their books as means to bring him to the orthodox faith. This generosity toward pagan insights will be a marked feature of Christian missionary activity, and of Christian appraisal and use of non-Christian texts, customs, and arts. That does not mean, however, that there was no difference between Neoplatonism and Christianity. There is all the difference in the world—a difference that centers not on what Neoplatonists and Christians think about the material world, merely, but on the very action of God, who came among us in the flesh.

[250] Jn 1:1–5.

the Word, God himself, is "the true light, that enlightens every man that comes into this world," and that "he was in the world, and the world was made by Him, and the world knew him not."[251] But that "he came unto his own, and his own received him not, but as many as did receive him, he gave power to become children of God, who believed in his name"[252]—this I did not read there.

Again, I read there, that the Word, God, "was begotten, not by the flesh, nor by blood, nor by the will of a man, but by God." But that "the Word was made flesh, and dwelt among us,"[253] I did not read there.

I tracked down in those books, not in the same words, but expressed in many ways, that the Son "was in the form of the Father," and "thought it not robbery to be equal to God,"[254] because in his nature he himself was God. But that he "emptied himself" of that form, and "took on the form of a slave," and "was found in the fashion of a man," and "humbled himself, and became obedient even unto death, death upon a cross," wherefore God has raised him from the dead, and "given him a name which is above every name, so that at the name of Jesus every knee must bend, in heaven, on earth, and under the earth, and every tongue confess that Jesus is Lord, in the glory of God the Father,"[255]—those books did not have it.

Again, that your only-begotten Son abides unchangeable before all times and above all times, coeternal with you, and that of his fullness souls receive what makes them blessed,[256] and that they are renewed by participating in the wisdom that abides in itself, so that they too may be wise—that is there. But that "at the appointed time He died for sinners," and that you "spared not your only Son, but gave him up for us all,"[257] is not there. For you have hidden these things from the wise and

---

[251] Jn 1:8–10.
[252] Jn 1:11–12.
[253] Jn 1:13, 14.
[254] Phil 2:6.
[255] Phil 2:7–11.
[256] Cf. Jn 1:16.
[257] Rom 5:6, 8:32.

revealed them to little ones, that all they who labor and are heavy-burdened might come to him, and he might give them rest, for he is meek and humble of heart;[258] and he directs the meek in judgment, and to the mild he teaches his ways,[259] looking upon our lowliness and our labor, and forgiving all our sins. But those who deck themselves out in the grand style of some higher learning do not hear him who says, "Learn from me, for I am meek and humble of heart, and you shall find rest for your souls," and "though they know God, they do not give him glory as God, or give him thanks, but they grow vain in their imaginations, and their foolish heart is darkened; calling themselves wise, they become as fools."[260]

And I read there too that they changed the glory of your incorruptible nature into idols and various figures, into the image and likeness of corruptible man, and of birds and four-footed beasts and creeping things,[261] yes, into that Egyptian fare for which Esau lost his birthright.[262] For your firstborn people honored instead of you the head of a beast, turning their hearts back to Egypt, and stooping your image, their own soul, before the likeness of a calf that eats hay.[263] These things I found there, but I did not feed on them.

For it pleased you, Lord, to take away from Jacob the reproach of being the lesser, so that the elder should serve the younger;[264] and you called the Gentiles into your inheritance.[265] And I too had come to you from the Gentiles; and I set my mind upon that gold you willed your people to bring out of Egypt,[266] for the gold is yours wherever it may be. And by your apostle you said to the men of Athens, that in you we

---

[258] Cf. Mt 12:25–30.

[259] Cf. Ps 25:9.

[260] Rom 1:21–22.

[261] Cf. Rom 1:23.

[262] Cf. Gn 25:27-34, Heb 12:16.

[263] Cf. Ps 106:20.

[264] Cf. Gn 25:23.

[265] Cf. Eph 1:11.

[266] Cf. Ex 12:35–36. Indeed, whatever is good and true in the pagan cultures is fairly to be adopted and used by Christians; it is "gold out of Egypt."

live and move and have our being, as certain of their own had said.[267] And in fact, it was from Athens that these books came. But I did not attend to the idols of the Egyptians, which they furnished with your gold, they who changed the truth of God into a lie, and worshiped and served the creature instead of the Creator.[268]

10

Thus admonished to return to myself, I entered into my inmost parts, with you, my God, as my guide, and I could do so, because you had become my help. So I did enter, and by the eye of the soul, such as it may be, I saw, above that same eye of my soul, above my mind, the unalterable Light; not this light of common day that all flesh may look upon, nor something grander than that but of the same kind, as if this sunlight should shine out more and more brilliantly and fill the whole universe with its power. That Light was not this light, but other, wholly other from all these. Nor was it above my mind as oil lies above water, or as the heavens are above the earth. It was higher, because it was this Light that made me, and I was lower, because I was made by it.[269] Whoever knows the truth, knows this Light, and whoever knows it, knows eternity. Charity knows it.

O eternal Truth, and true Charity, and beloved Eternity![270] You are my God, and for you I sigh day and night.[271] And when I first came to know you, you raised me up that I might see that there was something for me to see, and that I was not yet the man to see it. And you flashed

---

[267] Cf. Acts 17:27–28.

[268] Cf. Rom 1:25.

[269] The distinction is critical. "God is Light," says Saint John (1 Jn 1:5), and the Light that is God is not the created light that the sacred author says was the first of creation (Gn 1:3). This Light is *ontologically* prior to all created things, including the created light and the human mind, and is itself the Creator, not as the first in a series of causes at the same level of being, but as the foundation of all existent things and of all their causes and effects.

[270] Notice the Trinitarian expression, whereby three nouns are bound to one another by the interlocking of their adjectives.

[271] Cf. Ps 42:3.

against my weak sight, shining upon me with piercing arrows of light, and I trembled with love and awe. I found that I was far from you, in a country of unlikeness, as if I heard your voice from on high: "I am food for the strong; grow, and you shall feed on me. You shall not change me into yourself, as you do with food for your flesh, but you shall be changed into me."

And I came to see that you have corrected man for his iniquity, and you made my soul to shrivel like a spider,[272] and I said, "Then is truth nothing at all, if it is not spread out through finite or infinite spaces?" And you cried out from afar: "I AM WHO AM."[273] And I heard you, as one hears in the heart, nor was there any room for me to doubt; no, rather I should doubt that I was alive, than to doubt the existence of that Truth which is clearly to be seen by the things that are made.[274]

11

And I peered into the other things that are beneath you, and I saw that they have neither absolute being, nor absolute non-being; they *are*, indeed, because they have come from you; but they *are not*, because they are not what you are. For that most truly *is*, which abides without possibility of change.[275] But for me it is good to hold fast to God, because if I do not abide in him, I shall never be able to abide even in myself. But he who abides in himself makes all things new;[276] and you are my Lord, because you have no need for good things from me.[277]

---

[272] Cf. Ps 39:11.

[273] Ex 3:14.

[274] Cf. Rom 1:20.

[275] All things that are subject to change depend for their continued existence upon some agent from outside of them; they do not possess their own beings, then, not in the instant, and not across the range of their alterations. But things whose existence depends upon some contingency from without cannot suffice to explain why they exist at all, and that includes a universe of such things. Augustine thus sees an infinite chasm in being between God, who abides without any possibility of change, and the universe made up of creatures that can be changed. The chasm cannot be bridged by the creatures, but only by the Creator, in love.

[276] Cf. Rv 21:5.

[277] Cf. Ps 16:2.

12

And it became manifest to me that things which can be corrupted are good. If they were the highest good, they could never suffer corruption, but they could never suffer corruption unless they were good. For if they were the highest good, they would be incorruptible, but if they were not good at all, there would be nothing in them to corrupt. For corruption does harm; and unless there is some good to diminish, no harm can be done. So then, either corruption harms nothing at all, which cannot be, or, what is most certainly the case, all things that are corrupted are deprived of some good. If they were deprived of *all* good, they would quite cease to be. Then if they continue to exist, and if they cannot be corrupted, they will be the better for it, because they will persist incorruptibly.

And what is more monstrous than to say that things deprived of all good become better? Therefore, if they are deprived of all good, they will become utterly null; as long as they do exist, they are good. It follows that whatever exists is good. Then evil, whose source I was always searching for, is not a substantial thing, because if it were, it would be good. For a substantial being is either incorruptible, a great good indeed, or it is corruptible, in which case it must be good, because otherwise there would be nothing to corrupt. Thus did I see, and it was manifestly clear, that you made all things good, nor are there any substantial beings that you have not made. And because you did not make all things equal, it follows that each individual thing is good, and that all things taken together are very good, because our God has made all things very good indeed.[278]

---

[278] Cf. Gn 1:31. Augustine is not denying that there is evil in the world, according to the common use of that word. He denies that it has any distinct existence: it is not a thing in itself, but a privation or a corruption of some distinctly existent good. If a house is ravaged by fire, we may say, somewhat loosely, that it is a "bad house," because it can no longer serve the function of a house. But the "badness" is a negative, a privation: the walls have buckled, or the roof has fallen. What still exists is good, even if existence is all that is left to it. Thus is Augustine aiming a deadly blow at all religious and philosophical systems that posit the actual existence of evil as a thing in itself; those include the Manichean system.

13

In you, nothing at all is evil, and not in you only but in your whole created universe, because beyond it there is nothing that can break in and corrupt the order you have set upon it. In parts of it, however, there may be some things that do not accord well with others, and they are thought to be bad, and yet those same things are in accord with others, and they are good; and good in themselves, too. And all these things that do not accord one with the other, do accord with a lower part of creation, which we call the earth, which has its own cloudy and windy heaven above it, befitting it well.

And let me never say, "These things should not exist," because even if I saw nothing but them and desired better things than they, still, if only for them, I ought to praise you. For all things show that you are to be praised: dragons and all the deeps, fire, hail, snow, ice, the blast of the storm, which fulfill your word; mountains and all hills, fruit-bearing trees and all cedars; wild beasts and all cattle; creeping things and feathered birds on the wing; kings of the earth and all peoples; princes and all judges of the earth; young men and maidens; old men and children, let them praise your name. And from the heavens themselves let them praise you, our God; let all the angels in the heavenly heights praise you, all your hosts, the sun and moon, all stars and light, the heaven of heavens, and the waters that are above the heavens, let them praise your name.[279]

No more did I long for better things, because I thought about them all, and as I weighed them with a sounder judgment, I held that the higher things are better than the lower, but that all things together are better than the higher things taken alone.

---

[279] Cf. Ps 148. All created things praise God by their very existence.

14

But there is no sound judgment in those who are displeased with any of your creatures, as there was not in me, when many things you made displeased me. And because my soul did not dare be displeased with my God, it refused to take as yours anything that displeased it.[280] That was why it trailed off into thinking there were two substances, and it found no rest, but spoke folly. And in returning from that place, it fashioned for itself a god spread out everywhere through endless space, and it thought that such a god was you, and it gave it a place in its heart, and became again a temple to its idol, an abomination to you. But after you caressed my head, though I was unaware, and you shut my eyes lest they look upon vanity,[281] I retired a little from myself, and my madness was lulled asleep. And I awaked, and you were there, and I saw that you were infinite, but in another way, and this vision was not drawn from the flesh.[282]

15

And I looked back at other things, and saw that they owe their being to you, and that all finite things are in you, but in another way, not as in a location; rather, you hold all things in your hand, in your truth. Because all things are true insofar as they exist, falsehood is not a thing, unless we think that something is which is not. And I saw that all things are fitting not only for their places but for their seasons also, and that

---

[280] Augustine sees that to be displeased with any created being is to place oneself in the position of God, who has ordered all things toward his providential ends. We cannot see with God's eyes, not in the instant and not from eternity.

[281] Cf. Ps 119:37.

[282] Even to suppose that God is infinite in spatial and temporal extent is to make him finite *in being,* bounded by the existence of space and time that would contain him. But the infinity of God consists in his complete independence beyond and above any created thing and its mode of existence, even if the thing is supposed to exist to an infinite extent. Obviously, such an insight cannot come from "the flesh," because it is suggested by nothing we can see or touch or form an image of; it is the mind, illuminated by God, that can be raised to it.

you, who alone are eternal, did not begin to work after some innumerable ages of time,[283] because all those ages, both those which have passed away and those which shall pass away, can neither come nor go except by your work, and your abiding still.

16

By experience I found that it was no wonder that the same bread that is sweet to a sound palate is offensive to a sick one, and that light is hateful to sore eyes, but to clear eyes it is lovely. And the wicked are disgusted by your judgment, no less than if it were a viper or a mere worm, which you created good, and well fit for the lower parts of your creation. The wicked are fit for those too, insofar as they are unlike you, but well fit for the higher, insofar as they become more like you. And I asked what iniquity really is, and I found it was no substantial thing, but rather a warping of the will, stubbornly turning away from you, O God, who are the summit of being, and turning instead to the lowest things, casting away its own parts within,[284] and all swollen without.

17

And I was struck with wonder that I loved you now, and not a phantasm instead of you. I did not stand still to delight in my God, but I was swept up to you by your beauty, and soon I was cast down from you by my own weight, and with a groan I hurtled down to the lower things. This weight was the habit of my flesh. But the memory of you was still with me, nor did I doubt at all that there was One to whom I should cleave,[285] or that I was not yet one who would so cleave. For the corruptible body weighs upon the spirit, and this earthly dwelling presses the mind down as it muses on many things. I was then most

---

[283] Again, time has no independent existence. Modern physicists say that time is coterminous with the physical universe. Augustine is suggesting much the same thing here.
[284] Cf. Sir 10:10.
[285] Cf. Jo 23:8.

certain that your invisible things from the creation of the world can be seen and grasped by means of the things you have made,[286] even your everlasting power and Godhead.

Searching, now, into what led me to approve of the beauty of bodily things, whether of heaven or of the earth, what solid truth was at hand for me as I judged and said, "This ought to be so, that ought not to be so," searching, then, into the grounds of my judgment, for I did judge, I had found the unalterable and true eternity of truth, above my changeable mind. Thus did I pass, step by step, from bodies to the soul that senses things by means of the body, and on to the soul's power within, to which the bodily sense reports of things without, which is as far as the beasts can go, and then farther on to the power of reasoning, to which is brought for judgment whatever the bodily senses take in. When this power of reasoning discovered that it too in me is change-able, it drew itself upright to look on its own intelligence. It took its thought away from mere habit, it withdrew from the crowding phan-tasms bickering against each other, in order to find the light that fell upon it like the dew,[287] when without any hesitation it declared that the unalterable is to be preferred to the changeable. By the changeable it first came to know what is unalterable, because unless it knew it in some way, there would be no way it could be certain in preferring it to the changeable. So it came at last, in the twinkling of an eye,[288] to *that which is.* Thus indeed did I catch sight of those invisible things of yours, that are understood according to the things that are made.[289] But I was not yet strong enough to fix my gaze there. In my infirmity, I was beaten back, and I returned to my old habits of thought. All I brought away was the memory, loving and longing for what it had, so to speak, caught the aroma of—the food I could not yet eat.

---

[286] Cf. Rom 1:20.
[287] Cf. Dt 32:2.
[288] Cf. 1 Cor 15:52.
[289] Cf. Rom 1:20.

18

Then I sought a way to build up my strength to be fit to enjoy you, and I did not find it, until I embraced the mediator between God and man, the man Christ Jesus,[290] who is above all things God, blessed forevermore, calling me and saying, "I am the way of Truth, and the life,"[291] mingling the food, which I was not hearty enough to take,[292] with the flesh, for the Word was made flesh, that your wisdom, through which you made all things, might give milk to our infancy.[293]

For I was not yet a humble man holding fast to the humble Jesus, my God, nor did I know what lesson his infirmity had to teach us. But your Word, the eternal Truth, exalted on high over all the highest parts of your creation, lifted up to himself those who were brought low,[294] while amid the lowest parts he built for himself a humble dwelling from our clay, by which he topples from themselves those who must be brought low, to draw them to himself, healing their swollen pride and nourishing their love, lest they go farther abroad in trusting to themselves. So might they go weak, seeing before their feet divinity weakened by participating in the robe of skin we wear; then, utterly spent, they might cast themselves upon it, so that as it arises it would raise them up too.

19

But my thoughts were otherwise. I conceived of my Lord Christ only as a man of wisdom so outstanding—especially as he was wonderfully born of a virgin, showing us how we should hold temporal things in scorn, as compared with attaining immortality—that by his divine care for us he seemed to merit the same eminence of authority as a teacher.

---

[290] Cf. 1 Tm 2:5.
[291] Jn 14:6.
[292] Cf. 1 Cor 3:1–3, Heb 5:14.
[293] Cf. Jn 1:14, Prv 3:19, Col 1:16, 1 Cor 3:2.
[294] Cf. Lk 1:52.

What sacred mystery there might be in this Word made flesh, I had not the slightest inkling. This is what I understood from the writings about him that have been handed down. He ate and drank, he slept, he walked, he rejoiced, he became sad, he preached, and his flesh did not cleave unto your word save by a human mind and soul. Everyone knows this, who knows that your Word cannot be changed, and by then I knew it too, as well as I could know it, and I never doubted a bit of it. I knew that he would now move the limbs of his body at will, and now not move them; that he was now stirred by a feeling that stirred him, and now not stirred so; now he might bring forth by signs his wise sayings, and now he might keep silent. All these things are proper to a changeable soul and mind. And if these things written about him were false, the truth of everything else would be put in jeopardy, and nothing would be left in those books to trust in for the salvation of mankind. But because the writings are true, I acknowledged in Christ a man in full; not just a human body, or a soul along with the body but without a human mind, but a very man. I judged him to be preferred above all others, not because he was the person of Truth, but because of some great excellence of human nature in him, and a more perfect participation in wisdom.

Alypius, meanwhile, thought that Catholics believed that God had donned the flesh in this way: there would be no human soul in Christ, nothing but God and flesh. He gathered that they preached that the mind of a man was not in him.[295] And because he was persuaded that the deeds recounted of him could only be done by a living and rational creature, he was the more sluggish in turning to the Christian faith. But once he learned that this was the error of the Apollinarian heretics, he was glad of the Catholic faith and he let himself be tempered by it. But I confess it took me a little longer to learn how, in interpreting "the

---

[295] This is the heresy of Apollinaris (d. 382), who was eager to oppose the Arian heresy, which held that Christ was a created being, though the most eminent of all created beings. Apollinaris was thus prompted to assert that in Christ there was true God and true flesh *but not true man:* neither a genuine human intellect nor a genuine human will.

Word was made flesh," the Catholic truth is to be distinguished from the false teaching of Photinus.[296] For in refuting the heretics, what your Church believes and what sound doctrine maintains is made to stand out. For even heresies are of use, so that among those who are weak in the faith, those who are approved will be made manifest.[297]

20

But now that I had read the books of the Platonists and had gotten from them the suggestion to search after a truth that was incorporeal, I caught sight of your invisible things that are understood by the things that are made.[298] And, thrown back upon myself, I saw what the darkness of my soul had not allowed me to gaze upon before. I saw that it was certain that you exist, and that you are infinite, but not as if you were poured out across finite or infinite locations. I saw that you indeed are he who is ever the Selfsame,[299] in no part and by no motion another, or existing in another way. I saw that all other things come from you, by this one strongest and most binding proof, that they exist. Of these things I was sure, but I was still too weak to delight in you. I chattered casually as if I were quite the expert, and if I had not been seeking your way in Christ, our Savior, I would not have been expert; I would have expired.

For I now wanted to look like a wise man. I was full of my punishment, and I wept no tears, but I welled up in pride for all that I knew. Where then was that charity that builds upon humility's foundation, which is Christ Jesus? Or when would *those* books of the Platonists ever have taught me that? I believe that you wanted me to run into those

---

[296] Photinus (d. 376) held that the Word and the Father were one person, and that the Son of God came into existence only at the birth of Christ. Thus does he seem to have been more Arian than Arius (d. 336), who taught that there was a time when the Son of God was not, but that the Son was a sort of secondary or lesser God, who then made all things. Both heresies are ultimately unitarian, and Arianism in particular may have been behind Mohammed's virulent rejection of the divinity of Christ.
[297] Cf. 1 Cor 11:19.
[298] Cf. Rom 1:20.
[299] Cf. Ps 102:27.

books before I took your Scriptures into consideration, so that how I was affected by them would be etched in my memory, and later, how I was made meek when I read your books and your healing fingers soothed my wounds. Then would I be able to discern the difference between presumption and confession. I would distinguish those who see where they should go but do not see the way, from the way that does lead to the Father's blessed country, and not just for seeing, but for dwelling there. But what if I had been first formed by your Scriptures, and you had grown sweet to me as I grew familiar with them, and then later on I had fallen upon these other books? They might have torn me up from the solid ground of piety. Or if I had stood firm in that wholesome affection I had drunk from your Scriptures, I might have thought that someone else could have gotten the same, even if he had only read those books of the Platonists.

21

Most eagerly then did I lay hold of the venerable pen of your Spirit, and above all the apostle Paul. And all those questions faded away, when I had thought sometimes that Paul contradicted himself, or when the text he preached seemed not to accord with the testimonies of the law and the prophets. And all their eloquence showed one single face to me, and I learned to rejoice, and tremble.

So I set forth, and I found that every truth I read there was uttered with commendation of your grace, so that whoever sees it might not glory in it, as if it were not your gift—not only *what* he sees, but *that* he sees at all. For what does he have, that he has not received?[300] And he is not only admonished to see you, who are ever the same, but also to hold fast to you, that he may be healed. And he who is still too far away to see can yet walk along the way to go that he might see and might grasp. For even if someone should delight in the law of God according to the inward man, what will he do with the other law that

---

[300] Cf. 1 Cor 4:7.

reigns in his members, warring against the law in his mind, and hal-
ing him as a captive to that law of sin which is in his members?[301] For
you are just, O Lord, but we have sinned and done what is evil,[302] we
have carried on in wickedness, and your hand has weighed heavy upon
us.[303] Justly have we been handed over to that old sinner, the prince of
death,[304] who induced our will to become like unto his, who did not
stand in your truth.

Wretch that he is, what shall man do? Who shall deliver him from
the body of this death?[305] Only your grace, through Jesus Christ our
Lord, whom you have begotten co-eternal with yourself, and set in the
beginning of your ways; in whom the prince of this world found nothing worthy of death,[306] and yet he slew him; and the handwriting that
was against us was blotted out.[307] The Platonist books have none of this.
Those pages do not show the face of this piety, the tears of confession,
your sacrifice, a spirit deeply troubled, a humble and contrite heart, the
healing of the people, the city that is the Bride, the earnest of the Holy
Spirit, the cup of our ransom.[308] No one there sings, "Shall not my soul
wait upon God? From him comes my salvation," "for He is my God
and my salvation, my defense; no farther shall I be moved."[309] No one
there hears the voice, "Come to me, all you who labor." They disdain to
learn from him, for he is meek and humble of heart. You have hidden
these things from the wise and the prudent, and have revealed them
unto little ones.[310]

And it is one thing from some wooded mountaintop to see the
land of peace, but not to find the road that leads there, and to struggle

---

[301] Cf. Rom 7:14–25.
[302] Cf. Ps 51:4.
[303] Cf. Ps 32:4.
[304] Cf. 1 Cor 5:5.
[305] Cf. Rom 7:24.
[306] Cf. Jn 14:30, Lk 23:15.
[307] Cf. Col 2:14.
[308] Cf. Ps 51:17, Rv 21:2, 2 Cor 1:22.
[309] Ps 62:1–2.
[310] Cf. Mt 11:25–30.

along byways in vain, beset roundabout with enemies, those deserters in flight, with their prince the lion and the dragon;[311] but another to hold to the road that leads there, defended by the care of the heavenly Emperor, where are no highwaymen who have deserted the heavenly host; for they shun it like a torment. These things in wonderful ways penetrated my inmost parts when I read the least of your apostles and I meditated upon your works, and I trembled with fear.[312]

---

[311] Cf. 1 Pt 5:8, Rv 13:2.
[312] Cf. 1 Cor 15:9, Ps 143:5.

BOOK EIGHT

1

With gratitude to you, my God, may I recall and confess the mercies you bestowed upon me. Let my bones be filled with your love, and say, "Lord, who is like you? You have shattered my bonds; I shall offer to you the sacrifice of praise."[313] How you shattered them, I shall relate, and when they hear these things, let all who adore you say, "Blessed be the Lord in heaven and on earth; great and wonderful is his name."[314] Your words had taken hold of the heart of my heart, and you ringed me with ramparts roundabout. I was certain about your eternal life, though I saw it as an enigma, as in a glass, darkly.[315] Still, all my wavering back and forth about incorruptible being, and how all other beings come from it, was taken away. I desired, then, not to be more certain of you, but to be more steadfast in you. Everything about my life in time was shaky, and my heart had to be purged of the old leaven.[316] The way, the Savior himself, pleased me, but I still found it disagreeable to go to him by the narrow paths.[317]

---

[313] Ps 35:10, Ps 116:16–17.
[314] Cf. Ps 99:3.
[315] Cf. 1 Cor 13:12.
[316] Cf. 1 Cor 5:7.
[317] Cf. Mt 7:13.

But you put me in mind, and it seemed good in my sight, to go to Simplicianus,[318] who to me seemed a good servant of yours, and your grace shone in him. I had heard too that from his youth he had consecrated his life to you. By now he had grown old, and from his many years of following your way with such good zeal, it seemed to me he had gained experience of many things and had become a most learned man. And so he was, for a fact. I went to talk to him about my troubles, so that he might offer me something from his wisdom, as to what was the readiest way for somebody in my condition to walk in your path.

For I saw that the Church was full of people who went this way and that. I did not like what I was doing in the world. It was a very heavy burden to me. I no longer felt those old flames of desire, with the hope of honor or wealth, that used to make that ponderous servitude at least tolerable. They no longer delighted me, by comparison with your sweetness and the beauty of your house, which I loved. But I was still bound fast by the love of woman, nor did the apostle forbid me to take a wife, though he did urge me on to something better, very much wishing that all men should be as he was.[319] But I was a weakling, and I chose the softer place. And because of that one thing, I was tossed and tumbled into other business too, and I went slack, and I wasted away with cares that shriveled me up. For I would have to put up with things I did not want in order to be fit for married life, to which I had handed myself over to be bound.

I had heard from the mouth of Truth that there were eunuchs who had cut themselves for the sake of the kingdom of heaven, but also, "Let him who can receive this, receive it."[320] Surely all men are empty-headed, if the knowledge of God is not in them; men who cannot,

---

[318] Simplicianus—revered in the Church as Saint Simplician—succeeded Saint Ambrose as bishop of Milan in 397; he died in the year 400 or 401. Augustine looked upon him with great tenderness as his spiritual father. At Simplicianus's urging, Augustine wrote two books shortly after his return to Africa as a baptized Christian, on Paul's letter to the Romans, and on passages from the books of Kings.
[319] Cf. 1 Cor 7:1–7.
[320] Cf. Mt 19:11–12.

from the good things they see, find him who is good itself. But I was no longer in that state of vanity. I had gotten beyond it, and from the testimony of the whole created universe I had found you, our Creator, and your Word who was with you, God, one God with you, through whom all things were made.

And there are impious men of another kind, men who know God but do not give him glory as God or give him thanks. Into this error I too had fallen, and your right hand raised me up and set me apart from it, where I might grow well again, for you have said to man: "Behold, piety is wisdom," and, "Do not wish to seem wise," for "professing themselves to be wise, they have been made fools."[321] And I had found the goodly pearl, and I should have sold all I had to buy it.[322] But I hesitated.

2

Therefore I went to Simplicianus, the spiritual father of Bishop Ambrose when he received your grace, and Ambrose did love him as a father, too. I recounted to him how I had wandered round and round in error. But when I mentioned that I had read some books of the Platonists, whom Victorinus,[323] an erstwhile professor of rhetoric in Rome, who had died a Christian, as I had heard, had translated into the Latin tongue, he congratulated me for not stumbling into the writings of the other philosophers. For they were full of unreason and deceit, written in the

---

[321] Ws 13:1, Rom 1:21.

[322] Cf. Mt 13:45–46.

[323] Gaius Marius Victorinus, a Neoplatonist and a pagan, and a man who had defended the civic usefulness of the old Roman religious rites, converted to the Christian faith in or about 355; he was one of the greatest men of letters of his time, indeed Saint Jerome's teacher of rhetoric when Jerome was a young man. His conversion was a great triumph for the Church. Thereafter, Victorinus wrote many works defending or expounding the faith. These included defenses of the Nicene position on the Trinity, and an analysis of grace and predestination in the letters of Saint Paul. It was Victorinus who had translated the Neoplatonist works that Augustine had read. Victorinus was notably not like the charlatan Faustus, whose knowledge of the liberal arts was spotty.

alphabet of this world. But the books of the Platonists in all kinds of ways implant in the bosom God and his Word.

Then, to urge me on to the humility of Christ, hidden to the wise and revealed to little ones, he told me the story of Victorinus himself, with whom he had been most familiar when he lived in Rome. Of what he told me, I shall not be silent, as it affords cause to confess to you in great praise of your grace. Victorinus was a most learned old man, a master of all the liberal arts, deeply read in the philosophers, and a fine judge of what he read there. He had been a teacher to so many noble senators, that for the brilliance of his instruction he had earned and accepted what the citizens of this world esteem most highly, a statue of himself in the Roman forum. Into his old age he had done reverence to the idols and had partaken of the sacrilegious things held sacred, which at that time had gone to the heads of almost the whole Roman nobility, whose every breath was of prodigies and portents of every kind of god, of yapping Anubis, who had once brandished weapons against Neptune and Venus and Minerva, whom Rome had vanquished, and to whom she now bent the knee in prayer.[324] And this old man Victorinus had for so many years defended them with speeches to shake the earth. But at last he did not blush to become the child of your Christ, a baby at your font, bending his neck to the yoke of humility, and lowering his brow to the reproach of the cross.[325]

O Lord, Lord, who have bowed the heavens, and come down, who have touched the mountains, and they smoke,[326] by what way did you steal into that man's bosom? He used to read, said Simplicianus, the holy Scripture, and had with most careful study investigated and pored through all the Christian books. And he said to Simplicianus, not in the open, but secretly, as a friend, "You should know that I am a Christian." But Simplicianus responded, "I will not believe it, and

---

[324] Anubis, the dog-headed, was the Egyptian god of the dead. His worship had entered Roman society along with that of the Egyptian goddess Isis. Augustine remarks on the bitter irony of it, as Virgil had cast Augustus Caesar as the victor, with the true Roman gods, over Mark Antony, Cleopatra, and the rabble of Egyptian gods (cf. *Aeneid,* 8.696–99).

[325] Cf. Heb 11:26.

[326] Cf. Ps 144:5.

I will not number you among the Christians, until I see you in the church of Christ." "Is it the walls that make men Christians?" he said, with a laugh. So did he often say that he was a Christian already, and always Simplicianus gave the same reply, and then came always the joke about walls.[327] For he was shy of offending his friends, arrogant demon-worshipers. He thought that their enmity, from the summit of their Babylonian dignity—as from the cedar-tops in Lebanon, not yet crushed by the Lord[328]—would rain down upon him in storms.

But after much reading and longing, he drank strength in, and he was afraid Christ would deny him before his holy angels if he was afraid to confess him before men.[329] It struck him that he was guilty of a great crime, to be ashamed of the sacred mysteries of your humble Word, when he had not been ashamed of the sacrileges of demons in their pride. For he had been proud to imitate them and to accept their rites. But now he was ashamed of such vanity, and he blushed before the truth. And all at once, in a complete surprise, he said to Simplicianus, "Let us go to the church. I want to become a Christian." Simplicianus, who could hardly contain himself for joy, went along with him.

There he was steeped in the first mysteries of Christian instruction, and not long after that he gave in his name, that he might be reborn in baptism. Rome was stunned; the Church rejoiced. The proud saw it and raged, they gnashed their teeth, and they wore themselves thin;[330] but the Lord God was the hope of his servant,[331] who did not look back upon vanities and deceitful follies.

---

[327] Victorinus wished to believe that intellectual conviction was sufficient. But a Christian is one who has been made, by God's grace, a member of the Body of Christ, the Church; to believe that one's own intellectual efforts are enough to set oneself above God or apart from him. The parallel between Victorinus and Augustine is strong. The old man was held in bondage by a bad moral habit, and by his not wanting to give up the respect of his peers among the pagans, not to mention those who were powerful in the state. The young man was held in bondage by another bad moral habit, his addiction to the pleasures of the bed.
[328] Cf. Ps 29:5.
[329] Cf. Mt 10:33.
[330] Cf. Ps 112:10.
[331] Cf. 2 Cor 1:4.

At last came the hour when he was to profess his faith. It was the custom at Rome for those who were about to enter your grace, that they should stand on a high stage, in full sight of the faithful, and declare their faith in certain words they had gotten by heart. But Simplicianus said that the elders gave Victorinus the chance to do so in a more private place, as was their custom for people they thought might be embarrassed and timid. Victorinus, however, said that he would rather profess his salvation in the sight of the holy congregation. There was no salvation, after all, in the rhetoric he had taught, yet he had professed it in public. How much less then should he be ashamed to declare your Word in front of your meek flock, when he had not been ashamed of his own words in front of mobs of madmen?

So when he went up to make his profession, everyone who knew him began to whisper his name to one another, whispers of congratulation. But who there did not know him? And the sound ran softly from the lips of one happy person to another, "Victorinus, Victorinus!" And straightaway came the sound of rejoicing when they saw him, but then they fell silent, all ears, intent to hear him speak. With radiant confidence did that man utter the true faith, and everyone there wanted to seize him and take him to his heart. And they did seize him, by loving and rejoicing; those were the hands that seized him.

3

Bountiful God, what is at work in man that he should rejoice more at the salvation of a soul past hope, and set free from a greater danger, than if he had always had hope for the man, and the danger was less? Even you, merciful Father, rejoice more for one penitent man than for the ninety-nine just men who do not need to repent.[332] We too hear the tale with great cheer, when we hear that the shepherd is bringing the lost sheep back on his shoulders, rejoicing, and that the lost coin has been returned to your treasure-chest, and the neighbors gather to

---

[332] Cf. Lk 15:1–7.

celebrate with the woman who found it;[333] and the joy of the solemn service at your house brings tears to the eyes, when in your house we read about your younger son, how he was dead and is alive again, how he was lost, and now is found.[334] You do indeed rejoice in us, and in your holy angels who abide in holy charity. You are the Selfsame forever, for in one same way you know all things which are not the same forever, and which do not exist always in the same way.

What then is at work in the soul, that it delights more in things that are found again and returned home, than if it had possessed them always? Other things bear witness to it also, and all are full of testimonies that cry out, "It is so!" The victorious commander is led forth in parade; and he would never have won, had he not fought; and the greater the peril of the battle, the greater the joy in his triumph. A storm hurls the mariners and threatens them with shipwreck; everyone turns white at the prospect of death; then the sky and the sea grow calm, and everyone is overjoyed, as much as they were terrified before. A dear friend is sick, and his pulse discloses how ill he is; all who wish to see him healthy again grow sick at heart with him; let things go right with him, even if he cannot yet walk with the strength he had before, and there will be more joy than there was before he got sick, when he could walk around hale and strong.

Why, men will often gain these pleasures of human life not only from unexpected things that fall their way, without their choosing them, but even by difficulties they do choose and set in place. There is no pleasure in eating and drinking, unless there is first the unease of hunger and thirst. Drunkards will often eat salty dishes to stoke the flame, and to get the pleasure of dousing it with drink. And it is a standing custom that the new wife should not be given over to her husband immediately, lest he think too little of her, not having sighed for her as a wooer while he was made to wait.

---

[333] Cf. Lk 15:8–10.
[334] Cf. Lk 15:11–32.

We can see the same thing in foul and unholy gladness, as in what is granted by the moral law; the same, in the most sincere and decent friendship; the same, in him who was dead and is alive again, who was lost and is found. Everywhere we look, the greater trouble comes before the greater joy. What does this mean, O Lord my God? For you are eternal to yourself, you yourself are your joy, and some of your creatures rejoice forever roundabout you. What does it mean, that this part of nature alternates, falling away and rising again, clashing and returning to harmony by turns? Is this their mode of being, is this the measure you have given them, when from the heights of heaven to the depths of the earth, from the beginning to the end of the ages, from the angel to the smallest worm, from the first motion to the last, you have settled all manner of good things and all your own just works in their proper places, and have wrought all things in due season? Ah me, how high you are in the heights, how deep you are in the depths![335] Nowhere do you depart from us, and yet we hardly manage to return to you.

4

Come, O Lord, work in us, rouse us up, call us back, kindle us, ravish us, be fragrant, grow sweet; let us love, let us run! Do not many people come back to you out of a deeper hell of blindness than Victorinus did, and catch fire, and shine with the light they have received, the light that gives to all who receive it the power to become your children?[336] But when they are less well known to the people, even those who do know them take less joy in their return. For when joy wells up in many people at once, even the joy of each single person will be the more bountiful, because each man enkindles himself, and they all inflame one another. Besides, when they are known to many people, they can be an example of salvation to them, and many will follow in their path; and even those

---

[335] Cf. Eph 3:18.
[336] Cf. Jn 1:12.

who have gone before them are most glad, because their gladness is not for them alone.

Let it never be thought that in your dwelling place rich men are welcomed before poor men, and men of note before the commoners, when after all you have chosen the weak things of the world to confound the mighty, and you have chosen things of no account in the world, things that are scorned, that are as nothing, to bring to nothing the things that are.[337] But consider what that very same Paul did, the least of your apostles, by whose tongue you have sounded forth these words of yours. When the proconsul Paulus, his pride beaten down by the apostle's soldiership, was to be set beneath the easy yoke of your Christ and be made but a provincial in the great King's realm, the apostle was pleased to set aside his old name, Saul, and be called Paulus also, as a banner of so great a victory.[338]

For the enemy suffers a worse defeat when he loses a man whom he had the greater hold of, and through whom he had hold of many others too. But he keeps tight hold on proud men by the title of nobility, and on others, through them, by the title of authority. So much the greater grace it was, so much more welcome was the heart of Victorinus, as the devil had held it as an unassailable stronghold, and the tongue of Victorinus, the sharp and mighty weapon that had slain so many. Fitting it was indeed that your sons should abound in great joy. For our King had taken the strong man bound,[339] and they saw his vessels seized and cleansed, and made fit in your honor, and useful for every good work in the house of the Lord.[340]

---

[337] Cf. Jas 2:1–6, 1 Cor 1:27–29.

[338] Cf. Acts 13:7–9. Tradition had it that the official Sergius Paulus, who had summoned Barnabas and Saul to hear what they had to say, became a Christian, and that that is why Saul adopted the name, Paul. In Aramaic, the name may mean "Worker," but Paulus was a common Roman name.

[339] Cf. Mt 12:29.

[340] Cf. 2 Tm 2:21.

5

But when your man Simplicianus had told me about Victorinus, I was afire to imitate him—and that was why Simplicianus had told me the story in the first place. In fact, he told me more. In the days of the emperor Julian, a law was passed to prohibit Christians from teaching literature and rhetoric.[341] Victorinus obeyed the law, preferring to leave the ever-talking school rather than leave your word, whereby you make eloquent the tongues of babes. As brave as I thought he was, he seemed more fortunate still, because he found an occasion to be at leisure, only for you. I sighed for such a thing, bound as I was in no one else's irons but my own iron will. The enemy had control of my will, and out of it he forged the chain to shackle me. From a perverse will came lust, and from serving the lust came habit, and from not resisting the habit came necessity. Link upon interconnected link—this is why I have called it a chain—a hard servitude held me in its straits. And as for that new will that had begun to rise in me, O God, who are the only assured delight, it was not yet in trim to overcome my former will, made tough by old habit. So my two wills, one old, one new, this one fleshly, that one spiritual, came to blows with one another, and by their discord they wasted my soul away.

Thus did I come to understand by experience what I had read, how the flesh lusts against the spirit and the spirit lusts against the flesh.[342] As for me, I lusted in each, but more in the one I approved in myself than in the one I disapproved. In the latter, it was not so much I who lusted, because for the most part I suffered it unwillingly rather than acting in

---

[341] Flavius Claudius Julianus, called the Apostate (331363), was the half-nephew of Constantine the Great, and had been educated as a Christian, but he harbored a secret hatred for Christians, arising from the massacre of most of his near relations after the death of Constantine. When he became emperor in 361, he gave his hatred wide scope, abrogating all state donations of monies and lands to the Church since Constantine, demanding that the money be repaid, prohibiting Christians from being chosen as teachers of rhetoric and literature, and reinstating many pagan rites, including those requiring animal sacrifices. He was slain in a war he waged against the Persian Empire, and his last words were reported to have been, "Thou hast conquered, O Galilean."
[342] Cf. Gal 5:17.

accord with my will. But for all that, my usual habit became a greater bully than ever, and I had helped it along, because I had arrived willingly at a place where I did not now want to be. Who can justly speak against it, if a just punishment follows where the sinner goes? I no longer had my old excuse, that I was not yet ready to forsake the passing world and follow you, because I was not yet sure I had perceived the truth. For I was sure of it now. I was enlisted in the ranks of the earth, and I refused to fight for you. I was afraid to be relieved of all the baggage that held me back, when I ought to have worried about the baggage instead.

That burden of the passing world weighed me down with a lulling sweetness, as of sleep, and every time I tried to meditate upon you, my thoughts were like the struggles of someone who wants to wake up, but he is overcome and plunges back down into a deep sleep. No man wants always to be asleep, for everyone of sound judgment would much rather be awake, but still he will often put off shaking his sleep away, when sluggishness weighs heavy on his limbs, and he is all the quicker to grab hold of that sluggishness even though it irks him and it is time for him to get up. So too I was now sure that it was better for me to give myself to your love than to yield to my lust. That love pleased me and was winning me over; but the lust allured me and locked me in chains. I had no answer for you when you called to me, "Rise up, O sleeper, and arise from the dead, and Christ will give you light."[343] Everywhere I turned, you showed me that all you said was true, and I was convinced by the truth, and still I had nothing at all to respond but a few lazy and drowsy words: "In a little while," "Right away," "Give me a moment or two." But my "little while" was not little, and my "moment or two" stretched out for a long time.

It was no good that your law delighted the inner man, when another law in my members waged war against the law of my mind and led me as a prisoner into the law of sin, the law that reigned in my members. For the law of sin is the violence of long habit, which drags the unwilling soul and holds it bound. Deservedly so, for willingly did

---

[343] Eph 5:14.

the soul slide into the habit to begin with. Wretch that I was! Who would deliver me from this body of death?[344] Only your grace, through Jesus Christ our Lord.

6

Now I shall tell and confess to your name, O Lord, my help and my redeemer, how you ransomed me from slavery to worldly business, and freed me from the bonds of the bedchamber and its desires, that had held me in so tight a grip. My anxiety grew worse and worse, and every day I sighed to you; often did I go to your church, whenever I could get clear of my business duties, under whose weight I groaned. Alypius was with me, at leisure from his work as a lawyer, after his third term as an assessor, looking about for clients to whom he might sell his advice, as I was selling skill in speech, if such a skill can be taught. Meanwhile, Nebridius had yielded to our friendly request, to teach under Verecundus,[345] a citizen of Milan and a grammarian, who was on most familiar terms with us all. For Verecundus was begging us, as a friend, to give him one of us as an assistant, which he very much needed. It was not a desire to be well-off that led Nebridius to agree, for he could have done better, had he wanted, by teaching literature. He was a friend most gentle and meek, and in his good will he did not want to turn down our request. But he went about it with much foresight, shy of being noticed by people of influence in this world, shunning all the disquiet of mind they would cause him. For he wanted his mind to be free, on holiday as many hours as possible, to seek out or read or hear something about wisdom.

One day, when Nebridius was not around—I do not recall the cause—a man named Ponticianus came to visit me and Alypius at home.

---

[344] Cf. Rom 7:23–24.

[345] Verecundus, like Rominianus, was a wealthy man and a friend of Augustine and the others. Soon after the conversion of Augustine, he too would convert to the Christian faith, as he lay dying.

He was a fellow African, and a high officer in the palace guard. He wanted something or other from us, and we sat down to chat. And by chance he spied a book on a card table nearby. He picked it up, opened it, and found, much to his surprise, the apostle Paul. He had supposed it would be some book pertaining to that profession of mine that was grinding me down. But he broke out into a broad smile and looked at me, amazed and gratified to find what he did not expect, that such books and such alone lay in my sight. He was a Christian, and a faithful one too, and many a time he went to church for daylong prayers, prostrating himself before you, our God. When I told him that I devoted much care to those Scriptures, he began to tell me the story of the Egyptian monk Anthony, whose name shone bright among your servants, though till that hour it lay hidden to us.[346] When he heard that, he took his time in telling it, recommending to our hearts a man so great, astonished that we had never known about him. We stood agape, hearing that you had wrought wonders, well testified and acknowledged, fresh in the memory and near our own times, in the true faith and the Catholic Church. We were all struck with wonder—we, that such great things had happened, and he, that we had never heard of them.

After he told the story, he turned to the monastic congregations, and their customs that savor of your sweetness, and fruitful fields in

---

[346] Saint Anthony the Great, of Egypt, considered the founder of Christian monasticism (c.251–356). Our main source of information on his life is the biography by his fellow Egyptian, Saint Athanasius (c.293–373). Anthony's parents died when he was twenty years old, and he inherited a great deal of wealth, but one day Anthony heard the gospel about the rich young man, and he applied the words of Jesus to himself, "If you would be perfect, go sell all that you have, give to the poor, and come follow me" (Mt 19:21). He went on to lead a life of extraordinary asceticism, prayer, and charity. It is remarkable that the learned Augustine had never heard of him, but the real power of Anthony's example, here, lies in its youthful enthusiasm and decisiveness, as opposed to Augustine's delay, questioning, and fear of leaving behind the fleshly pleasures he had grown accustomed to. We should also notice that the biography of Anthony has an instant and radical effect on the two men of action, members of what we might call the emperor's secret service, and then on their two fiancées; but it takes far longer for Augustine to be moved by what he has read—until, that is, the instant of his conversion. God in his providence thus weaves the words and the stories of human beings into our own stories, as he is the author of all things.

the desert; and we knew nothing of all this. There was a monastery in Milan, full of good brothers, outside the walls of the city, nursed up by Ambrose. We did not know that, either. He pressed on with his speech, and we listened in silence, intent. He came to tell of a time when he and three of his barracks-mates were at Trier, and the emperor had gone that afternoon to watch the chariot races. They were strolling about the gardens beside the city walls, and there, by chance, they split into two groups, one man walking with him and the other two likewise walking by themselves. But as the others were strolling about, they happened on a house where some servants of yours dwelt, the poor in spirit of whom is the kingdom of heaven. There they found the book that tells of the life of Anthony.

One of them began to read it, and he marveled, and he took fire, and even while he was reading, he started to consider leaving the world's army and taking up a life like Anthony's, to serve you. These men were what are called special agents. All at once, filled with a holy love, soberly abashed, he grew angry with himself and cast his eyes upon his friend and said, "Tell me, please, where do we hope to get with all our work? What are we going after? What cause are we fighting for? What is the best we can hope for at court? To become 'friends of the emperor'? What is there in that, which isn't brittle and full of peril? And how many perils must you get through just to reach an even greater peril! And how long will that take? But if I want to be a friend of God, look, I want it, and so I am!"

So he said, in the birth-labors of a new life, and he turned his eyes to the pages again, and he read and he was changed within, where you saw him, and his mind was shed of the world, as it soon appeared. For while he read on and the sea of his heart was swirling, he growled a little and he discerned and decided what was better. Now your servant, he said to his friend, "I've torn myself free of that hope of ours. I'm determined to serve God. I am taking the step right now, right here. If you don't want to follow my example, don't try to oppose me." Then the other man said he would stick by his side, a comrade in such an army, for such a reward. And the two of them, now yours, raised up a tower with the treasure that it requires,[347] that of relinquishing all they had and following you.

Just then, Ponticianus and the other man who was walking with him in another part of the garden came looking for them, and when they found them in that very place, they told them it was high time to go back, because the sun was already low in the sky. But their friends calmly told them what they had resolved to do, and how that desire had arisen in them, and how it was made firm and sure, and they begged them not to trouble them, supposing they declined to join them. Ponticianus and his friend did not change their own purposes, but they wept, he said, and they gave them pious congratulations, and commended themselves to their prayers. Then they dragged their hearts back along the earth, and they left for the palace. But their friends fixed their hearts upon heaven,[348] and they remained in that house. Each man had a bride-to-be, but when the women heard of this, they also devoted their maidenhood to you.

7

That was the story Ponticianus told. But while he was speaking, you, Lord, wrenched me round to face myself, taking me from behind my back, because I had stationed myself so that I would not have to do that. You set me in my own sight, so I could see how base I was, hunchbacked and filthy, spotted and covered with festering sores.[349] I saw it, and I shrank back in horror, and I had nowhere to fly. And if I tried to turn aside, he kept on telling his tale, and again you set me in my sight, you shoved me forward, so that I would discover my iniquity and hate

---

[347] Cf. Lk 14:28–30. There is a rich irony here. The soldiers, acting by a brave impulse, are like wise men who prudently count up the cost before they go to build a tower, and the cost here is no less than to give up all their treasure in this world. They are far different from the timid man of letters.

[348] Cf. Mt 6:21.

[349] Cf. Is 1:6.

it. I had noticed it, but I pretended not to; I held back, and put it out of mind.

But the more warmly I loved those two whose wholesome affections I heard of, who gave themselves up wholly to you to be healed, the more I detested myself by comparison. Many years of mine had slipped away with me, twelve or so years since I was nineteen, when I read Cicero's *Hortensius* and was stirred up to study wisdom. And still I put off the time when I would hold earthly fortune in scorn and be free to follow wisdom's trail. Even to search for wisdom, let alone to find it, was to be preferred before all the treasures a man might find, with all the kingdoms of the world, and an ocean of bodily pleasures, even if you could have them at a nod. But I, a miserable young fellow, miserable at the onset of my youth, had even then begged from you the gift of chastity, and I said, "Give me chastity and continence, *but not yet.*"[350] I was afraid you would hear me right away and heal me right away from the disease of concupiscence, which I wanted more to satisfy than to snuff out. And I straggled along crooked ways, in a sacrilegious superstition, not because I was sure it was right, but because I preferred it to other ways that I did not seek out in piety, but fought, as enemies.

And I supposed that I had deferred from one day to the next to disdain all hope in the world and to follow you, because nothing certain appeared to me to steer my course by. But now came the day when I was stripped bare for myself to see, and my conscience grumbled against me, saying, "Where is my tongue now? Did you not always say you did not want to shrug off that load of vanity, because the truth was not certain? Well then, now it is certain, and the burden still weighs you down. Other people have gotten wings for their freer shoulders, people who have not worn themselves thin in the search by mulling these things over for ten years and more."

---

[350] Augustine's error continues to be that of wishing to master his own time, as those who delayed baptism for their children so that they could get their sinning done first. But the acceptable time is now.

It gnawed at me inside, and I was confounded, covered with a dreadful shame, all while Ponticianus was telling the story. When he finished, and he had done what he came for, he went away—and what then did I not accuse myself of! With what scourges of condemnation did I not whip my soul, to prod it along to follow you! But it dug in, it refused, and made no excuse for it. All arguments were exhausted, defeated. All that remained was dumb fear, dreading as death to be haled back out of the flow of habit, that was wasting me to death.

8

In the middle of this wrangling of my interior house, which I had so boldly raised up against my soul, in that chamber we call the heart, troubled in both mind and countenance, I turn to Alypius and I cry out, "What's wrong with us? What have you just heard? People of no learning rise up and take heaven by storm,[351] and we with all our learning, what do we do but wallow in flesh and blood! Are we ashamed to follow them because they went first, but we are not ashamed if we do not follow them at all?" I said a lot of such things, and in that upheaval, I tore myself away from him, when he stared at me in silence, thunderstruck. For I had never sounded like that before. My forehead, my cheeks, my eyes, the color of my face, the tenor of my voice, all spoke more of my mind than did the words I came out with.

Now there was a small garden where we lived, which we were free to use as well as the whole house, because our host, the landlord, did not live there. The tempest within my breast had carried me into it, where no one would get in the way of the fiery conflict that I had mounted against myself, until it should come to an end. How it would end, you knew, but I did not. But meanwhile I was in the grip of a healthy madness, and I was filled with life in dying, and I knew what an evil thing I was, but I did not know what good thing I was soon to become. So I went off into the garden, and Alypius came after me, hot

---

[351] Cf. Mt 11:12.

on my feet. And what I kept secret was secret still, though he was there. And how would he ever leave me, seeing me so moved?

We sat as far away from the house as we could. I fretted in the spirit, I seethed against myself in a storm of indignation, because I did not enter your good pleasure and covenant,[352] O my God, while all my bones cried out to me to enter, and they praised it to the skies. And one goes there not by ship or chariot or on foot, not even so far as we went from the house to the place where we were sitting. No, to go there, even to arrive there, we need do no more than to will to go. But we must will it bravely and wholly, and not thrash about here and there with a half-wounded will, struggling along, one part rising while another part falls, each against each.

In the middle of these sweltering passions of delay, I did a lot of things in the body that people do when they will a thing but are not strong enough to do it. Maybe they do not have the limbs they need, or their limbs are strapped, or they are weak and slack, or they are thwarted in some way. If I tore at my hair, if I beat my forehead, if I knit my fingers together and clutched my knee, I did it because I willed to do it. Yet I could have willed it and not done it, had my members not been limber enough to obey. There were, then, many things I did, when to will was not the same as to be able. But I did not do what I had my heart set on with an incomparably more powerful desire, and that was something I could do as soon as I willed it, because if I willed it, I would have already willed to will it. For here the power is in the willing, and to will is itself to accomplish the will. Yet it was not done. The body was readier to obey the slenderest prompting of the will, to move the limbs at a mere nod, than was the soul to obey its own high will, which it could accomplish merely by willing it.

---

[352] Cf. Phil 2:13.

9

Where does such a bizarre thing come from? Why should it be so? Let your mercy enlighten me, that I may put the question—if perhaps I can get a response from the hidden dens of human suffering, and the anguish of Adam's sons, shrouded in darkness. Where does such a bizarre thing come from? Why should it be so? Mind gives body a command, and body obeys at once. Mind gives itself a command, and it resists. Mind commands the hand to move, and so prompt it is, you can hardly distinguish the command from the compliance. Yet mind is mind, while the hand is of the body. Mind commands mind to will. The mind is nothing else but the mind, and yet it is not done. Where does this come from? Why should it be so? It commands itself to will, I say, and it would not give the command unless it willed it; and yet it does not do what itself commands.

Then it must not will it fully, and therefore it does not command it fully. For insofar as it commands, it wills, and insofar as what it commands is not done, it does not will, since the will commands that the will should be exactly so, and not something else. So it does not command in full, and therefore what it commands is not fully done. For if the will were full, it would not give the command, because it would already be what it willed to be. Hence it is not some monstrous thing partly to will, and partly not to will. It is an affliction of the mind, which cannot stand all upright, raised by the truth, so long as it is heavily laden[353] with old habit. And so there are two wills, because one of them is not whole, and what one has, the other lacks.

10

Let them begone from your sight, O God, as they do perish who babble and who seduce men's minds, who because they notice that we have two wills when we are weighing two courses of action, insist that there

---

[353] Cf. Mt 11:28.

are two natures of mind in us, one good and the other bad.[354] They themselves are bad when they hold these bad opinions, and they themselves shall be good if they come to hold true opinions and consent to the truth, so that your apostle may say to them, "You were once darkness, but now you are light in the Lord."[355] For as long as they will to be light, not in the Lord but in themselves, reckoning the nature of the soul to be what God is, they become a darkness denser than ever. They fall back farther from you in their monstrous arrogance—from you, the true light that enlightens every man who comes into this world.[356] Take heed what you say, and blush for shame: and come to him and be enlightened, and your faces will not be ashamed.[357]

As for me, all while I was weighing whether to serve the Lord as I had long resolved to do, I was the one who willed to do it, and I was the one who did not will. It was I, all the time. For I did not will in full, and I did not refuse in full. I was at war with myself, and I put myself to flight, and this rout was against my will. But that was not evidence of another man's mind. It was evidence of the punishment of my own. So it was not I who wrought it, but the sin that dwelt in me, as the punishment for a more freely chosen sin.[358] For I was a son of Adam.

For if there are as many contrary natures as there are wills that resist each other, there will not be two only, but many more. Suppose someone is weighing whether to go to the Manichean meeting or to the theater instead, the Manicheans will start shouting, "Look here, two natures! The good nature leads this way, the evil nature leads that way. Where else do we get this swaying in place while two wills are tugging at each other?" Well, I reply that both these wills are bad, the

---

[354] Augustine has the Manicheans in mind again. It is an easy way out, for sinners to assign their bad desires and bad habits to a will that is not really theirs, but that opposes them.

[355] Eph 5:8.

[356] Cf. Jn 1:9.

[357] Cf. Ps 34:5.

[358] Cf. Rom 7:20. If we are made by God for the enjoyment of the good, then we should expect sin to divide us against ourselves, as if we had set forth on a civil war among our own members and faculties.

one that leads to their meeting and the one that leads to the theater. But they believe that if a will leads their way, it must be good. All right then, suppose one of us should be swaying between two opposing wills, weighing whether he should go to the theater or to our church. Will they not then themselves waver a little, while they are thinking how to respond? They might say what they do not want to say, that it is a good will which leads to our church, as it is with people who are steeped in her sacraments and who go there in obedience. Or they might say that two evil natures and two evil minds are at strife in one man. But then what they always say will not be true, that one nature is good, and the other evil. Or they may be converted to the truth, and no longer deny that when someone deliberates, it is a single soul that tosses and turns between diverse wills.

So let them quit saying that when two wills are striving against each other in the same one man, there are two contrary minds contending, sprung from two contrary substances, two contrary principles, one good and the other evil. For you, truth-uttering God, condemn them, confute them, and defeat them, when, for example, both wills are bad; as when a man deliberates whether to kill someone by poison or the sword, or whether he should encroach upon one man's land or another's, or whether he should buy his pleasures by lavish expense, or become a slave to money by avarice, or whether he should go to the games or the theater, if both of them are on the same day. Even add a third: whether he should rob another man's house, if he has a chance; add a fourth, whether he should commit adultery, if the opportunity occurs at the same time with all the rest, and he wants them all alike, but cannot do them all at once. They tear the mind into four different wills at odds with one another, or more than that, into just as many wills as there are plenty of things to desire. But the Manicheans do not go around saying that there is so great a multitude of diverse substances.

It is the same way with good wills. I ask them whether it is good to enjoy a reading of the apostle, or to enjoy a sober psalm, or to talk about the gospel. To each one they will reply, "It is good." What then?

Suppose they all please alike, and at one same time. Will not then diverse wills rack a man's heart while he tries to decide which would be best to take up? They are all good, and still they are in contention, until one of them is chosen, to set at liberty one whole will, which had been divided into many. So it is also when eternity delights us from above, but the pleasure of a temporal good grips us from below: the same soul wills both this and that, but not with the whole of the will. It is torn asunder, with grievous unease, preferring the first thing for its truth, but, because it is familiar with it, not setting the second thing aside.

11

So I was sick at heart and in torment, accusing myself far more bitterly than usual, twisting myself round and round in my chain, till it should be snapped at last. For only a little held me—but it did hold. And you, Lord, kept after me in my hidden places, in your severe mercy doubling your lashes of fear and shame, lest I fall back again, and that last slight and slender tie should not be cut, but rather grow strong again and strap me down with all the tougher bonds. For I said to myself within, "Let it be right away, let it be right away," and as I said the word, I was at the point of settling the deal. I did it, almost, and I still did not do it; I did not slide back into my old ways, but I stood near the goal and caught my breath. And I made another attempt, and I was only a little way off, and littler still, and I was right there to touch it and take hold; but I was not there, I did not touch it, I did not take hold, hesitating to die to death and to live to life. The worse, ingrown in me, was stronger than the better, which I had not tried. And that very nick of time, when I would become other than I was—the nearer it came, the more did it strike me with horror. But it did not thrust me backward or turn me aside. It kept me hanging.

What held me back were my friends of old, trifles of trifles, vanities of vanities, and they tugged at my fleshly coat and whispered in my ear: "Are you going to send us away?" And, "From that moment on, we will never be with you again, not ever, forever!" And, "Look at this, look at that—from this moment on you will never get to do them, never again!"[359] And what were they suggesting, by "this" and "that," what were they suggesting, my God? May your mercy turn them away from your servant's soul! What filthy things they suggested, what ugly things! And I only half listened to them now, and hardly even that, for they did not face me down in the way, freely contradicting me, but they murmured behind my back, pinching me as I walked off, to get me to turn and look at them. And still they slowed me down, as I delayed, I put off the moment when I would tear myself free and shake them off and leap where I was called to go, while that bully, my habit, kept saying to me, "Do you think you can live without them?"

But by this time its voice had grown faint. For in the direction where I had set my face, where I trembled to cross, Continence appeared in her chaste dignity, serene, of good cheer, but not loosely so, speaking sweet words in all honesty, that I might come to her and doubt no more, stretching out her pious hands to take me to her embrace, full of the flocks of good examples that went before me. All the boys and girls were there, and so many young people, people of every age, grave widows and elderly virgins, and she the same Continence in all of them, by no means barren, but a fruitful mother of children, of joys she conceived by her husband, by you, O Lord.

And she laughed at me with a kind of beckoning laugh, as if she were saying, "You, can't you do what these lads and lasses have done? Or were they able to do it of their own power, and not in their Lord God? The Lord God has given them to me. Why do you stand on your own self, or not stand? Cast yourself upon him, and do not be afraid.[360]

---

[359] Augustine's insights into human psychology are astonishing. It is easy enough to deny yourself a pleasure for the time being, but it is tremendously difficult to look forward in time, as we have the power to do, and to will to never to enjoy that pleasure again. For we desire to be the providers of our own future, the authors of our lives.

[360] Cf. 1 Pt 5:7.

He will not pull away and let you fall. Cast yourself upon him, have no care! He will catch you and heal you."

And I blushed red indeed, because even now I was still listening to the trifles and their mutter, and I hung back, delaying. Then she again seemed to say to me, "Stop up your ears against all those unclean members of yours, that they may be mortified. They tell you tales of delight, but nothing like what the law of your Lord God has to tell." Such was the controversy in my heart; and it was all myself against myself. But Alypius stayed by my side in silence, awaiting the outcome of my strange commotion.

12

Deep reflection then drew up from its secret gulf the whole of my misery, and heaped the whole thing in my heart's sight, and a mighty storm surged up, bringing along a great rain of tears. And because I wanted to pour them out freely with all their sound, I got up and left Alypius, as it seemed fitter to be alone for the business of weeping, going far enough away so that even his presence would not be a burden to me. Such was I, and he felt it. I had said something or other, I think, and something in my voice was already big with tears. So I had risen, and he, astonished, stayed behind where we had been sitting. But I flung myself out under a fig tree, and I gave my tears free rein, and streams burst forth from my eyes, an acceptable sacrifice to you.[361] Perhaps not in these words, but with the same meaning, I said to you: "And you, O Lord, how long? How long, O Lord, will you be angry to the end? Remember not our iniquities from of old!"[362] For I felt that I was still in their grip. I hurled out these miserable cries: "How long, how long will it be 'tomorrow, tomorrow'! Why not right now? Why not this very hour, an end to my filth?"

---

[361] Cf. Ps 51:17.
[362] Ps 79:5, 7.

I was saying these things, and I wept in the bitterest contrition of my heart. Then, behold—I hear a voice from a house nearby, singsong, repeating over and over, whether a boy or a girl, I do not know: "Take and read, take and read."[363] At once, with a changed countenance, I began to think hard about whether children ever chant such a thing in one of their games, and I could not remember having heard so. Forcing back the tears, I got up, interpreting it as no other than a divine command, that I should open the book and read the first chapter I lit upon. For I had heard about how Anthony once chanced to come in where the gospel was being read, and he was admonished, as if the reading spoke directly to him: "Go, sell all that you have, give to the poor and you shall have treasure in heaven, and come, follow me."[364] And by that oracle he was instantly converted to you.

So I hurried back to where Alypius was sitting, as that was where I had laid down the apostle's book when I got up and went off. I seized it, opened it, and silently read this short verse, the first I cast my eyes on: "Not in rioting and drunkenness, not in the bedchamber and shamelessness, not in strife and envy, but put on the Lord Jesus Christ, and make no provision for the flesh and its lusts."[365]

No further did I want to read; it was not necessary. At once, at the very end of this sentence, as if by the light of confidence pouring through all my heart, all the dark shadows of doubt were put to flight.

---

[363] Latin: "Tolle, lege." We might translate it as, "Pick it up and read it." Augustine is about to do what the secret service agents did, and what happened in effect to Saint Anthony. This moment is the climax of the *Confessions*. It too is deeply ironic. The pagan Romans had long used Virgil's *Aeneid* as a sacred text, consulting it by means of what was called the *sortes Virgilianae*, the Virgilian drawing of lots. Someone trying to decide on a course of action would open the *Aeneid* at random, and let himself be guided by whatever his eye lighted upon. But that is not exactly what Augustine is doing here. God is guiding him, drawing him, pulling him toward that book of Paul's letters, so that, as God has foreseen, he would read the very passage that applied most directly to his sin. Nor is it that Augustine himself resolves afterwards, against his desires, to act accordingly; for the desires themselves are gone. The chain is knocked asunder.

[364] Lk 18:22.

[365] Rom 13:13–14.

Then I shut the book, putting my finger or some other marker in the place, and with my countenance now at peace I showed it to Alypius. But then he told me what was going on within him, which I knew nothing of. He asked to see what I had been reading, and he looked farther on than the passage I read. I did not know what followed. But what followed was this: "Take unto yourself him who is weak in the faith."[366] He applied the words to himself, and he opened the page to me. He drew strength from this admonition, and with a good resolution and purpose—wholly in accord with his moral habits, wherein he was always far different from me, and far better—he joined with me, without any confusion and delay.

To the mother then we go, and we show her what has happened; she rejoices. We tell her how it came about; she leaps for joy, she triumphs; and then she blessed you, who can do far beyond what we ask and what we understand, because she saw that you had granted to her far more about me than she used to beg with her pitiful and tearful groans. For you had converted me to yourself, so that I might no longer seek a wife or any other hope in this passing world. But I would stand on that rule of faith where you had revealed me to her so many years before. And you turned her mourning into joy, a far more bountiful joy than she had desired, far dearer, far more chaste, than what she had once sought from grandchildren begotten of my flesh.

---

[366] Rom 14:1. The rest of the verse is germane: "But not for doubtful disputations."

BOOK NINE

1

Your servant am I, O Lord, your servant am I, and the son of your handmaid. You have burst my bonds; I shall sacrifice to you the sacrifice of praise.[367] Let my heart praise you, and my tongue, and let all my bones say, "O Lord, who is like you?" Let them say it, and may you then respond to me, and say to my soul, "I am your salvation."[368]

Who am I, and what sort of man? What manner of evil have I not done, or if not done, spoken, or if not spoken, desired? But you, O Lord, are gracious and merciful, and your right hand took heed of how deeply I had fallen into death, and from the bottom of my heart you drew up its gulf of corruption. And that was no more than this: not to will what I had always willed, but to will what you willed. But where was my free will all those years? And out of what secret place deep down did you summon it forth in one moment, to bend my neck beneath your easy yoke, and give my shoulders to your light burden, O Christ Jesus, my helper and my redeemer?[369] All on a sudden how sweet you made it for me to go without the sweets of insignificant things! What I had dreaded to lose, I now rejoiced to put away. For you cast them out

---

[367] Cf. Ps 116:16–17.
[368] Ps 35:10, 3.
[369] Cf. Mt 11:30, Ps 19:15.

of me, you the true and supreme sweetness, you cast them out, and you entered within me instead, sweeter than every pleasure, though not to flesh and blood, more brilliant than all light, but more deeply hidden than any hiding place, loftier than all honor, but not to those who set themselves aloft. Now at last my soul was free from the biting cares of ambition, from getting wealth, and wallowing in the mud, and scratching at the scab of lust. And I prattled to you, my brilliance, my riches, my salvation, my Lord God.

2

And I thought it good in your sight not to be in an uproar to tear the service of my tongue away from the talking-markets, but to withdraw it gently. For I did not want boys to purchase any longer, from my lips, weapons for their fury, while they meditated not upon your law or your peace,[370] but upon deceitful follies and battles in the forum. Fortunately, there were only a few days before the grape-harvest vacation,[371] and I decided to put up with it till then, so that I could take a solemn leave once and for all, and, ransomed by you, never go back to being the salesman.

Our plan, then, was known to you, but not to men, except for our friends. And we had agreed not to spread it abroad to anybody. Still, all while we were making our way up from the vale of tears, singing the song of ascents,[372] you had given us sharp arrows and fiery coals to use against the sly tongues of people who might oppose us, pretending to give us good counsel, but consuming us in their love just as people do with their dinner.

---

[370] Cf. Ps 119:15. Augustine contrasts these young men with the young man in the psalm, whose meditation upon the law of God makes him wiser than his teachers.

[371] The *Vinalia Rustica,* August 19. The feast had long been held sacred to the god Jupiter and the goddess Venus.

[372] Cf. Ps 84:5–6. The songs of ascent are psalms 120–134, sung as the priests mounted the stairs of the Temple, or, according to some scholars, sung by pilgrims on the road to Jerusalem for one of the great feasts.

You had shot our hearts through with your charity, and we bore your words within us, fixed fast in our inward parts,[373] along with the examples of your servants, the black you had made bright, and the dead you had made alive. These were all crowded together in the bosom of our thoughts, where they burned and consumed any lingering sluggishness, lest we plunge again into the deeps. And they kindled us with such a lively fire, that any puff of contradiction from a subtle tongue would stoke our flames to burn more fiercely, rather than extinguish them. Nevertheless, because on account of your name, which you have hallowed throughout the earth, plenty of people would praise our vow and proposal, it seemed a kind of boasting not to wait for the time of vacation so near, but instead to leave off my profession beforehand and make a public profession in common sight. Then everyone might stare at what I was doing and go on about how I wanted to get the jump of the approaching season, because I wanted to look like an important man. And how would it have profited me, that people should be bandying opinions about my state of mind, and speak evil of the good we were going to do?

There was another thing, too. That summer, my lungs began to fail from overwork at school, and it was hard for me to draw breath, and pains in my chest showed that they were hurt, and I could not speak loud or for very long. At first it disturbed me that I might be compelled by necessity to lay down the burden of teaching, or, supposing I could be cured and get back my strength, at least to set it aside for a while. But once I had wished in full to take my ease and see that you are Lord, once that will had arisen in me and had been confirmed—and you know this, my God—I began to feel glad that this excuse, and not a feigned one, was available. It would temper the offense men would take, who for the sake of their freeborn sons wanted that I myself should never be free. So then, filled with this joy, I bore with the interim, about twenty days I suppose, till it should run its course. But it took some

---

[373] Cf. Jer 31:33.

strength to bear them, because the lust for gain had gone which used to share with me the heavy weight of the business, and I would have been crushed, had not patience come in its place. Will one of your servants, my brethren, say that I sinned in this, that after I had enlisted whole-heartedly in your army, I should suffer myself to sit a single hour in the seat of lies?[374] I shall not contend. But, most merciful Lord, have you not forgiven me this sin along with my other horrible and deadly sins, and in the holy water washed it from your knowledge?

3

Verecundus was wearing himself to the bone with anxiety about the good we now enjoyed. He saw that because of the chains that held him in such tight bonds, he was likely to lose our company. He was not yet a Christian, though his wife was one of the faithful, though it was she herself, more than anything else, that fettered him and hindered him from journeying along the road we had started on; and he said that he did not want to become a Christian by any other way than the very one he could not take.

Still, he made us a kindly offer, letting us use his house so long as we wanted to stay. You shall reward him for that, Lord, in the reward of the just; for with that portion you have already rewarded him. For when we were absent—we had gone just then to Rome—he was seized with a bodily illness, and in that condition he became a Christian and a faithful man, and then he set forth from this life. So did you have pity not only on him but on us too, for it would have been an unbear-able woe for us to suffer, to remember the outstanding courtesy our friend showed us, but not to be able to count him among your flock. Thanks be to you, our God! We are yours: your exhortations and your consolations tell us so. You, faithful promise keeper, shall render unto Verecundus the delightfulness of your paradise ever green, for his coun-try house at Cassiciacum, where we rested in you from the welter of the

---

[374] Cf. Ps 1:1.

world. For you forgave him his sins on earth, upon that mountain rich in curds, your mountain, your fruitful mountain.[375]

So he was wrung with concern, but Nebridius shared our gladness. Even though he too was not yet a Christian, and he had fallen into the pit of that most pernicious error, to believe that the flesh of the Truth, your Son, was a phantasm, he had got himself up out of the mire so far as to become a most ardent searcher for truth, while still not steeped in the sacraments of your Church. Not long after our conversion and our being reborn through your baptism, he too became a faithful Catholic, and with perfect chastity and continence he served you in Africa with the rest of his people, for his whole household followed his example and became Christian; and then you freed him of the flesh, and he now lives in the bosom of Abraham.[376]

Whatever that may be, whatever is signified by the word "bosom," there does my Nebridius live, my sweet friend, but your adopted son, the son of a slave no more. There he lives. What other place should there be for such a soul? There he lives, in the place he used to ask me about, me, a little and ignorant fellow. No longer does he lay his ear to my mouth, but he lays his spiritual mouth to your fountain, and he drinks as much as he can, he drinks wisdom according as he is eager for it, happy without end. Nor do I think he is so inebriated with it that he forgets about me, when you, Lord, whom he drinks in, keep us in mind.

So this is how we were. We consoled Verecundus in his sorrow, remaining good friends despite our remarkable conversion, and urging him to be faithful to his station, that is, his married life. We waited for Nebridius, expecting him to follow us. And he could easily do it, he was so near, he was right on the verge, when those days at last unrolled to their end. Many and long they seemed to me, as I was in love with that leisurely freedom, to sing out from my very marrow: "My heart has said to you, I have sought your face; your face, O Lord, I will seek."[377]

---

[375] Cf. Ps 68:15–16.
[376] Cf. Lk 16:22.
[377] Ps 27:8.

4

And now came the day when I was to be set free in fact from teaching rhetoric, as I had already been set free from it in my thought. And so it was done. You brought my tongue out of bondage, as you had already brought my heart, and I blessed you and rejoiced, and I set out for the country house with all my people. What I then did in a literary way, the books I wrote give witness, which, though they were meant to serve you, still panted with scholarly pride, as if in a pause between rounds of a fight. These books were on discussions we friends then present had among ourselves, and on what I discussed alone, before you.[378] What I discussed with Nebridius, who was absent, our letters show.

And how can I ever have time enough to commemorate all the great benefits you showered upon us, at that time above all, when I must hasten on to other and even greater things? For my memory calls me back, and it is sweet to me, Lord, to confess to you with what inward spurs you tamed me to your will, and how you leveled my pride to the plain, humbling the mountains and hills of my thoughts, and how you made straight my crooked ways, and made the rough places smooth;[379] and also how you subdued Alypius himself, that brother of my heart, to the name of your only-begotten Son, our Lord and Savior Jesus Christ, which he at first did not deign to mention in our writings. For he would rather have had them redolent of the gymnasia and their cedars, which the Lord had trodden down to dust, than of the Church's health-giving herbs against serpents.[380]

What cries, my God, did I send up to you, when I read the psalms of David, songs of faith, sounds of piety that shut the door on a pride-swollen spirit! I was yet a simpleton, untaught in your brotherly

---

[378] We have, from the letters of Augustine's student Licentius, descriptions of the conversations the young men had at Verecundus's villa. From those delightful mornings and evenings came three books: *Against the Academics,* Augustine's philosophical attack on the Skeptics; *On the Blessed Life*; and *On Order,* dealing with the problem of evil.
[379] Cf. Is 40:4.
[380] Cf. Ps 29:5, Lk 10:19, Mk 16:18.

love, a catechumen on holiday in the country house with my fellow catechumen Alypius. My mother stuck close to us, womanly in her bearing, manly in her faith, elderly in her freedom from care, motherly in her love, Christian in her devotion. What cries did I send up to you when I sang those psalms! How they set me aflame for you! How I was afire to recite them, if I could, over all the world, against the arrogance of mankind! And indeed they are sung throughout the world, and no one can hide away from your warmth.[381] With what sharp and passionate sorrow was I angry with the Manicheans! But I pitied them too, because they did not know those holy sacraments, those medicines, and they raged like madmen against the very antidotes that might heal them! I wished they would be at my side then, without my knowing they were there, so they could look into my face and hear my voice when I read the fourth psalm in that time of my leisure, and see how that psalm applied to me: "When I called upon you, you heard me, O God of my righteousness; in my distress you have enlarged me; have mercy on me, O Lord, and hear my prayer."[382] They might hear me without my knowing whether they heard or not, so they would not think that I had said those words on their account; and in fact, if I knew that they were listening to me or looking at me, I would not say those same things, or I would not say them in the same way, or, even if I did, they would not take it as showing how I spoke with myself and to myself in your presence, just from the familiar affection of my mind.

I trembled with fear, and at the same time I was in a ferment of hope and rejoicing, Father, in your mercy. All these came out in my voice and my eyes, when your good Spirit turned toward us and said, "Sons of men, how long will you be dull of heart? Why do you love vanity, and seek after a lie?"[383] For I had loved vanity, and I had sought after a lie. And you, Lord, had already magnified your Holy One, raising him from the dead and seating him at your right hand, whence he

---

[381] Cf. Ps 19:6.
[382] Ps 4:1.
[383] Ps 4:2.

would send forth the promised Comforter from on high, the Spirit of truth. And he had sent him, but I did not know it. He had sent him, because he was now magnified, rising from the dead and ascending into heaven. For till then the Spirit was not given, because Jesus had not yet been glorified.[384] And the prophet cries out, "How long, you dull of heart? Why do you love vanity and seek after a lie? Know you, that the Lord has magnified his Holy One."[385] He cries, "How long," he cries, "Know you," and I, so long unknowing, loved vanity and sought after a lie, and that is why I heard and trembled, because the words were spoken to such as I remembered myself to have been. For in the phantasms that I held for truth lay vanity and a lie. And I gave weighty and forcible sound to many things, in the sorrow of my remembrance. If only they had heard, they who still love vanity and seek after a lie! They might be sick with it, they might vomit it up, and you might hearken to them as they cry to you. For with a true death in the flesh He died for us, who now intercedes before you on our behalf.[386]

I read on: "Be angry, and sin not."[387] How deeply was I moved, my God, I who had now learned to be angry with myself for past sins, that I might not go and commit others! And I was deservedly angry, for it was not some other nature from a race of darkness that sinned when I sinned, as they say who are not angry with themselves, who are hoarding up wrath for themselves in the day of wrath and the revelation of your just judgment![388] Nor was my good, now, outside of myself, or to be sought under the sun by eyes of the flesh. They who rejoice in things outside of themselves easily dwindle away, spilled out upon what they can see, the things of time, and in their starving thoughts they lick the mere images. If only they would grow weary of having no food to eat, and say, "Who will show us good things?" Then we will say, so that

---

[384] Cf. Jn 7:39.
[385] Ps 4:3.
[386] Cf. Rom 8:34.
[387] Ps 4:4.
[388] Cf. Rom 2:5.

they may hear us, "The light of your face is sealed upon us, O Lord."[389] For we are not ourselves the light which enlightens every man, but by you are we enlightened, so that we who were in darkness may become light in you.[390] If only they would see the Eternal within, which I had tasted! And it made me gnash my teeth because I could not show it to them, if perchance they should bring me their heart in their eyes, still far from you, and say to me, "Who will show us good things?" For in that same place where I had grown angry, in my chamber, where I had been pierced to the quick, where I offered up a sacrifice, slaying my old man,[391] and hoping in you, with newly beginning meditation on my newness of life, you began to grow sweet to me, and you gave my heart gladness. And I cried out as I read these words without and acknowledged them within, and I wanted no more to be multiplied with earthly goods, devouring the times and having the times devour me, when I had, in everlasting oneness, other corn and wine and oil.[392]

And I shouted out the verse that followed, with a loud cry of my heart, "O, in peace! In the Self-same! What has he said, 'I shall lie down, and fall asleep'?[393] For who will resist us, when what is written comes to pass, 'Death is swallowed up in victory'?[394] And you, you indeed are the Self-same, who do not change, and in you is rest that forgets all labors. For there is nothing else beside you, and you, Lord, have established me in singleness of hope, and not to seek to obtain other things that are not what you are."

I read on, and I burned, nor did I find there what I could make of those deaf dead men, whose company I once shared—I, a plague, a snarling and ill-tempered dog, a blind man barking at the Scriptures, though they are honeyed with the honey of heaven, and lightsome with your light. And I pined away over their enemies.

---

[389] Ps 4:6.
[390] Cf. Jn 1:9, Eph 5:8.
[391] Cf. Rom 6:6, Eph 4:22.
[392] Cf. Jl 2:19, Ps 4:7.
[393] Ps 4:8.
[394] 1 Cor 15:54.

When shall I bring to heart all that happened in those days of my reprieve? I have not forgotten them, nor shall I keep in silence the sting of your flail, and the wondrous speed of your mercy. At that time, you tormented me with toothache, and when it grew so serious that I could no longer speak, there rose in my heart the desire to beg all my friends around me to pray to you for my sake, O God of every kind of healing. I wrote it on a wax tablet and gave it to them to read. As soon as we had bent our knees in simple affection, the pain went away. But what pain was it? Where had it gone? I confess that I was full of dread, my Lord and God, for from my childhood I had never experienced anything like it. And your decrees wound their way deep into my breast, and I rejoiced in the faith and praised your name. And the faith did not permit me to be careless about my bygone sins, which had not yet struck from my account by your baptizing.

5

When the vintage holidays were over, I gave up my position, telling the citizens of Milan to provide their schoolboys with another seller of words. I said it was because I had decided to serve you, and because my shortness of breath and the pain in my chest made me unable to keep up that profession. And I wrote to your vicar, the holy Ambrose, laying before him my errors of old and my present vow, and asking him to advise me on which of your books it would be best for me to read, so that I would be readier and better fit to receive a grace so great. He told me to read the prophet Isaiah. I think his reason was that among all the other writers, Isaiah is the clearest foreteller of the gospel and the calling of the Gentiles. But I did not understand the first part of his book, and, thinking that the rest was just like it, I put it aside for a while, till I might be better exercised in the eloquence of the Lord.[395]

---

[395] Isaiah certainly is the greatest of the prophets in foretelling the spread of the word of God throughout the world, and in many respects he is the most accessible of them all, since his prophecies are often not bound to a certain people and a specific historical situation. Yet it

6

So when the time came for me to submit my name, we left the countryside and returned to Milan. Alypius was happy to be reborn in you with me. He was now garbed in the humility that accords with your sacraments, and he was a valiant master over his body, going so far as to tread the frosty Italian soil with bare feet, an unusual thing to dare. We joined with us also the boy Adeodatus, whom I had begotten carnally, from my sin. You had fashioned him well. He was almost fifteen years old, but for native intelligence he surpassed many grave and learned men. I confess to you your own gifts, O Lord my God, creator of all things, and all-capable of reforming our deformities; for in making up that boy, I had no part but the crime. That we nursed him up in your schooling, you inspired us to do, and no other: they are your own gifts I confess to you. We have a book titled *The Schoolmaster*;[396] in it he speaks with me. You know that all the thoughts presented there as coming from my interlocutor are his own, when he was sixteen. Many more wonderful things from him did I experience. His intelligence left me in awe. Who but yourself can be the craftsman of such wonders?

Soon did you take away his life from the earth, and I recall him now with without worry, with no fear for anything in his boyhood or his youth, or anything about his person at all. We brought him into our society, all the same age in your grace, to be brought up in your school. Then we were baptized, and all our anxiety over the life we had lived before fled away. Nor could I have my fill, in those days, of considering with a wondrous sweetness how deep your counsel is, for the saving of mankind. How freely did I weep during your hymns and songs, stung to it by the sweet-sounding voices of your Church! Those voices flowed into my ears, and the truth

---

is a mark of Augustine's docility that he, a well-known teacher of rhetoric, assumes that he is but a neophyte when it comes to understanding the true eloquence of Scripture.

[396] *De Magistro* (389) was written a year before the lad Adeodatus died. It is a charming but also subtle conversation regarding what we do when we speak; regarding the signs we use to refer to realities, or to other signs; and whether we learn from these signs or from the intellect itself, informed by God.

melted into my heart, and the passions of devotion surged up within me, and made my tears run—and to be with those tears was well for me.[397]

7

The church of Milan had only recently begun to celebrate in this way, for consolation and exhortation, with the brethren eagerly singing with hearts and voices together. It was only a year or so since Justina,[398] mother of the boy-king Valentinian, persecuted your Ambrose in favor of her heresy, as she had been seduced by the Arians. The devout kept watch in the church, ready to die with their bishop, your servant. There my mother, your handmaid, bearing the chief part of the cares and the vigils, lived on prayer. At that time we were still cold, not warmed by your Spirit, but we were stirred when we beheld the astonished and troubled city. It was then that the practice was instituted of singing psalms and hymns in the manner of the Church in the east, so that the people would not faint away for weariness in their sorrow. To this day the practice has been retained, and is imitated by many churches, indeed by almost all, throughout the world.

Then in a vision you revealed to your vicar where the incorrupt bodies of the martyrs Protase and Gervase were hidden,[399] which you had

---

[397] It is clear that the early Church was always a singing Church: Saint Paul says that we are to speak to one another in "psalms, hymns, and spiritual songs" (Eph 5:19). Saint Ambrose himself was a composer of hymns, introducing the tradition to Christian worship in Milan.

[398] Justina was the second wife of Valentinian I, and the mother of Valentinian II. She was an Arian and an inveterate enemy of Ambrose, whom she tried and failed to replace with an Arian bishop, as she tried and failed to seize the churches and their property. She was, for a time, the real political power in Italy, but when she had to seek the assistance of Theodosius, the orthodox Catholic emperor in the East, she could accomplish nothing in full, and it was Theodosius who vetoed an edict in 386 that would have protected the Arians who affirmed the disastrous Council of Rimini (359). It was that council that moved Jerome to say, famously, that the world awoke and groaned to find itself Arian. After Justina died, the young man turned to orthodoxy and begged Ambrose to baptize him, but he died before the sacrament could be administered. That moved Ambrose to preach a funeral oration on Valentinian's behalf, dwelling upon the efficacy of the desire for the sacrament.

[399] We do not know when Gervasius and Protasius were martyred. It could not have been within living memory, as the site of their burial had been forgotten. They were young men,

secreted away in your treasure trove for so many years. You brought them forth at that opportune time to check a woman's rage—a woman, but an empress. So with all due honor they were discovered and exhumed, and transferred to Ambrose's basilica, and people who were oppressed by unclean spirits were healed, with the demons themselves confessing it. Not only that, but a certain well-known citizen who had been blind for years heard the crowds cheering for joy, and when he found out why, he leapt up and asked his guide to lead him there too. When he got there, he begged to be permitted to touch with his handkerchief the coffin of your holy ones, whose death was precious in your sight. And when he did so and he wiped his eyes, they were opened at once. Then the news ran everywhere, then your praises glowed and shone out bright, and the soul of that enemy woman, though not brought to the wholesomeness of right belief, was at least dampened in its rage for persecution.

Thanks be to you, my God! Whence and whither have you led my memory, that I should confess these great deeds to you, which I had forgotten and passed by? But despite it all, when your oils were sending forth so fine a fragrance,[400] we did not run after you; and that is why I wept all the more when I sang your hymns, now breathing in you and at last catching my breath, as far as one can breathe freely in this dwelling place made of straw.[401]

8

You who make men of one mind to dwell in a house together[402] also brought into our fellowship Evodius,[403] a young man from our home-

---

twins according to one account, whose father Vitalis was said to have been martyred in Ravenna, and whose mother Valeria was martyred in Milan. Gervase and Protase were the patron saints of Milan. Ambrose wanted to build a basilica, but he wanted first to have relics fit for it, and that was when he had the dream Augustine recounts here.

[400] Cf. Sg 1:3.

[401] Cf. 1 Cor 3:12.

[402] Cf. Ps 68:6.

[403] Evodius was a dear friend of Augustine, who returned with him to North Africa, becoming bishop of Uzala (c. 396), a small town near Carthage. Evodius was, like Augustine,

town. He had been enlisted as a special agent, and then he was converted to you and was baptized before we were, and having left the army of the world, he girded his loins to fight in yours. We were all of us together, all of us planning to live under a sacred pact. We sought some place where we might serve you to best effect, so we all were going to return to Africa. When we got as far as Ostia on the Tiber, my mother died.[404]

I am passing by many things, because I wish to make haste. Accept my confessions, my God, and my thanksgiving, even for the countless things I am silent about. But I will not pass by what my soul brings to birth about that handmaid of yours—she who gave birth to me in the flesh that I might be born into this world of time, and in the heart, that I might be born into light eternal. Not her own gifts do I speak of, but yours in her. For she neither made nor educated herself: you created her, and neither her father nor her mother knew what kind of child would come from them. And you brought her up in your fear by the rod of your Christ, the rulership of your only-begotten Son, in a faithful household, as a good member of your Church.

Yet she did not speak so much of how her mother worked hard to discipline her, as of a certain female servant far on in years, who used to carry her father around when he was a baby, as the bigger girls often carry little children on their backs. And this servant was well honored by her master and mistress in that Christian home, on account of her old age and her excellent manners. And so they committed their own daughters to her diligent care, and she was on the lookout to rein them in, when the need arose, with a holy severity, or to teach them by her

---

a learned man, and we have some of the letters they wrote to one another on matters of Scripture and doctrine.

[404] The year is 387. Ostia was the port of Rome, now in ruins; you can see the old amphitheater, and walk along the street of the shipwrights, and otherwise experience a trace of what Augustine and Monica felt as they looked out toward the sea. What follows in Book 9 is likely the first literary tribute to an ordinary woman—not a queen or a princess, and not the object of erotic love—ever written; Saint Gregory of Nyssa's biography of his elder sister and teacher, Saint Macrina (d. 395), would soon follow.

sober prudence. For outside of the time when they took their modest meals at table with their parents, she would not let them drink any water, even if they were parched with thirst, warding off a bad habit and adding this sound advice: "For now, you drink water because you can't have any wine, but when you are married, you will be ladies in charge of the pantries and the wine cellars, and then you'll find it dull to drink water, but the habit of drinking will be too strong for you." By this way of warning, and by the authority she had in commanding them, she restrained the eagerness of their tender years, and brought their very thirst to an honest moderation, so that from then on, they took no pleasure in what was not seemly.

Nevertheless, as your maidservant used to tell me when I was a boy, a taste for wine did worm its way into her. For whenever her parents asked her to do what sober little girls do, to draw some wine out of the vat, she would hold a cup under the tap above, and would wet the outside of her lips a little from it, before she poured any wine into the flagon. She did not do it out of any hankering to be drunk, but out of the overflowing high spirits of youth, which often froth over in play, and which our grave elders try to tamp down when we are young. So she added every little daily taste to the one before—for when a person scorns what is modest, little by little does he fall[405]—until she fell into the habit of guzzling down her cups nearly full to the brim with wine.

Where then was that hound the old woman and her stern forbidding? Can anything avail, Lord, over a hidden illness, if your doctoring did not keep watch over us? Her father and her mother and her nurses were not by, but you were there, you who created her, who called her, who can even use our superiors to do something for the health of our souls. What did you do then, my God? How did you cure her? How did you make her whole? Did you not bring forth from another soul a harsh and sharp insult, like an iron lancet from your secret medicine chest, to lance the boil with one stroke? It happened that a maidservant who used

[405] Cf. Sir 19:1.

to go with her to the wine vat fell out with her little mistress, one against one, and with a bitter scoff she cast the crime in her teeth, calling her a wine-guzzler. That struck her and stung her, and she thought about her nasty habit, and at once she condemned it and shed it for good.

Just as friends who flatter us can make us go wrong, so the reproaches of enemies can make us go right. But you pay them out not for what you do by their means, but for what they themselves have willed to do. For that angry girl wanted to rattle her young mistress, not heal her, so she did it in secret, either because she found the time and place were just right for a quarrel, or because she was afraid she too would get into trouble, being so slow to make the matter known. But you, O Lord, steersman of things in heaven and on earth, who wrest the deeps of rushing rivers to your ends, and order the whelming flood of the ages, can heal the mad fury of one soul by that of another, lest anyone, noting that someone he wants to correct has in fact been corrected by something he has said, should attribute the healing to his own power.

9

So she was brought up modestly and soberly, and you made her subject to her parents more than they made her subject to you. When she came of marrying age, she was given to a man whom she served as her lord, and she set about gaining him for you, speaking to him about you by her way of life.[406] Therein you had made her beautiful, an object of reverent love to her husband, and even of wonder. For she even bore with the wrongs he did to their bed, and never had any jealous quarrel with her husband over them. She looked ahead to the mercies you would have upon him, when he would believe in you and be made chaste. He was, besides, a man of remarkable good will, though he had a hot temper. But she knew well enough not to stand against her husband when he was angry, not even in a word, let alone by a deed. But when she

---

[406] Monica is a perfect embodiment of the wisdom of a good Christian woman matched with a difficult or unbelieving husband; cf. 1 Pt 3:5–7.

saw that he had calmed down and was quiet, she took the opportunity
to give him a reason for what she had done, if perchance he had gotten
riled up before he had considered the matter well.

To sum it up, when many wives who had milder-tempered husbands showed the marks of blows on their bruised faces, and in their
common gossip would complain about how their husbands carried on,
she would admonish them and their loose tongues. She said, in a grave
and jesting way, that from the time when they first heard the words
of the marriage contract, they should have thought of them as deeds
that made them servant women, so they should keep their condition in
mind and not rise up in pride against their masters. They were amazed
at what she said, knowing what a fierce fellow she had to put up with
in her husband, and yet no one ever heard that Patricius had beaten his
wife, or seen a single sign of it, or that they had ever differed in opinion or quarreled in the house for a single day. When they asked her as
friends why this was so, she taught them the rule I have recalled above.
The women who observed it saw that it worked and thanked her for it.
The women who did not were harassed and kept under.

By her obedient ways, she also won over her mother-in-law, who
at first had been incited against her by the whisperings of malicious
female servants. But she persevered in her tolerance and her meekness,
so that finally the mother-in-law, on her own, told her son about the
double-talk of the servants and how it had troubled the household peace
between her and her daughter-in-law, and she urged him to punish them
for it. At that, taking his lead from his mother, setting about good order
in the household, and wishing to bring his people into harmony, he had
the culprits whipped at the pleasure of her who had found them out.
And she added this promise, that if any of them should ever be pleased
to say a single bad thing about her daughter-in-law, they should hope
for the same kind of reward—which none of them dared to do. So, after
that, the two lived together with a memorable sweetness of good will.

There was another great gift, my God, my Mercy, that you gave
to your good steward, in whose womb you created me. Sometimes

she would hear one woman saying a lot of bitter things about another woman—as when swollen and undigested discord turns someone's stomach, and in the heartburn of it she tells a present friend about an absent enemy, and her breath is all raw hatred. But my mother would never utter a word of it, one to the other, unless it would help to reconcile them. This might seem a small virtue to me, had I not had sad experience of countless groups of people, when some kind of horrible pestilence of sin is spread abroad, not only blurting out to angry enemies what *their* angry enemies have said, but even to add things that were never said at all. But to a humane man it should be little enough to refrain from stirring up hatreds among men, or from making them worse by speaking ill; he should try to douse them by speaking well. That is what she was like, with you as her intimate teacher, in the schoolhouse of the heart.

At last she won her husband over for you, when he was at the final verge of his life in time,[407] nor, once he had become one of the faithful, did she complain about anything she had had to put up with from him when he was not. For she was indeed the maidservant of your servants. Any one of them who knew her had much to praise in her, and would honor and praise you, because he would feel your presence in her heart, with all the fruits of her holy life bearing witness. For she had been the wife of one man, she had paid the duty she owed her parents, she had been pious in her handling of household affairs, and her good works bore her witness. She had nursed up her children, bringing them to birth in labor as often as she saw them swerving away from you.

Finally, O Lord, for all of us your servants whom you have given permission to speak, for all of us who before she fell asleep lived together, having received the grace of your baptism, she took such care, as if she had given birth to us all, and she served us, as if she had been a daughter to us all.[408]

---

[407] Patricius became a Christian shortly before he died, and thus, by her persistent prayer and love, Saint Monica was made the means whereby God saved her husband, her son, several of his friends, and her grandson.

[408] A lovely expression of the truth revealed by Christ, that we grow greater by love. Saint

10

The day was now looming when she would depart this life, which day you knew, but we did not. It happened, I believe by your secret providential care, that she and I were leaning alone at a window, looking out over the garden in the house where we were staying. We were at Ostia on the Tiber, away from the crowds, trying to rest up after being on the road so long, and getting ready for a sea voyage. We were by ourselves, and we talked very softly, forgetting about things past, and stretching our minds toward what lay before us.[409] And we wondered, between ourselves, before the present Truth that you are,[410] what the future eternal life of the saints would be like, which eye has not seen, nor ear heard, nor has it entered into the heart of man.[411] And we panted, with the mouth of the heart, after the highest streams of your fountain, the fountain of life,[412] which is in your presence, so that, sprinkled by it as much as we could be, we might somehow ponder a mystery so great.[413]

When we had reached that end in our conversation, when the sweetest delight of the bodily senses, set forth in the most brilliant material light, seemed not only unworthy to be compared with the joy of that life, but even to be remembered at all, raising ourselves up with a more ardent longing toward the Selfsame, step by step we took our course through all corporeal things, even that heaven whence the sun and the moon and the stars shine upon the earth.[414] And we rose

---

Monica was the mother to them all because she was the servant and daughter to them all; we do not understand the one without the other.

[409] Cf. Phil 3:13.

[410] Cf. 2 Pt 1:12.

[411] Cf. 1 Cor 2:9.

[412] Cf. Ps 36:9, Ps 42:1.

[413] Cf. 1 Cor 15:51–52.

[414] Notice that the heavens above are corporeal creatures, and not the heaven that is the dwelling place of God. Augustine and Monica, lifted up by grace into a contemplation of God, traverse in their minds and souls the range of being from earthly things and moments of time to God and his eternity, and thus they are led to accomplish what Plotinus and the other Platonic philosophers held forth as the highest end of the philosophic life. But for the Platonists, whatever they achieved in this vein, or thought they achieved, was by

yet higher, turning our thoughts more inward, speaking about your works, marveling at them, and we came to our minds, and we ascended beyond them also, till we attained the land whose plenty never fails,[415] where you feed Israel forever with the food of truth,[416] where life is that wisdom through which all things are made,[417] both those that have been and those that are yet to be. And this Wisdom is not in the process of becoming, but it is as it always has been, and as it always shall be. For having been and coming to be are not in it, but being only, because it is eternal; for to have been and coming to be are not eternal. And while we were speaking and longing, we gained a slight touch of it by a thrust of our whole heart; and we sighed, and we left behind the first fruits of the spirit,[418] bound to that life, and we returned to the sounds of our voices, where a word has both beginning and end. How unlike your Word, our Lord, abiding ever in himself, without age, and making all things new![419]

And so we said, "If for someone the uproar of the flesh should fall silent, silent also the fancies of earth and the waters and the air, silent the poles, silent the very soul as it transcends itself by not thinking about itself, silent all dreams and imaginary revelations, silent every tongue and every sign and all things that pass away—for if he should give ear, they all say, 'We did not make ourselves, but he made us who abides forever'[420]—if when they have said this, they too fall still, raising the ear to him who made them; and if *he* alone should speak, not by their means, but by himself, so that we might hear *his* word, not by a tongue of flesh or the voice of an angel or the sound of thunder, not by

---

their own effort, since the One to which they aspired was an impersonal fount of being. Plotinus himself had the experience only once or twice, calling it the flight of the alone to the Alone. How great a gulf separates that bare and lonely philosophical flight from the joy and communion of the Church—and of mother and son, together here.

[415] Cf. Is 58:11.
[416] Cf. Ps 78:24.
[417] Cf. Jn 1:3.
[418] Cf. Rom 8:23.
[419] Cf. Rv 21:5.
[420] Cf. Ps 100:3.

the riddle of a likeness,[421] but by his own self, whom we love in these things, whom we love without these things, just as we were straining ourselves upward and with a fleeting thought touched upon the eternal Wisdom abiding above all things[422]—and if this could be prolonged, and all visions of a far other kind were swept away, and this one vision should ravish the beholder and take him within and fold him up in its profoundest joys, if everlasting life should be like this single moment of understanding for which we sighed, would it not be, 'Come, enter into the joy of your Master?'[423] But when shall this be? Shall it not be when we all rise, though we shall not all be changed?"[424]

I said these things, though not exactly in this way and in these words. But you, O Lord, know that on that day when we talked about these things, the world with all its pleasures seemed petty to us. And my mother said, "Son, as far as I am concerned, I have no more to delight me in this life. I do not know what I am to do here any longer, or why I am still here, now that all my hope in this world is done. There was only one reason why I wished to linger a little while longer in this life, and that was to see you become a Catholic Christian before I died. God has granted my desire more plentifully than I had hoped, because I now see that you are his servant, and you hold worldly happiness in scorn. What am I doing here?'"

11

I do not well recall how I responded to her, but in the meantime, after five days or a little more, she took to her bed with fever. And one day during her illness she fell into a faint, and for a while she was unconscious of the things around her. We ran to her, but she soon came to her senses again, and she looked at me and my brother standing by her as if

---

[421] Cf. 1 Cor 13:12.
[422] Cf. Ws 7:22–26.
[423] Mt 25:23.
[424] Cf. 1 Cor 15:51–52.

to ask us, "Where was I?" We were stricken with grief, but she fixed her eyes on us and said, "Put your mother here." I fell silent and held back my tears. But my brother said something to the effect that it would be a happier thing if she died not in some strange place, but in her home country. When she heard him say so, her countenance was troubled, and she gave him a sharp look right back, because he still had a taste for such things, and then she turned to me and said, "Look at what he is saying." And soon, to us both: "Put this body anywhere. Don't trouble yourselves over it. The only thing I ask is that you remember me at the altar of the Lord, wherever you may be." And when she had made her wishes as clear as she could in words, she lay still again, in agony with the disease that grew heavier and heavier.

When I considered the gifts, O invisible God, which you instill into the hearts of your faithful, and I saw what admirable fruit they bring forth, I rejoiced and gave you thanks, for I recalled what I had long known, that my mother had been fervent in her care about the tomb she had prepared for herself, next to the body of her husband. Seeing that they had lived together in great harmony, she wanted to join to that happiness (as the human soul has no great room for things divine) the hope that people would remember them, and say that God had granted to her, after her pilgrimage across the sea, that the same earth would cover the earthly part of husband and wife. I do not know when, in the fullness of your bounty, this silly wish began to fade in her heart. But I was amazed and glad to see it so clearly now, though when we were at the window, talking together, and she said, "Why am I still here?", she showed no desire to die in her homeland. Later, I did hear of something that happened when we were at Ostia. It was on a day when I was not there, and with a motherly trust she was talking with some of my friends about contempt for this life, and the good gift of death. They gaped in astonishment at the woman's manly courage—your gift to her. And they asked whether she was afraid to leave her body so far from her own city. "Nothing is far away from God," she said, "and I needn't be afraid that at the end of the world he will not know where I am lying, to raise me up again."

And so, on the ninth day of her illness, and the fifty-sixth year of her life, and the thirty-third year of mine, that devout and religious soul was released from the body.

12

I closed her eyes, and an immense sorrow flowed into my heart of hearts and overflowed in tears. Then by a violent command of my mind, my eyes forced the well-springs back and they were dry again, and in that struggle it was ill with me indeed. As soon as she breathed her last, the boy Adeodatus broke out into loud weeping, but we checked him, and he held his peace. Something boy-like in me too, which had fallen into weeping, was checked by a young man's voice, the voice of my heart, and at last was silent. For we did not think it becoming to throng that funeral with laments and tears and groans, as people do when they bewail the miseries of those who die, or as if the dead were utterly extinguished. For she did not die in misery, nor did she wholly die. This we held for certain, from the witness of her way of life, from a faith not feigned,[425] and from reasons sure and true.

What was it then that made me so heavyhearted? No other than the fresh wound, when what I had been accustomed to was so suddenly torn away, our life together, so sweet and dear. For I was filled with joy when, in the last hours of her illness, while I was attending to her wishes, she bore me good witness and said sweet things to me, and she called me a dutiful son. And she called to mind, with a great feeling of love, that she never heard from my lips a single harsh or reproachful word. But, my God who made us, how could the honor I rendered her ever compare with the service she rendered me? And in fact, because I had been bereft of a solace so great, my soul was wounded and my life was as if torn in shreds, for hers and mine had been made as one life together.

---

[425] Cf. 1 Tm 1:5.

Now that the boy had been kept from weeping, Evodius took up the psalter and began to sing a psalm, and the whole house responded to him so: "I shall sing of mercy and justice to thee, O Lord."[426] And when they heard what we were doing, many brethren and religious women gathered there, as was their practice, to take charge of the funeral. Meanwhile, I retreated to another part of the house, where I could in decency discuss with my friends, who thought that I should not be left alone, what I thought was most fit for the time. By that warm poultice of truth I eased the agony I felt within, known to you, but not to those who listened to me intently and thought I was without any feeling of sorrow. But in your ears, while none of them heard, I blamed the womanish softness of my affection, and I restrained my flood of grief, and it receded, little by little. And it rushed back upon me, but not to the shedding of tears or to any change in my countenance, though I knew well what I was pressing down in my heart. And I was deeply distressed, that such merely human things could have such power over me, because in due order they are the lot of mankind and they must come to pass. So I grieved over my very grief, and wore myself out in a double sadness.

But at last the body was carried out, we went to the burial place, and we came back, without tears. For I did not weep, not when we poured our prayers out to you as we offered for her the sacrifice of our redemption, nor when, as is the custom there, the corpse was set down beside the grave before it was buried—not even amid those prayers did I shed a tear. But all that day, in secret, I was most heavy of heart, and with a troubled mind I begged you as well as I could to heal my sorrow. You did not do so, and I believe it was because you wanted to have me remember, by this one trial, how strong the bond of habit is, even against a mind that feeds no longer upon a deceitful word.

It seemed to me I should go and bathe, as I had heard that the Greeks called the bath a *balaneion*, because it casts, *ballei*, anxiety, *ania*,

---

[426] Ps. 101:1.

from the soul. See, this too I confess to your mercy, Father of orphans,[427] because I washed, and I was the same as I was before, nor did I sweat the bitter sorrow from my heart. Then I fell asleep, and I woke again, and I found that my grief was made a good deal milder. And as I was lying alone in my bed, there came to my mind those truth-telling verses of Ambrose.[428] For you are the

> *Creator of the earth and sky,*
> *Ruling the firmament on high,*
> *Clothing the day with robes of light,*
> *Blessing with gracious sleep the night,*
>
> *That rest may comfort weary men,*
> *And brace to useful toil again,*
> *And soothe awhile the harassed mind,*
> *And sorrow's heavy load unbind.*

And little by little, the old thoughts of your handmaid came to me again, her devotion to you, and her mild and comely behavior toward us, and how I was all at once deprived of it, and I took comfort in weeping in your sight, about her and for her sake, and about myself and for my sake. And I let the tears I had held back flow freely, as much as they would, laying them as a pillow under my heart. And it rested upon them, because you were there to hear, and not the ears of some man taking my weeping as a thing to look down on. And now, O Lord, I will confess it to you in writing, read it who will, and interpret it as he will. If he finds it a sin that I wept for my mother some little part of an hour, a mother now dead to my eyes, who had wept so many years for me so that I might live in your eyes, let him not laugh. But rather, if he is a man of ample charity, let him even weep to you for my sins, to you, the Father of all the brothers of your Christ.[429]

---

[427] Cf. Ps 68:5.

[428] The hymn *Deus Creator omnium*. The translation is by Charles Bigg, in *The English Hymnal* (1933).

[429] Cf. Mt 12:50.

13

But now that my heart is healed of that wound, for which I would later blame the affections of the flesh, I pour out to you, our God, tears of a very different kind, for your handmaid. These tears trickle from a broken spirit, pondering the perils that beset every soul that dies in Adam.[430] And even though, made alive in Christ before she was delivered from the flesh, she lived so that your name might be praised in her faith and her habitual works, still I dare not say that from the time when you gave her new birth by baptism, no word against your law ever came from her mouth. For it has been said by Truth, your Son: "If anyone says to his brother, 'Fool,' he shall be guilty of hellfire,"[431] and woe even to a laudable human life, if you should keep back your mercy and examine it piece by piece! But because you do not insist upon searching our crimes to the utmost,[432] we can confidently hope to find a place with you. And if anyone recounts to you his own merits, what does he recount but your gifts to him? If only men would know they are but men, and he who boasts would boast in the Lord![433]

Therefore, O God of my heart, O my praise and my life,[434] I shall set aside for a little while her good deeds, for which I rejoice and give you thanks, and shall now entreat you for my mother's sins. Hear my prayer, by that healing Balm for our wounds, who hung upon the tree, and is seated at your right hand, and intercedes for us.[435] I know that she was a merciful woman, and that she forgave from her heart the debts of her debtors.[436] Please, then, forgive her debts too, if she contracted any through all the many years after she was cleansed in the water of salvation. Forgive them, O Lord, forgive them, I beseech you,

---

[430] Cf. 1 Cor 15:22.
[431] Mt 5:22.
[432] Cf. Ps 130:3.
[433] Cf. Ps 9:20, 1 Cor 1:31.
[434] Cf. Ps 118:14.
[435] Cf. Rom 8:34.
[436] Cf. Mt 6:12.

nor enter into judgment with her.[437] Let mercy rejoice in triumph over justice,[438] for your words are true, and you have promised mercy to the merciful.[439] It was your gift to them that they were merciful, for you shall have mercy on whom you have had mercy, and you shall show mercy to whom you are mercifully inclined.[440]

And I believe that you have already done what I beg of you, but still, look with favor, O Lord, upon the free words of my mouth. For when the day of her dissolution was at hand, she did not think about having her body covered with sumptuous robes or hoarded up in spices, nor did she crave a choice monument, or care for a tomb in her native land. She did not demand these things of us. She desired only that her name be remembered at your altar, which she had served without letting a day go by. There, she knew, the holy Victim was dispensed, by whom the handwriting that was against us was blotted out;[441] by whom the enemy, reckoning up our crimes, was led off in triumph.[442] For the enemy sought for some offense and found none in him, in whom we are conquerors.[443] Who shall pour back to him his innocent blood? Who will restore to him the price he paid for us,[444] to take us from his keeping? Unto that sacrament of our ransom, your handmaid bound her soul with the bond of faith. Let no one break that bond and take her from your protection. Let neither the lion nor the dragon[445] thrust themselves in the way by force or guile. She herself will not reply that she owes nothing, lest she be refuted and seized by the cunning accuser.[446] But she will reply that her debts have been forgiven by him whom no one can repay for what he paid for us, when he owed us nothing.

---

[437] Cf. Ps 143:2.
[438] Cf. Jas 2:13.
[439] Cf. Mt 5:7.
[440] Cf. Rom 9:15.
[441] Cf. Col 2:14.
[442] Cf. Eph 4:8.
[443] Cf. Jn 14:30, Rom 8:37.
[444] Cf. Ps 49:7.
[445] Cf. Ps 91:13.
[446] Cf. Mt 5:26.

Let her then rest in peace with her husband, before whom and after whom she married none other, whom she served, bringing forth fruit to you by her patience, so that she might win him too for your treasury. And inspire, O my Lord, inspire your servants my brothers, your sons and my masters, whom I serve with heart and voice and the written word, that whenever they read this, they remember at your altar your handmaid Monica,[447] with her onetime husband Patricius, by whose flesh you brought me, I do not know how, into this life. May they remember my parents with devout affection in this light that passes away; may they remember my brothers under you, Father, in our Catholic mother the Church, and my countrymen in that eternal Jerusalem for which your pilgrim people sigh from their setting forth until their return, so that the last request she made of me may be granted to her by these confessions of mine through the prayers of many, granted more richly than through my own.

---

[447] This is the only time Augustine gives his mother's name—at the climax of his tribute and his prayer. Monica is a Punic (and therefore Semitic) name. What ethnic group her husband Patricius belonged to, we cannot tell, as it was common for non-Italic people to adopt Roman names.

BOOK TEN

1

Let me know you, O Lord, who know me; let me know you even as I am known.[448] Virtue of my soul, enter it and make it a fit dwelling for you, that you may have it and hold it without spot or wrinkle.[449] This is my hope, for this I speak, in this hope I rejoice, whenever I rejoice in a wholesome way. As for all the other things in this life, the ones we weep the more for, we ought to weep less for, and the ones we weep the less for, we ought to weep more for. For behold, you have loved truth,[450] and he who does what is true comes into the light.[451] I wish to do so in my heart, in these confessions before you; and by my pen, before many witnesses.

2

And even if I did not want to confess it to you, O Lord, is there anything in me that can hide from your eyes, to which the deepest pit of human conscience lies naked?[452] I would be hiding you from me, and not myself

---

448 Cf. 1 Cor 13:12.
449 Cf. Eph 5:27.
450 Cf. Ps 51:6.
451 Cf. Jn 3:21.
452 Cf. Ps 139:12.

from you. But now that my groaning is witness that I am displeasing to myself, you shine forth, you please me, you are loved and desired, so that I blush for shame, and I cast myself off and choose you instead, and I shall never please myself or you, unless it is because of you.

So then, Lord, I am manifest to you, whatever I may be. And I have said with what fruit I confess to you. For I do so not with words and sounds the flesh makes, but with the words of the soul, and the outcry of thought, which your ear understands.[453] When I am wicked, to confess to you is none other than to displease myself, but when I am devout, to confess to you is none other than to refuse to attribute the good to myself. For you, Lord, bless the just man,[454] but first you take him when he is impious and you make him just. That is why, my God, the confession I make in your sight is both silent and not silent. It makes no noise, but it cries out with affection. I am not saying anything to men that is right and just, except what you have heard from me before, nor do you hear any such thing from me but what you have spoken to me first.

3

What therefore do I have to do with men, that they should hear my confessions, as if they were going to heal all my debilities? A race eager to spy into other people's lives, but sluggish to correct their own! Why should they want to hear from me what I am, when they do not want to hear from you what they themselves are? And when they hear me talking about myself, how can they know that I am speaking the truth, when no man knows what is in a man, but the spirit of man that is in him?[455] But if they should hear about themselves from you, they will not be able to say, "The Lord is telling a lie." If a man hears about himself from you, that is no other than to know himself. And if he does

---

[453] Cf. Rom 8:26.
[454] Cf. Ps 5:12.
[455] Cf. 1 Cor 2:11.

know, and he presses on and says, "This is false," he himself is lying. But because charity believes all things[456]—among those whom it knits together, making them one—I too, O Lord, shall confess to you so that men may hear. I cannot demonstrate to them that what I confess is true; but they will believe me, if charity has opened their ears to hear me.

Nevertheless, O my most inward Physician, make clear to me what fruit I reap by doing these things. For when the confessions of my bygone sins are read and heard—sins you have forgiven and covered,[457] to make me blessed in you, changing my soul by faith and your sacrament—they rouse up the heart, lest it drowse in hopelessness and say, "I cannot do it." Let the heart be wakeful in a love of your mercy, and in the sweetness of your grace, wherein every feeble person is made mighty, when by that grace he comes to know well how feeble he is.[458] Good men delight to hear of the past sins of those who are rid of the sins now. It does not delight them that the sins were evil, but that the sins once *were*, and are no longer.

What fruit then do I hope to reap, my Lord, to whom my conscience confesses every day, more secure in the hope of your mercy than in its own innocence, what fruit, I ask, shall I reap when in your presence by these writings I confess to mere men what I now am, and not what I once was? For I have seen that other fruit and I have spoken of it. But what I am now, at this very time when I write these confessions, many people desire to know, both those who know me and those who do not, who have heard something from me or about me. But their ear is not at my heart, where I am whatever I am. That is why they want to hear, from my confession, what I am within, where neither eye nor ear nor mind can peer. They are ready to believe, for how else will they know it? For charity says to them, the charity that makes them good men, that I am not lying when I confess about myself, and it is their charity that trusts me.

---

[456] Cf. 1 Cor 13:7.
[457] Cf. Ps 32:1, Rom 4:7.
[458] Cf. 2 Cor 12:9–10.

4

But why do they want this? What fruit will they reap? Do they wish to join me in thanksgiving when they hear how far I have come toward you, by your free gift? And to pray for me, when they hear how much my own heaviness slows me down? To such people I will reveal myself. For it is no mean fruit to have many people give thanks to you for us, and to have many people pray for us. Let the brotherly mind love in me what you teach us is to be loved, and grieve for what in me you teach us is worthy of grief. Let that brotherly mind do this; not the mind of a foreigner, or of strange children, whose mouth speaks vanity,[459] and whose right hand is a right hand of iniquity, but that brotherly mind which, when it approves of me, rejoices for me, and when it disapproves, is sad for me, because whether it approves or disapproves, it loves me still. To such people I will reveal myself. Let them breathe easy when they hear of the good in me; let them sigh when they hear of the bad. All my good deeds are yours, the gifts you have planted in me; all my wicked deeds are my own, and your judgments against me. Let them breathe easy for those and sigh for these, and from their brotherly hearts, your thuribles, let the incense of hymns and weeping rise into your presence. Then, Lord, delighted with the fragrance of your holy temple, may you have mercy upon me according to your great mercy,[460] for your name's sake, and do not abandon what you have begun, but bring to its consummation all that in me is unfinished.[461]

This is the fruit to reap when I confess not what I was, but what I now am, when I confess it not only before you, with secret joy touched with trembling, or with secret sorrow touched with hope, but also in the ears of the sons of men, the faithful, sharers in my joy and partners in my mortality, my countrymen, my fellow pilgrims, those who have gone before me in the way, those who will follow me, and those who

---

[459] Cf. Ps 144:11.
[460] Cf. Ps 51:1.
[461] Cf. Phil 1:6.

walk at my side. These my brothers are all your servants, whom you have desired to make your sons; they are my masters, whom you have commanded me to serve if I wish to live with you and according to your will. And your Word would be little good to me if he preached this service only, and he did not go before me in performing it. And so I perform it in deeds and words, under the protection of your wings; and perilous indeed it would be, save that under your wings my soul takes shelter,[462] and my weakness is known to you. I am a little one, but my Father lives forever, and my Protector is sufficient for me,[463] for He is the same who begot me and who defends me; and you yourself are all my goods, you the almighty, who are with me, even before I am with you. Therefore I shall publish myself to such people whom you have commanded me to serve, telling them not what I was but what I have been and what I still am, nor do I sit in judgment on myself.[464] In this way then let me be heard.

5

For it is you, Lord, who judge me. For even though no one knows what is in a man save the spirit of man that is in him,[465] still there is something in a man that not even the spirit in him knows, but you, Lord, know all that is in him, you who made him.[466] As for me, though I despise myself in your sight, and I account myself but dust and ashes,[467]

---

[462] Cf. Ps 57:1.

[463] Cf. 2 Cor 12:9.

[464] Cf. 1 Cor 4:3.

[465] Cf. 1 Cor 2:11.

[466] We are indeed an abyss of mystery to ourselves, not merely because of sin, but because, made as we are in the image of God, we transcend time as no other bodily creature does; we do more than remember, because we recollect; we do more than anticipate, because we foresee, we plan; we feel more than affection, because we can love those who are not lovable; we do more than act, because we grasp our acts in imagination, performance, and judgment. We take such depths for granted, skimming the surface of self-awareness. What follows in Book Ten is a remarkable meditation upon, and analysis of, the human mind; I know of none more acute and incisive, either from the ancient world or from our own time.

[467] Cf. Job 42:6.

still I do know something about you that I do not know about myself. And surely we see now as through a glass, in ambiguity, and not yet face to face.[468] Then as long as I am on my pilgrim way toward you, I am nearer to myself than I am to you; yet I know you cannot be violated in any way, while I do not know which temptations I am strong enough to resist, and which not. But I have hope because you are faithful, and you will not suffer us to be tempted beyond what we can bear,[469] but when the temptation comes you make for us a way out, so that we can endure. Therefore I will confess what I know about myself, and I will confess what I do not know about myself, because whatever I do know, I know by your light, and what I do not know, I will never know, until my darkness is made in your countenance like the noonday sun.[470]

6

Not with a wavering but with a sure conscience do I love you, Lord. You smote my heart with your word, and I loved you. And heaven and earth and all that is in them, behold, they all say to me that I should love you, nor do they cease to say it to all men, so that they are without excuse.[471] But more profoundly will you have mercy on whom you will have mercy, and show compassion to those whom you will show compassion;[472] and otherwise do heaven and earth utter their praises to the deaf.

What then do I love, when I love you? Not the comeliness of a body, not the grace of a season, not the gleam of light so friendly to the eyes, not the sweet melodies of songs in all their modes, not the pleasant fragrance of flowers and ointments and spices, not manna and honey, not winsome limbs for the embraces of the flesh; these are not the things I love, when I love my God.

---

[468] Cf. 1 Cor 13:12.
[469] Cf. 1 Cor 10:13.
[470] Cf. Ps 37:6.
[471] Cf. Rom 1:20.
[472] Cf. Rom 9:15, Ex 33:19.

And yet I do love a kind of light, a kind of voice, a kind of fragrance, a kind of food, and a kind of embrace, when I love my God, the light, the voice, the fragrance, the food, and the embrace of my inward man, where a light that no place can contain fills my soul, where a voice sounds that no time can rush away, where a fragrance is found that no breeze can scatter, where a sweetness is tasted that no feeding can diminish, where something cleaves that satiety never pulls apart. This is what I love, when I love my God.

And what is this? I asked the earth, and it said, "I am not he," and everything else in it confessed the same thing. I asked the sea and the deeps and the creeping things that live, and they responded, "We are not your God; seek him above us." I asked the winds that blow, and all the air and all things that dwell in it said, "Anaximenes[473] was deceived; I am not God." I asked the sky, the sun, the moon and stars, and they said, "Neither are we the God you seek." And I said to everything that stood about the doors of my flesh, "Tell me about my God, since you are not he. Tell me something about him." And they cried out in a loud voice, "He made us!"[474] My question, my gaze; their reply, their beauty.

And I turned my attention to myself and I asked, "You—who are you?" And I replied, "A man." And see, body and soul are ready at hand, one without, the other within. By which of those two should I have sought my God, when I sought him by means of the body, searching from earth to heaven, wherever I could send my scouts, the beams of my eyes? But the better part was the one within. For that was really the presiding part to which all my bodily scouts reported, the judge of

---

[473] Anaximenes of Miletus (d. 526? BC) was one of the most significant of the pre-Socratic philosophers, men who attempted to identify the *arche* of the universe—that is, the underlying essence (usually physical) or explanatory principle. Anaximenes said that it was air, because air could be condensed to form water and then ice, and thus, he conjectured, could we understand the three phases of matter—that is, solid, liquid, and gas. He also believed that the human soul could be equated with the breath, a common enough notion across human cultures.

[474] Cf. Ps 100:3. Against those philosophers, such as the Epicureans, who argued against divine action in the world on account of what they found wrong and ugly in it, Augustine inquires of the world and finds that the beauty of its creatures testifies to their Creator.

the responses of heaven and earth and all that is in them, when they said, "We are not God!" and "He made us!" My inner man came to know these things through its adjutant, the outer man. I within, I knew these things, I the mind, through the senses of my body. I questioned the whole mass of the world about my God, and it answered me, "I am not he, but he made me."

Is this beauty, their response, not plainly apparent to all whose senses are sound? Why does it not say the same thing to everyone? All living creatures great and small see it, but they cannot put the question to it. For in them, reason has not been placed as judge over what the senses report. But men can put the question, so that they may see and understand the invisible things of God from the things that are made,[475] but by their love they make themselves subject to these created things, and as subjects they cannot pass judgment. The created things do not respond to those who question them unless they judge them too, nor do they change what they say, that is, how they appear to the senses. One man sees, and that is all; another sees and asks; it does not appear one way to this man and another way to that man, but appearing the same to both, it is dumb to this man, and speaks to that man. In reality, it speaks to everyone, but they alone understand it who take up the reply from without and compare it with the truth within. For truth says to me, "Your God is not heaven or earth or any bodily thing." Their nature says so. All men see that a thing of mass is less in a part than it is in the whole. Yet you, my soul, are better than that, I say, because you quicken the mass, your body, supplying it with life, which no mere body can do for another body. But your God for you is the very life of life.

7

What then do I love when I love my God? Who is he, above the head of my soul? By that same soul of mine I shall climb up to him. I shall soar

---

[475] Cf. Rom 1:20.

beyond that power by which I cleave to the body and fill its frame with life. Not by that power shall I find my God. For then the horse and the mule that have no understanding[476] might find him, for they have that same power by which their bodies live. There is another power, whereby I not only enliven my flesh but make it capable of sense, a power which the Lord has fashioned for me, commanding the eye not to hear, and the ear not to see, but giving the eye for me to see, and the ear for me to hear, and granting to each of the other senses its proper seat and function. All these diverse functions, by means of the sense organs, I put in act, I who am one mind. I shall go beyond this power of mine too, because the horse and the mule possess the like, for they also sense things by means of the body.

8

I shall soar, then, beyond this power of my nature, ascending by degrees to him who made me. And I come to the fields and the spacious country seat of the memory, where are treasures of innumerable images of all kinds of things, imported by the senses. Whatever we think, too, is hoarded up there, by enlarging or diminishing or somehow varying what the sense has touched on, and whatever else is commended to it and laid in place, which has not been swallowed up and buried in forgetfulness.

When I go there, I ask that something I want be brought to me, and some things come forth at once, some things take a little longer, as if they had to be dug out from some more obscure cubbyholes; some things sally forth in troops and, when you are looking for something else, leap right in the middle as if they were saying, "Maybe we're the ones you want?" And I wave them away with the hand of my heart, driving them from recollection, till finally the clouds dissolve and what I want appears to sight, coming forth from its hiding places. Some things come easily, in untroubled order, one by one, just as they are

---

[476] Cf. Ps 32:9.

bidden, and the ones in front give way to the ones that follow, and when they give way they are put back in place again, to come out whenever I want them again. The whole of that happens whenever I recite something by heart.

Where are all the things saved, one by one and according to their kinds, that are taken in from their proper entryways, as light and all colors and the shapes of bodies come through the eyes, and all the kinds of sound come through the ears, all smells through the entryway of the nose, all taste from the entryway of the mouth, and from the sense of the whole body comes what is hard or soft, hot or cold, smooth or rough, heavy or light, pressing upon it from within or without?[477] All these things does that vast recess of the memory take in, with all its secret places and its winding ways no one can describe, to summon up when needed, or to stow away again. And they all enter by their own doorways and are put in place there. And yet the objects themselves do not enter, but the images of the things we sense are there, ready for us to think about when we bring them back to mind.

And who can tell how these images are formed, even though we know which senses have seized upon them and smuggled them away inside? Even while I am settled in darkness and silence, I can bring forth colors in my memory if I want to, and I can tell the difference between white and black and any others I wish, nor do sounds break in and disarrange what I have taken in from my eyes and am now considering, even though the sounds are there too, laid away by themselves, so to speak. For I can call for them if I please, and there they are, and with a tongue at rest and a silent throat I can sing as much as I wish, and those color-images, which are no less present there, do not get in the way, do not break in when that other treasure is brought out which came in through the ears. So it is with everything else I have ingested

---

[477] It will not do to say that our memories are stored in the brain as we might store things in cabinets and drawers. The brain is not the mind, but the means by which the mind acts, though there is a mutual interaction between the two, and unlike the beasts, man can *change his mind*, by exertions of the mind itself.

or digested through the senses. I can recall them if I like, and I can tell the scent of lilies from the scent of violets even while I am not smelling anything, and I prefer honey to spiced wine, and the soft to the harsh, though I am not tasting anything or handling anything. I do it by remembering.

All these things I do within, in that vast hall of my memory. Ready for me there are heaven and earth and the sea, with everything in them that I can sense, besides the things I have forgotten. I happen upon myself there too. I recall myself, what I did or when or where, or what I was feeling when I did it. Everything I remember is there, whether I myself experienced it or I took it on trust from someone else. From that same bounty I connect the likelihoods of things I have experienced, or of things I have believed because of my experience, with the likelihood of future actions and events and hopes, and I meditate upon them all as if they were present before me. "I shall do this and that," I say to myself in that immense bay of my soul, full of images, so many, so great, and this or that follows. "Oh, if it were only this or that!" "God forbid it should be this or that!" I say such things to myself, and when I say it, there they are, the images of everything I am talking about, from that storehouse of the memory, nor could I talk about any of them if the images were not there.

Great is this power of memory, exceedingly great, O God, a vast and endless sanctuary. Who can plumb its depths? And this is the power of my mind, and it belongs to my nature, and I myself cannot grasp all of what I am. Therefore, the mind is too narrow to contain itself.[478] But where is the part of it that it cannot contain? Surely within it, not without. Why then does it not contain it? A great wonder rises in me when I think of it—I am seized with astonishment. And men go to gaze upon mountain heights, and the whelming waves of the sea, and rivers

---

[478] The mind is of potentially limitless extent; it can imagine what it has never seen, considered, or imagined; it can learn of what it had never supposed could exist. It does so without being fully aware of the wonders it is performing as it performs them. Of no merely material thing can we posit such power.

flowing afar, and the all-surrounding ocean, and the winding paths of the stars, and they leave themselves behind, nor do they wonder that while I was naming all these things, I did not see them with my eyes. Nor could I have named them—those mountains and waves and rivers and stars I have seen, and the Ocean[479] that I take upon trust—unless I had seen them in my memory within, and seen them far apart from one another, as if I had seen them outside. Yet I did not swallow them up by sight when I saw them with my eyes; nor are the objects themselves with me, but their images. And I know by which sense of the body each thing is impressed upon me.

9

But those are not the only things that this immense capacity of my memory holds in its bosom. Here we find also all those precepts of the liberal arts that have not fallen away, stored in a place deeper within, but not really a place at all, nor is it their images I hold, but the things themselves.[480] For what grammar is, or skill in argument, how many kinds of questions there are, whatever I know about them lies in my memory not as if I had to retain the image and leave the object behind, nor as if it made a sound and passed by, as a voice that prints its trace upon the ears, so that you can recall it to mind as if it were sounding when it is not; nor like an odor when it passes and dwindles away in the wind, affecting the sense of smell so that it casts its image upon the memory, which we can have again when we bring it to mind; or like

---

[479] The ancients believed that the Ocean—what we call the Atlantic—surrounded the land masses of Europe, Asia, and Africa, on the globe of the world.

[480] This is an important point. It is one thing, perhaps, to have memories of sense impressions, such as the sight of a fir tree or the taste of hazel nuts. Man remembers also *things he has never sensed,* because they are not bodily things, though he may first learn of them by means of senses: he hears a teacher, he reads a book, he draws a diagram. Mathematical objects, such as lines and circles, are of this sort, and that is why Plato, in the *Republic,* says that mathematical knowledge is of a higher order than is our knowledge of things we can sense. It is close to philosophical knowledge, because its objects are immaterial and thus not subject to change.

food, which when it is in the belly has no taste, and yet it savors of something in the memory still; or like anything we feel when we touch a bodily object, and when the object is taken away we can form an image of it in the memory. For indeed these things were not sent into the memory themselves, but only their images, caught up with marvelous speed, and laid up, so to speak, in wonderful cabinets, and brought back out by the wondrous power of remembering.

10

But when I hear that there are three kinds of questions—whether it is, what it is, what kind of thing it is—I do retain the images of the sounds we make when we pronounce the words, and I know that they pass through the air with their noise, and then they no longer are. But as for the things these sounds signify, I have never touched them with any bodily sense, nor have I ever seen them at all except by my mind. Yet I have treasured up in my memory not their images, but the things themselves. But by what road they came into me, let them say, if they can. For I consider all the gateways of my flesh, and I do not find which one of them they came in by. The eyes say, "If they had color, we brought news of them." The ears say, "If they made a sound, we gave notice of them." The nostrils say, "If they had any smell, they came in by our passage." The sense of taste says likewise, "If they had no taste, do not ask us about them." The touch says, "If there is no body to it, we could not handle it, and if we did not handle it, we gave no notice of it." Whence and how did these things get into my memory? I do not know how. For when I learned them, I did not take them on credit from someone else's mind, but I recognized them in my own mind, and I approved them as true, and I commended them to my heart, as if I were setting them in place, to fetch them when I wanted. Somehow, they were there even before I learned them, but they were not in my memory.[481] Where then were they? When they

---

[481] Here Augustine comes close to affirming what Plato believed, that the soul has innate

were uttered, how did I recognize them, saying, "It is so, it is true"? How, unless they were already in the memory, but faraway, hidden down in caves so deep, if no reminder comes to dig them up, I might never have been able to think of them at all?

11

Therefore we find that to learn things when we do not draw their images from the senses, but rather we discern them within us as they are and without any images, is no other than, by thinking, to gather up what the mind had held here and there and helter-skelter, and by careful attention to make sure that they are readily available in the memory, so that what had been lurking about in a scattered and careless way will now, grown familiar, make a quick and easy appearance.

And how many things of this kind does my memory bear, ready to hand, as I have said, things we are said to have learned and to know! And if I leave off recalling them for just a little while, they plummet again and slip away into the deepest and most private hideaways, and I must think them all over again afresh to get them back out of there—for they have no other place to go—and to assemble them together (*cogere*) so they can be known, that is, to collect them from a certain scattering. That is where we get the word *cogitare* from, *to think*. For *cogo* is to *cogito* as *ago, I act*, is to *agito, I act constantly*, and *facio, I make*, is to *factito, I make habitually*.[482] Even so, the mind has appropriated this word to itself, because only what is collected in the mind and not from elsewhere can properly be called an object of cogitation.

---

knowledge. For Plato, this knowledge has perhaps come from a previous existence, so that learning may be considered a form of recollection; cf. *Meno*, 81c-d.

[482] The augmented forms of the verbs are what linguists call "frequentative," denoting action that occurs again and again, or back and forth. English has a similar feature in verbs with the frequentative or iterative suffixes -er and -el (-le): e.g., *fluster, haggle, glimmer, wriggle*.

12

The mind also contains innumerable reasonings and laws of numbers and dimensions, which no bodily sense has pressed upon it, for they have no color, no sound, no smell, no taste, no touch. I have heard the sounds of the words that signify them when someone is discussing them, but the sounds are one thing, and the laws are another. For the sounds are one way in Greek and another in Latin, but the things themselves are neither Greek nor Latin nor any other language. I have seen lines drawn by carpenters that are as slender as the strands of a spider web. But the lines themselves are something else, and not the images that the eye of my flesh reports to me. For to know them is to recognize them within, without any cogitation about a body. I have also sensed with all my bodily senses the numbers we *name* when we count, but the numbers we *use* in counting are far otherwise. As they are not the images of those names, they must have real existence.[483] Someone who does not see them may laugh at me, and I will be sorry for him as he laughs.

13

I hold all these things in the memory, and I even remember how I learned them. Why, many things that are wrongly argued against them have I heard, and I remember those too. They are false, no doubt, but it is not false that I remember them. And I remember that I have distinguished between these truths here, and what is objected against them falsely there; and I see that it is one thing for me to make the distinction now, and another for me to remember the distinction I used to make so often when I thought about them. Therefore, I remember that I have often understood these things, and what I now discern and understand, I commit to memory, so that afterwards I shall remember that I now do

---

[483] Plato believed that mathematical objects possess genuine existence, and are not mere constructions of the human mind. As soon as we admit that mathematicians *discover truths about a mathematical reality*, rather than just working out the implications of a man-made system, we must leave materialism behind.

understand. And I remember that I have remembered, so that, in time to come, if I can recall that I was at this time able to bring these things to mind, it will be by the power of memory that I shall recall it.[484]

14

My memory also contains the affections of my mind, but not as the mind itself possesses them when it feels them, but in a far different way, rather as the power of memory possesses itself. For when I am not glad, I remember that I was once glad, and though I am not sad I call to mind my bygone sadness, and sometimes I remember without fear that I was afraid, and I am mindful of my desire of old though I feel the desire no more. By contrast, I am happy when sometimes I recall a sadness gone forever, and sad to recall a gladness gone forever.

That is nothing to wonder at, if we are dealing with a bodily thing. For the mind is one thing, the body another. Then if I rejoice as I remember a bodily pain that is no more, it is a matter of course. But supposing that the mind is the same thing as the memory—for when we command someone to remember something, we say, "Make sure you keep this in mind," and when we forget something, we say, "I didn't have it in mind," and, "It slipped my mind," and so do we call the memory the mind—supposing that this is so, how can it be that when I am glad as I remember my past sadness, the mind possesses the gladness and the memory the sadness, and the mind is glad because there is gladness within it, but the memory is not sad, even though the sadness is in it? Does the memory then not belong to the mind? Who would say such a thing? Well then, the memory must be a kind of belly for the mind, and gladness and sadness are like sweet and bitter food, in this sense, that when they are committed to the memory, they can

---

[484] The point here is far more than a rhetorical flourish or a curiosity. Other creatures remember; man can stand as it were outside of himself to regard his own memory. He remembers that he has remembered; he recollects; he commits to memory; he even attempts to forget. Thus his mind cannot simply be a function of memory, or a mingling of memory with desire and instinct, as it is in the more intelligent beasts.

be stowed away in the belly, where they will have no taste. It is silly to think that these things are like those, and yet they are not utterly unlike, either.

But I bring this from my memory too. When I say that there are four passions that disturb the mind, desire, gladness, fear, and sorrow, and when I discuss them by dividing each one into the several forms it takes according to its kind, defining the forms, it is in my memory that I find what I am going to say and what I bring forth. And while I am calling them back to mind by my memory, none of these disturbing passions disturbs me. Yet before I called them back to myself and handled them again, they were there, and that is why they could be recalled. Maybe, when the memory brings these things up by recalling them, it is as when food is brought back from the belly, for ruminating—chewing the cud. But why then does the person discussing them, that is, remembering them, not taste them in the mouth of his cogitation, the sweetness of joy or the bitterness of sorrow? Perhaps the things are just not similar in every way. For who would willingly speak about it, if every time we mentioned sadness or fear, we were forced to grieve or to be afraid? Even so, we would never speak of them, except that in our memory we do find the concepts of these very things, and not just the sounds of the names impressed as images upon the body's senses. These concepts we have not admitted through the doorways of the flesh, but it is the mind itself, perceiving them through the experience of their passions, that commends them to memory, or the memory retains them, even when they are not commended to it.

15

But who shall say with easy confidence whether we perform these actions by means of images? I name a stone, I name the sun, when the things I name are not present to my senses. No doubt, their images are readily available in my memory. I name some bodily pain, and it is not there, so long as nothing is hurting me; but unless its image were in my memory, I do not know what I would say, or how in talking about the pain I could distinguish it from pleasure. I name bodily health, when I am sound in the body. The thing I name is with me, but still, its image too must be in my memory, or I would never be able to recall what the sound of this name is supposed to signify. And sick people would not know what you were talking about by the name "health," unless its image were grasped by the power of memory, even though the thing itself is absent from the body.

I name the numbers we count with, and look, they themselves are in my memory and not just their images. I name the *image* of the sun, and it is in my memory, and I recall not an image of the image, but the thing itself—it is right there, ready for me when I call it to mind. I name the memory, and I recognize what I am naming. And where do I recognize this fact, but in that same memory? Is it possible that the memory can be present to itself by means of an image, and not by its own power?

16

Now then, when I name "forgetfulness" and I recognize what I am naming, how do I recognize the thing if not by remembering it? I am talking not about the sound of the name, but the thing the name signifies. For if I forgot that, I would never be able to understand what the sound was good for. When I remember memory, memory itself is at hand for me, by its own power; but when I remember forgetfulness, both memory and forgetfulness are right there: the memory, which I use in remembering, and the forgetfulness, which I remember. But what is forgetfulness if not a privation of memory? How then can it be present to me as something to remember, seeing that I cannot remember, when forgetfulness is upon me? Now, granting that what we remember we retain in the memory, unless we remembered forgetfulness, we could never recognize what it means when we hear the word "forgetfulness," and so forgetfulness is in fact retained in the memory.

236

Therefore something is present, lest we forget; something which, when it is present, we do forget. What can we understand from this? Is it that forgetfulness in itself is not in the memory when we remember it, but rather it is present in its image? For if forgetfulness were present in itself, it would cause us not to remember, but to forget. Who shall now hunt this down at last? Who can comprehend how it can be?

For my part, Lord, I toil at this, and I toil in myself. I have become for myself a soil hard to till, land that requires much sweat.[485] For we are not now searching into the regions of the sky, or measuring the distances between the stars, or asking how the earth hangs in balance; I am the one who is remembering, I, the mind. It is no cause for wonder if something that I am not should be far away from me. But what is nearer to me than I am? Yet, see here, I cannot comprehend the power of my memory, even though without it I cannot even name myself. For what do I want to say, when I am certain that I do remember forgetfulness? Can I possibly mean that what I remember is not in my memory? Or that forgetfulness is in the memory, only so that I may not forget it? Most absurd, both of these.

What about a third possibility? Can I say somehow that when I remember forgetfulness, forgetfulness itself is not in my memory, but only its image? How can I say so, when, if the image of a thing is to be impressed upon my memory, it is first necessary that the thing itself should be present, to impress its image? That is how I remember Carthage and every other place where I have been. That is how I remember the faces of men I have seen. So too with everything reported by the senses; so with the health or the pain of the body. When these things are present, the memory catches images from them, images that I can stare at when the things are present, or that I can draw up out of the mind by recollection even when they are absent. Then if forgetfulness is retained in the memory not by its own presence but by its image, then surely forgetfulness itself must once have been present, for

---

[485] Cf. Gn 3:19.

the memory to seize upon its image. But when it was present, how did it etch its image in the memory, when forgetfulness by its very presence must blot out what it finds noted down there? Nevertheless, whichever way it is, incomprehensible and inexplicable though it be, I am certain that I do remember forgetfulness, which buries what we remember.

17

Great is the power of memory, this thing to make us tremble, my God, a boundless multiplicity, profound as the sea. And this is the mind, and I myself am it. What then am I, my God? What kind of nature? A life of many modes and changes, astoundingly immense! Behold, in the innumerable fields and dens and caverns of my memory, innumerably filled with kinds of things past numbering, either by their images, as is the case with all bodily things, or by their very presence, as with all of the arts, or by certain notions or marks, as with the affections of the mind—for even when the mind does not feel them, the memory retains what it was like, for whatever is in the memory is also in the mind—I run through all these things, I fly here and there, I pry into them as deeply as I can, but never to the bottom. Such is the power of memory, such is the power of life in man whose very life is a way of dying!

What then shall I do, you my true life, my God? I shall pass beyond this power of mine called the memory, I shall pass beyond it, that I may touch you, sweet light, at last. What do you say to me? By my mind I mount up to you who abide above me, I shall pass beyond this power of mine called the memory, desiring to attain to you, to touch you where you may be touched, and to cleave to you, where it is possible to cleave to you. For even cattle and birds have memory, or they would never seek their dens to sleep in, or their nests, or the many other things they are accustomed to; for they never could become accustomed to anything at all were it not for the memory. Therefore, I shall pass beyond the memory, that I may touch him who set me apart from the four-footed beasts and made me wiser than the birds of the air.[486] Shall I pass beyond the memory, O true good and sweetness secure, to find you—where? Where shall I find you? If I set my memory aside when I find you, I will not keep you in mind. And how can I find you, unless I am mindful of you?

18

For the woman had lost her coin,[487] and she searched for it by the light of her lamp, and unless she had kept it in mind, she would not have found it. And when she did find it, how could she know that it was that coin, if she had not kept it in her mind? Many a thing do I remember having lost and then found again. Here is how I know it. I might be looking for something, when someone says to me, "Maybe this is it?" or "Is it that?" and I say no, until someone shows me the thing I have been looking for. Unless I had kept in mind what it was, even if someone showed it to me I would not find it, because I would not recognize it. And that is how it always is when we look for something we have lost, and we find it again.

Still, if by chance something is lost to the eyes but not from the memory, as can happen with any visible body, we do retain its image within, and we seek the object until it is restored to the sight. And when we find it, we recognize it by the image within us. We do not say we have found what we have lost, unless we recognize it, and we cannot recognize a thing we do not remember. But it was lost to the eyes, and not to the memory.

19

What then? When the memory itself loses something, which happens when we forget and we rummage about in order to remember, where

---

486 Cf. Job 35:11.
487 Cf. Lk 15:8–10.

at last do we look for it if not in that very memory? There, if one thing is offered instead of another, we toss it away, until we happen upon the thing we were looking for. And when it turns up, we say, "This is it," which we would not say unless we recognized it, and we would not recognize it unless we remembered it. Now, we had in fact forgotten it. Maybe it is like this. The thing had not entirely slipped away, and from the part we still hold on to, we seek after the other part. For the memory senses that it is not reflecting upon all of it at once as it used to do, but it is amputated in its habit, so to speak, and it limps along while it demands that what it has lost be restored.

For example, suppose we see a man we know or we are thinking about him, but we have forgotten his name and are trying to remember it. Another name comes to us, but we do not connect it with him, because we are not used to thinking about him with that name in mind. So we toss it away, till some name comes to us, and by some customary mark the mind accepts it as just the right thing. But where does that name come from, if not from the memory? For even if someone else puts us in mind of it and we recognize it, it comes from the memory. We do not credit it as a new name, but we approve it as we recall it, and we are assured that the name spoken is the right one. But if the name had been blotted out of the mind through and through, we would not remember it even if someone reminded us of it. For as long as we still remember that we have forgotten something, we have not forgotten it completely. Therefore, if we have forgotten something completely, we cannot even look for it when we have lost it.

20

In what way then do I seek you, Lord? For when I seek you, my God, I seek the blessed life. I will seek you, that my soul may live.[488] For my body lives by my soul, and my soul lives by you. In what way then do I seek the blessed life? It shall not be mine until I say, "Enough, there

---

[488] Cf. Ps 63:1.

it is," when it is fitting that I should say so. How do I seek it? By some memory of it, which I have forgotten, but I still remember that I have forgotten it? Or by a hankering to learn something unknown, either because I have never known it or because I have forgotten it so far as not even to remember that I have forgotten it? Is not the blessed life what everyone wants, and there is no man who does not want it in full? But where did they come to know it, that they should want it so much? Where did they see it, to fall in love with it? We do possess it, no question, but I do not know how.

And there is another way to have it, so that when you have it that way, you are blessed, and there are also those who are blessed in hope.[489] They have it in a lesser way than do those who are blessed by the thing itself, and yet they are better off than those who are blessed neither in possession nor in hope. Even these, nevertheless, would never desire to be blessed unless they possessed it in some way—for most assuredly, they do desire it. In some way they know it, I do not know how, and they possess it by some sort of knowledge. And I try my hardest to figure out whether it is in the memory, because, if that were so, then at some time we all must have been blessed. I do not now ask whether either each of us was blessed one by one, or all of us together were blessed in that man who first sinned, in whom we all are dead, and from whom we were born into misery.[490] I am asking whether the blessed life is in the memory. For we would not be in love with it unless we knew it. We hear the name and we desire the thing, and we all say so, for we take no delight in the mere sound of it. When a Greek hears its name in Latin, it does not delight him, because he does not know what is being said. But it does delight us, just as it would delight him if he heard it in Greek. For the thing itself, which the speakers of Greek and Latin and every other human language seek, is not itself either Greek or Latin. So it is known to all men, who, if you could ask them in one voice whether they want to be happy, would respond without any hesitation that they do. And that would not be, unless the thing itself signified by this name were held in their memory.

21

But is it held in the same way as when I remember Carthage, which I have seen? No, for the blessed life is not seen by the eyes, because it is not a body. What about how we remember numbers? No, for if you have them in your knowledge, you do not still go seeking them; but we have the blessed life in our knowledge, and that is why we love it, and still we want to gain it so that we may be blessed. What about how we remember eloquence? No, for even granting that there are many people who are not yet fine speakers and who recall the thing itself when they hear the name, and who want to be eloquent too, so that they clearly have some knowledge of it, still, they must by their bodily senses have observed other fine speakers, and it pleased them, and they desired to be fine speakers too. But some inward knowledge must have moved them, or they would not have been pleased, nor would they have desired the thing if it had not pleased them. But we gain no experience of the blessed life from other people by any sense of the body.

Is it then as we remember joy? Maybe so. For even when I am sad, I remember my joy, as I remember the blessed life, though I am wretched. I have never, by any sense of the body, seen my joy, or heard it, or smelled it, or tasted it, or felt it by touch, but I have experienced it in my mind when I have been happy, and some mark of it has stuck so fast to my memory, that I am well able to bring it to mind, sometimes with scorn, and sometimes with desire, according to the differences among the things that I remember to have rejoiced for. I have been steeped sometimes in a sort of joy from filthy things, and when I recall them now I detest them and abominate them; and also sometimes in good and decent things, and when I recall them I desire them again if by chance they are not there, and so am I sad as I recall that old joy.

When and where, then, have I experienced that happy life, so that I should bring it to mind again and love it and desire it? And I am not alone in this, or among but a few, since every man indeed wants to be happy. And if we did not know it by some sure mark, we would not desire it with a will so sure. But what is this? Why, if you ask two men whether they want to be soldiers, one might respond yes, he does, and the other no. But if you ask them whether they want to be happy, each one, instantly, without any wavering, would say that he would choose it, and in fact the man who wants to be a soldier and the man who wants not to be a soldier desire these things only so that they may be happy. Maybe it is that one person rejoices here, and another rejoices there? So all men agree that they want to be happy, just as they would agree, if they were asked, that they want to rejoice, and they call that same joy the blessed life. So that even though one person catches up with it here and another there, it is still one same thing that everyone strives to attain—that they may be joyful. This being so, no man can say he has never had the experience, because when we hear the phrase "the blessed life," we find it in the memory and we recognize it.

22

Far be it, O Lord, far be it from the heart of your servant who is confessing to you, far be it from me to count myself blessed merely because something or other is bringing me joy. For there is a joy that is not granted to the ungodly, but only to those who worship you freely, and you yourself are their joy. And that is the blessed life, to rejoice in you, to you, and because of you; that is what it is, and there is no other. And those who think it is something else are pursuing another joy and not the true one. Still, their will is not turned completely aside from some image of joy.

23

So it is not actually certain that all men desire to be happy, because those who do not desire to rejoice in you, which alone is the happy life, do not really desire a happy life. Or is it that all do desire it, but because the flesh lusts against the spirit and the spirit against the flesh,[491] so that men do not do what they desire, and they fall back upon what they can attain and they rest content with that, because what they are not strong enough to attain they do not desire as much as they must in order to acquire the strength?

For if I put the question to everyone, whether they would rather rejoice in the truth than in falsehood, they are as quick to say, without hesitation, that they would rather rejoice in the truth, as they are to say they want to be happy. And that blessed life indeed is a rejoicing in the truth, a rejoicing in you who are the Truth, O God, my light, the health of my countenance, and my God.[492] This is the blessed life that all men desire, this life which alone is blessed; all men desire it, all men desire to rejoice in the truth.

I have known many men who wish to deceive. But who wishes to be deceived? No one. Where then have they gotten knowledge of this blessed life? It must be where they have gotten knowledge of the truth. For they love that too, because they do not wish to be deceived, and when they love the blessed life—which is no other than a rejoicing in truth—they also love the truth, nor would they love it if they did not have some mark of it in their memory. Why then do they not rejoice in it? Why are they not happy? Because they are more powerfully occupied with other things, and these will sooner make them wretched than their slender memory of blessedness will make them happy. Still, for

---

[491] Cf. Gal 5:17. The pagan philosophers were unanimous in saying that all men desire to be happy, and not instrumentally but for its own sake. Then the question presses: since that is so, why do they not attain what they desire?
[492] Cf. Ps 43:3, 5.

a while, there is among men a dim light; let them walk in it, let them walk, lest the darkness overtake them.[493]

Why, then, does the truth give birth to hatred, and why do people take for an enemy your man who preaches the truth, if they love the blessed life, which is none other than a rejoicing in truth? It must be that this is how they love the truth: they love something else, and they want what they love to be the truth, and because they do not want to be deceived, they do not want to be convinced that they are wrong. So they hate the truth, because of the thing they love in truth's place. They love the truth when it gives them light, but they hate it when it rebukes them. Because they do not want to be deceived, but they do want to deceive others, they love truth when it shows itself to them, but they hate it, when it shows them to themselves. But this will be the pay they earn: the truth will reveal all those who do not want to be revealed in the truth, but it will not reveal itself to them.

Such is the human soul, such it is, blind, slovenly, base, and disgraceful, wanting to hide, but not wanting anything to be hidden from it. It gets the opposite in return; it cannot hide the truth, but the truth hides itself. But even so, even while it is wretched, it would rather rejoice in true things than in false things. Blessed then shall it be when, without any trouble and obstruction, it rejoices in that truth alone, by which all other true things are true.

24

See what a long way I have walked in my memory, seeking you, Lord, and beyond it I have not found you. For everything I find concerning you is something I have stored in my memory, ever since I first learned about you. For ever since that time, I have not forgotten you. Wherever I found truth, I found my God, the very truth, which I have not forgotten from the time I first learned it. Therefore, ever since I learned about you, you have dwelt in my memory, and that is where I find

---

[493] Cf. Jn 12:35.

you when I call you to mind and when I delight in you. These are my holy pleasures, which your kindheartedness has given me, when you regarded my poverty.

25

But where in my memory do you dwell, Lord—where do you dwell? What kind of nest have you fashioned for yourself? What sanctuary have you built? You have given my memory the honor of your dwelling there, but in what part you dwell, I must consider. For I soared beyond those parts that even the beasts have, once I brought you to mind (for I could never find you there among the images of bodily things), and I came to the parts where I store up the affections of my mind, but I did not find you there either. And I entered the seat of my mind itself (which also is in my memory, because the mind remembers itself), but you were not there, because you are neither a bodily image nor an affection of a living person, such as when we are glad, or we grieve, or desire, or dread, or remember, or forget, or anything else of that sort. You are not even the mind itself, because you are the Lord God of the mind. And all these things change, but you abide unchangeable above all things, and you have deigned to dwell in my memory, ever since I first learned of you. And why do I ask where you were dwelling in it, as if location exists in it at all? But surely you do dwell in it, because I have remembered you from the first time I learned of you, and when I call you to mind, I find you there.

26

Where then did I find you, so that I might learn about you? For you were not in my memory before I learned about you. Where then did I find you, so that I might learn about you, unless it was in yourself, above me? Not in any place; for we can come to you and go from you, and still there is no place. Everywhere, O Truth, you preside, and you respond simultaneously to all who ask counsel of you, though they ask counsel regarding a variety of things. Your responses are quite clear, but not everyone hears you clearly. Everyone consults you about what they want, but they do not always hear what they want to hear. Your best minister is he who does not so much look to hear from you what he wants to hear, as to want what he has heard from you.

27

Late have I loved you, Beauty so ancient and so new, late have I loved you! And behold, you were within me and I was without, and I sought you there, and I, though uncomely, rushed upon the comely things you have made. You were with me, but I was not with you. They held me far away from you, though if they had not been in you, they would not have been at all. You called to me, you cried, you broke through my deafness; you gleamed, you shone in splendor, and you put my blindness to flight; you sent forth a fragrance, and I breathed it in, and I pant for you; I tasted, and now I hunger and thirst; you touched me, and I burned for your peace.

28

When I shall cleave to you in every part of me, I shall never grieve or toil again, and my life will be alive and filled with you. As for now, because you lighten the load of those you fill, and because I am not yet filled with you, I am still a burden to myself.[494] The joys I should lament are at strife with the sorrows that should make me glad, and I do not know which way the victory will go. Woe is me! Have mercy on me, O Lord! My evil sorrows are at strife with my good joys, and I do not know which way the victory will go. Woe is me! Have mercy on me, O Lord! Woe is me! See,

---

[494] Cf. Job 7:20.

I do not hide my wounds from you. You are the physician, and I am ill; you are merciful, and I am a poor man in need of mercy.[495]

Is not man's life on earth a trial?[496] Does anyone wish for troubles and difficulties? You command us to bear up under them, not to love them. No one loves what he must endure, even if he loves the act of enduring. Even though he may rejoice at his endurance, he would rather there be nothing to endure. When I am in adversity I desire to prosper, and when I prosper I dread adversity. Where is the middle ground between them, where the life of man is not a trial? Woe to the prosperities of the world, woe again and a third time woe, from fear of adversity and from the corruption of gladness! Woe to the adversities of the passing world, woe again and a third time woe, for we desire to prosper, and adversity is hard, and it may break down our endurance. Is not the life of man on earth a trial, without reprieve?

29

All my hope is in your great mercy alone.[497] Give what you command, and command what you will. You order us to be continent. "And when I came to know," as someone has said, "that no one can be continent unless God should give it this too was a point of wisdom, to know whose gift it was."[498] By continence we are gathered together and brought into the One, from whom we had spilled away into the many. He loves you less, who loves something else along with you, something which he does not love because of you. O Love ever burning and never to be quenched, O Charity, my God, set me afire! You command continence: give what you command, and command what you will.

---

[495] Cf. Ps 109:22.
[496] Cf. Job 7:1.
[497] Cf. Ps 33:22.
[498] Cf. Ws 8:21.

30

You certainly do command that I contain myself from the lust of the eyes, the lust of the flesh, and the ambition of this world.[499] You ordered me away from keeping a mistress, and though you allow for wedlock, you have put me in mind of what is better. And because you gave it, it was done, even before I became a steward of your sacrament. But the images of all the many things I have spoken about live in my memory to this day, such images as my long habit fixed there. They try to storm me when I am awake, and then they have no force, but when I am asleep, they prevail so far as to bring pleasure, and sometimes even consent, as if I were doing the deed. The trick of that image in my soul is so powerful in the body, that these false sights entice me when I am asleep, when true sights could never do so when I am awake.

Surely I am still myself then, O Lord my God! Yet there is a great difference between myself and myself, in that moment when I pass from waking to sleeping, or back again from sleeping to waking. Where is reason at that time, by which a man can stand firm against such suggestions when he is awake, and even if the objects themselves were brought before him, he would remain unshaken? Is it shut away with the eyes? Does it slumber with the senses of the body? And how is it that even in sleep we often resist, remembering our resolve and holding to it most chastely, yielding no assent to those enticements? And still the great difference is there, so that when something happens otherwise in our sleep, when we wake up we return to our peace of conscience, and in that same passage we discover that we have not done what somehow, to our sorrow, was done in us.

Is not your hand, almighty God, able to heal all the infirmities of my soul, and by a more abundant gift of grace to snuff out even the lascivious movements of my sleep? You shall increase, Lord, all your gifts in me, more and more, so that my soul may follow along with me toward you, its feet set free from the lime of concupiscence, so that it

---

[499] Cf. 1 Jn 2:15.

will not be a rebel to itself. Even in dreams, then, far from committing in animate images these base deeds of corruption all the way to the spilling of the flesh, it will not consent to them at all. For it is no great thing for the Almighty to do, who can do far greater things than we ask for or understand, to make it so that such a thing has no pleasure in it at all, or so little pleasure that the chaste affection of someone in his sleep can thwart it by a single nod of the will, and not only when we are far on in years, but when we are young too.

For the time being, I have confessed to my good Lord what I still am when it comes to this kind of evil. I tremble as I rejoice in what you have given me, and I mourn because I am still unfinished, hoping that you will make perfect your mercies in me,[500] till I attain that fullness of peace which my inward and my outward man will have with you, when death is swallowed up in victory.[501]

31

There is another evil of the day, and would it were sufficient unto it.[502] We repair the daily crumbling of the body by eating and drinking, while we wait for the time when you shall destroy both the belly and its food,[503] when you shall slay our neediness with a wondrous satiety, and clothe this corruptible body with what is incorruptible forever.[504] Meanwhile, the necessity is sweet to me, and I fight against this sweetness lest I be caught, and I wage a daily war by fasting, bringing my body into subjection, and the pains I suffer from it are driven off by the pleasure it brings me. For hunger and thirst are really kinds of pain; they burn hot and they kill like a fever, unless the medicine of nourishment relieves us. But because, out of the comfort of your gifts, the

---

[500] Cf. Phil 1:6.
[501] Cf. 1 Cor 15:54.
[502] Cf. Mt 6:34.
[503] Cf. 1 Cor 6:13.
[504] Cf. 1 Cor 15:53.

nourishment is readily available to us from the earth and the water and the sky that serve our weakness, our calamity is called our delight.

You have taught me that I should take my food in the same way I take medicine. But while I am passing over from the quiet of fullness to the disquiet of need, a snare of concupiscence is laid in that very passage. For the passage is pleasure, and there is no other way to go, but by this passage that necessity compels us to take. And though health is the reason why we eat and drink, still a certain dangerous mirth tags along after it, and often tries to get in front so that it will be the reason instead, while I say that I do these things or want to do them for my health. Nor do they keep to the same measure. What is enough for the health is hardly enough for delight, and I am often unsure whether the needful care of my body is asking for help, or a deceitful pleasure-seeking demands to be served. And my luckless soul is quite glad of the uncertainty, and uses it for some special pleading and excuse, happy that it is not clear what would be enough for a moderate and healthy diet. So do we cloak the business of pleasure under the cover of health. I struggle every day to resist these temptations, and I call upon your right arm, and I bring my confusions to you. For I still have no good counsel on this matter.

I hear the voice of my God, commanding, "Let not your hearts be overcharged with surfeiting and drunkenness."[505] Drunkenness is far from me; you will have mercy on me, so that it may never draw near. But feasting, well, that has sometimes crept up on your servant; you will have mercy on me, that it may be put far from me. For no one can be continent, unless you give it.[506] You grant us many things we pray for, and every good thing we receive before we pray for it, we receive from you; and yours also is the gift of knowing that to be so. I was never a drunkard, but I have known drunkards whom you have made into sober men. So too it is your doing, that people who have never

[505] Lk 21:34.
[506] Cf. Ws 8:21.

been drunkards stay that way; your doing, that people who have been drunkards do not stay that way; your doing, that both sorts should know whose doing it is.

I have heard another of your sayings: "Do not go after your lusts, but turn away from your wantonness."[507] And by your favor I have heard this too, and I love it dearly: "Neither if we eat, shall we enjoy plenty, nor if we refrain from eating, shall we lack,"[508] which is to say, the one will not make me rich, and the other will not leave me destitute. I have heard another: "I have learned to be content in whatever state I am in; I know how to abound, and I know how to suffer poverty. I can do all things in him who strengthens me."[509] Behold, a soldier of the heavenly armies, not dust, which we are. But remember, Lord, that we are dust, that from the dust you have made man, and he was lost and is found.[510] Nor could that man do these things by his own power, for he too was dust, whom I have heartily loved as by the breath of your inspiring he said this, "I can do all things in him who strengthens me." Strengthen me, that I may have that ability. Give what you command, and command what you will. He confesses that he has received this also, that when he glories, he glories in the Lord.[511] I have heard another man begging you, that he may receive: "Take from me," he says, "the greed of the belly."[512] Whence it is clear, O holy God, that you are the giver, whenever what you command is done.

Good Father, you have taught me: "All things are pure to the pure, but to the man who eats with offense, it is evil."[513] And that every one of your creatures is good, and nothing to be cast away, so long as it is received with thanksgiving. And that our food does not commend us to God, and so let no man judge us for our food and drink. And that

---

[507] Sir 18:30.
[508] 1 Cor 8:8.
[509] Phil 4:12–13.
[510] Cf. Ps 103:14, Gn 2:7, Lk 15:32.
[511] Cf. 1 Cor 1:31, Jer 9:24.
[512] Sir 23:6.
[513] Ti 1:15.

he who eats should not scorn him who does not eat, and he who does not eat should not judge him who does.[514] I have learned these things, thanks to you, praise to you, my God, my Teacher, you who knock at the door of my ears, you who fill my heart with light; deliver me from all temptation!

It is not the uncleanness of the dinner that I fear, but the uncleanness of the lust for it. I know that Noah was permitted to eat any kind of flesh that was suitable for food,[515] and that Elijah was fed with meat,[516] and that John, endowed with a marvelous abstinence, ate the locusts granted to him for food and he was not polluted;[517] but I know also that Esau was deceived by his craving for lentil stew,[518] and David reproached himself for wanting a drink of water;[519] and our King was tempted not by meat, but by bread.[520] And so the people in the desert deserved to be reproved not because they desired to eat meat, but because in their desire for food they grumbled against the Lord.[521]

Every day, set amidst these temptations, I wrestle against the craving to eat and drink. It is not like what I could do with the pleasures of the bed, that I could resolve to cut them off once and for all. And so the reins of the throat are to be held in temperance, sometimes relaxing them, sometimes pulling them tight. And who is he, Lord, who is never swept up a little bit beyond the bounds of his need? He is great, whoever he is, and he should magnify your name. But I am not he; I am a man, a sinner. But I too magnify your name, and he who has overcome the world[522] pleads to you for my sins. Let him number me among the

---

[514] Cf. Rom 14:3.
[515] Cf. Gn 9:3.
[516] Cf. 1 Kgs 17:6.
[517] Cf. Mk 1:6.
[518] Cf. Gn 25:34.
[519] Cf. 2 Sm 23:16.
[520] Cf. Mt 4:3–4.
[521] Cf. Ex 16:8.
[522] Cf. Jn 16:33.

weaker members of his body, for your eyes behold that body not yet perfect, and in your book all its members shall be written down.[523]

32

I do not trouble myself too much with the enticements of the sense of smell. When they are absent, I do not go seeking them. When they are present, I do not refuse them, but I am quite ready to do without them for good. So it seems to me; perhaps I am deceived. For a deplorable darkness hides my faculties from me, so that when my mind interrogates itself about its powers, it judges that it should not be given credence too easily. Even what is in it is often stowed away, so that only experience can make it manifest. And no one should hold himself secure in this life, which is called one continual trial. He may be someone who can go from the worse to the better, but who ends up going from the better to the worse. Our one hope, our one trust, the one firm promise we are given, is your mercy.

33

The pleasures of the ear once tangled me in bonds and put me under the yoke, but you have loosed the bonds and set me free.[524] I do confess that when I hear the songs your words breathe life into, sung with a sweet and skillful voice, I take my ease a little, not so much that I must cling to them, for I can still get up and leave, if I wish. Still, along with the words that are their life and that give me reason to welcome them in, they seek a place of no small dignity in my heart, and I can hardly offer them one they are due. Sometimes it seems I grant them more honor than is becoming. That happens when I feel that our minds are stirred by those holy verses to a more religious and brightly burning flame of devotion when they are sung in that way, than if they had not

---

[523] Cf. Ps 139:16.
[524] Cf. Ps 116:16.

been so sung. And all the various movements of the human spirit have their own corresponding measures in the voice and in song, and they are aroused by a kind of secret affinity. But it is not fitting to give over to the delight of the flesh an unstrung mind, and this delight often beguiles me, whenever sense does not accompany reason in a patient way, following behind it. It even strives to run ahead of reason and lead it along, when only on account of reason did it deserve to be admitted in the first place. So it happens that I sin in these regards, not sensing it at the time, but later.

Yet sometimes I err by being too severe, wary, beyond due measure, of this manner of being beguiled. Why, sometimes I would have it that every pleasant melody to which the psalms of David are sung should be banished from my ears and from those of the Church herself. And then the safer way seems to me what I remember Athanasius,[525] the bishop of Alexandria, used to say, when he had his lector intone the psalm with so slight an inflection of the voice that it was nearer to ordinary speech than to singing. Still, when I recall the tears I wept at the songs of the Church in those first days of my recovered faith, and when I think that I am now moved not by the singing, but by the things that are sung, when they are sung with a clear voice in a most suitable melody, I recognize once again the great usefulness of this institution. So do I toss and turn, the danger of pleasure here, the restorative experience there; but I incline more, not as if I were delivering an unretractable verdict, to approve the custom of singing in the church, so that when we entertain the ears, we may help the weaker soul to rise to a feeling of devotion.

---

[525] Saint Athanasius (c.296–373), bishop of Alexandria and tireless defender of the orthodox faith, both as regards the Trinity and the full divinity and humanity of Christ. He was a crucial voice at the Council of Nicaea (325), hated and plotted against by the Arians and their sympathizers. As for music in the Church, Athanasius believed that the worshipers themselves should become like stringed instruments upon which the Word of God plays, so that when the psalms were chanted, the words themselves would be like musicians bringing harmony into and from the soul, rather than being a mere occasion for melody that would overcome them and their meaning.

And yet whenever it happens that I am moved more by the song than by what is sung, I confess that I have sinned and am worthy of punishment, and then I would rather not hear the singing. See where I am! Weep with me and weep for me, all you who stir with something good within, something that results in good action. If no such good stirs in you, these matters will not move you. But you, O Lord my God, I pray, hear my plea, look upon me, see me, have mercy on me and heal me. For in my eyes I have become a riddle to myself; and that is my infirmity.

34

One pleasure of this flesh of mine, the pleasure of the eyes, remains for me to speak of in these confessions. Let the ears of your temple, brotherly, devout, hearken to them, so that we may have done with these temptations of fleshly desire, which as I groan still bang at my door, while I long to be clothed with my dwelling place that is from heaven. The eyes are smitten with lovely shapes in all their variety, and colors that glow and delight. Let them not take possession of my soul! Let God be its master, who indeed made all these good things, but he himself is my good, not they. They touch me every day while I am awake, and I get no rest from them, as I can rest from melodious sounds, and sometimes, in silence, from sounds of every kind. For this queen of the colors, this light, soaking everything we look upon, wherever I may be in the daytime, glides beside me in many a way and tickles my fancy while I am doing something else and not paying attention to it. For it enters our bosoms with such force, if it is suddenly taken away we want it back and demand it, and if it is gone for a long time, it grieves the mind.

O Light that Tobit saw, when with these eyes shut up in blindness he taught his son the way of life, and he walked before him in the steps of charity and never went astray![526] Light that Isaac saw, when his fleshly eyes were laden and dimmed with old age, and he gained

---

[526] Cf. Tb 4.

the reward, not of blessing his sons though he did not recognize them, but of recognizing them in his blessing![527] Light that Jacob saw, he too taken blind in his old age, when from his light-filled heart he shone upon the destinies of peoples to come, sealed from beforehand in his sons, and when he laid his hands on his grandsons, Joseph's sons, mystically crossing them, so that he blessed them not as their father corrected him from without, but as he discerned by the light within![528] This same is the Light, the one Light, and all are one who see it and love it!

But this corporeal light we are speaking of sheds its dangerous and enticing spice on the life of the passing world, for the blind souls that love it. But they who know how to praise you for the light take it up in your hymn, "O God, creator of all things,"[529] and are not taken in by it in their sleep. That is how I want to be. I stand against the seductions of the eyes, lest my feet be tripped up as I enter upon your way; and to you I lift up eyes that cannot be seen, that you may pluck my feet from the snare.[530] And you never cease to pluck them, because ensnared they often are. You never cease to free my feet, while I am caught all the time in traps scattered everywhere. For you do not sleep nor shall you slumber, you that keep guard over Israel.[531]

Innumerable are the things men have added to tease the eyes; things made by various arts and their artisans, in robes, shoes, vessels and manufactures of that kind, in paintings and feigned images in other forms, going far beyond need, and far beyond any modest and pious meaning. They follow along after the outward things they make, abandoning from within the One who made them, and destroying what they have been made to be. As for me, my God and my Beauty, I shall even for these things sing to you and offer a sacrifice of praise to you who are sanctifying me, since all the beautiful things brought by the

---

[527] Cf. Gn 27.
[528] Cf. Gn 48:10–20.
[529] The first words of St. Ambrose's evening hymn; see Book 9, ch. 12.
[530] Cf. Ps 25:15.
[531] Cf. Ps 121:4.

soul of the craftsman into his hands come from that beauty which is above the soul, for which my soul sighs day and night. But the followers and fashioners of things that are beautiful on the outside derive from the higher beauty the rule for what will please, but not the rule for what will be of good use. Though they do not see it, it is there, so that they may not go far astray but rather keep watch over their powers for your sake, and not squander them upon tiresome delicacies.

And even while I am saying and discerning all this, I am tangling my every step in these things of beauty. But you shall root me up out of them, you shall, because your mercy stands before my eyes. Pitifully am I caught, and you shall have pity and root me up. Sometimes I shall not feel it, because I had hardly touched upon them, and sometimes I will feel real pain, because I had long been clinging to them fast.

35

At this point, another and far more perilous form of temptation assails me. Besides the concupiscence of the flesh, which lurks in the delight of the senses and all their pleasures, which they who set themselves far from you serve as slaves, and perish, there is a concupiscence of the soul, present by means of those same bodily senses. It is a vain and curious itch that seeks not to delight the flesh, but to gain new experiences through the flesh, and it drapes itself in the garb of understanding and knowledge. Now, because it comes from the appetite to know, and because for knowledge the eyes are princes among the senses, in the holy discourse it is called the concupiscence of the eyes.[532]

For the proper object of the eyes is to see; and we apply the word to the other senses too when we want to refer to knowledge. After all, we do not say, "Hear how red it is," or, "Smell how white it is," or, "Taste how brightly it glows," or, "Feel how it flashes." All these things are said

---

[532] Cf. 1 Jn 2:15. Augustine is not talking here about visual excitations, but about temptations that entice the mind, that feed a hankering to know, regardless of the goodness or the usefulness of what one wishes to know.

to be *seen*. But we do not only say, "See how it shines," which only the eyes can sense, but also, "See how it sounds," "See how it smells," "See how it tastes," "See how hard it is." So the general experience of the senses is called, as I have said, the concupiscence of the eyes, because the function of seeing, wherein the eyes hold pride of place, is usurped by the other senses by a sort of resemblance, when they are exploring some object of knowledge.

From this consideration, we can more clearly see the difference between the objects of pleasure and of curiosity, both of them coming to us through the senses. Pleasure pursues what is lovely, melodious, sweet-smelling, flavorful, and soft. But curiosity pursues things quite contrary to these, just to try them out, not because it wants to endure the trouble, but because it lusts to experience and to know. What pleasure is it to look at a cadaver torn apart and see what gives you the shudders? Yet whenever such a thing is lying in the street, people race to see it, to be made sad, to blanch with horror. Why, they are afraid they might see it in their dreams, as if someone had forced them to look at it when they were awake, or some rumor of its beauty had enticed them to go! So too with the other senses; it would take a long time to go through them all.

From this morbid hankering we get all those spectacles to gape at in the theater. From it we get people who squint at works of nature that are not beyond our capabilities, but that are of no profit to us if we know them; all they want is to know them, no more. Hence too the practice of magic, if anything can be sought by that warped form of learning. Hence even in religion, God is put to the test, when people demand signs and prodigies, not because they desire something that might save them, but only for the experience.

It is a vast wilderness, full of snares and dangers. And behold, God of my salvation, many of them have I cut away and cast out of my heart, as you have given me the strength to do. Even so, when, when dare I say, while so many things of this sort go humming all around our daily life, when dare I say I have never been held spellbound by one of them, to gaze at it and to catch at it, with idle care? It is true that the theater no longer carries me away, and I take no pains to know the crossings of the stars, nor has my soul ever sought any answers from the shades of the departed; all such sacrilegious rites I detest. My Lord God, to whom I owe my humble and simple service, how many shifts and suggestions does the enemy ply me with, to get me to demand some sign from you![533] But I beseech you, by our King and by our homeland Jerusalem, so single-hearted and chaste, no matter how far I have been from consenting to these suggestions, let it be even farther, and farther! But when I pray to you for the salvation of someone else, the end I seek is much different. Then, in doing what you will, you shall grant me what you will, and you shall grant me, willingly as ever, the grace to follow you.

Nevertheless, who can count all the many petty and contemptible things that try our curiosity every day? Who can tell how often we fall? How often do we put up with someone telling a frivolous tale, at first because we do not want to offend the weak, but then little by little we attend to it with a will? I do not go to the racecourse anymore to watch a dog run after a rabbit, but if, while I am in the countryside and in the middle of serious thought, I chance upon the same sort of hunting, it turns all my attention that way, and I go off the road, not because my horse is compelled to, but because my heart is so inclined. And unless you admonish me straightaway, making me see how weak I am, or rousing me up from that spectacle to think about you, or to scorn the whole thing and pass it by, I gape at it like an empty-headed dolt. And what about when I am at home, and a lizard catching flies or a spider tangling them in her nets will captivate me? Yes, they are little animals, but is it not the same sort of thing? I do go on to praise you, creator of wonders and governor of all things, but that is not why I began to stare at them. It is one thing to get up again quickly, another not to have fallen.

My life is full of such stuff, and my only hope is your abundant mercy. For when our heart has become a catch-basin of things of this

[533] Cf. Mt 16:4: "A wicked and adulterous generation seeks a sign."

sort, when it swarms with troops of vanity, they will often break out and interrupt and disturb our prayers. In your presence, even while we are directing the voice of our heart to reach your ears, a matter of such importance will be cut short by frivolous thoughts that rush in upon us from I do not know where.

36

Shall I reckon this also as something to hold in contempt? Or what shall lead us back into hope, if not your well-known mercy? For you have begun to change us. And you know how much you have changed me, because first of all you healed in me the lust to avenge myself, that you might look graciously upon all my other iniquities, and heal all my infirmities, and ransom my life from corruption, and crown me with pity and mercy, and fill my longing with good things,[534] you who have bridled my pride by godly fear, and who have tamed my neck to your yoke. And now I wear it, and it weighs lightly upon me, as you have promised,[535] as you have made it to be; and so it always was, but I knew nothing of it back when I was afraid to bow beneath it.

But is it true, Lord, you who alone rule as master without arrogance, for you who have no lord are alone Lord,[536] is it true that a third kind of temptation has ceased to assail me, or shall ever cease in this life? It is the desire to be feared or loved by men for no other reason than to get the joy of it, which is not joy at all. What of that? A wretched life, a base sort of boasting. Hence it comes about that we do not love you best of all, and we do not fear you in a pure way, for you resist the proud, but you give grace to the humble;[537] you thunder above the ambitions of the world, and you shake the mountains to their roots.[538]

---

[534] Cf. Ps 103:3–5.
[535] Cf. Mt 11:30.
[536] Cf. Neh 9:6.
[537] Cf. Jas 4:6, Ps 138:6.
[538] Cf. Ps 46:3.

Granted, certain offices of human society make it necessary for one to be loved or feared by men. But then the adversary of our true blessedness steps in, sprinkling, "Well done, well done," in his snares everywhere, so that when we eagerly gather them up, we may be caught unawares. Then we set our joy apart from the truth, and we place it in the deceiving opinions of men, and we delight in being loved and feared not for your sake but instead of you. And that is how the enemy makes people to be like himself, joining him not for the concord of love, but to be consorts in punishment. For he set his seat in the north,[539] so that, as he mimics you in his perverse and twisted way, cold and benighted men might be his slaves.

But we, Lord, are your little weakling flock; take us as your own. Stretch your wings over us and let us fly to our refuge beneath them.[540] Be our glory; let us be loved and feared among ourselves for your sake. If anyone wishes to be praised by men while you reproach him, he will not be defended by men when you judge him, and they will not rescue him when you damn him. Now, suppose we are not dealing with a sinner who is praised in the desires of his soul, or who is blessed for working injustice, but rather a man who is praised for some gift you have given him, and suppose he rejoices more in the praise he gets than in the gift that people praise him for. He too is praised while you reproach him, and the man who praises him is better than he. For the one is pleased by God's gift to a man, while the other is better pleased with a man's gift than with God's.

37

We are tried by these temptations every day, Lord, every day without cease. And the human tongue is the daily furnace where we are tried.[541] In this matter too you command us to be continent: give what

---

[539] Cf. Is 14:13.
[540] Cf. Ps 17:8.
[541] Cf. Prv 27:21.

you command, and command what you will. You know how I have
groaned in the heart and shed streams of tears, praying to you about
it. Nor is it easy for me to tell how well I have been cleansed of this
plague, and much do I fear my secret sins,[542] which your eyes can see
but mine cannot.

For other kinds of temptations, I have some capacity to examine
myself, but for this one, hardly any. I see how near I have come to
being able to restrain my mind from the pleasures of the flesh and from
the curious study of idle things, when I decide to do without them, or
when they are not about. Then I ask myself how much or how little an
annoyance it is to me, not to have them. Or take riches, for example.
People seek them to serve one of the three forms of concupiscence, or
two of them, or all of them at once. If we cannot tell for certain whether
we scorn them while we possess them, we can cast them aside and test
ourselves that way.

But what can we really do with the desire for praise? How can we
test ourselves by going without it? By living a life so wicked, so desperate, and so savage, that everyone who knows us must detest us? Can
anything more insane be uttered or thought? But if praise is ever and
ought to be the comrade of a good life and good works, it is no more
fitting to abandon its fellowship than to abandon the good life itself.
But I cannot tell whether I can take a thing's absence with an easy or an
irritated mind, unless the thing is not there.

What shall I confess to you, Lord, about this kind of temptation?
What else, but that I am delighted by praise, but I am delighted more
by the truth itself. For if I were given a choice, whether to be a raging
madman, someone far gone from the truth in all things and yet praised
by everyone, or to be constant and most assured in the truth but reviled
by everyone, I see what I would choose. Still, I could wish that the
approval I get from someone else's lips did not increase my joy for any

---

[542] Cf. Ps 19:12.

little good I have done. But I confess that it does increase it; not only that, but reproach diminishes it.

And whenever I am troubled by this wretchedness, an excuse steals in to plead for me. You know, O God, what the excuse is worth; I am not sure. For you have demanded of us more than continence, showing us for which things we must pull back on the reins of our love. You have demanded justice too, showing us where we are to bestow that love, and it is your will that we love not only you but our neighbor also. And often I think I delight in my neighbor's good prospects and his having come far, when he understands something well and he delights me with his praise, and, by contrast, I think I am saddened by his deficiency, when I hear him blame what he is ignorant of, or what is good. And sometimes too I am sorry to be praised, when I am praised for something in me that displeases me, or when lesser and slighter goods are esteemed more highly than they ought to be. But how can I really know whether I feel this way because I do not want the man who praises me to differ from my own reckoning of myself, not because I wish to be of profit to him, but because the good things in me that please me are more pleasant to me when they please someone else too? For, in a way, I am not really being praised when the praise is not in accord with my opinion about myself, because then either the objects of praise displease me, or they please me less than other objects do. Am I not then unsure of myself about this?

When I look to you, O Truth, I see that I should be moved by praise not on my own account, but for the good it may do my neighbor. But I do not know whether I am. In this matter I know less about myself than I know about you. I beg of you now, my God, that you will show my own self to me, so that to my brothers who will pray for me I may confess what malady I have discovered within me. Let me once again take great pains to interrogate myself. If it is my neighbor's good that moves me when I am praised, why am I less moved if it is someone else who is unjustly reproved, than if it is I? Why am I stung the more sharply when the slander is flung at me, than when with the same injustice it is flung at someone else, and in my presence? Is this too something I do not know? Or is this my last resort, that I should seduce myself and neither think nor speak the truth in your presence? Put this madness far from me, Lord, lest my own lips become for me the ointment of sinners, to make my head sleek with oil.[543]

38

Needy and poor am I,[544] yet better off while in my secret sighs I displease myself and seek your mercy, till my defect shall be made up and brought to perfection in your peace, which the eye of the arrogant man does not know. For the word that comes from men's lips, and the works they commemorate, have in them a most dangerous temptation from the love of praise, which for a private excellence goes abroad begging for votes. It tempts me even when I rebuke myself for it, for then I may praise myself for the rebuke. And often a man will glory the more in his very contempt for empty glory, so that in the end he cannot be said to glory in his contempt for it at all, since he does not really scorn it if he glories in it.

39

Deep within us, deep within, there is another evil in this sort of temptation, whereby vain men puff themselves up, pleased with themselves though they please no one else, and even displease them, nor do they care to please others anyway. But they who are pleased with themselves are quite displeasing to you. It is not only that they take as good what is not good, but that they take the goods you have given them as if they were their own; or, if they admit that you have given them, they consider them as what they have merited; or if they admit that you have given them freely, they still do not rejoice in them as things to be shared

---

543 Cf. Ps 141:5.
544 Cf. Ps 40:17.

with others, but they are jealous and look at others askance. In all these matters, in the toils and perils of this sort, you see the trembling of my heart, and I feel indeed that I have been wounded, but that you have healed me straightaway.

40

Where have you not walked along with me, O Truth, teaching me what I should beware of and what I should desire, when I have brought before you as well as I could these lower things I have seen, and asked for your counsel? By my outward sense I have taken stock of the world as well as I could, and I have examined the life of my body and these very senses of mine. Then I entered the inner chambers of my memory, many and spacious, and wondrously full of innumerable riches, and I considered it, and was struck with awe, and I could make nothing of it except by your help, and I found that no object in it was you. Nor was I myself—I, the finder, I who went far afield to examine everything, struggling to distinguish one thing from another, and to esteem each one according to its proper worth, taking up some things to question while my senses were dizzy with them, feeling out other things that were mingled with my own self, distinguishing and enumerating the messengers themselves, and then taking stock of the vast storehouse of my memory, drawing some things out, and stowing some things away within—nor was I, while I did so, nor was even the power I used the same as what you are. For you are the ever-abiding light I sought counsel from, as I asked whether these things exist, what they may be, and how we ought to weigh their worth. And you taught me and commanded me, and I heard you.

Often do I do this. It is a delight, and whenever I can relax from necessary work, I take refuge in this pleasure. But in all these things I run through as I seek your counsel, I find no secure place for my soul except in you, where all my scatterings may be gathered up, and where no part of me shall ever fall away from you. And sometimes you open the door for me into a feeling far unlike anything I am accustomed to, a kind of sweetness which, if it were brought to perfection in me, I have no idea what it would be, but this life it would not be. But then I stumble under all the awkward loads I carry on my shoulders, and I am swallowed back into my old ways, and they hold me down, and I weep, and still they hold me fast. What a proper burden habit is! I can be here with the burden, but I do not want to be; I want to be in that other life, but I cannot; so I am wretched both ways.

41

And so I have considered my sins and their infirmity, born of concupiscence in its threefold variety,[545] and I have called upon your right arm to come to my salvation.[546] For with a wounded heart I have seen your splendor, and it has set me reeling, and I said, "Who can ever behold that place?" I have been cast away from your eyes. You are the Truth, presiding over all things. And I, in my greed, did not want to lose you, but along with you I wanted to possess a lie; for no one wants to speak falsely in such a way that he himself will not know what is true. So I lost you, because you do not deign to be possessed along with a lie.

42

Whom could I find to reconcile me to you? Was I to go about pleading with the angels? By what prayer? What sacred rites? Many people, as I hear, who struggle to return to you and who cannot do it on their own, try out such mysteries,[547] and fall into a longing for

---

[545] Cf. 1 Jn 2:16: "The lust of the flesh, and the lust of the eyes, and the pride of life."
[546] Cf. Ps 18:35.
[547] Augustine is thinking here of the Manicheans along with all other peddlers of "mysteries"—that is, secret knowledge imparted in often bizarre rites of religious initiation, most famous among them the so-called Eleusinian mysteries, devoted to the goddesses of grain (Demeter, whose name means "Mother Earth") and the underworld (Persephone). The

peculiar visions, and end up fit for delusion. High and mighty they are, and they seek you by their lofty learning, puffing out their chests rather than beating them in penitence. And, as their hearts are alike, they attract to themselves comrades and fellow conspirators in pride, namely the powers of the air,[548] who take them in by magic forces, all while they were looking for a mediator to purify them, and there was none. For it was the devil, assuming the shape of an angel of light.[549] And what enticed the proud flesh most of all was that he possessed no fleshly body.[550]

They were mortal and sinful, but you, Lord, with whom they wanted to be reconciled, are immortal and sinless. Hence it was fitting that the mediator between God and men should possess something in common with God and something else in common with men.[551] If in both ways he were like men, he would be too far from God, and if in both ways he were like God, he would be too far from men, so he would be no mediator at all. That mediator full of lies,[552] then, by whom in your secret judgment pride deserves to be deluded, has one thing in common with men, that is, sin; and he desires to have something else in common with God, showing himself off as immortal because he is not clothed with mortal flesh. But because the wages of sin is death, he has that too in common with men, as both at once shall be condemned to death.[553]

---

apostate emperor Julian reinstated the mysteries in Rome, and he was himself an initiate.

[548] Eph 2:2. Augustine attributes the mad visions such people pursued—likely by means of a combination of spells and narcotics—to the malevolence of demons that deceived them.

[549] Cf. 2 Cor 11:15.

[550] Note the shrewd point here: carnality can well be manifested as a prideful contempt for the body.

[551] Cf. 1 Tm 2:5, Heb 4:15. Saint Anselm will develop Augustine's insight in his work *Cur Deus homo?* (c. 1095).

[552] Satan; cf. Jn 8:44.

[553] Cf. Rom 6:23, Rv 20:14. Augustine is thinking of the "second death," which is damnation.

43

But the true Mediator, whom in your secret mercy you have shown to men, and whom you sent that they might learn humility from his own example, that Mediator between God and men, the man Christ Jesus, made his appearance between mortal sinners and the just and immortal God; mortal, as men are, and just, as God is. And because the wages of righteousness is life and peace, by the righteousness that joined him with God he rendered null and void the death of the ungodly whom he would make righteous,[554] a death he willed to share with them. He was revealed to the saints of old, that they might be saved by faith in his passion yet to come, as we are saved by faith in his passion that has passed. As man, He is the Mediator; as the Word, he is not midway, for he is equal to God, and God with God, and both together, one God.[555]

How dearly have you loved us, gracious Father, who did not spare your only Son, but gave him up for us, the ungodly![556] And with what a love, that for us he who did not think it robbery to be equal with God was made subject to death, even death on a cross;[557] he alone, free among the dead,[558] having the power to lay down his life and the power to take it up again,[559] for our sakes, the Victor and the Victim unto you; the Victor, because he was the Victim; for our sakes, unto you both priest and sacrifice, the priest, because he was the sacrifice;[560] making us who were slaves into sons for you,[561] by being born from you, and by serving you. Well may I then hold my hope firmly in him, because you will heal all my infirmities[562] through him who sits at your right hand and intercedes for us. Otherwise, I must despair. Many and

---

[554] Cf. Rom 5:6.
[555] Cf. Jn 1:1, Phil 2:6.
[556] Cf. Rom 8:32.
[557] Cf. Phil 2:6.
[558] Cf. Ps 88:5.
[559] Cf. Jn 10:18.
[560] Cf. Heb 9:11–12.
[561] Cf. Gal 4:7.
[562] Cf. Ps 103:3.

great are those infirmities, many and great, but your medicine is more potent. And we might have thought that your Word was too far from any connection with men, and lost all hope for ourselves, but that he was made flesh, and he dwelt among us.[563]

Stricken with trembling for my sins and the heavy load of my misery, I had been restless in my heart and I had thought to flee into the lonely wilderness,[564] but you forbade me, and you gave me strength, saying, "Christ died for all men, so that they who live should live no longer for themselves, but for him who died for all."[565] See, Lord, I cast all my care upon you, that I may live, and ponder the wonders of your law.[566] You know how unskillful I am, and how weak; teach me and make me whole.[567] He, your only Son, in whom are hidden all the treasures of wisdom and knowledge,[568] has redeemed me by his blood.[569] Let the proud not slander me now, as I consider the price of my redemption, as I eat and drink, and give my wealth away, and poor as I am, wish to be filled with Him among those who eat and are satisfied; and they shall praise the Lord, who seek him.[570]

---

[563] Cf. Jn 1:14.
[564] Cf. Ps 11:1.
[565] 2 Cor 5:15.
[566] Cf. Ps 119:18.
[567] Cf. Jn 5:11.
[568] Cf. Col 2:3.
[569] Cf. Eph 1:7.
[570] Cf. Ps 22:26.

BOOK ELEVEN

1

Can it possibly be, Lord, who dwell in eternity, that you are ignorant of what I am saying to you? Or that you must wait for the time to come to see what is happening in time? Why then do I set out for you in order all the things I have recounted? Surely not that you will know them by my means. I do it to rouse up my affection toward you, and the affection of those who read these accounts, so that we may all say together, "Great is the Lord, and greatly to be praised!"[571] For I have said it, and I shall say again, "I do this for the love of your love."

For likewise we pray, and yet Truth says, "Your Father knows what you need, before you ask him for it."[572] Therefore let us lay our affection open before you, confessing to you our miseries and the mercies you have showered upon us, that you may set us wholly free. For you have begun it, so that we may leave off being miserable in ourselves and may be blessed in you. And you have called us, that we may be poor in spirit, and meek, and mournful, and hungering and thirsting for righteousness, and merciful, and clean of heart, and peacemaking.[573] See, I have recounted to you many things, such as I could and would, for you were

---

[571] Ps 145:3.
[572] Mt 6:8.
[573] Cf. Mt 5:3–9.

beforehand in your willing that I confess to you, O Lord my God, for you are good, and your mercy endures forever.[574]

2

But when shall I ever suffice to tell with my pen all your exhortations, all your terrors and consolations, all your directions at the helm, by which you have led me on to preach your word and to dispense your sacrament to your people? And if I can suffice to tell them all in order, the droplets of time are precious to me, and for a long time I have been burning to meditate upon your law,[575] to confess to you my knowledge of it and my poor skill, the first fruits of your enlightening me, and the last leavings of my darkness, until feebleness is swallowed up in strength. I do not want the hours to trickle away in doing something else, whatever hours I may find free of what I need to refresh my body and my sharpness of mind, and free of the service we owe to men, and the service we do not owe, but we give nevertheless.

O Lord my God, pay heed to my prayer, and let your mercy hearken to my desire, in a ferment not for myself alone but for my brothers, that it may be of use to them in charity—and you see in my heart that it is so. I would sacrifice to you the service of my thought and my tongue: give me then what I shall offer to you. For I am needy and poor,[576] and you are rich to all who call upon you, and you who are free from care take care for us. From all rashness and all falsehood, circumcise my inward parts and those outward parts, my lips.[577] Let my chaste delights be your Scriptures, and let me not be deceived in them, or by them deceive others.

Give ear, Lord, and have mercy, O Lord my God, light of the blind, strength of the weak,[578] and at once also light of those who see, and strength of the strong; give ear to my soul and hear it calling from the

---

[574] Cf. Ps 118:1.
[575] Cf. Ps 1:2.
[576] Cf. Ps 40:17.
[577] Cf. Rom 2:29.
[578] Cf. 2 Cor 12:9.

deep.[579] For if your ears are not also in the deep, where shall we go? To whom shall we cry? Yours is the day and yours is the night,[580] and the moments fly past at your bidding. From them, give us a broad space[581] to meditate upon the hidden treasures in your law, nor shut it against us who are knocking.[582]

It was not for nothing that you willed that so many pages of secrets shrouded in shade should be written down, nor shall those forests be without deer that make their retreat there,[583] and refresh themselves, ranging about, and feeding, and lying down to rest, and chewing the cud. Perfect me, Lord, and reveal them to me. Behold, your voice is my joy, your voice, beyond a flood of pleasures. Give me what I love—for I do love, and this love too have you given. Do not forsake your gifts, and spurn not him who thirsts for your green fields.[584] Let me confess to you whatever I shall find in your books, and let me hear the voice of your praises. Let me drink you in, and let me ponder the wonderful things in your law from the very beginning, when you made heaven and earth, unto the everlasting kingdom with you in your holy city.

Lord, have mercy on me and hear what I desire. For I think it is not for the earth, not for gold and silver and precious stones and handsome clothing, or for honors and powerful positions or the pleasures of the flesh, not even for the necessities of the body and this pilgrim life on earth—which shall all be added unto us who seek your kingdom and your righteousness.[585] See, my God, whence comes my desire! The unrighteous used to tell me of their delights, but not as your law does, O Lord. See, whence comes my delight! See, Father; look upon me, see and approve, and in the sight of your mercy may I find grace with you, so that the inner rooms of your word may be opened to me when I knock.

[579] Cf. Ps 130:1.
[580] Cf. Ps 74:16.
[581] Cf. Ps 18:19.
[582] Cf. Mt 7:7.
[583] Cf. Ps 42:1.
[584] Cf. Ps 23:2.
[585] Cf. Mt 6:32–33.

I beg it of you by our Lord Jesus Christ your Son, that man of your right hand,[586] the Son of Man, whom you have confirmed as the mediator between you and us, through whom you sought us when we were not seeking you,[587] and sought so that we might seek you, your Word through whom all things were made,[588] and I among them; your only Son, by whom you called into your adoption the whole nation of believers,[589] among whom am I; I beg you, by him who sits at your right hand and intercedes for us,[590] in whom are hidden all the treasures of wisdom and knowledge.[591] Those do I seek in your books. Moses has written of him. He himself says it: Truth says it.

3

Let me hear and understand how in the beginning you made heaven and earth.[592] Moses wrote this, he wrote it and he passed away, he

---

[586] Cf. Ps 80:17.

[587] Cf. Is 65:1. God's grace is always first: he does not wait for us to seek him, let alone to find him. It is his gift to us that we seek him at all.

[588] Cf. Jn 1:3.

[589] Cf. 1 Pt 2:9–10.

[590] Cf. Rom 8:34.

[591] Cf. Col 2:3. One of the most powerful and, for us, striking names for Christ, in the writings and the sermons of the Fathers, is simply "Truth." They mean more than that Christ speaks the truth. He is, personally, substantially, fully, the Truth.

[592] Cf. Gn 1:1. We must not suppose that, since Augustine is finished with the biographical portion of his work, he is now free to engage in theological speculation. From the beginning, he has been meditating on what it means for God, the eternal God who has redeemed him from his sins in time, to be the Creator, the providential Ordainer, and the consummation of all the things he has made. All things come from God, all are guided by him, and all, according to their kinds, according to the laws of their being, return to him. We should note, too, that Augustine takes for granted that profound mysteries are hidden in those simple words in Genesis. There is no question here of a naive and purely literal reading, for Moses himself, whatever he intended by those words, intended more than meets the eye on the surface. Besides, the true author is not Moses but God, by whose providence and inspiration Moses may have said far more than even he intended; indeed, if we believe that the Scripture is sacred, we may be guided by such historical concerns but we must not permit ourselves to be limited by them. God is above history, and therefore he is above the understanding and the intentions of human beings bound to their history.

passed hence from you to you, and he is not here before me now. If he were, I would take hold of him and plead to him and in your name beseech him to make these things plain to me. I would present the ears of my body to the sounds bursting from his lips, and if he spoke in the Hebrew tongue, he would knock against my sense to no avail, and not a thing could proceed from there to touch my mind. But if he spoke in Latin, I would know what he was saying. But how would I know whether he was speaking the truth? And if I did come to know this too, would I have to know it from him? No, for deep within me, deep in the dwelling place of thought, Truth, which is neither Hebrew nor Greek nor Latin nor any strange language, would speak without lips and the organs of speech, without the sounding of syllables, saying, "He speaks the truth." Then at once, assured and confident, I would say to that man of yours, "You do speak the truth."

Since, then, I cannot put my questions to him, I beg you, Truth, with whom he was filled when he uttered true things, I beg you, my God, to pardon my sins, and as you once gave your servant the power to say these things, give to me also the power to understand them.

4

Behold, heaven and earth exist, and they cry out that they have been made; for they are changed and they vary from what they were. For anything that exists and that has *not* been made has nothing within it that was not there before. But to have something that was not there before is just what it means to be changed and to vary. They cry out also that they have not made themselves: "We exist insofar as we were made. Therefore, we did not exist before we came to be, such that we might have made ourselves." And the voice of the creatures that say so is its own proof.[593]

---

[593] If a thing is subject to change, it cannot account for its own existence, and that includes a whole universe of such things. Then it must have been *made*, directly or indirectly through mediating causes. It cannot have come from nothing. That law, that nothing comes from

Then it was you, Lord, who made them, you who are beautiful, for they are beautiful; you who are good, for they are good; you who are, for they are. Yet they are not beautiful or good in the way you their Creator are, nor do they exist as you exist, for as compared with you, they are neither beautiful nor good, nor do they exist at all. It is thanks to you that we know these things, and our knowledge compared with your knowledge is mere ignorance.

5

But how did you make heaven and earth, and what was your instrument for this grand architecture of yours? You were not like a human craftsman, who shapes one body from another body, at the discretion of his soul, which peers into itself by its internal eye and finds there a figure that it can in some way impose upon the object—and where would the soul get the power to do that, except that it was you who made it? And it imposes that figure on a thing already existing and possessing the means to continue so, such as earth or stone or wood or gold or the like. And whence did these materials come to be, save that you have established them? You made the craftsman's body, you made his soul that commands his members, you made the matter he makes his works from, you made the inborn intelligence whereby he takes hold of his art and sees within what he shall make without, you made the bodily senses he uses as interpreters to convey from his mind to the material what he is making, and to report back to the mind what he has made, so that he may consult the truth that presides within him, as to whether he has made it well.

All these things praise you, Creator of all things. But how do you make them? How did you make heaven and earth, O God? Surely it

---

nothing, was not preached first by Christians or Jews, but by the early materialist philosophers themselves, such as Democritus (c.460–c.370 BC). They supposed that atoms—literally, objects that cannot be divided—made up all things and were themselves perpetually existent and indestructible. Modern physics has given atomists the lie, though for what I suspect are mainly social reasons, physicists are often shy of drawing the conclusion that the universe must therefore have been set into existence by the self-existent God.

was not in heaven or earth that you made heaven and earth, nor in the air or the waters, for these things belong to heaven and earth, nor was it in the whole universe that you made the whole universe, because there was no place yet where it might be made, before it was made so that such a "where" might exist.[594] Nor did you take any tool in hand, to make heaven and earth, for where would you get this thing you had not made, so that you might make something else? What can be, unless you are? Therefore, you spoke and they were made, and it was in your Word[595] that you made them.

6

But how did you speak? Was it the same way as when the voice came from the cloud, saying, "This is my beloved Son"?[596] For that voice was in act and then it was done, begun and completed. Syllables sounded and passed away, the second after the first, the third after the second, and so on in order, until the last came after all the rest, and then silence. It shines out in plain sight, then, that the motion of a created thing expressed that voice, serving your eternal will, though it was itself a creature in time. And the outward ear announced these words of yours, fit for the time, to the provident mind whose inward ear was listening for your eternal Word. But that inward ear compared these words sounding in time with your Word in eternal silence, and said, "This Word is far other, far other is it. These words are far beneath me, rather they *are not*, because they fly and pass away. But the Word of God above me abides forever."[597]

---

[594] An important point, anticipating modern physics by 1500 years. We must not think of "place" and "time" as already existent but empty receptacles waiting for God to fill them. Space and time are both features of the created universe, and God was not dependent upon them, no more than he was dependent upon some already existent but unformed matter.
[595] Cf. Jn 1:3.
[596] Mt 3:17.
[597] Cf. Is 40:8, 1 Pt 1:25.

If, then, you spoke in words that make a sound and pass away, when you said that heaven and earth should be, and if that is how you made heaven and earth, then there would have been a corporeal creature before heaven and earth, by whose temporal movements that voice could have run its course in time. But there was no corporeal thing before heaven and earth, and even if there were, you surely must have made it a thing without a voice that passes away, so that you could then make a voice that passes away, the voice you would have used when you said that heaven and earth should be made. And what could that thing be, for making such a sound? Had you not made it, it would not exist at all. Well then, what word did you speak, to make the corporeal thing these other words would come from?

7

That is how you call us to understand the Word, God who is God with you, the Word spoken from eternity, in whom from eternity all things are spoken.[598] It is not, in the Word, that what was spoken came to an end, and then came something else, so that all things might eventually be spoken; but all things were spoken at once and from eternity.[599] Had it not been so, there would have been time and change, and no true eternity, no true immortality.

I understand this, my God, and I give you thanks. I understand this, I confess, my Lord God, and whoever is not thankless for the assured truth understands it with me and blesses you for it. For we know, Lord, we know that insofar as a thing is not what it was, and is what it was not, it dies and it rises. Nothing in your Word, then,

---

[598] Cf. Jn 1:1–3.

[599] God's creation of the world is an eternal act: we are not to think of God as doing something first, and then doing something else, even though the things he does make themselves manifest in time, in a series of events. Eternity, too, is not the same as perpetual duration in time, either backwards or forwards or both. Whatever exists in time is subject to change. For a fuller development of this line of thought, see Boethius, *The Consolation of Philosophy*, Book 5.

recedes and proceeds, because it is truly immortal and eternal. And so you speak all the things you speak, at once and eternally in your Word that is coeternal with you, and whatever you speak that it might be, comes to be. Nor do you make in any other way than by speaking it. Still, the things you make by speaking do not all come to be at once and forever.

8

Why, I ask, O Lord, my God, is it so? Somehow I see it, but I do not know how to put it in words. Thus, perhaps: Whatever begins to be and ceases to be, begins just at the time and ceases just at the time it must, as is known in your eternal reason, where nothing begins and nothing ceases. Now, this reason is your very Word, which is also the beginning, because he speaks to us too. Thus in the gospel he speaks by means of the flesh, and it resounded outwardly in the ears of men, that it might be believed and sought for within, and found there in eternal truth, where that good and only Master teaches all his disciples.

There I hear your voice, Lord, speaking to me. For he who teaches us speaks to us, but he who does not teach us is not speaking to us, even if he does speak. Now then, who teaches us but the ever-standing Truth? Even when he warns us by means of a changeable created thing, we are led to the Truth ever-standing, where we truly do learn, when we stand and hear him, and we rejoice with the joy of the bride who hears the bridegroom's voice,[600] which returns us to the place from which we came. Hence he is the Beginning, and unless he abides forever, there would be nowhere for us to return to when we go astray. But when we return from our error, it is by knowing that we are returning, and that we may know, he teaches us, for he is the Beginning and he speaks to us.

---

[600] Cf. Sg 2:8–10.

9

In this beginning, O God, you made heaven and earth, in your Word, your Son, your Power, your Wisdom, your Truth,[601] wondrously speaking, wondrously creating. Who can comprehend it? Who can tell of it? What is it that shines right through me and batters my heart without a bruise? I shudder, I am all afire; I shudder, inasmuch as I am not like it; I am all afire, inasmuch as I am like it. Wisdom, wisdom it is, which shines into me, shredding that cloud of mine that shrouds me again as I faint away under the smoke and heavy sludge of my punishment. For my vigor is made so feeble in my need, I cannot bear even what is good for me, until you, Lord, who have been gracious to all my iniquities, should go on to heal all the diseases that make me weak. For you shall redeem my life from corruption and crown me with mercy and lovingkindness, and you shall fill my longing with good things, and my youth shall be made new, like the eagle's.[602] For in hope we are saved,[603] and in patience we await what you have promised.[604] Let him who can do so, listen to you discoursing within him, while in confidence I shall proclaim the words of your oracle: "How magnificent are your works, O Lord! In wisdom you have made all things!"[605] And this Wisdom is the beginning, and in this beginning you made heaven and earth.

10

Are they not full of their own rickety old age, who say to us, "What was God doing before He made heaven and earth?"[606] If he lay about doing nothing, they say, why not keep it up from this point on and forever,

---

[601] Cf. 1 Cor 1:24.

[602] Cf. Ps 103:3–5.

[603] Cf. Rom 8:24.

[604] Cf. Jas 5:7–8.

[605] Ps 104:24.

[606] Again, there is no "before" or "after" in God. If there were, then time would be, in essence, "before" or alongside God, independent of him. Then he would not be truly eternal, and thus not truly God.

just as he had abstained from work before? For if some new motion came forth in God, some new will to fashion a created world he had never fashioned before, how can we be talking about a genuine eternity? For a will must have arisen that had not existed before. For the will of God is not a created thing, but is before any creature, because nothing can be created if the will of the Creator does not come first. Now, the will of God belongs to his very essence. But if something springs up in the essence of God that was not there from before, his essence cannot genuinely be said to be eternal. But if God's will to create was from everlasting, why is the creation not also everlasting?

11

Those who talk this way do not yet understand you, O Wisdom of God, light of all minds. They do not yet understand how those things are made which are made by you and in you. They struggle to know eternal things, but their heart still flutters between the past and future motions of things, to no avail.

Who shall hold fast this heart of man, and fix it in place, that it may stand still a little while, and catch a little of the splendor of eternity ever-standing, and compare it with times that never stand still, and see how it cannot be compared with them at all? That it may see that time can be long only by the coming and passing away of many motions, which cannot all be drawn out at one same time? That therefore there is no coming and going in eternity, but the whole is present all at once? That no time is wholly present all at once? That it may see that every past time is driven along by the time to come, and every time to come follows upon time past, and that all past and future time is created and begins its course from that which is present ever? Who will hold fast the heart of man, that it may stand and see how eternity that is neither future nor past stands and decrees the times that are future and past? Can my hand do it? Can the hand of my mouth do it, telling in little words of a work so grand?

12

See now, I shall respond to the man who says, "What was God doing before he made heaven and earth?" I will not respond as someone is said to have done, in jest, to elude the force of the question. "He was getting a hell ready," he said, "for people trying to pry into the deeps." It is one thing to see, another to mock. I will not respond so. I prefer to respond, "I do not know," if I do not know, rather than to say what will make him who sought after deep things a butt of mockery, while he who gave a false answer is praised.

Instead, I say that you, our God, are the creator of every creature, and if we are to understand by "heaven and earth" every created thing, then I make bold to say that before God made heaven and earth, he did not make anything. For if he did make something, what would it be but a created thing? If only I knew whatever I wish for my profit to know, as well as I know that no creature was made before any creature was made!

13

Now if any mind flitting here and there should go roving over the images of backward time, wondering that you, God the almighty, all-creating, all-upholding, should through innumerable ages have refrained from so great a work before you made it, let him wake up and pay attention, because he is wondering at things that are simply false. Where could those innumerable ages have come from, when you yourself had not made them yet, since you are the founder and creator of all ages? What times could ever exist, unless you had set them in place? How could they have passed by, if they did not exist? Since, then, you are the fashioner of all times, if there was any time before you made heaven and earth, how can it be said that you were resting from work? For you would have made that same time, nor can any times pass by before you have made times at all. But if there was no time before heaven and earth, why should we bother to ask what you were doing then? For there was no *then*, when there was no time.

It is not by time that you precede the times; else you would not precede all times. But you precede all past times by the loftiness of your ever-present eternity, and you surpass all future times, because they are future, and when they have come, they will have passed; but you are ever the self-same, and your years shall not fail.[607] Your years do not come and go, but these years of ours do come and go, that all years may come. Your years stand all together, because they do *stand*; nor do years arriving push years on their way out, because they do not pass at all. But our years shall all be, only when all our years shall be no more. Your years are one day, and your day is not *each* day, but *the today*; because your today does not yield to tomorrow, just as it did not succeed upon yesterday. Your today is eternity: therefore you begot the Coeternal one, to whom you said, "This day I have begotten you."[608] You made all times and before all times you are: nor was there any particular *time* when time was not.

14

So then, there was no time in which you were not making anything, because time itself is something you have made. And no times are coeternal with you, who abide the Selfsame; and if they could so abide, they would not be times.

What then is time? Who can explain it, quickly and easily? Who can even grasp it in thought, let alone find the words to express it? But what in our common speech do we make more familiar mention of than time? And surely, we do understand it when we speak of it, and we understand it likewise when we hear someone else do the same.

What then is time? If nobody asks me, I know what it is. If I want to explain it to somebody who asks me, I do not know. But I can say

---

[607] Cf. Ps 102:27.
[608] Cf. Ps 2:7, Mk 1:9–11, Heb 5:5.

with confidence that I know this: If nothing should pass by, there would be no past time, and if nothing were coming to be, there would be no future time, and if nothing existed at all, there would be no present time. Take then those two times, the past and the future. How can they *be*, when the past no longer exists and the future does not yet exist? As for the present, if it were always present and did not pass on into the past, it would not be a present time, but eternity. If then the present, in order to be a time, comes to *be* only insofar as it passes away, how can we say that even this time *is*? For its cause of being is that it shall *not be*. Is it then that we can only say, in truth, that time *is*, because it tends *not to be*?

15

And yet we talk about a "long time" and a "short time," and only when we are talking about the past or the future. A hundred years ago, for example, we call a long time past, and in the same way, a hundred years in the future we call a long time to come. Likewise, we might call ten days ago a short time past, and ten days in the future a short time to come. But in what sense can it be short or long, when it is not *in being*? For the past is now no more, and the future is not yet. Then we should not say, "It *is* a long time." We should say of the past, "It *was* long," and of the future, "It *shall be* long."

My Lord, my Light, shall not your truth here also laugh at man? That long time past—was it long once it had gone into the past, or was it so before then, while it was still present? For it could be long when there *was* something to it that admitted of length. But when it had gone into the past, it no longer *was*. So then it could not *be* long in the past, because it had no *being* at all. Then let us not say, "The time past was long," for we cannot find anything that was long, since, once it has gone into the past, it has ceased to be. Let us say instead, "That time was long when it was present," because so long as it was present, it was long. For it had not yet passed into nonexistence, and there was something to it that admitted of length. But as soon as it had gone into the past, it ceased to be long, because it ceased to be.

Let us see, then, soul of man, whether the present time can be long. For it has been granted to you to sense and to measure the durations of time. How shall you answer me? Are a hundred present years a long time? But first you must see whether there can even be a hundred *present* years. For if the first of those years is now in play, then it is present, and the ninety-nine are in the future, and do not yet exist. If the second year is in play, then the first is past, the second is present, and the others are still to come. Take any year from the middle of this number, and let it be present; the others before it are past, and those after it are in the future. Therefore a hundred years cannot all be present.

Now see, at least, whether the single year ongoing can be present. For if the first month is in play, the others are still to come, and if the second, then the first is past and the others do not yet exist. Thus it is that even a year now in play cannot all be present, and if it is not all present, then the year is not present. There are twelve months to a year, and if you take any one month from it and let it be present, the others must be either past or future. Yet that single month in play is not present, but only a single day of it. If it is the first day, then the others are in the future; if the last, then the rest are past; if a day in the middle, then it will lie between the past days and the future days.

Look how the present time, which alone we found worthy of being called "long," has been contracted to the length of scarce one day. But let us take that day apart too. For not even the whole of one day can be *present*. It is made up of twenty-four hours of day and night. The first hour has all the rest to come; the last has all the rest gone before; and any of the hours set in between has the hours before it in the past, and the hours after it in the future. And that same hour runs its course in moments that fly away; those that have flown are past, and those that remain are future. If we can grasp some measure of time that cannot be divided into parts no matter how tiny, it alone is fit to be called *present*. And yet it flies off so quickly into the past, it cannot be extended by the slightest duration. For if it were extended, it could be divided into past and future. The present takes up no space.

Then where is this time we may call "long"? In the future? Surely we do not say, "It *is* long," because what is supposed to be long does not yet exist. Rather we say, "It *will be* long." So then, when will it be? If even in a future time it is yet to come, it will not be "long" then, because what is supposed to have length will not yet exist. But if we say that it will be "long" when it comes out of the future that does not yet exist, and it begins to exist and is present, then the present time cries out against us in what I have said above, saying that it is impossible for any present time to be long.[609]

16

Nevertheless, Lord, we do sense intervals of time, and we compare them with one another, saying that some are longer and some are shorter. We also measure how much longer or shorter one time is than another, and we say it is twice as long or three times as long or only just as long. Now then, it is times passing by that we measure, and we measure them by perceiving them. But who can measure times past, which no longer exist, or times to come, which do not yet exist? Dare anyone say that something which does not exist can be measured? Therefore, while time is passing, it can be perceived and measured, but once it has passed, it cannot be measured, because it does not exist.

---

[609] If nothing but the present exists, supposing that the past no longer is and the future has not yet come to be, and if the present time is infinitesimal, how can we speak reasonably about the perduring existence of anything? Heraclitus (fl. c. 500 BC), struck by the phenomenon of ceaseless change, is reported to have said that you cannot step into the same river twice; and so he taught that the fundamental principle of the cosmos is fire. But if we believe that things do retain their identity despite change and time, where shall we "locate" such an identity, since the present time is insufficient for it, and since material change is ceaseless? Again, merely material attempts to describe the identity fail.

17

Father, I am asking, not affirming; my God, govern me and steer my ways.[610] Who shall dare say to me that there are not three times, as we learned when we were boys, and as we taught to other boys, the past, the present, and the future, but only the present, because the other two do not exist? Or do they really exist, but the future leaves some secret dwelling when it becomes the present, and the present returns to some secret dwelling when it becomes the past? Those who sang of things to come—where did they see them, if such things do not yet exist? For what does not exist cannot be seen. And those who tell the stories of the past would not be telling them truly unless they could discern them in the mind. But if these things were nothing at all, they could never be discerned. Hence, the future and the past do exist.

18

Permit me, O Lord my hope, to inquire more deeply, and let not my effort be disturbed. If the future and the past exist, I wish to know *where* they may be. But if I do not yet have the strength for it, I still know that wherever they are, they are not there as future or past, but as present. For if even there they are future, they cannot yet *be* there, and if even there they are past, they no longer *are* there. Then wherever they are, whatever they are, they cannot exist except as present. Whenever we tell true stories of things past, we bring from the memory not the things themselves, which have passed away, but words conceived by their images. These images impress, as they pass through the senses, their footprints in the mind. For example, my boyhood, which no longer exists, is in past time, which no longer exists, and yet its image, when I recall it and tell of it, I behold in the present time, because it still exists in my memory.

---

[610] Cf. Ps 32:8.

Whether a like cause applies for those who foretell things to come, that they sense beforehand the presently existing images of things that do not yet exist, I confess, my God, I do not know. This I do know for certain, that we often meditate on our actions beforehand, and that this premeditation is present, but the action we premeditate does not yet exist, because it is future. But when we have taken the first steps and begun to do what we have premeditated, then the action will exist, because then it will not be future, but present.

No matter how the secret fore-sensing of future things may come about, a thing cannot be seen unless it does exist. But what already exists is not future, but present. Therefore, when it seems that people foretell the future, they do not see the things themselves which do not yet exist, that is, the future things, but their causes or perhaps their signs, which do already exist. Then it is not things future but things present that they see, and from them they foretell what they have conceived in the mind. Those conceptions too are present, and those who foretell the future are looking into things that are right there in front of them.

The sheer number of such predictions can give me an example. I look upon the light of dawn, and I foretell that the sun is about to rise. What I am looking at is present, and what I am foretelling is future; not the sun, which now is, but its rising, which is not yet. But unless I could form an image in my mind of its rising, as I am doing right now while I am speaking of it, I could never foretell it. But the dawning light I see in the sky is not itself the sunrise, though it does precede it, nor is the image I form in my mind; but the two are seen now in the present, so that the future sunrise can be foretold. Future things, therefore, do not *yet* exist, and since that is so, they do not *exist*, and since that is so, *they* cannot be seen at all. But they can be foretold by present things that now exist and can be seen.

19

Tell me then, you who govern your creation, in what manner you teach souls the things that are to come? For you did teach your prophets. In what manner do you teach the future, when nothing is future to you? Or is it rather that you teach them present things that have to do with the future? For surely what is not, cannot be taught. This way of yours is too far from my ken, it is too mighty;[611] of my own I cannot attain it; but by your power I can, when you grant that I may, you the sweet light of my soul's secret eyes.[612]

20

In any case, it is now as clear as day that neither future things nor past things exist, nor do we properly say that there are three times, the past, the present, and the future. But perhaps we can properly say that there are three times: the present of things past, the present of things present, and the present of things future. For three things of this sort are in the soul, and I see them nowhere else: a present memory of past things, a present beholding of present things, and a present expectation of future things. If we are permitted to speak in this sense, then I see three times, and I confess that they are three. Let it be said, too, that there are three times, past, present, and future, as custom misuses the words. So let it be said. I do not trouble myself about it, I will not resist it or blame it, so long as we understand what we are saying, and not that what is to come exists now, or what is past. Few are the things we speak of in a proper sense; many are those we speak of improperly, and yet we still understand what we mean.

---

[611] Cf. Ps 131:1.
[612] Cf. Eccl 11:7.

21

I said a little while ago that we measure times as they pass by, and we can say that this time is twice as long as that, or this is just as long as that, and so too with anything else we might say of portions of time as we measure them. Therefore, as I said, we measure times passing by, and should someone ask me how I know this, I would say, I know it because in fact we do measure, nor can we measure things that do not exist; and past and future things do not exist. As for the present time, how can we measure it, since it takes up no space? It must be measured, then, as it passes by, because when it is gone, it is not measured; because there will be nothing to be measured.

But where does it come from, what way does it take, and where does it go, while it is being measured? Whence, but from the future? What way, but through the present? Where to, but into the past? What then? *From* what does not yet exist, *through* what has no extension, and *into* what exists no longer. But what are we measuring, if not time, in some sort of extended space? For we do not say, when we are speaking about time, it is single or double or triple or equal or whatever else of this sort, unless we are speaking of temporal extent. In what extended space, then, do we measure time as it passes? In the future from which it comes? But we cannot measure what does not yet exist. In the present through which it is passing? But we cannot measure what has no extent. In the past, where it is going? But we cannot measure what no longer exists.

22

My soul is all on fire to solve this most intricate riddle. Do not shut, O Lord my God, gracious Father, I beg you in the name of Christ, do not shut from my desire these commonly used and yet secret things, do not hinder it from entering their inner chamber; but let them shine out to me, Lord, by your mercy that shines upon them. From whom can I demand an answer about these matters? To whom shall I more profitably confess my clumsiness than to you? For you do not find it bothersome, this burning passion of mine to study your Scriptures.

Give me what I love: for I do love, and you have given me this love. Give, Father, who truly know to give good gifts to your children,[613] give, because I have undertaken to understand; and heavy labor is upon me, until you shall open the door. In the name of Christ, I beg you, in the name of that Holy of Holies,[614] let no man shout me down. I have believed, and that is why I am speaking. This is my hope, for this I live, that I may gaze upon the beauty of the Lord.[615] Behold, you have made my days old, and they pass away, I do not know how.[616]

And we talk of time and time, and times and times: "How long has it been since he said this?" "How long since he did that?" "This long syllable takes twice as long as that short simple syllable." We say these things, we hear them, we are understood, and we understand. As plain as day they are, and we use them all the time. But these same things hide in the depths, and their discovery is new.

23

I once heard a learned man say that the movements of the sun and moon and stars are what times are, but I did not nod in agreement.[617] Why those alone? Why not rather the motions of all bodily things? Really, now, if the lights of heaven should cease, but a potter's wheel kept turning, would time not exist, time for measuring those rotations? Would we not say that it was moving with the same small lapses of time, sometimes more slowly, sometimes more quickly, some longer "days," and some shorter? And even while we were saying so, would we

---

[613] Cf. Mt 7:11.
[614] Cf. Heb 9:11–12.
[615] Cf. .Ps 27:4.
[616] Cf. Ps 39:5.
[617] Another crucial point, and one that dethrones the heavenly bodies from any position of divinity. The sun and moon and stars are, as regards their creaturely nature, no other than a potter's wheel or the clay the potter shapes.

not also be speaking in time? How could there be in our words some long syllables and some short ones, unless the longer ones took more time to sound, and the shorter ones less? Give to men, O God, the intelligence to see in a little thing the common intelligible features of little and great things both. The stars and the luminaries of heaven are for signs and seasons and days and years.[618] So they are; but I would never say that the circuit of that little wooden wheel was a day, nor should that learned man say that time must therefore not exist at all.

But I wish to know the force and the nature of time, whereby we measure the motions of bodies, and we say, for example, that one motion is twice as long as another. Here is one thing I ask. We call by "day" not just the stay of the sun above the earth, whereby day is one thing and night another, but the whole complete circuit from dawn to dawn in the east, and so we say, "These many days have gone by." For we reckon complete days along with their nights, and do not set the space of the nights to the side. Well, since one day is made complete by the motion of the sun and its circuit from east to east, I ask, "Is that motion itself what a day is, or how long it takes to complete the motion, or both at once?"

If the first is what a day is, then it would be a day even if the sun completed its round in but a single hour. If the second, then it would not be one day if from one sunrise to the next took only one hour, but the sun would have to go round twenty-four times to make up one day. If both at once, then we could not give it the name of "day" if the sun went round its whole revolution in the space of an hour, nor if the sun stood still while as much time passed by as it usually takes for it to make the round from morning to morning.

Therefore I will not ask what it is we call a "day," but what time is, whereby we measure the circuit of the sun and we might say that it had gone through it in half the usual time, if it had gone through it in the space that twelve hours takes up; and when we compare the times and

---

[618] Cf. Gn 1:14.

say that this is one stretch, and this other is twice that, if the sun ran its course from east to east sometimes with the one stretch and sometimes with the other. Let no one tell me then that the motions of the heavenly bodies constitute the times, for at the prayer of a certain man the sun stood still, that he might complete his victory in battle.[619] The sun stood, but time went on, went on for its own span, enough so that the battle might be waged and fought to the finish. Therefore, I see that time is a kind of distension. But do I see it? Or do I merely seem to see it? You, O Light, O Truth, shall show it to me.

24

Do you command me to agree, if someone says that time is the motion of a body? You do not. For I hear that no body can be moved unless it is moved in time. You say so. But I do not hear that this same motion of the body is what time is. You do not say so. For when a body is moved, I measure by time how long it is moved, from when it begins in motion to when it stops. And if I have not seen when it began to move, and if it keeps on moving so that I do not see when it stops, I am not able to measure the time, unless perhaps I measure it from when I first see it to when I stop seeing it. And if I take a long time looking at it, I can say only that it was a long time, but not how long it was, because whenever we talk about that, we do so by comparison, as, "This took as long as that," or "This took twice as long as that," or something else of the sort. But if we can make note of the distance between where the moving body or its parts comes from and where it is going, as if it were moved on a lathe, we can say how much time it takes the body or a part of it to go from this place to that place.

Since, then, the motion of a body is one thing, but the thing we measure it by is something else, who can fail to see which of the two ought rather to go by the name of "time"? For if a body is various in its movements, sometimes standing still, we measure not only its motion

---

[619] Joshua, in the vale of Ajalon; cf. Jos 10:12–14.

but its standing, and we say, "It stood still for just as long as it moved," or, "It stood still twice as long or three times as long as it moved," or any other extent our measuring can grasp or guess at, when we talk about more and less. Therefore, time is not the motion of a body.

25

And I confess to you, Lord, that I still do not know what time is, and yet again I confess to you, Lord, that I know I am saying these things in time, and that I have long been speaking about time, and that this "long" cannot be long unless by some span of time. How, then, can I know this, when I do not even know what time is? Or is it that I do not know how to express what I do know in fact? Ah me, I do not even know what it is that I do not know! Behold, my God, you see before you that I am telling no lie: I speak what is in my heart. You, you shall light my lamp, O Lord my God, you shall enlighten my darkness.[620]

26

Does not my soul confess to you, telling the truth in confession, that I do measure times? So it is, O Lord my God. I measure, and I do not know what it is I am measuring. I measure the motion of a body by time. Do I not then also measure the time? Can I really measure the motion of a body, how long it has been, how long it takes to go from here to there, unless I am also measuring the time in which it moves? What then can I use to measure time? Do we measure a longer span of time by some shorter unit, as we measure the length of a crossbeam by the cubit? That is how it seems we measure the extent of a long syllable, saying that it is twice the extent of a short syllable. So too we measure the stanzas of a poem by the verses in each stanza, and we measure the verses by their feet, and the feet by the syllables, and the long syllables by the short syllables. I am not talking about how they look on the

---

[620] Cf. Ps 119:105.

page, for then we would be measuring spaces, not times. I mean when we utter the sounds and they pass by, so we say, "This song is lengthy, because it is composed of so many verses," and, "These verses are long, because they consist of so many feet," and, "These feet are long, because they are stretched out into so many syllables," and, "This syllable is long, because it is twice what a short syllable is."[621]

But that still does not give us a grasp on a sure measure of time. For it may happen that a shortish verse may be sounded out over a longer time, if we drawl it as we pronounce it, than a longish verse, if we hurry it up. So with a poem, a foot,[622] a syllable. That is why it seems to me that time is nothing else but a certain distension. A distension of what, I do not know—and I wonder if it is not of the mind itself. My God, I beg you—what do I measure, when I say, vaguely, that this time is longer than that, or, precisely, that this time is twice as long as that? I am measuring time, I know. But I am not measuring the future, which does not yet exist, I am not measuring the present, which has no extent, and I am not measuring the past, because it no longer exists. What then am I measuring? Times as they are passing, and not times past? That was what I had said.

27

Stand firm, my mind, and attend with all your strength. God is our help; he made us, and not we ourselves.[623] Attend and see where truth begins to dawn. Look at the matter thus. The voice of a bodily thing begins to sound, it continues to sound, and so it goes on until it stops, and then there is silence, and the voice is past, and is a voice no more.

---

[621] In Latin and Greek quantitative verse, two short syllables were considered to make up exactly one long syllable, taking up the same time to pronounce, as in western music two half-notes make up one whole note. A long syllable possessed a long vowel or a diphthong, or a short vowel followed by two consonants.

[622] Greek and Latin verses were made up of "feet," each with a specified pattern of long and short syllables.

[623] Cf. Ps 100:3.

It was a future thing before it began to sound, and it could not be measured because it did not yet exist. Nor can it be measured now, because it no longer exists. While it was sounding, then, it could be measured, because something existed that could be measured. But even then it was not standing still, for it was coming on and passing by. Did that passing by make it more apt for being measured? For while it was passing by, it was being stretched out along a certain extent of time, whereby it might be measured; for the present has no extent.

Now, if we say that it could be measured then, let us change the terms, and suppose that another voice has begun to sound and continues to sound without any interruption. Let us measure it while it is sounding, for as soon as it ceases to sound, it will have passed by, and there will no longer be anything to measure. Let us then measure it, plain and simple, and say how long it is. But it is still sounding, and it can be measured only from the point when it began to sound to the point when it stops. That interval is what we measure, from some initial point to some end. And for that reason, a voice that never does end cannot be measured, so that we can say how long or short it is, or that it is equal in length with another, or twice as long, or three times, or whatever. But when it does come to an end, it will have ceased to be. How then can it be measured? And yet we do measure times; not those times which do not yet exist, nor those which do not exist any longer, nor those which are not stretched out over any extent, nor those that have no boundaries. So we do not measure future or past or present or passing times, and yet we do measure times.

O God, Creator of all things! That very verse of eight syllables, *Deus Creator omnium,*[624] alternates between short and long syllables. Four of them—the first, the third, the fifth, and the seventh—are single, by comparison with the four long syllables—the second, the fourth, the sixth, and the eighth, each of which takes double the time as does each of the first. I pronounce them over and over, and so it is, as plain and

---

[624] The first line of Saint Ambrose's hymn; see Book 9, ch. 12.

clear as sense can show it. As far as sense can show, I measure the long syllable by the short and I see that it has twice the length. But when one syllable sounds after the other, if the first is short and the second is long, how do I hold on to the short one, how shall I apply it to the long one in order to do my measuring, so that I can say that the long is twice the short, when the long syllable does not begin to sound until the short syllable has ceased? And can I even measure that long syllable while it is present, since I measure it only when it has been completed? For its completion is its passing away.

Then what is it I am measuring? Where is the short syllable I used as a unit of measurement? Where is the long syllable I am to measure? Both have sounded, have flown off, have passed on, and are now no more. Yet I reply with firm conviction that I do measure them, insofar as we may rely on a well-exercised sense, and I say that this is single and that is double, that is, in their temporal extent. And I could not do this unless they had passed on and come to their end. Hence, I do not measure the things themselves, which no longer exist, but something in my memory that abides and holds fast.

It is in you, my mind, that I measure my times.[625] Do not shout me down—that is, do not let yourself be shouted down by the mobs of your impressions. In you, I say, I measure times. I measure the present impression which passing things make upon you and which remains when they have gone, and not the things that pass by so as to make the impression. I measure this impression when I measure times. Either the times I measure are these things, or I do not measure times.

But what about when we measure periods of silence, and we say that this silence took up as much time as that sound did? Do we not then extend our thought to the measure of a voice, as if it were sounding, so that we can say something about the intervals of silence in an

---

[625] Our sense of time, our ability to measure time, is an intellectual operation, acting not upon some material thing, but upon an immaterial thing, a memory or an imagination. Time, to exist at all, Augustine concludes, must then exist as an immaterial and intellectual object, abiding in the mind of God.

extent of time? For even when the mouth and the voice are at rest, we can go over poems and verses in our thought, along with any discourse whatever, and anything whose length we can measure, so that when it comes to how much time this or that utterance takes, we report no other than if we had spoken it aloud. Suppose someone wants to utter a longish sound, and suppose he thinks about it beforehand and settles how long it is going to be. He has already in silence gone through this extent of time, and, commending it to his memory, he begins to utter the sound until he has led it on to the end proposed. It has sounded, yes, and it shall go on sounding, for the part of it which is completed has sounded, and what is left over shall sound, and so it goes forward until the present intention has carried the future into the past, the future dwindling while the past increases, until all of what was to come is consumed, and the past is all.

28

But how can the future dwindle and be consumed, since it does not yet exist, and how can the past grow, since it exists no longer? It would be impossible, except that in the mind that does this there are three functions. For it looks forward, it attends, and it remembers, so that what it looks forward to goes to what it attends to, and from there to what it remembers. Who then denies that things to come do not yet exist? And yet the expectation of things to come already exists in the mind. And who denies that the past exists no more? And yet the memory of past things is in the mind still. And who denies that the present time has no extent, because it passes in a moment, a point? But the attention endures, and what is going to be present passes through it to become what is absent. Then it is not a future time that is long, because it does not exist at all, but a long future is a long expectation of the future, nor is there a long past time, for the past no longer exists, but the long past is a long memory of what is past.

Say I am going to repeat a song I know. Before I begin, my expectation stretches out to take in the whole. But as soon as I begin, whatever portion of that song I have taken away and put in the past is retained in my memory. And so the life of my action is extended into the memory on account of what I have uttered, and into my expectation on account of what I am going to utter. But my attention is still present, through which what had been future must cross in order to go into the past. And the farther I go into the song, the shorter my expectation becomes, and the longer my memory, until the whole of the expectation is consumed, and the entire action has been brought to an end and has passed into the memory. As the whole song, so also every part, so also every syllable. And so also in some longer action whereof this song may be but a small part; so also in the whole life of a man, whose parts are all his actions; so also in the whole passing age of the sons of men, whose parts are all the lives of individual men.

29

But because your loving kindness is better than all those lives, behold, my life is a distension, a drawing-apart, and your right hand has taken me up in my Lord, the Son of Man, the mediator between you who are one and us who are many,[626] drawn out by many things in many ways; by whose means I may lay hold of him who has laid hold of me, and from my days of old be gathered up to follow but One, forgetting the things that are behind;[627] not drawn apart but stretching forth, not toward things that will come and pass away, but to the things which are before us; no, not by distension but by firm intention I follow to gain the palm of my calling from above, where I shall hear the sound of praise, and gaze upon your beauty, which neither comes nor goes. But now my years are spent in groaning,[628] while you, Lord, my consolation,

[626] Cf. 1 Tm 2:5–6.
[627] Cf. Phil 3:12–14.
[628] Cf. Ps 31:10.

are eternal; and I trickle away with the times,[629] whose order I do not know, and my thoughts are torn asunder by all the tumultuous chances of life, even the most inward parts of my soul, until at last I shall melt and flow into you, washed clean and clear by the fire of your love.

30

And I shall stand and grow solid in you, in my mold, your truth, nor shall I suffer the questions of men who are punished with disease, and who thirst for more than their bellies can hold, when they say, "What did God do before he made heaven and earth?" Or, "How did it come into his mind to make something, when he had never made anything before?"

Lord, grant them to consider well what they are saying, and to find out that they cannot say "never," when time does not exist. For when someone says that he "never had made," what can he mean other than to say that he had "made at no time"? Let them then see that there can be no time without creation, and let them stop saying such a silly thing. Let them stretch forth their minds to the things that are to come,[630] and let them understand that before all times you are the eternal creator of all times, and that no times are coeternal with you, nor is any creature coeternal with you, even should there be a creature *above* the times.

31

O Lord my God, how deep is the gulf of your secret place,[631] and how far away from it the consequences of my sins have flung me! Heal my eyes, that I may share the joy of your light. Certainly if there is some mind so mighty in knowledge and foreknowledge as to know everything past and everything to come, and to know it just as I know the

---

[629] Cf. Ps 90:9.
[630] Cf. Phil 3:13–14.
[631] Cf. Ps 18:11.

song I know best, that mind would be a sheer marvel, something to stun us into trembling, for nothing past would be hidden from it, and nothing of all the ages to come, just as that song is not hidden from me while I am singing it, what and how much of it has gone from the beginning, and what and how much remains until the end. But never let us think that you, the Creator of souls and bodies, know all future and past things in this way—never let us think it! Far more marvelously do you know them, in a far, far more secret way! It is not as someone sings a song he knows, or hears someone else singing it, that his feelings change, and his sense is drawn one way and another, by his expectation of sounds to come and his memory of sounds gone by. That is not how it befalls you, who are unchangeably eternal, indeed the eternal creator of minds. You knew, in the beginning, heaven and earth without any variation in your knowledge; so too did you make, in the beginning, heaven and earth without any division of your action. Let him who understands it confess to you, and let him who does not understand it also confess to you. O how lofty you are, and yet the humble of heart are your home! For you raise up those who had tumbled down; and they whose place aloft is you are shall not fall.[632]

---

[632] Cf. Ps 145:14.

BOOK TWELVE

1

My heart, Lord, smitten by the words of your Holy Scripture, is yet busy with many things[633] in this poverty of my life; and that is why human intelligence mostly goes a-begging in a lavish show of words, for questioning has more to say than finding out does, and we are longer about petition than about possession, and the hand has more to do with knocking than with taking up. But we hold on to the promise—and who shall break it?[634] If God is for us, who shall be against us?[635] Ask, and you shall receive; seek, and you shall find; knock, and it shall be opened unto you. For everyone who asks, receives, and everyone who seeks, finds, and to everyone who knocks, it shall be opened.[636] These promises are yours, and who shall fear to be deceived, when it is Truth who makes the promise?

2

Unto you, Most High, the lowliness of my tongue confesses that you made heaven and earth; this heaven I see, this earth I tread upon, whence

---

[633] Cf. Lk 10:41.
[634] Cf. Heb 10:23.
[635] Cf. Rom 8:31.
[636] Cf. Mt 7:7.

comes this other earth, my body, that I carry about. You have made them. But where, Lord, is that heaven of heaven which we hear of in the psalm, "The heaven of heavens is the Lord's, but the earth has he given to the sons of men"?[637] Where are you, O heaven we cannot see, to which all that we do see is earth? For this whole universe, which in no single place exists as a whole, has received form and beauty even in its least parts, the very bottommost of which is this our earth. But to that heaven of heavens, this earthly heaven of ours is mere earth. Indeed, it is not absurd to call both of these bodily creatures "earth," in comparison with that heaven I know nothing of, which belongs to the Lord, and not to the sons of men.

3

And of course this "earth" was invisible and without shape, a profound abyss, of what sort I do not know, upon which there was no light, for as yet it had no form.[638] That is why you commanded it to be written that darkness was upon the abyss, and what else is darkness but the absence of light? For if there had been light, where would it have been but above, shining forth and filling things with brightness? But since light did not yet exist, what else was the presence of darkness but the absence of light? The darkness then was "above," "upon," because the light "above" was not there, just as when there is no sound, there is silence. And what else does it mean that silence is somewhere, but that sound is not?

Is it not you, Lord, who have taught the soul that confesses to you? Have you not taught me, Lord, that before you gave form to this unformed matter and made distinctions in it, there was no "something," neither color, nor shape, nor body, nor spirit?[639] But it was not altogether nothing, either, for there was a certain unformed-ness, without any feature to look upon.

---

[637] Ps 115:16.
[638] Cf. Gn 1:2.
[639] This unformed matter was also created by God: think of it as pure potentiality, pure receptivity to whatever form God might impose upon it, that discrete *things* might come to be.

4

What then shall we call this thing, to instill it into the minds of people whose wits are a little slow? We must use some word they are accustomed to. What, in all the parts of the world, can we find that is nearer to being without form in any way than "earth" and "the deep"? They are less lovely to behold, on account of their low level of being, than are those other higher parts, gleaming with light that shines from within. Why then should I not take it that the unformedness of the matter you made without form, out of which you then made this world of lovely form, might well be called "earth invisible and without form," to suggest the truth to men in the most commodious way?

5

When thought looks for something about this thing that sense can latch upon, it says, "It is not an intelligible form, such as life or justice, because it is the matter of bodies. It is not capable of being sensed, because what is seen or sensed cannot exist in what is invisible and in confusion." When human thought says this to itself, is it not struggling to know it by not knowing it, or to be ignorant of it by knowing what it is?

6

Let me, Lord, confess to you by my lips and my pen everything you have taught me about this material substance. I used to hear its name without understanding it, and other people who did not understand it would tell me tales about it, and I conceived it as full of innumerable and diverse forms, and therefore I was not thinking about it at all.[640] Ugly and horrible forms, all in disorder, went rolling about in

---

[640] He is referring to the Manicheans. When we say that the "earth" was without form, we do not imagine some repugnant and horrible chaos, seething constantly in one ugly shape after another, but complete formlessness.

my mind, but they were forms, and I called them "without form," not because they lacked all form, but because the forms they had were such as, if I caught sight of them, would make my senses turn away, appalled at what I found unusual or disagreeable, and my human frailty would be deeply troubled. But the truth is, what I was thinking about was "without form" not by a privation of all form, but by comparison with what had a more handsome form. And true reason persuaded me that I must withdraw from it every least trace of any form whatever, if I meant to think about what was "without form," and I could not do it. I would sooner judge that the thing I was trying to think about—the something between form and nothing, neither formed nor nothing, formless and the next thing to nothing—did not exist at all, than think that it could exist deprived of all form.

So my mind ceased to question my imagination about the subject, filled as it was with images of bodies with form, which it changed and exchanged at will. And I strained to peer more deeply into the bodies themselves and their mutability, whereby they cease to be what they were and begin to be what they were not. And I suspected that when they crossed from one form to another, the passage was through a sort of unformed state, and not through an absolute nothing. But I desired to know whether it was so, and not merely suspect it. And if my voice and my pen should confess to you all that you have unraveled for me regarding this question, what reader will bear it long enough to understand? But not for this shall my heart cease to give you honor, and to sing a song of praise for what it cannot express. For the mutability of mutable things is itself capable of assuming all the forms into which the mutable things may be changed. And this mutability, what is it? Is it mind? Is it body? Is it some figure of a soul or a body? If we could say, "a *something nothing*," and "an *is is-not*," that is what I would call it. And yet it surely *was*, that it might take on those visible and well-composed forms.

7

But whatever it was, where did it come from, that it should be a some-thing capable of taking on those visible and well-composed forms? Where did it come from, whatever it was, but from you, from whom all things come, insofar as they have existence? But the farther a thing is from you, the more unlike it is to you, for we are not talking here about location. Therefore, you, Lord, who are not one thing now and another thing then, but the Self-same, the Self-same, the Self-same, the holy, holy, holy Lord God almighty, you, in the beginning which is of you, in your Wisdom begotten of your substance, made something, and you made it from nothing.[641]

For you made heaven and earth; not of you, because then it would be equal to your only-begotten Son and, through him, equal to you; and in no way could that be just, that something which was not of you should be equal to you. And besides yourself there was nothing, O God, one Trinity and threefold Unity, out of which you might have made these things. Therefore, it was from nothing that you made heaven and earth, a great thing and a little thing, for you are almighty and good, to make all things good—the great heaven and the little earth. You were, and nothing else existed from which you made heaven and earth, two things, the one near to you, the other near to nothingness; the one, than which you alone would be higher, and the other, than which noth-ingness alone would be lower.

8

But that heaven of heavens was yours, Lord, and this earth which you gave to the sons of men[642] to see and to touch was not then as we now see it and touch it. For it was invisible and uncomposed, a deep that no light shone above, but darkness was *above* the deep—*above*, that is,

---

[641] Note the Trinitarian formulas; cf. Jn 1:1.
[642] Cf. Ps 115:16.

rather than *in*.[643] For in fact this watery deep which is now visible has a light even in its lowest regions that is proper to its form, which the fish and the creeping things at its bottom can in some way sense. But that first abyss was altogether a next-to-nothing, because it did not yet *have* any form, though it was already something that could *receive* form.

For you, Lord, made the world from formless matter, which you made from nothing as a thing next to nothingness, out of which you then made the great things that we sons of men look upon in wonder. Surely this corporeal heaven is wonderful, which you spoke into being on the second day, after the creation of light, as a firmament between the water and the water, saying, "Let it be made," and it was made.[644] You called that firmament "heaven," that is, the heaven of this earth and sea, which you then made on the third day, giving a visible form to the formless matter that you made before any of the days. For you had already made a heaven before any of the days, but that was the heaven of this heaven, for in the beginning you made heaven and earth. But *that* "earth" you made was formless matter, for it was invisible and formless, and darkness was upon the deep. From that invisible and formless earth, from that formlessness, from that next-to-nothing you made all the things whereof this mutable world consists without consistence. For that same mutability appears in the world, and by it can times be observed and numbered, for times come by the changes of things, when their forms vary and turn; and the matter they are made of is that invisible earth I have mentioned above.

9

That is why, when the Spirit, the teacher of your servant, declares that in the beginning you made heaven and earth, he says nothing about times and is silent about days. No wonder; for the heaven of heaven, which you made in the beginning, is an intellectual creation, and although it

---

[643] Cf. Gn 1:2.
[644] Cf. Gn 1:6–8.

is in no way coeternal with you, the Trinity, still it does partake of your eternity, holding its mutability bound before the sweetness of its bliss as it contemplates you; and without any lapse from when it was first made, cleaving to you, it stands beyond all the rolling changes of the times. And to tell the truth, this formlessness, the earth invisible and unformed, is likewise not numbered among the days. For where there is no form and no order, neither does anything come and go. And where that does not happen, there clearly are no days, nor any periods of time succeeding one upon the other.[645]

10

O Truth, light of my heart, let it not be my own darkness speaking to me! I slid down into those material things, and darkness came upon me, and yet even there did I come to love you. I went astray, and I remembered you. I heard your voice calling after me to return, and I could hardly hear it on account of the enemies of peace at riot within me. And now, behold, I do return, burning and panting for your flowing spring.[646] Let no man forbid me! This shall I drink, this shall I live. Let me not be my own life. Of my own, I have lived ill, I have been death to myself. In you I come to life again. May you speak to me, may you discourse with me. I have put my faith in your books, and their words are most mysterious.

11

You have said to me, Lord, declaring with a strong voice to my inward ear, that you are eternal, you alone possess immortality, because you suffer no change in form or motion, nor does your will vary with the times, because no will is immortal if it is sometimes this and sometimes

---

[645] The heaven of heavens is beyond change, cleaving to the eternity of God; the formless "earth" is beneath change, since there are as yet no discrete objects, no unities of form and matter, that can pass from one state to another.
[646] Cf. Ps 42:1.

that. By the light of your countenance this is clear to me, and I pray, let it shine more and more clearly, and in that manifest clarity let me continue to stand, sober, under the protection of your wings.[647]

Again, you have said to me, Lord, declaring with a strong voice to my inward ear, that you have made all natures and substances, things that are not what you are, and that nevertheless exist. The only thing that does not come from you is what does *not* exist, along with any movement of the will from you who *are*, to what is less than you. Such a movement is a dereliction and sin. You have told me that no one's sin harms you or disrupts the order of your governance, not in the first and highest, not in the last and least. By the light of your countenance this is clear to me,[648] and I pray, let it shine more and more clearly, and in that manifest clarity let me continue to stand, sober, under the protection of your wings.

Likewise, you have said to me, with a strong voice declaring it to my inward ear, that not even that creature[649] whose delight you alone are is coeternal with you; which as it drinks you in with a most persevering chastity, has never and nowhere made show of its own mutability; which, because you are present to it always, you whom it holds to with all its affection, has no future to look forward to and conveys nothing it remembers into the past, and never suffers any alteration, and is not distended in time. O blessed creature, if such a creature there may be, cleaving unto your bliss, blessed in you who dwell within it forever, blessed in you who give it light! I can find nothing it pleases me more to reckon worthy of being called the Lord's heaven of heaven, than your own house, contemplating your beauty without any falling away to look at another; a pure mind, made one in utter harmony, the established peace of those holy spirits, those citizens of your city in the heavens above this heaven we see.

---

[647] Cf. Ps 91:4.
[648] Cf. Ps 89:15.
[649] The "heaven of heavens," created, but with no mere physical location; existent in the mind of God.

The soul is a pilgrim from far away, but if she thirsts for you now, if tears have become her bread while she hears, day after day, "Where is your God?",[650] if she now desires and seeks from you one thing alone, that she may dwell in your house for all the days of her life[651]—and what is her life, but you, and what are your days but your eternity, as are your years that never fail, because you are the Selfsame forever?—then she, the soul that is able, may well understand how far beyond all times you the eternal are, seeing that your house, which never wandered far afield, even though it is not coeternal with you, still by cleaving to you without pause and without falling away does not suffer any changeableness of time. By the light of your countenance this is clear to me, and I pray, let it shine more and more clearly, and in that manifest clarity let me continue to stand, sober, under the protection of your wings.

And see, there is a certain formlessness in these mutations of the least and lowest things. And who shall say to me—unless it is someone who roves round and round with his own fancies, by the folly of his heart—who else but someone such as that shall say to me that if all form has diminished and wasted away, and if only formlessness remains, the formlessness through which a thing is changed and turns from one form to another, this formlessness can show the courses of the times? Never could it do so. For without a varying in motions, times do not exist, and there is no varying where there is no form.

12

These things I have considered, my God, as far as you have granted it to me, as far as you have stirred me to knock for them, as far as you have opened them to me when I knocked.[652] Now then, I find two things you have made that are outside the scope of time, although neither of them is coeternal with you. One was so formed as, without any

---

[650] Ps 42:3.
[651] Cf. Ps 27:4.
[652] Cf. Mt 7:7.

falling away from contemplating you, without any interval of change, being changeable but never changed, it enjoys the fruit of eternity and immutability to the full. The other was so formless, it had in it nothing in motion or at rest that could be changed from one form into another, and so it could not be subject to time. But you did not leave this thing to be formless forever, for before any day, in the beginning, you made heaven and earth, the two things I have spoken of. Now the earth was invisible and without form, and darkness was above the abyss. By these words, formlessness is suggested to us—to lead along, step by step, those who cannot conceive of a privation of all form which still does not fall into utter nothingness. Out of this formlessness was to be made another heaven, and this visible and well-formed earth, and the lovely water, and everything else in the constitution of this world that is recorded as having been created in "days."[653] For they are the kinds of things in which the changes of the times may take place, on account of their ordained commutations of movement and form.

13

This, meanwhile, is what I understand, O my God, when I hear your Scripture saying, "In the beginning God made heaven and earth, but the earth was invisible and without form, and darkness was above the abyss," and not mentioning on what day you made them. I understand the "heaven of heaven" as that intellectual heaven, where the intellect knows all at once, not in part, not as through a glass darkly, but in full, in manifest clarity, face to face;[654] not this thing now and that thing later, but, as I have said, it knows all at once, without any succession of times. And I understand that "earth invisible and without form" to refer to an earth without any succession of times, since a succession

---

[653] Notice that Augustine assumes that the sacred author of Genesis—traditionally held to be Moses—did not intend the word "day" to be interpreted literally, but that he did imply that "days," that is, time itself, could pass by only when form had been imposed upon the formless matter.

[654] Cf. 1 Cor 13:12.

must go from this thing now to that thing then, and where there is no form, there is no "this thing" and "that thing."

Because of these two, the one first-formed and the other utterly formless—heaven the one, but the heaven of heaven; earth the other, but the earth invisible and without form—because of these two, I understand meanwhile what your Scripture is saying when without any mention of days it says, "In the beginning God made heaven and earth." For it adds immediately which earth it was speaking of. And when it mentions that the firmament was made on the second day, and it was called "heaven," it suggests which heaven it was speaking of before, when there was no mention of days.

14

Wondrous is the depth of your beautiful words, when, behold, even their surface before us draws your little ones gently onward—but what wondrous depth, O my God, what wondrous depth! It strikes one with awe to gaze upon it, the awe of honor, the trembling of love. Fervently do I hate its enemies:[655] O, that you would slay them with the double-edged sword,[656] that they may be enemies no longer! That is how I love them, to be slain to themselves, so that they may live for you.

But see, there are others who find no fault with the book of Genesis, but who praise it, and they say, "The Spirit of God did not mean the words he wrote through his servant Moses to be understood in the way you say, but in another way, as we say." To them I shall respond thus, God of us all, and let you be the judge.

15

Will you people really call false what Truth has said spoken with a strong voice to my inward ear, about the true eternity of the Creator,

---

[655] Cf. Ps 139:19–22.
[656] Cf. Heb 4:12.

that his essence never varies with the times, and that his will is not something else besides his essence? He does not, then, will one thing now and another thing later, but once, and all at once, and forever does he will all the things he wills, not now and again, not this now and that then. Nor does he will what he did not will before, or be unwilling when before he was willing, for such a will is mutable, and no mutable thing is eternal. But our God is eternal.

Will you call it false too, what is spoken to me in my inward ear, that the expectation of things to come turns into present sight when they have come, and present sight becomes memory when they have passed by? But every power of thinking that varies in such a way is mutable, and no mutable thing is eternal. But our God is eternal. These things do I gather up and join together, and I find that my God, the eternal God, did not establish his creation because some new will came to him, nor is his knowledge subject to anything transitory.

What then are you saying, you who contradict me? Are these things really false? "No," they say. What then? Is it false, that every formed nature and all matter capable of receiving form derive their being from him alone, who is supremely good, because he supremely is? "We do not deny this, either," they say. What then? Do you deny that there is a certain sublime creation, cleaving unto the true God, the truly eternal God, with so chaste a love, that even though it is not coeternal with him, it never in any chance and change of the times releases its hold on him to spill away, but rests content in the utterly true contemplation of him alone?[657] For you, God, show yourself to a being that loves you as much as you command, and you are sufficient for it, and so it never leans away from you or toward itself. This is the house of God, not of earthly material, nor even built of any heavenly body, but a spiritual house,[658] and a partaker of your eternity, because it remains without blemish forever.[659] For you made it fast forever and ever; you have given

---

[657] The "heaven of heavens," that is.
[658] Cf. 1 Pt 2:5.
[659] Cf. Eph 5:27.

it a decree, and it shall not pass away.[660] Still it is not coeternal with you, because it is not without a beginning; for it was made.

Although we find no time before it, for wisdom was created before all things, it is surely not the Wisdom that is equal and coeternal with you his Father, the Wisdom, my God, through whom all things were made, and in whose beginning you made heaven and earth.[661] It is instead the created wisdom, intellectual in its nature to be sure, which by its contemplation of the light, is light; for this too, though it is a created thing, is called wisdom.

But consider the difference between the light that illumines and the light that receives the illumination. So great is the difference between the wisdom that creates, and the wisdom that is created, as also between the justice that justifies, and the justice that is made so by justification. For we too are called "your justice," as says a certain servant of yours, "that we may be made the justice of God in him."[662] There was, then, a certain created wisdom before all other created things, that is, the rational and intellectual mind of your chaste city, our mother, which is above, and free, and eternal in the heavens. And what are these heavens, but the heaven of heavens that praise you, because this too is the heaven of heaven that is the Lord's? Therefore, even though we find no time before this created wisdom, since what was created first must precede the creation of time, still the eternity of the Creator is before it. From that eternity, when it was created, it took its inception, not as the beginning of its time, for time did not yet exist, but as the beginning of its very being.

So, then, it comes from you, our God, as quite a different thing from you, and not the Selfsame. Yet we find no time before it or even within it, because it has been made most fit to behold your face forever and never to be turned aside from it. That is why it is never altered by

---

[660] Cf. Ps 148:6.

[661] Augustine distinguishes a created wisdom (cf. Sir 1:4) from Christ, the second Person of the Trinity, the co-eternal Wisdom of God (cf. Jn 1:1, 1 Cor 1:24).

[662] 2 Cor 5:21.

any change. And yet the capacity to be changed inheres in it, and it might grow dark and cold, but that it cleaves to you with so powerful a love, it shines and burns from you as from a noonday everlasting. O lovely and lightsome house, I have loved your beauty,[663] and the dwelling place of the glory of my Lord, who built you up and possesses you! Let my pilgrim way sigh for you, and I say to him who made you, let him possess me also in you, for he made me also. I had gone wayward like a lost sheep,[664] but upon the shoulders of my shepherd, your builder, I hope to be carried back to you.[665]

You contradictors to whom I have been speaking, what do you say to me now? You do believe that Moses was a devout servant of God and that his books are oracles of the Holy Spirit. Does this house of God exist? A house which is not coeternal with God, but eternal in the heavens according to its mode of being, where you shall seek the successions of times in vain, because you will not find them there? For it surpasses any kind of distension, and any fleeting age, as its good is ever to cleave to God. "It does exist," they say. What, then, of the things that my heart has cried out to my God, when it heard within itself the voice of his praise, what then do you contend that I have spoken falsely? Perhaps that there was a sort of matter without form, and because it had no form, it had no order? But where there was no order, there could be no succession of times. And yet this near-nothing, insofar as it was not utterly nothing, was surely from him from whom everything that exists is, whatever and however it may be. "This too," they say, "we do not deny."

16

With these people I wish to converse a little in your presence, my God, these who concede that all those things are true, which your truth has not been silent about, speaking them deep within my mind. As for those

---

[663] Cf. Ps 26:8.
[664] Cf. Ps 119:176.
[665] Cf. Lk 15:5.

who deny these things, let them bark as much as they like and shout at each other; I shall try to persuade them to be quiet, and to prepare the way for your Word to come to them. But if they refuse to do that, and they reject me, I beg you, my God, do not keep silent from me.[666] Speak truly in my heart; you alone speak so; and I shall send them out the door, as they blow the dust into their own eyes. And I shall enter into my chamber,[667] and sing you a song of love, groaning with groans that cannot be told as I make my pilgrim way,[668] remembering Jerusalem with my heart raised up to her, Jerusalem my fatherland, Jerusalem my mother,[669] and you who reign over her, who give her light, you her Father, her protector, her spouse, her chaste and brave delights, her single and steadfast joy, her all good things that cannot be captured in words; and all these at once, because you are the one all-embracing and true good. And I shall not turn aside, till at last you have gathered up from my scattering and my disorder all that I am, and brought me to the peace of that mother most dear, where the first-fruits of my spirit already are,[670] giving me assurance of these things. I shall not turn aside till you have conformed me to her, and confirmed me forever,[671] O God, my mercy.

But I speak to those who do not say that these true things are false, and who honor your holy Scripture given to us by Moses the holy, and who set it at the summit of authority for us to follow, and who yet contradict me in some point. And I say, "Be yourself, our God, the judge between my confessions and their gainsaying."

17

For they say, "Although the things you say are true, Moses still did not intend those two created things when by the revelation of the Spirit he

---

[666] Cf. Ps 28:1.
[667] Cf. Mt 6:6.
[668] Cf. Rom 8:26.
[669] Cf. Gal 4:26.
[670] Cf. Rom 8:23.
[671] Cf. 2 Sm 7:24.

said, 'In the beginning God made heaven and earth.' He did not signify, under the name of 'heaven,' that spiritual or intellectual creature
ever contemplating the face of God, nor under the name of 'earth' did
he signify formless matter." What then? "What we say," they reply, "is
what that man had in mind, when he spoke those words." And what is
that? "By 'heaven and earth,'" they say, "he meant to signify by a brief
and universal term the whole of this visible world. After that, he would
go on to treat of the universe as it were joint by joint, by the enumera-
tion of days, just as it pleased the Holy Spirit to express it. For the people to whom he was speaking were rude and fleshly, so that he judged it
fit to mention to them only those works of God that were visible." They
do agree that it is not incongruous to say that the invisible earth and the
unformed and darksome abyss may be understood as referring to that
unformed matter, out of which, during the six days afterwards, all the
visible things known to everyone were made and set in order.

Well then, what if someone else should say that this same formlessness and confusion of matter was first suggested to us by the name
of "heaven and earth," because from it was created and completed this
visible world, with all the natures that appear so manifestly in it, the
world we are accustomed to call by the name of "heaven and earth"?

And what if still another man should say that it was not improper
to call this invisible and visible nature "heaven and earth," for those two
words comprehend the whole universal creation that God made in his
wisdom, that is, in the "beginning"? But, he says, since all things have
been made not out of the substance of God, but out of nothing—for
they are not the self-same, as God is, there being a certain mutability in
them, whether they abide forever, as does the everlasting house of God,
or they suffer change, as do the soul and body of man—it was the *matter common to all things visible or invisible*, as yet formless but certainly
capable of receiving form, the matter from which "heaven and earth"
were made, that is, both the invisible and the visible creation once they
have received a form, that was called by those two names. They were
the same names the earth was called by, when it was said to be invisible

and without form, and darkness was over the abyss. But, he says, there is this distinction: we understand "earth invisible and without form" to refer to the *corporeal* matter before any quality of form was imposed upon it, and "darkness upon the abyss" to refer to the *spiritual* matter before any restraint, so to speak, upon its unchecked flood, and before wisdom shone upon it.

And there is something else to say, if someone likes. When we read, "In the beginning God made heaven and earth," we do not take the names to signify the visible and invisible natures, already formed and brought to their finish, of heaven and earth. We take them to signify the same formless first-beginning of things, the matter capable of receiving form and capable of being the stuff of creation, because in it already in a confused way, not yet made distinct by their features and forms, were all those things which we call "heaven" and "earth," now that they have been set in proper order: the first a spiritual creation, the second a corporeal creation.[672]

18

Having heard and considered all these things, I do not wish to quarrel about words, which is good for nothing but to subvert the souls of those who listen. But the law is good for building up, if someone puts it to lawful use, as its end is charity from a pure heart and a good conscience and a faith unfeigned. And our Teacher well knew upon which two precepts he would hang all the law and the prophets. O my God, light of my soul's hidden eyes, how does it harm me, when with a burning love I confess these things, how does it harm me that the words may be understood in different ways, yet all of them true? How does it harm me, I say, if I think that the writer was thinking about one thing, and

---

[672] This last interpretation posits that the primordial "seeds" of things were created in the beginning, their future shapes and natures present, but undeveloped and latent, in the matter that God first created. We might suggest that the whole universe wherein man would be placed was present in the first burst of time and matter and light, and man likewise, and all other creatures.

another person thinks he was thinking about something else? All of us readers strive to follow his path and to grasp what the writer intended, and as we believe he tells only the truth, we never make bold to say that he thought something we know or think to be false. Then as long as every man tries to understand in the Holy Scriptures what the writer himself understood in them, what harm is there if he should understand what you, Light of all truth-telling minds, show him to be true, even if the author he reads did not understand it so? For the author understood a truth, though it may not have been that particular one.

19

For true it is, Lord, that you made heaven and earth. True it is also that the beginning is your Wisdom, in which you made all things. True, again, that this visible world has for its two great parts the heaven and the earth, which in brief encompass every made and created nature. And it is true that every mutable thing suggests to our understanding a certain lack of form, whereby it either receives a form, or is changed or turned into something else. True likewise that whatever cleaves to the unchangeable form suffers no succession of times, and even though it is susceptible of change, it never does change. True also that the formlessness which is next to nothing cannot suffer a succession of times. True, that the stuff from which a thing is made can in a certain manner of speech be called by the name of the thing that is made from it, whence the formlessness out of which heaven and earth were made can be called "heaven and earth." True, that of all formed things, nothing is closer to having no form than earth and the deep. True, that you from whom all things exist made not only every created and formed thing, but also the material capable of receiving form and being the stuff of creation. True, that everything that has been formed from the formless was itself formless, and then it was formed.

20

From all these true things, which they do not doubt, they to whose inward eye you have given the gift to see them, they who steadfastly believe that Moses your servant spoke in the Spirit of truth—from all these, I say, one man takes up this sense, as he says, "In the beginning God made heaven and earth," that is, "In the Word that is coeternal with himself, God made the intelligible creation and the sensible creation, the spiritual and the corporeal." And another sense, he who says, "In the beginning God made heaven and earth," that is, "In his Word coeternal with himself, God made the universal mass of this corporeal world, with all the manifest and well-known natures it contains." Still another sense, he who says, "In the beginning God made heaven and earth," that is, "In the Word coeternal with himself, God made the formless matter of the spiritual and corporeal creation." Still another, who says, "In the beginning God made heaven and earth," that is, "In his word coeternal with himself, God made the formless matter of *corporeal* creation, wherein heaven and earth already lay confused, which now we perceive as distinct and formed, in the mass of this world." Still another, who says, "In the beginning God made heaven and earth," that is, "In the very inception of making and working, God made the formless matter, containing heaven and earth but in a confused way, whence they now stand forth in broad sight as having been formed, with all the creatures that are in them."

21

And the same thing goes for understanding the words that follow. From all their true senses, he takes up one of them for himself, when he says, "But the earth was invisible and without form, and darkness was over the deep," that is, "The corporeal thing God made was still only the formless stuff of corporeal things, without order, without light." Another, who says, "But the earth was invisible and without form, and darkness was over the deep," that is, "The whole creation, which here is called heaven and earth, was still a formless and darksome matter, whence the corporeal heaven and the corporeal earth would be made, with all the things therein, known to our bodily senses." Still another, who says, "But the earth was invisible and without form, and darkness was over the deep," that is, "This whole creation, which is called heaven and earth, was still formless, and there was a darksome matter, whence the *intelligible* heaven would be made, which elsewhere is called the heaven of heaven, and whence the earth would be made, that is, *all* of corporeal nature, including in one name even the corporeal heaven; so then, from this matter would be made the whole of the invisible and visible creation." Still another, who says, "But the earth was invisible and without form, and darkness was over the deep," that is, "Scripture has not called that formlessness by the name of heaven and earth, because that formlessness already existed, which Moses called the invisible earth without form, and the darksome deep. From that, God made the heaven and earth the author mentioned at first, namely, the spiritual and corporeal creation." And yet another, who says, "But the earth was invisible and without form, and darkness was over the deep," that is, "A kind of formlessness already existed which was the stuff from which God made the heaven and earth the author mentioned at first, the whole corporeal mass of the world, divided into two great parts, the higher and the lower, with all the usual and well-known creatures in them."

22

Now, someone may try to resist these last two interpretations, thus, "If you will not allow that this formless matter may be called *heaven and earth*, then you are suggesting there was something God did not make, out of which he made heaven and earth. For Scripture does not tell us that God made this matter, unless we understand it to be signified by the words 'heaven and earth,' or perhaps by the single word 'earth,'

when it is said, 'In the beginning God made heaven and earth.' So also
in what follows, 'But the earth was invisible and without form.' Though
it was his pleasure to refer to the formless matter in that way, we still are
to understand it as no other than what God made in the verse before it,
when it says he 'made heaven and earth.'"

Those who assert either one of the two opinions we gave last will,
when they hear this objection, respond in this way: "We do not at all
deny that God made this formless matter, God, from whom are all things
exceedingly good. As we say that what has been created and formed is
the greater good, so too we say that what can receive form and be the
stuff of creation is also good, but a lesser good. But Scripture does not
trouble to mention that God made this formlessness, just as it does not
mention that he made many other things, such as the cherubim and the
seraphim, and the other orders which the apostle distinguishes, thrones,
dominations, princedoms, powers.[673] Yet it is manifestly clear that God
made them all. But if we understand that all things are included, when
it is said that he 'made heaven and earth,' what shall we say of the
waters upon which the Spirit of God was brooding? For if all things
are named under the one word 'earth,' how then can we take the name
'earth' to imply formless matter, when we look upon the waters in all
their loveliness? But if we do take it that way, why is it written that from
that same formlessness the firmament was made, and called 'heaven,'
while it is not written that the waters were made from it? For they are
formless and unseen no longer, these waters we see flowing, so lovely to
behold. Or if you say that they received this beauty when God said, 'Let
the waters beneath the firmament be gathered together,' thus taking the
gathering-together as this same receiving of form, what is to be said of
the waters that are above the firmament? Had they been without form,
they could never have merited so honorable a station. Yet Scripture
does not give us the command whereby they received their form.

---

[673] Cf. Col 1:16.

"So then, if Genesis is silent about God's having made what neither sound faith nor sure reasoning doubts that he made, neither will any sober doctrine dare say that those waters must have been coeternal with God, just because we hear them mentioned in the book of Genesis but we do not find where they were made. Since that is so, why can we not understand also, with Truth as our teacher, that God made the formless matter, which this verse calls the 'earth invisible and without form' and the darksome abyss, and that he made it from nothing, and that therefore it is not coeternal with Him, even though the account omits to tell us when it was made?"

23

Well then, having heard these things and examined them according to my weak capacity (which I confess to you, my God, for you do know it), I see that two sorts of dissensions can arise when something is expressed in signs by those who report the truth. One concerns the truth of the things, the other, the meaning intended by the person reporting them. For we are doing one thing when we ask what is true about the creation of a thing, and another, when we ask what by these words Moses, that outstanding steward of your faith, intended the reader or the hearer to understand.

From the first sort, let them depart from me who reckon that they know things that are false. From the second, too, let them depart from me who reckon that Moses ever said things that were false. Let me, Lord, join with those who feed upon the pasture of your truth in the wide fields of charity,[674] delighting with them in you, and let us all together approach the words of your book, and in them search for the meaning you intend, through the meaning intended by your servant, whose pen you have used to spread those words abroad.

---

[674] Cf. Ps 37:3.

24

But which of us can find out this meaning from among all those many true things which meet us when we seek them in these words, understanding them in this way or that, so that he can say with confidence that this is what Moses thought, or that that is what he intended to be understood in that account, and just as confidently as he might say, "This is true," even if Moses was thinking about something else?

For behold, my God, I am your servant, and I have vowed to you a sacrifice of confession in these pages, and now I entreat you, that you may have mercy on me and may let me pay my vows to you.[675] And see how confident I am as I say that you made all things in your unalterable Word, all things invisible and visible, but I am by no means so confident as to say that Moses intended this but not that when he wrote, "In the beginning God made heaven and earth." No, not at all, because though I see it to be certain in your truth, I cannot see it in his mind in the same way, to be sure he was thinking of it when he wrote those words.

For he could have been thinking of the very onset of creation, when he wrote, "In the beginning." Or he could have wanted "heaven and earth" in this sentence to be understood as referring to no one nature already formed and brought to completion, whether spiritual or corporeal, but both still without form, inchoate. I see that whichever of these things he might have said, he would have spoken the truth, but which of the two he was thinking about, I cannot be so sure. But whatever that great man was gazing upon in his mind when he uttered those words, whether this or that or something else I have not mentioned, I do not doubt that he saw it truly and that he expressed it in a fitting way.[676]

---

[675] Cf. Ps 116:14.

[676] If we believe that Scripture is the word of God, we must not reduce it to the word of man, taking as significant only what we suppose the human author intended. Scripture always means more than man, with his creaturely limitations, can understand. Of course, some interpretations are wrong; all heretics get things wrong. The point is that a range of

25

Let no man vex me now by saying, "Moses did not think as you say, but as I say." For if he should ask me, "How do you know that Moses was thinking what you infer from his words?" I should bear it with an even mind, and respond to him by saying what I have said above, and I might go into it a bit more fully, should he be stubborn about it.

But when he says, "Moses did not think as you say, but as I say," while he does not deny that what either one of us says is true, then, O life of the poor, my God, whose bosom gives shelter to no contradiction, shower a soothing rain into my heart,[677] that I may put up with such people patiently. For they do not say this to me because they are themselves divine and they see in the heart of your steward what they say, but because they are proud. They do not know Moses's opinion, but they do love their own, not because it is true, but because it is theirs. Otherwise, they would love equally another true opinion, as I love what they say when they say the truth, not because it is they who say it, but because it is true; and therefore, because it is true, it does not really belong to them at all. But if they come to love it because it is true, then it is both theirs and mine, as it is the common possession of all who love the truth.

But when they quarrel and say that Moses did not mean what I say, rather what they say, I will not have it, I do not love it. For even if they are correct, their rashness springs not from knowledge but from brazenness. Overblown pride, not insight, has begotten it. Therefore, O Lord, must we tremble at your judgments, since your truth is neither mine nor this man's nor that man's, but it belongs to us all, whom you have called as a people to share it in communion, and terrible is your

---

valid interpretations is possible, not contradicting one another and not treating the word with contempt. What is most impressive about the discussion here is that we get a glimpse into interpretations of Genesis that were common among the educated Christians of Augustine's time—common among priests and bishops, and therefore not entirely unknown to the people in general.

[677] Cf. Dt 32:2.

warning to us not to hold it as a private thing, lest we be deprived of it. For whoever sues to hoard up for himself what you propose to be enjoyed by everyone, whoever wants for his own what belongs to all, is driven out of the commons back to what is merely his; that is, from the truth to a lie. For "whoever speaks a lie, speaks it from his own."[678]

Hearken, O God, best Judge, Truth itself, hearken to what I shall say to this man who speaks against me. For I say it in your presence, and in the presence of my brothers who make lawful use of the law, for the purpose of charity. Hearken to what I shall say to him and see if it pleases you. For I would return to him this brotherly and peaceable reply: "If we both see that what you say is true, and if we both see that what I say is true, where, I ask, do we see it? I surely do not see it in you, nor do you see it in me, but we both see it in that unalterable Truth that stands above our minds. Then since we are not quarreling over that same light of our Lord God, why should we quarrel over the thought of our neighbor, which we cannot see as we see the unalterable truth? Especially when, if Moses himself should appear to us and say, 'I was thinking about this,' still we would not see that it was so, but we would have to take it on trust."

Then let no one of us be puffed up against another,[679] going beyond what has been written down. Let us love the Lord our God with our whole heart, our whole soul, our whole mind, and let us love our neighbor as ourselves.[680] Unless we believe, no matter what he meant in his books, that Moses meant it in the light of these two precepts of charity, we shall make the Lord a liar,[681] because we will be imagining something about our fellow servant's mind that is other than what the Lord has taught. See here, how doltish it is, among such a great plenty of opinions most true that we can gather from those words, to be so bold as to affirm which one of them Moses most likely meant, and with per-

---

[678] Jn 8:44.
[679] Cf. 1 Cor 4:6.
[680] Cf. Mk 12:30–31, Lv 19:18, Dt 6:2.
[681] Cf. 1 Jn 1:10.

nicious contentions to offend against the very same charity that moved him to say all the things we are trying to expound.

26

Yet as for me, my God, O height of my humility, rest of my labor, who hear my confessions and forgive my sins: because you command me to love my neighbor as myself, I cannot believe that you gave to Moses, your most trusty household servant, a lesser gift than I would have chosen and desired for myself, had I been born at that time and had you set me in that place. I would have wished that, by the service of my heart and tongue, those books might be spread abroad which were for so long afterwards to be of profit to all peoples, from the peak of their authority overcoming throughout the world the mere words of false and proud teachings.[682] I would have wished, surely, had I been Moses then—for we all come from the same lump of clay, and what is man, unless you are mindful of him?[683]—I would have wished, had I been in his place, and had you laid upon me the task of writing the book of Genesis, that you would give me such eloquence in speaking and such a way of weaving words together, that even those who cannot yet understand how God creates would not reject sayings that far surpass their capacity, and that they who already understand it, no matter what true interpretation they have arrived at in thought, would find that it was not passed by in your servant's few words. And if another man should see something else by the light of truth, that too might not fail to be understood from the very same words.

27

It is like a rushing spring, pent up in a narrow place, whose flowing-forth is richer and feeds more streams over a wider expanse than does

---

[682] Cf. 1 Tm 6:3–5.
[683] Cf. Ps 8:4.

any one of the rivers that arise from it and that flow across many regions. So too your dispenser of truth, and his way of telling it, would profit many a preacher to come, and out of a narrow strait of speech would gush forth streams of truth pure and clear. From those streams every man may draw what truth he can, one man this and another man that, by longer river-bends of conversation.

For when some people read or hear these words, they think of God as like a man, or like some force endowed with an immense mass, and they suppose that he suddenly got a new notion, to make heaven and earth as if at some distance outside of himself, the two great bodies, one higher, one lower, to contain all things. And when they hear that God said, "Let it be so, and so it was made," they think the words had a beginning and an end, sounding and passing by in time, and once the words had passed, all at once what was commanded to exist did exist; and anything else they might think of in this way, on account of their familiarity with the flesh.

In the meantime, a wholesome faith is building up in them, though they are still only little souls, and their weakness is borne up by this lowly way of speaking, as children are carried upon their mother's lap. For they take and hold for certain that God made all the natural things which their senses behold roundabout them, in all their marvelous variety. And if any man should scoff at this style as if it were mean and base, and make his proud and weakling way from the cradle where he nurses, alas, the poor fellow shall fall. Lord God, have mercy on him, lest they who walk along the road should trample upon the featherless chick! Send your angel to lay it back in the nest, that it may live until it learns to fly.

28

But others, for whom these words are a nest no longer, but shady orchards, see the fruit hiding in the shade and flutter in gladness roundabout, and twitter as they find them and pluck them for their food. For whenever they read or hear these words, they see, O God, that all past and future times are surpassed by your eternal and stable abiding, and that nevertheless there is no creature of time that you did not make. And by a will that was in no way changed or newly arisen when it had not existed before, since your will is what you yourself are, you made all things. You did not make from yourself a similitude of yourself, the form of all things, but rather a dissimilitude without form, which then might be formed according to your similitude, returning to you, the One, in the capacity you have ordained for each kind of creature to do so. Hence would all things together be very good,[684] whether they abide in close revolution around you, or whether, by degrees, set farther away by times and places, they cause or they receive their beautiful changes. These things those others do see, and they rejoice in the light of your truth,[685] in what little measure they may.

And another focuses his mind on where it says, "In the beginning God made," and he takes it that wisdom is the beginning, because she herself says so to us.[686] Another attends to the same words and understands the beginning as the inception of creation, reading them thus, "In the beginning he made," as if to say, "At first he made." Among those who understand "in the beginning" as "in wisdom" he made heaven and earth, one person believes that "heaven and earth" name together the matter of heaven and earth that was to be used for creation, while another person believes that it names the already formed and distinct natures, and still another believes that "heaven" names one formed and spiritual matter, and "earth" the formless matter of bodily things. As for those who take "heaven and earth" as signifying the still formless matter out of which heaven and earth would be formed, they do not all understand it in the same way. One person understands by it the matter out of which *both* the intelligible and the sensible words would be brought to completion. Another person understands by it only the

---

[684] Cf. Gn 1:31.
[685] Cf. Ps 43:3.
[686] Cf. Prv 8:22–24.

matter from which would come this corporeal mass, which in its vast compass would contain natures already visible and ready to hand. Nor do they also understand it in the same way, who believe that "heaven and earth" signifies creatures already set forth and arranged. One person means both the invisible and the visible nature, while another person means only the visible nature, wherein we look upon the luminous sky above and the murky earth below, and all the things that are in them.

29

But let us consider him who takes "In the beginning he made," as if it said only, "At first he made." He has no true way to understand "heaven and earth," unless he understands it as the material of heaven and earth, that is, the whole universe, including both the intelligible and the corporeal creation. For if he wants it to refer to the whole universe already formed, he might justly be asked what God made afterwards if he made this first. After that universe, there is nothing to be found. And then he might not want to hear the next question, "Why do we say 'at first,' if afterwards there was nothing?"

Now, if he says that it was first formless, and only formed afterwards, he has said nothing absurd, so long as he is fit to tell things apart, and say what precedes by virtue of eternity, what precedes in time, what precedes by excellence, and what precedes by being the originating fount. So God precedes all things, by his eternity; the flower precedes the fruit, in time; the fruit precedes the flower, by excellence; and sound precedes the song, as its source and origin.

Of these four kinds of priority, the two in the middle are quite easy to understand, but the first and the last, only with great difficulty. For it takes a rare and persistent vision, Lord, to behold your eternity unchangeably making changeable things, and by that creation, its being *before* them. And who is of so keen mind as to be able to discern, without great labor, how sound is prior to song? For song is sound that has received a form, and while a thing without form can exist, what does not exist cannot receive a form. This is how matter is prior to what is made from it. It is not prior in the sense that it actively makes the thing, when rather it is itself in a state of being-made, nor is it prior by any lapse of time. For we do not first utter formless sounds without singing, and then later fit them together into the form of a song, as someone might make a chest from wood or a bowl from silver. Such materials do precede in time the forms of the things made from them. But it is not that way with singing. For as soon as one begins to sing, the sound is heard. It is not first a formless sound that then is shaped into song. Every sound passes on once it has been sounded, and you cannot then go back to it and take from it something you might compose by art into a tune.

Therefore, the song depends on its sound, and the sound is its matter. That matter receives a form, so that a song may come to be. And so, as I was saying, the matter to be sounded precedes the form to be sung. It is not prior because it has any power to make the song, nor is the sound the artist who fashions the song, but from its body something is furnished to the mind of the singer, to make a song. It is not prior in time, because it sounds as soon as the song does. It is not prior by virtue of excellence, for a sound is not preferable to a song, seeing that a song is not mere sound, but a lovely sound. But it is prior as an originating fount, because we do not form a song that there may be sound, but sound receives a form that there may be a song.[687]

By this example, let him who can do so understand that the matter of things was made first, and called "heaven and earth" because heaven and earth were made from them, not made first in time, because it is the forms of things that give rise to times, while that matter was then without form, and can now be perceived only in conjunction with the

---

[687] It is important for us to recover a sense of priority that is not merely temporal, and a sense of causality that is not merely like that of one billiard ball striking another. God's priority to the universe is not temporal, as if he were the imaginary machine-maker of the deists, kicking the world into action and then going his way. God's priority is, in its most fundamental form, *ontological:* He is the absolute Being who lends existence at all moments and in the most infinitesimal recesses of matter to all existent things.

times. Nor can anything else be told about that material, unless we say that it had a sort of priority that resembles priority in time, seeing that in value it was least of all, because surely things with form are better than things without form; and that it was preceded by the eternity of the Creator, so that the stuff from which anything could be made would itself have been made from nothing.

30

Amid this diversity of true opinions, let Truth itself beget concord, and may our God have mercy on us, that we may use the law in a lawful way, for the precept's end, which is pure charity.

So when it comes to this, if a man asks me which of these opinions your servant Moses had in mind, these are not the words for my confessions, if I did not confess to you that I do not know. And yet I do know that, except for those that are carnal, about which I have spoken as much as I thought opportune, the opinions I have described are all true. And even those who hold those carnal opinions are little children of good hope, since they are not frightened away by the words of your Scripture, humbly sublime and rich in their spareness.

But let us all love one another, all we who, I confess, do see truths in those words, and who speak them. And likewise let us all love you, our God, the fount of truth, if indeed we thirst for the truth and not for vanities. And let us honor your servant, the steward of your Scripture, who was filled with your Spirit, and let us trust that when he wrote these things which you revealed to him, he was most intent upon what in them shone brightest with the light of truth, and was richest in fruit to do us good.

31

So when someone says, "Moses meant what I mean," and someone else says, "No, he meant what I mean," I think I can say with more reverence, "Why not what you both mean, if both opinions are true?" Why not a third opinion, and a fourth, and whatever else someone may see in these words that is true? Why not believe that he saw all of them? For through him the one God has tempered the sacred writings for the understandings of many people, who would see diverse things in them, and true. Without fear I say it from my heart, that if I should ever write something from a position of high authority, I would rather write it so that my words would ring out with whatever part of the truth any reader might be able to grasp, than to set out one true opinion so plainly as to exclude other opinions that could not offend me by being false. I do not want to be so headstrong, my God, as to doubt that that man merited from you the gift I have described. Surely, when he wrote, he perceived and he considered whatever truths might be found in his words, including what we have not been able to find, or rather not yet, and still they are there to be found.

32

Finally, O Lord, who are God and not flesh and blood, supposing that a man sees less than there is to see, could it lie hidden from your gracious Spirit, who shall lead me into the land of righteousness?[688] Could it lie hidden, what you yourself in those words were going to reveal to readers yet to come, even if he through whom they were spoken was thinking of only a single meaning out of the many that are true? If it is so, let that one meaning be the loftiest of all, and show us that one, Lord, or any other truth you please, so that if you make plain to us what you made plain to that great man of yours, or something else perchance by the same words, it will still be you who are feeding us, and not error deluding us.

Behold, O Lord my God, I pray, how much, how much we have written about only a few words! How could our strength, how could our years ever suffice to treat all your books in the same way? Deign

---

[688] Cf. Ps 143:10.

then to let me more briefly confess to you regarding them, and let me choose the one truth, sure and good, that you shall have inspired me to speak of, even if many should occur to me, as well they may. Let there be such good faith in my confession, that if I happen to say the same thing that your minister intended, I will say it right and in the best way—and it is my duty to strive for that. But if I do not attain to that, still let me say what your Truth will teach me from his words, the same Truth that spoke to him what it was pleased to speak.

BOOK THIRTEEN

1

I call upon you, my God, in your loving kindness to me, for you made me and you did not forget me, even when I had forgotten you.[689] I call you into my soul, which you are furnishing to receive you by the desire you have breathed into it. Do not forsake me now as I invoke you, you who came to me first that I might invoke you, who visited me again and again, besetting me with many kinds of voices, that I might hear from afar and turn back to you, and call to you who were calling me.[690]

O Lord, you have blotted out all my evil deservings,[691] lest you should pay back into my hands all I did when I fell away from you,[692] and you have been beforehand with all my good deservings, so that you might pay back into your hands the works you made in me. Before I ever was, you were, nor was I anything at all to which you might grant the gift of being. Yet, behold, I do exist, from your bounty that came before everything you made me to be, and before everything out of which you made me. Nor did you have any need of me, nor am I any such good thing that you might use for your help, my Lord and my

[689] Cf. Is 49:15.
[690] Cf. Ps 80:19.
[691] Cf. Is 44:22.
[692] Cf. Ps 28:4.

God; not that I might serve you lest you grow weary in your works, not that your power would be the less if you went without my obedience; not that I should cultivate you as a man does the earth, as if you would lie fallow were it not for my tillage; but that I might serve you, and attend to you, that it might be well with me, by your gift. For it is also your gift that I am such as can be well.

2

From the fullness of your bounty does your creation subsist, so that there might not be lacking a good which could be so because you are its origin, though it would be of no profit to you, and would not be equal to you as being of your substance.

For what could heaven and earth, which you made in the beginning, merit from beforehand from you? Let the spiritual and corporeal creations, which you made in your Wisdom, tell what they merited. For they were inchoate and without form, each in its kind, whether spiritual or corporeal, apt to fall headlong into utter distance and unlikeness from you, the unformed spiritual more excellent than if it were corporeal and formed, and the corporeal, even without form, more excellent than if it were nothing at all. But thus without form they depended upon you, they hung upon your Word, they were without form, until by that Word you should call them back to your oneness, that they might receive form, and that the whole universe, from you who are the only and the sovereign good, might be very good indeed.[693] What did they merit from the first, even so much as to be formless, since apart from you they would not be such as they are at all?

What did corporeal matter deserve from you, even to be invisible and without form, since it would not even be that, except that you made it? Since it did not exist, it could not lay any claim on you that it should exist. And what could the inchoate spiritual creation deserve from you from the first, even that it should be darksome and flow like

---

[693] Cf. Gn 1:31.

the deep, unlike you? But by your word it was to be turned round to you who made it, and be made into light, by your illumination; not equal to you, but still, in its form, conforming to what is equal to you.

And just as, for a corporeal creature, to be is not the same as to be beautiful, for otherwise it could never be deformed, so, for a spiritual creature, to live is not the same as to live wisely, because then it would be wise unalterably. It is good for it to cleave to you, lest it should turn away from you and lose the light it gained from turning toward you, and fall back into a life like that of the dark deep. For even we, who are spiritual as to the soul, once dwelt in that life of darkness when we turned aside from you, our light. And still do we labor in our old dim ways, until in your only-begotten we shall be your righteousness, like the mountains of God.[694] For we have been the objects of your judgment, when we were like the great deep.

3

But when you said at the first of creation, "Let there be light,"[695] and there was light, I understand it, not unfitly, to refer to the spiritual creation, because there already was a sort of life you might illuminate. But just as it could lay no claim on you that it might be the kind of life that could be illuminated, so too, once it did exist, it could lay no claim on you to give it light. Nor could its formlessness please you, save that it would be made into light, and then it would please you not by its mere existence, but by its beholding the illuminating light and cleaving to it. So then, that it lives and that it lives in blessedness, it owes to your grace alone, turning by a better change to what cannot be changed for either the better or the worse. This you alone are, because you alone exist in sole simplicity, and to live, for you, is the same as to live in bliss, because you are your bliss.

---

[694] Cf. Ps 36:6.
[695] Gn 1:3.

4

What then could possibly have been lacking to your good, when you are your own good, even if these things had not existed at all, or had remained without form? You made them, not out of need, but rather out of the fullness of your bounty, imposing a form upon them, and not so that your joy would be made complete.[696] For their imperfection displeases you who are perfect, and so you shall make them perfect to please you, not as if you yourself were imperfect or were to be made perfect by their perfection.

For your gracious Spirit was stirring upon the waters;[697] he was not borne up by them, as if he should take his rest upon them. Those upon whom your Spirit is said to rest, he makes rather to rest upon him. But your incorruptible and unalterable will, sufficient unto itself, was stirring upon the life it had created. For that life, to live is not the same as to live in bliss, for it has life even as it floats in its own darkness. This remained for it, to be converted to him who made it, and to live nearer and nearer to the fount of life, and in his light to see light,[698] and to be made perfect, and illuminated, and blessed.

5

Behold, the Trinity appears to me in an enigma,[699] the Trinity which you are, my God, for you the Father, in him who is the beginning of our wisdom, your Wisdom born of you, equal to you and coeternal with you, that is, in your Son, you made heaven and earth.[700] And we have said many things about the heaven of heaven and the earth invisible and without form, and of the abyss, dark in the aimless flow of its spiritual formlessness, until it should be turned round to him who gave

---

696 Cf. Jn 15:11.
697 Cf. Gn 1:2.
698 Cf. Ps 36:9.
699 Cf. 1 Cor 13:12.
700 Cf. Jn 1:3.

it whatever life it had, and then be made a beautiful life by his illumining, to be the heaven of his heaven, which then was set between the water and the water.[701] And I now understood the Father by the name of God who made these things, and the Son, by the name of the beginning in which he made them. Believing my God to be a Trinity, just as I believed so did I search in his holy words, and behold, your Spirit was stirring above the waters.[702] Behold my God the Trinity: Father, Son, and Holy Spirit, the Creator of all creation.

6

But tell me what was the reason, O truth-speaking Light—I bring my heart before you, lest it teach me vanities, and I beg you by our Mother Charity, dispel its darkness and tell me, why did your Scripture first name your Holy Spirit only after it had named heaven and the earth invisible and without form, and darkness over the abyss? Was it only then fitting to first bring him to our minds, when it could be said of him that he *moved above*? That could not be said, unless something had been mentioned first, *above* which it could be understood that your Spirit moved. For he did not move above the Father or the Son, nor could he rightly be said to move *above* at all, were there not something for him to move above. Then that over which he moved had to be named first, and he afterward, as it was not fitting to name him without saying that he moved above. But why then was that so?

7

At this point, let him who has the intellect for it follow your apostle when he says that charity has been shed abroad in our hearts by the Holy Spirit who has been given to us,[703] and when he teaches us about

---

[701] Cf. Gn 1:6.
[702] Cf. Gn 1:2.
[703] Cf. Rom 5:5.

spiritual gifts and shows us the supereminent way of charity;[704] and when he bends the knee to you on our behalf, that we may come to know the supereminent knowledge of the love of Christ.[705] Therefore, even from the beginning did the supereminent Spirit move above the waters.

To whom shall I say it, how shall I speak of the weight of cupidity sinking us into the abyss and its yawning chasm, and of charity that lifts us up by your Spirit, who was moving above the waters? To whom shall I say it, and how? For these are not locations into which we plummet, and from which we are raised again. What can be more like, and yet what can be more unlike? They are affections, they are loves; the filth of our spirit flowing and sinking by the love of things that bring us care; and it is your holiness lifting us higher by a love free from care, that we may in turn lift up our hearts to you, where your Spirit is moving above the waters, and arrive at that supereminent repose, when our soul shall have crossed over those waters where there is no firm place to stand.

8

Sunk had the angel, the soul of man had sunk, and been shown the deep of all spiritual creation in the dark abyss, were it not that you said from the beginning, "Let there be light," and there was light, and every obedient intelligence of your celestial city cleaved unto you, and came to repose in your Spirit, who moves unchangeably over every change-able thing. Otherwise even the heaven of heaven would be, in itself, a dark abyss, while now it is light in the Lord.[706]

For even in that restless misery of the spirits that spilled away, dis-playing their darkness, stripped naked of the robe of your light, you show well how great you have made the rational creature, for which nothing that is less than you suffices to give repose in blessedness, and that is why they cannot even suffice to themselves. For you, our God,

---

[704] Cf. 1 Cor 12:31.
[705] Cf. Eph 3:19.
[706] Cf. Eph 5:8.

shall enlighten our darkness, from you arise our robes of light, and our darkness shall be as the noonday sun.[707]

Give yourself to me, my God, give yourself back to me! See, I love you, and if my love is too little, let me love you with more strength. I cannot measure my love, to know how much I am still wanting from what would suffice, so that my life would run to your embraces and never turn aside, till at last it should be hid in the hiding-place of your countenance.[708] I do know this much: it is ill with me apart from you, and not only outside of me but within me too, and all plenty which is not my God is penury to me.

9

But did not the Father or the Son also move above the waters? If we mean it as a body in a location, the Holy Spirit did not move that way, either. If we mean the unalterable eminence of Godhood, then all three, the Father and the Son and the Holy Spirit, were moving above the waters. Why then was this said only of the Holy Spirit? Why is a place, which was no place, attributed to him, of whom alone is it said that he is your gift?[709]

In your gift do we rest: that is where we enjoy you. Our repose is our place. Love lifts us there, and your gracious Spirit raises up our humility from the gates of death.[710] In your good will is our peace.[711] A body inclines by its weight to its proper place. For weight tends not to the lowest place, merely, but to the place that is its own. The fire rises, and the stone falls. By their weight they are driven, and they seek their proper places. Oil poured into water from below rises above the water;

---

[707] Cf. Is 58:10.

[708] Cf. Col 3:3.

[709] Cf. Acts 2:38.

[710] Cf. Ps 9:13.

[711] "Peace," says Augustine in *The City of God*, "is the tranquility of order" (Bk. 19, ch. 13). Since God is the creator of all things, including the soul of man, it follows that sin necessarily embroils us in war and restlessness.

water poured on top of oil sinks down below the oil; by their weight they are driven, and they seek their proper places. Things a little out of their order will not rest; set them in order again, and they do. My love is my weight; wherever I am carried, it is what carries me. By your Gift we are kindled and we are borne aloft; we grow warm within with fire, and we set on. We ascend the ascending steps of the heart, and we sing a song of degrees.[712] In your fire, in your gracious fire we burn, and we set on, for we are climbing to the peace of Jerusalem. For I was glad when they said to me, "Let us go to the house of the Lord."[713] There shall good will make a place for us,[714] that we may desire nothing else than to abide there forever.[715]

10

O blessed creation which knew nothing else—and it would in itself have been something else—save that by your Gift (which moves above everything that is changeable), as soon as it was made, without any lapse of time, it was raised up as you called it, saying, "Let there be light," and so there was light. In us, instead, there is a distinction of time, for we were darkness and we shall be made light.[716] But of that creation it is truly said what it would have been had it not been enlightened. That is why it is described at first as dark and ceaselessly flowing, in order to show what made it to be otherwise, that is, to be made light, turned to the Light that never fails.[717]

Let him understand this who can; let him seek it from you. Why should he trouble me about it, as if I were the light that enlightens any man who comes into this world?[718]

---

[712] The "songs of ascents" or degrees are Psalms 120-134; see Book 9, ch. 2.
[713] Ps 122:1.
[714] Cf. Jn 14:2.
[715] Cf. Ps 27:4.
[716] Cf. Eph 5:8.
[717] Cf. Jn1:5.
[718] Cf. Jn 1:9.

11

Who shall understand the all-powerful Trinity? And yet who does not speak of it—if it is indeed what he speaks of? Rare is the soul, whatever he says about the Trinity, who knows whereof he speaks. For men argue and fight about it, but unless he is at peace, no one sees this vision. I wish men would ponder some three things in their own selves. They are far different from the Trinity, but I mention them, so that men may exercise their minds and try them and come to understand how far away the things really are.

Here then are the three: *to be, to know, to will.* For I am and I know and I will. I am a knowing and a willing being, and I know that I am and that I will, and I will to be and to know. Now, just as in these three things there is a life that cannot be divided into parts, one life and one mind and one essence, so there is an inseparable distinction among them, and yet a distinction for all that. Let him see it who can. Surely a man stands face to face with himself. Let him attend to it in himself and see it and tell it to me.[719]

But after he has found something there, and told what he has found, let him not suppose he has found the unalterable Being that is above these things, that which unalterably *is* and unalterably *knows* and unalterably *wills.* Whether there is a Trinity in God because of these three powers, or whether the three are in each Person, so that each possesses all three, or whether both hold true, so that in wondrous ways, simple and manifold, it is its own bound in its boundless being, whereby it is and it is known to itself and it suffices to itself, unalterably itself in the bountiful greatness of its unity—who shall find it easy to conceive? Who shall find the words to express it? Who shall be so rash as to deliver in any way his opinion about it?

---

[719] Augustine is employing an analogy, and he is acutely aware that it is only an analogy. We must not reduce the Blessed Trinity to three modes or faculties of one Being, because that would efface the Persons and their distinctness.

12

Go farther in your confession, O my faith. Say to your Lord, "Holy, holy, holy Lord my God, in your name were we baptized, Father, Son, and Holy Spirit; in your name we baptize, Father, Son, and Holy Spirit."[720] For among us also, in his Christ, God made heaven and earth, the spiritual and carnal members of his Church. And before it received the form of doctrine, our earth was invisible and without form,[721] and we were covered with the darkness of ignorance, for you have disciplined man for his iniquity,[722] and your judgments are a great deep.[723] But because your Spirit moved above the waters, your mercy did not forsake our misery, and you said, "Let there be light; repent, for the kingdom of heaven is at hand; repent, and become light."[724] And because our soul was troubled within us, we remembered you, Lord, from the land of Jordan, and from the mountain which was equal to yourself but was made little for our sake.[725] And our darkness displeased us, and we turned round to you, and there was light. Behold, we were once darkness, but now we are light in the Lord.[726]

13

And we have come thus far by faith, not by sight.[727] For by hope have we been saved. But hope that is seen is not hope.[728] Till now, deep calls

---

[720] Cf. Is 6:3. Mt 28:19.
[721] Cf. Gn 1:1–2.
[722] Cf. Ps 39:11.
[723] Cf. Ps 36:6.
[724] Cf. Gn 1:3, Mk 1:15, Acts 2:38.
[725] Cf. Ps 42:6.
[726] Cf. Eph 5:8. Augustine applies the language of Scripture as regards creation to the re-creation of the human soul. Again, we must keep in mind that God, the author of Scripture, can, by means of the human beings his Spirit inspires, express the truth in words that signify several perfectly compatible things at once. Therefore what we say of the great cosmos we may say of the little cosmos, the human soul, that in important respects is greater than all the rest of physical creation: that God wills that his Light should enlighten our darkness.
[727] Cf. 2 Cor 5:7.
[728] Cf. Rom 8:24.

unto deep, but now it calls in the sound of your cataracts.[729] Till now, it is he who says, "I could not speak to you as to spiritual beings, but only as to the carnal,"[730] even as he himself does not believe he has comprehended it, forgetting things past, and straining toward things to come,[731] and he groans under his burden,[732] and his soul thirsts for the living God, as deer thirst for the running streams, and he says, "When shall I come there?,"[733] longing to be clothed with his dwelling place, which is from heaven.[734] And he calls upon the deeps below, saying, "Do not conform yourselves to this passing world, but be reformed in the renewing of your mind,"[735] and "Be not mere children in under-standing, but be children when it comes to malice, that you may be made perfect in your minds,"[736] and "You stupid Galatians, who has bewitched you?"[737]

But he speaks thus not in his own voice, but in yours. You sent your Spirit down from on high, through him who rose on high, and opened the floodgates of your gifts,[738] that the surge of the stream might glad-den your city.[739] For the bridegroom's friend sighs for him,[740] having now the first fruits of the Spirit within him, but till now groaning, looking forward to his adoption, the redemption of his body.[741] For him he sighs—for he is a member of the bride—for his sake he is jeal-ous—for he is the bridegroom's friend—for him he is jealous, not on his own account. For in the voice of your cataracts, not in his own, he

---

[729] Cf. Ps 42:7.
[730] Cf. 1 Cor 3:1.
[731] Cf. Phil 3:13.
[732] Cf. 2 Cor 5:4.
[733] Cf. Ps 42:1–2.
[734] Cf. 2 Cor 5:2.
[735] Rom 12:2.
[736] 1 Cor 14:20.
[737] Gal 3:1.
[738] Cf. Mal 3:10.
[739] Cf. Ps 46:4.
[740] Cf. Jn 3:29.
[741] Cf. Rom 8:23.

calls to that other deep,[742] which he fears in his jealous zeal, lest as the serpent deceived Eve by his guile, their senses might be corrupted and might fall from that chastity which is in our Bridegroom, your only-begotten Son. What a light of beauty, when we shall see him as he is,[743] and all the tears which have been my bread day and night shall have passed away, while they daily said to me, "Where is your God?"[744]

14

And I too say, "Where is my God?" Behold where you are. Let me catch my breath a little in you, while I pour out my soul in the sound of exultation and confession, the sound of one who celebrates a holy feast.[745] And still it is sad, because it slides back and becomes a deep once more, or rather it perceives that it is still a great deep. My faith speaks to it, the lamp you have lighted for my steps in the night,[746] saying, "Why are you sad, my soul, and why do you trouble me? Hope in the Lord; his word is a lamp unto your feet."[747] Hope and persevere, till the night is past, that mother of the wicked; till the wrath of the Lord is past. And we too were once children of wrath, we were darkness,[748] and we still carry the remnants of that darkness about with us, in the body that is dead because of sin,[749] till the day shall breathe upon us and all the shadows flee.[750]

Hope in the Lord;[751] in the morning I shall stand and contemplate him; evermore shall I confess to him. In the morning I shall stand

---

[742] Cf. Ps 42:7.
[743] Cf. 1 Jn 3:2.
[744] Cf. Ps 42:2–3.
[745] Cf. Is 30:29.
[746] Cf. Ps 119:105.
[747] Ps 42:11, Ps 119:105.
[748] Cf. Eph 2:3.
[749] Cf. Rom 8:10.
[750] Cf. Sg 2:17.
[751] Cf. Ps 42:11.

and see the health of my countenance, my God,[752] who shall bring to life our mortal bodies because of the Spirit that dwells in us,[753] for in his loving kindness He moved above our inner dark and whelming deep. From him in this pilgrim life we have received an earnest that we should even now be light, while we are yet saved by hope, made sons of the light and the day, not the sons of night and darkness that we once were.[754] In the uncertainty of human knowledge, it is you alone who can make division between us and them, you who probe our hearts and who call the light day and the darkness night.[755] Who can discern what we are but you? For what do we have but what we received from you, made into vessels of honor from the same lump from which others have been made for dishonor?[756]

15

And who but you, our God, made for us a firmament of authority, set above us in your divine Scripture?[757] For the heaven shall be rolled up like a scroll, which now is stretched like a tent-skin above us.[758] For your divine Scripture soars with an authority more sublime, now that the mortal men through whom you bestowed them upon us have departed this mortal life. And you know, Lord, you know, how you clothed men with skins as soon as they had become mortal, by sin.[759] Whence like a skin you stretched out the firmament of your book, those lessons of yours that ring so well together, which you set in place above us, using mortal men as your ministers. For by their very death, the firm authority of the words you spoke through them has been stretched out

---

[752] Cf. Ps 43:5.
[753] Cf. Rom 8:11.
[754] Cf. Eph 5:8.
[755] Cf. Gn 1:5.
[756] Cf. Rom 9:21, 2 Tm 2:20–21.
[757] Cf. Gn 1:6.
[758] Cf. Is 34:4, Rv 6:14.
[759] Cf. Gn 3:21.

in sublime height over all things below. But when they were still alive, that authority had not been raised to such height. For you had not yet stretched out that heaven like a skin; you had not yet spread abroad the fame of their death.

Let us look, O Lord, upon the heavens, the work of your fingers:[760] clear our eyes of the cloud you had cast upon them. Your testimony is there, bestowing wisdom upon little ones; perfect your praise, my God, out of the mouth of babes and sucklings.[761] For we know no other books that destroy pride as these do, that destroy the enemy and the defender, the man who resists being reconciled to you as he defends his own sins. Lord, I know no sayings so chaste, none which so persuade me to confess and to ease my stiff neck and bend it to your yoke,[762] and which invite me to serve you as a free gift. Let me understand them, gracious Father, as I am placed beneath them; for you have made them a solid firmament for those who are placed beneath.

There are other waters above this firmament, as I believe, immortal, and kept free from earthly corruption. Let them praise your name, let the super-celestial citizens, your angels, praise you; they who have no need to gaze up at this firmament, no need to read in order to know your word. For they always behold your face,[763] and there they read, without syllables in time, what your eternal will decrees. They read, they choose, they fall in love; they read evermore and what they read never passes away. For by choosing and loving they read the very immutability of your counsel. Their book is not shut, their scroll is not rolled up, for you yourself are their book for everlasting, because you set them in their orders above this firmament, that which you fixed above the infirmity of your people below. And they can gaze up at it and come to know your lovingkindness that proclaims, in time, you who made the times.

---

[760] Cf. Ps 8:3.
[761] Cf. Ps 8:2.
[762] Cf. Mt 11:30.
[763] Cf. Mt 18:10.

For your lovingkindness, Lord, is in the heavens, and your truth soars high as the clouds.[764] The clouds pass away, but heaven abides. They who preach your word pass from this life into the other life, but truly your Scripture is stretched above the peoples, to the end of the passing world. Even heaven and earth shall pass away, but your words shall not pass away,[765] for the vellum shall be rolled up, and the grass over which it was stretched shall pass away with all its beauty, but your word shall abide for everlasting. Now does it appear to us in a cloudy riddle,[766] and in the mirror of the skies above, and not as it is. For even though we are beloved by thy Son, it has not yet appeared what we shall be.[767] He gazed through the lattice of the flesh, and spoke sweet words, and set us afire with love, and we ran after his fragrance.[768] But when he shall appear, we shall be like him, for we shall see him as he is;[769] for our seeing shall be as he is, but for us it is not yet so.

16

For just as you wholly *are*, so do you alone *know*, for you unalterably are, you unalterably know, and you unalterably will. And your being knows and wills unalterably, and your knowledge is and wills unalterably, and your will is and knows unalterably. Nor does it seem just before you, that what is changeable and receives the light should know the Light in the same way as the unalterable Light should know itself. And so my soul is to you as a land without water,[770] because just as it cannot give itself light, so too it cannot slake its own thirst. Thus is the fountain of life with you, as it is by your light that we shall see light.[771]

---

[764] Cf. Ps 36:5.
[765] Cf. Is 40:8, Mt 24:35, 1 Pt 1:25.
[766] Cf. 1 Cor 13:12.
[767] Cf. 1 Jn 3:2.
[768] Cf. Sg 2:9–14.
[769] Cf. 1 Jn 3:2.
[770] Cf. Ps 63:1.
[771] Cf. Ps 36:9.

17

Who gathered up men's bitter waters into one society? For they all have the same end for everything they do, a temporal and earthly happiness, although they are tossed and tumbled by an innumerable variety of cares. Who, Lord, but yourself? For you said, "Let the waters be gathered up into one place, and let the dry land appear,"[772] thirsting after you, for the sea is yours, and you made it, and your hands formed the dry land.[773] It is not the bitterness of human wills, but the gathering of the waters that is called the sea. For you check the evil desires of men's souls too, and you fix bounds to how far the waters are permitted to go,[774] that their waves may be dashed against one another; and that is how you make the sea, by the order of your dominion over all things.

But you water the souls that appear before you and thirst for you, souls that another end has set apart from the society of the sea, by a hidden spring of sweet water, that the earth too may bring forth its fruit;[775] and she gives her fruit, and at your command, O Lord her God, our soul buds forth in works of loving kindness after their kind, loving our neighbor by coming to the aid of his fleshly needs; having seed within her, by way of her likeness to others, for by our own weakness we feel compassion for others in need, and we go to their relief, assisting them as we would wish to be assisted if we were in similar need.[776] And we do so not only when we find it easy, as with the herb that bears its seed within it, but also when it calls upon the mighty oak of our protection, as that of the tree bearing fruit: that is, to do good by plucking a man who suffers injustice from the hand of the powerful, and offering him the shade of protection, beneath that sound oak of just judgment.

---

[772] Cf. Gn 1:9.
[773] Cf. Ps 95:5.
[774] Cf. Job 38:11.
[775] Cf. Gn 1:11.
[776] Cf. Mt 7:12.

18

So, Lord, I beseech you, let truth spring up, as you are making it to do, as you give cheerfulness and the capacity to give, let truth spring up from the earth, and let righteousness look down from heaven,[777] and let there be luminaries in the firmament.[778] Let us break our bread for the hungry, and let us take into our home the needy man who has no roof over his head. Let us clothe the naked, and let us not despise them who live with us, who are of our own seed.[779] And once these fruits have been born from the earth, look, and see that it is good. And let our timely light break forth,[780] and as we pass from this lower fruit of action to the higher delights of contemplation, holding fast to the word of life,[781] let us appear like luminaries in the world, fixed fast in the firmament of your Scripture.

There you discuss things with us, so that we learn to divide intelligible things and things we sense, as between the day and the night, or between souls given to intelligible things and souls given to the things of sense. And the purpose is this: that it shall not be you alone who make division between light and darkness, but by your grace made manifest throughout the sphere where they turn, your spiritual children shall do so also, set in the same firmament and given their distinct places; that they shall shed light upon the earth and divide the day from the night, and shall them be signs for seasons,[782] because the old things have passed away, and behold, they are made new,[783] and because our salvation is now nearer than when we first believed, and the night is far spent, and the day draws near,[784] and because you are blessing the

---

[777] Cf. Ps 85:11.
[778] Cf. Gn 1:14.
[779] Cf. Is 58:7.
[780] Cf. Is 58:8.
[781] Cf. Phil 2:16.
[782] Cf. Gn 1:14.
[783] Cf. Rv 21:4–5.
[784] Cf. Rom 13:11.

crown of your year,[785] sending laborers into your harvest that others have sown before, and sending laborers into another field whose harvest will come at the end.[786] So do you answer the prayers of him who seeks, and you bless the years of the righteous man,[787] while you are the Selfsame, and in your years that never fail you build a granary for the years that come and go.

For in your eternal counsel, you bestow in their proper seasons heavenly goods upon the earth. To one man is given, by the Spirit, the word of wisdom, as it were the greater luminary, for those who delight in the brilliance of the clearest truth, to govern the day. To another, by the same Spirit, is given the word of knowledge, as it were the lesser luminary. To another, faith; to another, the gift of healing; to another, the power of working miracles; to another, prophecy; to another, the discernment of spirits; to still another, speaking in various tongues, and all these are like the stars. For the same one Spirit performs all these works, dealing out, as he wills, to each man his proper gifts, and causing the stars to shine bright, to the profit of all.[788]

But the word of knowledge, encompassing all the mysteries that vary with the seasons as the moon does, and the other gifts that are mentioned last, just as the stars were, are to govern the night, inasmuch as they differ from that brightness of wisdom which gladdens the day. These are necessary for those people whom that most prudent servant of yours could not speak to as spiritual men, but as to the fleshly[789]— and it was he who spoke wisdom among those perfected in the faith. But the natural man is like a little baby in Christ, who still drinks his mother's milk.[790] Until he grows big enough for solid food, and until he can look steadfastly upon the sun, let him not suppose that his night is forsaken, but let him rest content with the light of the moon and the

---

[785] Cf. Ps 65:11.
[786] Cf. 1 Cor 3:6–9.
[787] Cf. Ps 5:12.
[788] Cf. 1 Cor 12:4–12.
[789] Cf. 1 Cor 3:1.
[790] Cf. Heb 5:13.

stars.[791] Most wisely, our God, do you discourse with us in your book, your firmament, that by a marvelous contemplation we may learn to discern all things, though still in signs and seasons and days and years.

19

But "wash yourselves first and be clean, put away the evil from your souls and from the sight of my eyes,"[792] and let the dry land appear.[793] Learn to do good, to judge the orphan and vindicate the widow, that the earth may sprout up the green grass for food, and the fruit-bearing tree.[794] "Come, let us reason together,"[795] says the Lord, that there may be luminaries in the firmament of heaven, to shine upon the earth.[796]

That rich young man asked the good Teacher what he should do to gain eternal life.[797] Let the good Teacher—whom the lad believed was a man and no more, but he is good, because he is God—let the good Teacher tell him that if he wants to come unto life, he must keep the commandments, he must put away the bitterness of malice and wickedness; let him not kill, let him not commit adultery, let him not steal, let him not bear false witness, that the dry land may appear and sprout up honor for mother and father, and love of neighbor. "I have done all these things," he says. Where then do all those thorns come from, if the earth is fruitful? Go, root up and clear out the brambles of avarice,[798] sell what you have and fill your granaries by giving to the poor, and you shall have treasure in heaven, and follow the Lord, if you want to be perfect. Be a friend to those among whom he speaks wisdom, for he knows what to distribute to the day and to the night, that you also

---

[791] Cf. Gn 1:16.
[792] Is 1:16.
[793] Cf. Gn 1:9.
[794] Cf. Is 1:17, Gn 1:11.
[795] Is 1:18.
[796] Cf. Gn 1:17.
[797] Cf. Mt 19:16–22.
[798] Cf. Mt 13:7.

may know it, that there may be made for you too the luminaries in the firmament of heaven. But that will never be so, unless your heart is in it; nor will that be so, unless your treasure has been there,[799] as you have heard from the good Teacher. But the barren earth was sad to hear that, and the thorns choked out the word.

But you, a chosen generation,[800] weak in the eyes of the world,[801] you who have forsaken everything to follow the Lord[802]—go where he goes, and put the mighty to confusion; go where he goes, you beautiful feet,[803] and shine in the firmament,[804] that the heavens may tell his glory, dividing between the light of the perfect, but who are not yet like the angels, and the darkness of the little ones, who yet are not without hope. Shine over all the earth, and let the day that is splendid in sunlight utter to the day the word of wisdom, and let the night that gleams in the moon utter to the night the word of knowledge.[805] The moon and the stars of night shine, but the night does not quench their light, because they illumine it according to their modest degree. For behold, it was as if God had said, "Let there be luminaries in the firmament of heaven," and straightaway from heaven came a great sound, like the rush of a mighty wind, and there appeared cloven tongues as of fire, settling upon each of them, and there were made luminaries in the firmament of heaven, having the word of life in them.[806] Race everywhere, you holy fires, you beautiful fires! You are the light of the world, and you are not placed under a bushel.[807] He to whom you cleave is the Most High, and he has raised you high. Race, wildfire, and make yourself known to all nations!

---

[799] Cf. Mt 6:21.
[800] Cf. 1 Pt 2:9.
[801] Cf. 1 Cor 1:27.
[802] Cf. Mt 19:27.
[803] Cf. Is 52:7, Rom 10:15.
[804] Cf. Ps 19:1.
[805] Cf. Ps 19:2.
[806] Cf. Acts 2:2–4, Phil 2:15–16.
[807] Cf. Mt 5:14–15.

20

Let the sea also conceive and give birth to your works, and let the waters bring forth the creeping creature that has life.[808] For when you separate the precious from the base, you become the mouth of God, who said, "Let the waters bring forth," not the living soul the earth brings forth, but the creeping things that have life, and the birds of the air that fly above the earth. For your sacraments, O God, by the works of your saints, have crept forth among the waves of worldly temptations to dye the nations in your name, in your baptism.

And among these deeds, grand and wondrous works have been wrought, like the great whales, and the calls of your heralds that fly above the earth, ever near the firmament of your book, set above them as their authority, beneath which they were to fly wherever they went.[809] For there is no manner of speech, no language, where their voices are not heard, since their sound has gone through all the earth, and their words to the ends of the world, because you, Lord, have multiplied them by your blessing.[810]

Am I telling a lie? Am I mixing things up? Do I fail to distinguish the lucid knowledge of these things in the firmament of heaven from the corporal works in the choppy sea beneath the firmament of heaven? The first are things we have sound notice of, fully defined, not to be increased by the generations, such as are the lights of wisdom and knowledge. The second, their works in the flesh, are many and diverse, and as one thing grows from another, they are multiplied, O God, in your blessing, for you come to the comfort of our mortal senses that so easily grow weary; so that for the understanding mind, one thing may be uttered and figured forth in many ways, by the motions of corporeal creatures. The waters have brought these things to birth, but in your word. The needs of people alienated from the eternity of your truth

---

[808] Cf. Gn 1:20.
[809] Cf. Gn 1:21–22.
[810] Cf. Ps 19:3–4.

have brought them to birth, but in your gospel. For the waters have cast them up,[811] the same waters whose bitter sickness was the cause for their going forth in your word to begin with.

And all the things you have made are beautiful, and behold, you who made them all are more beautiful beyond words to tell it. And had Adam not fallen away from you, the brackish salt waters would not have flowed from his loins, that is, mankind, plunged in deep cares, swollen with great waves of pride, flowing and fleeting without any stay. Then your dispensers would not have needed to labor in the many waters, turning to what is corporeal and what can be grasped by the senses, to work their mystical works and words. For that is how those creeping and flying creatures now strike me. Made subject to bodily sacraments, initiated in them, steeped in them, men would go no farther, unless the soul should live spiritually on another stage, and pass from the word of their initiation to look ahead to its consummation.

21

That is why, in your word, it is not the depth of the sea, but the earth, separated from the bitter waters, that casts up not the creeping and flying creatures that have life in them, but the living soul.[812] And at this time, it has no need of baptism, which the nations need, as it did also when it was covered by the waters; for there is no way to enter the kingdom of heaven but this, from the time when you established it to be the way.[813] Nor does it demand great miracles to be its material for faith. For it is no longer such as will not believe unless it sees signs and wonders,[814] now that the faithful earth has been set apart from the sea-waters bitter with faithlessness, and tongues are meant to be a sign not to those who believe, but to those who do not believe.[815]

---

[811] Cf. Is 57:20.
[812] Cf. Gn 1:24.
[813] Cf. Jn 3:5.
[814] Cf. Jn 4:48.
[815] Cf. 1 Cor 14:22.

And the earth you have founded upon the waters needs no longer the sort of bird that the waters brought forth in your word. Send your word into the earth by your messengers. We tell stories of what they have done, but you, you are the one who work within them, that they might fashion a living soul. The earth brings that soul forth, because the earth is the reason why they act in it, just as the sea was the cause of the creeping things and the birds that fly beneath the firmament of heaven. The earth needs these creatures no longer, though it does feed upon the Fish raised up from the deep, on that table you have prepared in the sight of them who believe.[816] For that is why he was raised from the deep, that he might give nourishment to the dry land. And the birds, though they are the brood of the sea, are multiplied upon the earth. For man's faithlessness was the cause of the first calls of the evangelists; but even the faithful are urged on and are blessed by them in a multiplicity of ways, day by day. But the living soul takes its onset from the earth, for it profits none but the faithful to hold themselves aloof from the love of this passing world, that their soul may live for you. That soul was dead while it lived for pleasures, Lord, for deadly pleasures;[817] but you are the life-giving pleasure of the pure in heart.

Then let your ministers work on the earth, not as they used to do in the waters of faithlessness, announcing and speaking by miracles and mysteries and mystic words, where ignorance, the mother of wonder, is spellbound in reverent fear before the secret signs. For that is faith's entry for the sons of Adam who have forgotten you, while they hide from your face[818] and become a deep. Yes, let your ministers work as on the dry land set apart from the yawning deep, and let them be a pattern for the faithful,[819] living among them and stirring them up to imitate them. For the faithful listen not only to hear, but to take action: "Seek

---

[816] The Fish is a symbol of Christ. In Greek, the first letters of the words Iesous Christos Theou 'Yios Soter, Jesus Christ of God the Son, Savior, spell out ICHTHYS, the Greek word for fish.

[817] Cf. 1 Tm 6:20.

[818] Cf. Gn 3:8.

[819] Cf. 1 Tm 1:16.

God, and your soul shall live,"[820] that the earth may bring forth the living soul. Do not conform yourselves to this world,[821] but keep aloof from it. The soul lives by shunning what it dies by craving. Keep yourselves continent from the monstrous savagery of pride, from luxury and its slough, and from a false name for knowledge, that the wild beasts may be made meek and mild, and the cattle tamed, and the serpents harmless.[822] For these, in allegory, are motions of the soul. But disdainful arrogance, and a smack for lust, and the venom of inquisitiveness are motions of a dead soul. For a dead soul does not lose all its motion. It dies by departing from the fount of life, and so it is snatched up by the passing world and is conformed to it.

But the Word, God, is the fount of life eternal, and it does not pass away. And that is why this departure of the soul is held in check by your Word, when we are told, Do not conform yourselves to this passing world,"[823] so that the earth will bring forth in the fount of life a living soul, a soul made continent in your word, by the preaching of the evangelists, and by imitating the imitators of your Christ. This is what it means to be according to kind, because a man strives to emulate his friend. "Be as I am," he says, "because I too am as you are." Therefore in the living soul there will be good beasts, meek in their behavior. You have commanded as much, saying, "Do your work in meekness, and every man will love you."[824] And there shall be good cattle too, not too fat if they eat, nor too lean if they do not, and good serpents, not dangerous or hurtful, but subtle,[825] to be aware, searching into this temporal nature as much as is needful, so that by the things that have been made, eternity may be seen and understood.[826] For these animals

---

[820] Is 55:6.
[821] Cf. Rom 12:2.
[822] Cf. Is 11:6–9.
[823] Rom 12:2.
[824] Sir 3:19.
[825] Cf. Gn 3:1.
[826] Cf. Rom 1:20.

are servants of reason when their deadly aggression is restrained, and they live and are good.

22

For see, O Lord our God, our Creator, when the affections are held back from love of the passing world, the affections wherein we died by evil living, and when the living soul begins to exist by living well, then shall your Word be fulfilled, when you said by your apostle, "Do not conform yourselves to this passing world."[827] And then shall follow what you joined to it straightaway, saying, "But be reformed in the renewing of your mind," not now as living after our kind, as if we were to imitate our next neighbor, nor even living by the authority of some better man. For you did not say, "Let there be man after his kind," but, "Let us make man in our image, after our likeness,"[828] that we may prove what your will is.

That is why the dispenser of your word, begetting children by the gospel, not wanting them to be babes forever whom he must nourish with milk and tend as nurslings,[829] says, "Be reformed in the renewing of your mind," that you may prove what is the will of God, what is good and pleasing and perfect. Therefore, you do not say, "Let there be man," but, "Let us make," nor "according to his kind," but "in our image, after our likeness." Renewed then in his mind, and seeing and understanding your truth, he needs no man to demonstrate it for him, no one of his kind to imitate, but by your demonstration he himself proves what your will is, what is good and pleasing and perfect. And as he now can receive it, you teach him the Trinity of the Unity, and the Unity of the Trinity. That is why it says in the plural, "Let us make man," and the singular is added to it, "And God made man," and it says in the plural, "in our image," and the singular again is added to it, "in

---

[827] Rom 2:12.
[828] Gn 1:26.
[829] Cf. 1 Cor 3:1, Heb 5:12.

the image of God." Thus is man renewed in coming to know God, in the image of him who created him, and, now made spiritual, he judges all things that are to be judged, while he himself is judged by no man.[830]

23

As for his judging all things, it means that he has dominion over the fish of the sea, the birds of the air, and all cattle, and wild beasts, and over all the earth, and all the creeping things that creep upon the earth.[831] He does so by his mind's understanding, whereby he perceives the things that are of the Spirit of God. Otherwise man, though set in a place of honor, understands nothing, and is compared to the witless cattle, and he has become like them.[832]

Therefore, in your Church, according to the grace you, our God, have bestowed upon her, for we are your workmanship created for good works, there are not only spiritual persons placed in authority, but also spiritual persons who obey those who are set above them. So you made man male and female[833] in your spiritual grace also, where in bodily sex there is neither male nor female, neither Jew nor Greek, neither bond nor free.[834] Spiritual men, then, both those who are in authority and those who obey, judge spiritually. We do not judge those spiritual intelligences that shine in the firmament, for it is not fitting to sit in judgment upon authority so sublime. We do not judge your book, even when something in it does not shine out clear, because we submit to it our understanding, and we hold as certain what is shut from our vision, certain, and rightly and truthfully spoken.

For a man, spiritual though he may be and renewed in the knowledge of God, after the image of him who created him, ought to be

---

[830] Cf. 1 Cor 2:15.
[831] Cf. Gn 1:28.
[832] Cf. Ps 49:20.
[833] Cf. Gn 1:27.
[834] Cf. Gal 3:28.

a doer of the law, not a judge.[835] Nor does he pretend to distinguish between those spiritual and carnal men who are known to your eyes, our God, and whose works have not yet appeared to us that we might know them by their fruits.[836] But you, Lord, already know them, and you have already in secret made your division and called them, before there ever was a firmament. Nor does the man, though spiritual, pass judgment upon the disorderly peoples of this passing world. What has he to do with judging those who are outside,[837] when he does not know which of them is going to come into the sweetness of your grace, and which shall remain in the everlasting bitterness of impiety?

Man, then, whom you have made after your image, is not given dominion over the lights of heaven, let alone over that heaven that is secret, nor over the day and the night, which you called into being before the foundation of the heavens, nor over the gathering of the waters that is the sea. But he has been given dominion over the fish of the sea and the birds of the air, and all cattle, and all the earth and all the creeping things that creep upon the earth. He judges and approves what is rightly done, and disapproves what he finds amiss; whether in the solemn performance of the sacraments whereby your lovingkindness initiates into the Church those whom it has traced in the many waters; or in that Sacrament that shows the fish raised up from the abyss for the devout earth to feed upon; or in the signs of words and their sounds, made subject to the authority of your book, like the birds that fly beneath the firmament—judging them by interpreting, expounding, discussing, disputing, blessing, and calling upon you, in signs that sound and break forth from the lips, that the people may respond, Amen.

And all these must be pronounced aloud, by the body, on account of the abyss of this world and the blindness of the flesh. They make it so that thoughts cannot be seen, so we must beat the ears with sound.

---

[835] Cf. Jas 1:22.
[836] Cf. Mt 7:16.
[837] Cf. 1 Cor 5:12.

And so, though the birds of the air are multiplied upon the earth, they take their origin from the waters.

Moreover, the spiritual man judges and approves what is right and disapproves what he finds amiss in the works and the ways of the faithful, in their almsgiving, like the fruitful earth. He also judges the living soul, its affections made meek in chastity, in fasts, and in devout meditations, insofar as these can be perceived by the bodily senses. He is said to be the judge also over those matters wherein he has the power of correction.

24

But what is this—and what a mystery! Behold, Lord, you bless men, that they may increase and multiply, and fill the earth.[838] Is this not a nod to us, that we should understand why you did not so bless the light that you called "day," or the firmament of heaven, or the sun and moon, or the stars, or the earth, or the sea? I might say, our God, who made us in your image—I might say you wanted to bestow this blessing upon man only, except you gave the same to the fish and the whales, that they might increase and multiply and fill the waters of the sea, and to the birds, that they might be multiplied upon the earth. I might say, too, that the blessing properly pertains to those kinds of things that are begotten of themselves, if I found that you had given it to the vines and the fruit trees and the cattle. But neither to the grasses and the trees, nor to the wild beasts and the serpents, did you say, "Increase and multiply," even though all these too, like the fish and the birds and human beings, increase by generation, and preserve their kinds.

What then shall I say, O Truth, my Light? That it was idle, that it was said without any sense? Never, Father of piety! Far be it from a servant of your word to say so. And if I do not understand what you mean by this speech, let others who are better than I am make better use of it—that is, who have more understanding than I do, according to what

[838] Cf. Gn 1:28.

you have given each man to understand. But let this my confession be pleasing in your sight, for I confess to you, Lord, that I believe you did not speak so to no purpose. Nor shall I keep silent about what the words suggest to me as I read them. For what they suggest is true, and I do not see what should prevent me from understanding the figurative sayings in your books in this way.

I know, for example, that a thing can be signified in many ways by the body though it is understood in one single way by the mind, and that the mind can understand in many ways what is expressed in a single way by the body. Take the love of God and neighbor. It is a single thing, but in what a wide variety of sacraments is it expressed, and in countless languages, and in any one language in countless bodily figures of speech! So do the fry of the sea increase and multiply. Take heed again, my reader. Look what Scripture gives us in one way, in one sounding voice: "In the beginning God made heaven and earth." Is that not understood in many ways, and not deceitfully or erroneously, but with different kinds of true understanding? So does the offspring of man increase and multiply.

So, if we think of the natures of things not allegorically, but in their proper literal sense, the saying, "Increase and multiply," befits all things begotten from seed. But if we treat the words as set forth figuratively— and I am readier to suppose that Scripture intends them so, because then it would not have been pointless to attribute this blessing only to the creatures of the sea and the offspring of men—we find multitudes, among both spiritual and corporeal creatures, as in heaven and earth, and among souls both righteous and unrighteous, as in light and darkness, and among the holy authors who have ministered the law to us, as in the firmament fixed between the waters and the waters, and in the society of the bitter heathen, as in the salt sea, and in the careful devotion of pious souls, as on the dry land, and in works of mercy performed in this present life, as seed-bearing plants and trees bearing fruit, and in spiritual gifts made manifest for our profit, as in the luminaries of heaven, and in affections shaped by temperance, as in the living soul. In all these, we meet with fertility, and increase, and multiplication.

But what can increase and multiply in such a sense that one thing can be expressed in many ways, or one expression can be understood in many ways? We will find what can do so only among signs given in corporeal form, or among things the intellect has conceived. For signs given in corporeal form, we understand the brood of the waters, on account of things made necessary by the dark depths of the flesh; for things the intellect has conceived, we understand the brood of men, on account of the fecundity of reason. And that, we believe, is why you, Lord, spoke thus to both kinds of creatures, saying, "Increase and multiply." In this blessing, I take you to have granted us the power and the authority to express in many ways what we understand in one way alone, and to understand in many ways what we read as expressed, darkly, in but one way. Thus are the waters of the sea made full, which do not move except by a variety of significations, and thus too is the earth replenished with human offspring, whose dryness appears in its eager desire, and reason is its governor.

25

I wish to say, O Lord my God, what the Scripture that follows brings to mind, nor do I fear to say it. For I shall speak the truth, when you inspire me and give me to say what you wish me to say about these words. Nor do I believe I shall speak the truth with any other inspiration than yours, seeing that you are the Truth, and every man is a liar.[839] And that is why it is said, "He who speaks a lie, speaks of his own."[840] So I speak from your gift, so that I may speak the truth.

Behold, you have given to us for food every green herb bearing seeds which is upon all the earth, and every tree that bears fruit with its seed in it.[841] And not only to us, but to all the birds of heaven and the beasts of the field and the creeping things; but you have not given

---

[839] Cf. Rom 3:4.
[840] Jn 8:44.
[841] Cf. Gn 1:29.

these things to the fish and the great whales. For we were saying that the works of mercy were signified and figured forth allegorically by the fruits of the earth, which the fruitful earth provides us for the necessities of this life. Such an earth was the pious Onesiphorus, to whose house you gave mercy, for many a time he gave refreshment to your Paul, and he was not ashamed that Paul was in chains.[842] So too the brethren who came from Macedonia, who blossomed out with such fruit when they supplied Paul's needs.[843] But certain trees grieve him, because they did not give him his due fruit, when he says, "At my first defense no one stood by me, but everyone forsook me. Let it not be held against them."[844] For we owe these fruits to those who minister the rational doctrine to us, by their understanding of divine mysteries; and we owe the fruits also to them, as they are men; and also as to the living soul, as they give themselves to us as patterns of continence to imitate. Again, they are due to them as to the birds that fly, for their blessings that are multiplied over the earth, as their sound has gone forth to every land.[845]

26

And those who delighted by these foods feed upon them, but they do not delight those whose belly is their god.[846] Nor are they the real fruit to those who offer them, but rather the mind with which they give. So I see clearly what gave joy to him who served God and not his belly, I see it and I rejoice with him. For he received from the Philippians what they had sent to him by Epaphroditus;[847] but I still see what really gave him joy. What gave him joy, he fed upon, as he speaks about it in truth: "I rejoiced greatly in the Lord, because your care for me has

---

[842] Cf. 2 Tm 1:16.
[843] Cf. 2 Cor 11:9.
[844] 2 Tm 4:16.
[845] Cf. Ps 19:4.
[846] Cf. Phil 3:19.
[847] Cf. Phil 4:18.

come to bloom again, though it was bothersome to you."[848] They had, then, shriveled up with a long weariness, as if they had gone dry of this fruit of good work, and he rejoices for them because they have come to bloom again, and not for himself, whose wants they have supplied. Hence he goes on, thus: "I am not saying this because I am lacking anything, for I have learned to be content with the conditions in which I find myself. I know how to do with little; I know how to do with plenty. I have become accustomed to all and each; to be full, and to go hungry, to abound, and to suffer want. I can do all things in him who strengthens me."[849]

What then do you rejoice in, Paul? What do rejoice in, you great man, what do you feed upon, you who have been renewed in the knowledge of God, according to the image of him who created you, a living soul, alive with such continence, with a voice speaking mysteries, like a bird in flight? For to such living souls is this food due. What then feeds you? Gladness! I shall listen to what follows: "Even so," he says, "you have done well to share in my tribulation." That is what brings him joy, that is what he feeds on, that they did him a good turn, not that his straits were eased—he who says to you, "You have enlarged me when I was in distress," for he knew how to abound and how to suffer want, in you who strengthen him. "For you Philippians know," he says, "when I began to preach the gospel, after I came from Macedonia, no church shared with me in giving and receiving, except for you only. For even when I was in Thessalonica, you sent me things I needed, not once but twice."[850] So he rejoices now that they have returned to these good works, and he is glad that they are in bloom again, as when a field revives in its fertility.

Was it really for his own needs, that he said, "You sent me things I needed"? Is that why he rejoiced? Not for that. How do we know?

---

[848] Phil 4:10.
[849] Phil 4:11–13.
[850] Phil 4:15–16.

Because he adds, "Not that I am looking for a gift, but I desire fruit."[851] I learned from you, my God, how to tell the difference between a gift and fruit. A man gives a *gift* to provide necessary things, such as money, food, drink, clothing, shelter, assistance. But *fruit* is the good and right will of the giver. For our good Teacher does not say, "He who receives a prophet," merely, but he adds, "in the name of a prophet," nor does he say, "He who receives a just man," merely, but he adds, "in the name of a just man."[852] And indeed, the one will receive the reward of a prophet, and the other the reward of a just man. Nor does he say, "He who gives a cup of cool water to one of my little ones," merely, but he adds, "in the name of a disciple," and he joins these words to it, "Amen, I say to you, he shall not lose his reward."[853] The *gift* is to receive the prophet, to receive the just man, to offer a cup of cool water to the disciple, but the *fruit* is to do this in the name of a prophet, in the name of a just man, in the name of a disciple. With fruit was Elijah fed by the widow who knew she was giving food to a man of God, and that is why she fed him; but it was a gift he fed on when the raven came. Nor was the inner Elijah fed, but only the outer, who might have broken down for want of that sort of food.[854]

27

So shall I speak, Lord, what is true in your sight, so that when unlearned men and infidels—who need the initiating mysteries when they are coming into the Church, and mighty miracles to win them over,[855] which we believe are signified under the name of "fishes" and "whales"—take on themselves to refresh your children, or to assist them in any way this present life calls for, as long as they still do not know why it is to be done and what it pertains to, they neither feed the

---

[851] Phil 4:17.
[852] Mt 10:41.
[853] Mt 10:42.
[854] Cf. 1 Kgs 7:7–16.
[855] Cf. 1 Cor 14:22.

children nor are they fed by them, because they do not do them from a right and holy will, nor are the others gladdened by the gifts, where they do not yet see any fruit. For gladness comes from what feeds the soul. And so the fishes and the whales do not feed upon such food that only the earth brings forth, once it has been set apart and divided from the bitter waves of the sea.

28

And you, God, saw all you had made, and behold, it was very good,[856] for we also see the same things, and behold, all is very good. As for your works taken one by one, when you said, "Let them be made," and they were made, you saw this or that, and you said that it was good. I have counted seven times when it was written that you saw that something you made was good; and the eighth time, because you saw all you had made, behold, it was not merely good, but *very good*, as taken all together. For as single things they were good, and that was all, but taken all together, both good and very good. This is how we say that all kinds of bodies are beautiful, but far more beautiful is a body made up of many beautiful members, than are the same members considered by themselves. For the whole is made complete by a most orderly agreement among the members, though all of the members taken one by one are beautiful.

29

But I paid good heed to find out whether it was seven or eight times that you saw that your works were good when they pleased you, and in your seeing I could not find any time by which I could understand how often you saw what you had made. And I said "Lord, is your Scripture not true, since you are true and you who are the Truth have given it to us? Why then do you tell me that there is no time in your seeing, while

---

[856] Cf. Gn 1:31.

your Scripture tells me that you looked at what you made on various days and saw that it was good, and when I count up the instances, I find how often you said it?"

Regarding this, you say to me, for you are my God and you speak with a strong voice to the inward ear of your servant, bursting through my deafness, as you cry out, "O man, what my Scripture says, I myself say. Nevertheless, it speaks it in time, while time does not touch my Word, because my Word stands firm in equal eternity with me. So then, all that you men see by my Spirit, I too see, just as all that you speak through my Spirit, I too speak. So too, when you see them in time, it is not in time that I see them; and when you speak them in time, it is not in time that I speak them."

30

And I listened, O Lord my God, and I sucked a drop of sweetness from your truth, and I understood that there are people who dislike your works, and say that you were compelled by necessity to make many of them. The frame of the heavens and the ordering of the stars, for example: they say that they did not come from you, but that they had already been created somewhere else, from some other source. Then, they say, you crammed them together, you bound them up, and you wove a structure out of them, when out of your defeated enemies you built up the ramparts of the world, to trammel them within this construction so that they would never be able to wage war against you again.[857] And there are other things, they go on to say, that you never made or even fit together, such as flesh of all kinds, and the tiniest living things, and whatever grips the earth with roots. No, it was a mind in enmity with you that did it, an alien nature that you never created, working contrary to you, begetting and shaping them in the lowest regions of the world.

---

[857] Again, Augustine refers to the Manicheans and their insistence that some good substance they identified as God had to involve some of his enemies when he made the world, and that then the evil beings made the living things on earth.

Madmen say these things, because they do not see your works by your Spirit, nor do they recognize you in them.

31

But as for those who do see them by your Spirit, it is you in them who see. So when they see that the things are good, you see that they are good; and whatever delights them because of you, it is you that give the delight; and everything that pleases us by your Spirit, pleases you in us. "For what man knows the things of a man, but the spirit of man within him? So too no one knows the things of God but the Spirit of God. But we," he says, "have not received the spirit of this world, but the Spirit that comes from God, that we may know the gifts that God has given us."[858]

And I am careful here to say that surely no one knows the things of God but the Spirit of God. How then can we even know what gifts God has given us? And the response comes to me, that likewise what we know by his Spirit is not known to any man, but only to the Spirit of God. Just as it was rightly said to those who would speak in the Spirit of God, "It is not you who speak,"[859] so it is rightly said to those who know in the Spirit, "It is not you who know." Hence, we are no less justified in saying, "It is not you who see," to those who see in the Spirit. So whenever they see, in the Spirit of God, that something is good, it is not they but God who sees that it is good.

It is one thing, then, for someone to think that something good is bad, as did the Manicheans I have spoken of. It is another, when a man sees that something is good, because it really is good, as many people take pleasure in your creatures because they are good, but they take no pleasure in you in your creatures, so that they would rather enjoy the creatures than you. It is still another, when a man sees that something is good and it is God in him who sees it is good, so that God the Creator

---

[858] 1 Cor 2:11–12.
[859] Mt 10:20.

372

should be loved in what he has made. But he cannot be loved, were it not for the Spirit he has given, "for the love of God is poured out into our hearts by the Holy Spirit, who has been given to us,"[860] and through Him we see that all is good that exists to any degree. From him it exists, whose existence admits of no degree, but he is—he is.[861]

32

Thanks be to you, O Lord! We see heaven and earth, whether corporeal, the higher part and the lower, or the spiritual creation and the corporeal creation; and in the adorning of these parts, whether they make up the whole mass of this world, or the whole universal creation, we see light made, and divided from darkness.

We see the firmament of heaven, whether it is the principal body of the world, set between the spiritual waters above and the corporeal waters below, or whether it is this space of the air where the birds fly about, because this too is called heaven, dividing the waters that are borne aloft in vapors and that fall again in dew when the nights are clear, and those heavier waters that flow upon the earth. We see the face of those waters gathered on the fields of the sea, and the dry land, whether bare or given such shape as to be visible and well-ordered and fit to be the mother of green plants and trees.

We see the luminaries shining from above, the sun to supply the day, the moon and stars to solace the night, and all of them to mark and signify the times.

We see a moist element everywhere teeming with fishes and beasts and birds, because the bulk of air that bears up the birds in flight grows dense from the exhalation of the waters.

We see the face of the earth decked with earthly creatures, and man in your image and likeness, set higher than all the unreasoning animals, because he is made in your image and likeness, that is, in the power of

---

[860] Rom 5:5.
[861] Cf. Ex 3:14.

reason and understanding. And just as in his soul there are two powers, one that is lord by its wise direction, the other that is subordinate and that obeys, so too in his bodily nature the woman was made for the man, she who would share an equal nature of rational intelligence in the mind, but in the sex of the body would be subject to the masculine sex, just as the appetite to act is subject to the skill of the rational mind, to conceive what would be right to do. We see these things, each one of them good, and all of them together very good.

33

Your works praise you,[862] that we may love you, and we love you, that your works may praise you. They have their beginning and their end in time, their rise and fall, growth and decay, beauty and loss. So do they have their morning and their evening, partly in a hidden way, and partly plain to see. For you made them from nothing, not from yourself, not from some other thing that was not yours, not from some other preexisting thing. You made them from matter concreated with them, that is, from matter created simultaneously with them, and upon its formlessness you imposed a form without any interposition of time. For seeing that the matter of heaven and earth is one thing, and their form is another, you made the matter from absolutely nothing, and the form of the world from the unformed matter, and both simultaneously, so that form should follow upon matter without any intervening delay.

34

We have also looked into what you wanted to be figured forth by your making things in this order, or by your having them written down in this order. And we saw that each single thing was good, and the whole altogether very good, in your Word, in your only-begotten, heaven and earth, the Head and the Body of the Church, predestined before all times, with neither morning nor evening. But when you began to execute in time what you had predestined, to make hidden things manifest,[863] and to compose what we had discomposed—for our sins loomed over us, and into the dark deeps we departed from you, and your gracious Spirit moved upon the waters, to come to our help in due time—you took the ungodly and made them righteous, and you set them apart from the wicked, and you fixed the sound authority of your book between those who were above, who would be docile to your teaching, and those who were below, who were to be subjected to them, and you herded up the society of the unbelieving into one conspiracy, that the devotion of the faithful might shine out clear, bringing forth works of mercy to you, and dealing out their earthly riches to the poor to acquire riches in heaven.

And then you kindled certain luminaries in the firmament, your saints holding within them the word of life, and by the sublime authority bestowed upon them, beaming with spiritual gifts. And then you brought forth, from corporeal matter, the visible sacraments, the wonders to behold, and the sounds of words according to the firmament of your book, to steep the unbelieving peoples in the truth and to bless the faithful besides. Then you formed the living soul of the faithful, alive by affections well-ordered, in the lively vigor of continence. And then you renewed the mind in your image and likeness, to be subject to you alone, needing no human authority to imitate. And you subjected its rational action to the intellect and its excellence, as you subjected the woman to the man. And you willed all the officers of your ministry that are needful for perfecting the faithful in this life, so that from those same faithful might come works fruitful for temporal uses and for the time to come. We saw all these, and they are indeed very good, because you are the one in us who see them, you who have given us the Spirit, so that we might see them and love you in them.

---

[863] Cf. Lk 8:17.

35

Lord God, grant us peace—for you have bestowed all things upon us. Give us the peace of rest, the peace of the Sabbath, the peace without an evening. For this most lovely order of things so very good, when their measures have been run, shall pass away. For in them too have been made a morning and an evening.

36

But the seventh day is without an evening, and has no setting, because you have made it holy and to abide forever. And thus, after you had made all your very good works, though you were at rest when you made them, you rested, that the voice of your book might foretell to us that we too, after all our works that are very good because you have given them to us, might rest in you, in the sabbath of eternal life.

37

For then you also shall rest in us, just as now you work in us, and so shall that rest of yours be through us, as these works you work are through us. But you, Lord, are ever at work and ever at rest. Nor do you see for a time, or move for a time, or rest for a time; and yet you make those things that are seen in time, and the times themselves, and the rest that comes after time.

38

And so we see the things you have made, that they exist; but they exist, because you see them. And we see from outside ourselves that they exist, and from within ourselves, that they are good; but you saw them already made, where you saw them as to be made. And we at one time were moved to do well, after our heart had conceived of it by your Spirit; but at an earlier time, we were moved to do ill, having forsaken you. But you indeed, the one true God, never ceased to do well. And some of our works have been good, by your gift to us, but they do not last forever. After them we hope to rest in your great sanctification. But you, the Good, in need of no good, are always at rest, because you are your own rest. What man can give this to another man to understand? What angel can give it to an angel? What angel to a man? Let us beg it of you, seek it from you, and knock at your door for it. Thus, thus is it received, thus shall it be found, thus shall it be opened. Amen.[864]

---

[864] Cf. Mt 7:7–8.